Information Communication Technology Standardization for E–Business Sectors:
Integrating Supply and Demand Factors

Kai Jakobs
RWTH Aachen University, Germany

INFORMATION SCIENCE REFERENCE

Hershey · New York

Director of Editorial Content:	Kristin Klinger
Senior Managing Editor:	Jamie Snavely
Managing Editor:	Jeff Ash
Assistant Managing Editor:	Carole Coulson
Typesetter:	Chris Hrobak
Cover Design:	Lisa Tosheff
Printed at:	Yurchak Printing Inc.

Published in the United States of America by
  Information Science Reference (an imprint of IGI Global)
  701 E. Chocolate Avenue, Suite 200
  Hershey PA 17033
  Tel: 717-533-8845
  Fax: 717-533-8661
  E-mail: cust@igi-global.com
  Web site: http://www.igi-global.com/reference

and in the United Kingdom by
  Information Science Reference (an imprint of IGI Global)
  3 Henrietta Street
  Covent Garden
  London WC2E 8LU
  Tel: 44 20 7240 0856
  Fax: 44 20 7379 0609
  Web site: http://www.eurospanbookstore.com

Library of Congress Cataloging-in-Publication Data

Information communication technology standardization for e-business sectors :
integrating supply and demand factors / Kai Jakobs, editor.
     p. cm.
  Includes bibliographical references and index.
  Summary: "This book studies the nature, relevance, and quality of standards
with ICTs and the impact they have on businesses"--Provided by publisher.
  ISBN 978-1-60566-320-3 (hbk.) -- ISBN 978-1-60566-321-0 (ebook) 1.
Information technology--Standards. 2. Electronic commerce--Information
technology. I. Jakobs, Kai, 1957-
  T58.5.I5247 2009
  658.8'72--dc22
                           2008054191
British Cataloguing in Publication Data
A Cataloguing in Publication record for this book is available from the British Library.

All work contributed to this book is new, previously-unpublished material. The views expressed in this book are those of the authors, but not necessarily of the publisher.

Advances in IT Standards and Standardization Research (AISSR) Series

Editor-in-Chief: Kai Jakobs, RWTH Aachen, Germany
ISBN: 1935-3391

Information Communication Technology Standardization for E-Business Sectors: Integrating Supply and Demand Factors

Edited By: Kai Jakobs, Aachen University, Germany

- Information Science Reference
- Copyright 2009
- Pages: 301
- H/C (ISBN: 978-1-60566-320-3)
- Our Price: $195.00

Information Communication Technology Standardization for E-Business Sectors: Integrating Supply and Demand Factors studies aspects affecting the nature, relevance, and quality of standards, and the impact they have on businesses. This Premier Reference Source discusses the dynamics and mutual impact of factors that condition demand for standards and supply.

Standardization and Digital Enclosure: The Privatization of Standards, Knowledge, and Policy in the Age of Global Information Technology

Edited By: Timothy Schoechle, University of Colorado, USA

- Information Science Reference
- Copyright 2009
- Pages: 304
- H/C (ISBN: 978-1-60566-334-0)
- Our Price: $165.00

Standardization and Digital Enclosure: The Privatization of Standards, Knowledge, and Policy in the Age of Global Information Technology establishes a framework of analysis for public policy discussion and debate. Discussing topics such as social practices and political economic discourse, this book offers a truly interdisciplinary approach to standardization and privatization valuable to technical, economic, and political researchers and practitioners, as well as academicians involved in related fields.

Standardization Research in Information Technology: New Perspectives

Edited By: Kai Jakobs, Aachen University, Germany

- Information Science Reference
- Copyright 2008
- Pages: 300
- H/C (ISBN: 978-1-59904-561-0)
- Our Price: $180.00

Standardization Research in Information Technology: New Perspectives amasses cutting-edge research on the application of standards in the market, covering topics such as corporate standardization, linguistic qualities of international standards, the role of individuals in standardization, and the development, use, application, and influence of information technology in standardization techniques.

OTHER BOOKS IN THE SERIES:
Advanced Topics in Information Technology Standards and Standardization Research
Edited By: Kai Jakobs, Aachen University, Germany
• IGI Publishing • Copyright 2006 • Pages: 348 • H/C (ISBN: 1-59140-938-1) • Our Price: $89.95

The *Advances in IT Standards and Standardization Research (AISSR)* seeks to address the needs of the knowledge society through the betterment and expansion of available research. In covering emerging areas, such as, technological innovation, open source applications, intellectual property, and the standardization of technological applications, the series will create a platform for the continued development of these areas and the information technology standards arena in whole.

Order Online at ww.igi-global.com or call 717-533-8845 x100 – Mon-Fri 8:30 AM - 5:00 PM (EST) or
Fax 24 Hours a Day 717-533-8661

Editorial Advisory Board

Table of Contents

Section III
Successful Standards Development

Section IV
Case Studies

Section V
Policy Issues

Section VI
Additional Readings

Detailed Table of Contents

Section I
Introduction

Quite frequently, a distinction is made in the literature between "ICT infrastructure" and "applications". Yet, some definitions of the former also include applications (and even human resources). Moreover, applications increasingly rely on an underlying infrastructure that provides the necessary (quality of) services. Thus, this Section argues that any such distinction is artificial, and should be abandoned.

This chapter puts forward the view that ICT infrastructure and the applications using it – such as e-business – need to be considered together. It provides examples of the impact an ICT infrastructure may have on e-business applications.

Section II
E-Business Standards and Business Models

This Section represents part of the outcome of the No-Rest project (Networked Organisation – REsearch into STandardisation). This project was co-funded by the European Commission and, among others, develop tools for the assessment of the impact they have on networked organisations. This Section provides insights into the links that exit between standards and companies' business models.

This chapter structures the overall need for standards in the e-government sector along several dimensions. It also discusses various relevant national initiatives. The complex organisational structure of governmental organisations is identified the most important driving force for developing common standards

Based on a survey of a set of European service companies, this chapter identifies a taxonomy comprising five clusters of service standards. A closer look at companies active in e-commerce reveals that this taxonomy does not reflect their needs particularly well. This is primarily due to special needs that result from the geographic distance between firm and customers.

The relation of different stakeholder groups to standardisation is discussed in this chapter. It first examines their relations in ICT standardisation, focussing on the equity – or rather, the lack of it – of different stakeholders. It goes on to develop stakeholder-centred scenarios for how demand for standards is generated. Based on these scenarios the chapter then uses business models to re-assess the nature of standards demand that is expressed in terms of the complex vendor-applier-user relations, and to describe the emergence of standards demand.

Section III
Successful Standards Development

The chapters of this Section are also direct results of the No-Rest project. Against the background of the complexity of the Web of today's standards setting bodies in the ICT sector, they discuss how companies that either wish to either implement, or to pro-actively contribute to the development of (one of set of competing) standards should act to make efficient use of their – typically limited – financial and human resources.

The chapter observes that the users (of RFID technology) are typically under-represented in the relevant standards setting processes. It then discusses the role that RFID standards play in shaping the adoption of RFID systems in the automotive supply chain.

Chapter VI

Kai Jakobs, RWTH Aachen University, Germany

The question on how potential standards setters can select the best platform for their planned activities is discussed in this chapter. It proposes an attribute-based way to describe SSBs. This, in turn, will enable companies to map their requirements onto potentially suitable SSBs' characteristics.

Chapter VII

Kai Jakobs, RWTH Aachen University, Germany
Jan Kritzner, RWTH Aachen University, Germany

This chapter briefly outlines the outcome of a study that looked at potential links between ICT / e-business standards' origins and their subsequent success in the market (or lack thereof). It suggests that companies are not that much interested in the origin of a standard in the sense of "consortium vs SDO". Rather, considerable importance is assigned to the processes adopted by an SSB. Here, an SSB's characteristics need to be compatible with the company's strategy and its business model.

Section IV
Case Studies

The case studies presented in this part discuss various aspects relating to the supply of, and demand for, standards. They do so for various industries, for different technologies, and from different perspectives. Yet, they all show how closely supply and demand are interlinked in ICT standardisation.

Chapter VIII

W. Lemstra, Delft University of Technology, The Netherlands
V. Hayes, Delft University of Technology, The Netherlands

This chapter describes the evolution of the 802.11 family of standards. Specifically, it looks at the role NCR played during this process, and why and how the idea of an open standard was pursued. How subsequently this standard was turned into a market success is also addressed.

For a change, this chapter adopts an industry perspective. Following a description of the evolution of e-business, it finds that today's standards still fail to meet many fundamental business needs, including cost-effectiveness and adequate security. Therefore, some proposals for improvements are also made.

Chapter X

The Chinese government's 3G policy is the focus of this chapter. The country promotes its indigenous TD-SCDMA standard despite the strong market incumbents, WCDMA and CDMA2000. North's transaction cost theory is used to analyse this case study of ideology-driven interactive game of economics and politics.

Chapter XI

This chapter provides insights into the standardisation activities in the context of the FlexRay protocol designed for in-car use. It focuses on the division of labour between the two consortia FRC and JasPar. The Consumption Decision Model is used to analyse the reasons behind JasPar's decision to draft very narrow specifications.

Chapter XII

Despite expectations to the contrary, standards do change. In some instances, such change may be inevitable; in others, it is not. Some such changes are innovation-related, others stem from the standardisation process itself. This chapter develops a conceptual framework to determine under which circumstances, and how, standards change is avoidable. It also identifies means to reduce the negative impact of change.

Section V
Policy Issues

Adopting a more high-level perspective, this Section discusses the (future) role of governments in the ICT standardisation process. Not least because of public procurement policies and of government-initiated standardisation activities (at least in Europe) governments' views of (open) standards are of particular relevance.

Chapter XIII

Mogens Kühn Pedersen, Copenhagen Business School, Denmark

Vladislav V. Fomin, Vytautas Magnus University, Lithuania

Henk J. de Vries, Erasmus University, The Netherlandss

Standards, especially open standards, are becoming increasingly important for policy makers. This holds particularly for policies relating to national/regional information infrastructures, therefore, this chapter predicts that governments will seek more active role in standardisation. It identifies general directions for future developments of the trend towards open standards, as well as some associated critical issues.

Section VI
Additional Readings

This Section offers some additional chapters. They are not directly related to the specific topic of the book, but should furnish the reader with a better idea about what ICT standards research is all about.

Chapter XIV

Ioannis P. Chochliouros, Hellenic Telecommunications Organization S.A. (OTE), Greece

Anastasia S. Spiliopoulou, Hellenic Telecommunications Organization S.A. (OTE), Greece

Tilemachos D. Doukoglou, Hellenic Telecommunications Organization S.A. (OTE), Greece

Elpida Chochliourou, General Prefectorial Hospital "Georgios Gennimatas," Greece

The chapter discusses the policy measures and standard necessary to implement the European "Electronic Signatures Directive".

Chapter XV

Esther Ruiz Ben, Technische Universität Berlin, Germany

This chapter illustrates the importance of quality standards for the internationalisation of the ICT sector in general, and for offshoring in particular.

Preface

Analyses of ICT and e-business standardisation typically focus on phenomena either related to the demand for, or the supply of, standards. Based more on traditional scientific mono-disciplinary interests than industry (and research) concerns, studies tend to focus on either the initiation and elaboration of standards, or on issues relating to their subsequent adoption and implementation. This book starts from the observation that this segmented approach significantly hampers the broader understanding of how standards

- Are shaped by the environment from which they emerge,
- Interact with the environment within which they are to be deployed.

The book, therefore, integrates studies of supply and demand-side factors that affect the relevance and the quality of standards, and thus affect the impact they have. In this context, the book also addresses the dynamics between factors that condition demand for, and those that condition the supply of standards.

The ultimate aim is to provide the basis on which to better understand how ICT and e-business standards might be better articulated to the changing needs of networked organisations. The book, therefore, addresses, on the one hand, the issues that relate to the production of adequate standards. On the other hand, it is concerned with the interaction of standards with their broader environment during implementation and use.

This book emerged from the NO-REST (Networked Organisations – Research into STandardisation) project that was undertaken in the context of the 6 European Framework Programme for Research and Technological Development. In fact, documenting this project's findings is a core motivation behind the book. Accordingly, the majority of chapters reflect the findings and views of this project. Specifically, these include Chapters I – VIII. They are complemented by another six chapters that discuss various related aspects.

Overall, the NO-REST project investigated the applicability and dynamics of standards in the e-business and e-government sectors, and developed guidelines for tools for the assessment of their performance, and of the impact they have on networked organisations.

To this end, the project evaluated the various standards development platforms, examined how implementations affect standards and interoperability, and did a re-active performance analysis of standards as well as a pro-active integrated impact assessment. It also looked at the application of standards, and analysed how standards – and their implementations – are subject to change incurred by the environment within which they are implemented. The project devised an analytical framework for a causal model of such changes.

No-Rest also looked at the various standards setting organisations, with a focus on how they react to – and influence – the dynamics of the environment within which they work. This included an analysis of the relation between the 'credibility' of a standards setting organisation, i.e., to which extent does the origin of a standard influence its viability in the market place. No-Rest then established if, and how, a standard's origin affects its performance, and set up guidelines helping those who wish to create a standard decide which standards setting organisation to select.

However, no project is an island ... Therefore, in this book No-Rest's findings are complemented by insights from other authors, that look at specific aspects surrounding the link between supply of, and demand for, standards.

And now - over to the chapters.

Section I, '*Introduction*' comprises only one chapter. In this first chapter, entitled '*An Integrated View of E-Business and the Underlying ICT Infrastructure*', Martina Gerst, Eric Iversen, and Kai Jakobs argue that e-business systems cannot be considered independent form the ICT system into which they are imbedded, and whose services they use. This holds specifically for the underlying communication network, which is why these networks are also specifically targeted by individual chapters.

The three chapters of **Section II**, '*E-Business Standards and Business Models*', provide insights into the links that exit between standards and companies' business models.

In Chapter II, entitled '*The Demand for E-Government Standards*', Knut Blind and Stephan Gauch argue that the rather complex organisational structure of governmental organisations is the most important driving force for developing e-government standards. The chapter looks at a number of ongoing initiatives in this domain, and identifies a number of issues that still need to be resolved.

Chapter III, by Knut Blind, is entitled '*A Taxonomy of Service Standards and a Modification for E-Business*'. Through a survey among European service companies it aims to find out in which service-related categories service standards are implemented. A taxonomy of service standards is developed that comprises five clusters. The analysis of the sub-sample of companies active in e-commerce, however, reveals significant differences that reflect their special needs caused by the distance to their customers.

'*Business Models and the Dynamics of Supply and Demand for Standards*' is the title of Chapter IV. Here, Richard Hawkins examines the structural relationship of various stakeholder groups to standardisation, described both in terms of how different stakeholders demand and acquire standards and in terms of their corresponding motivations and/or capabilities to influence the standardisation process.

Section III, '*Successful Standards Development*' offers another three chapters that discuss the development process of standards from the point of view of those who would like to either pro-actively contribute to it, or would like to implement its outcome.

Chapter V, by Ian Graham et al., is entitled '*Emergence of Standardisation Processes: Linkage with Users*'. Looking at the standardisation process for RFID technology, they find that the engagement of the large majority of end users in standards development is limited. This attitude is traced back to several reasons, including the facts that RFID is still an immature technology, most of the prospective RFID users are too small to consider themselves as being able to influence standardisation, and that RFID technologies are not used to support day-to-day business.

In Chapter VI, entitled '*Perceived Relation between ICT Standards' Sources and their Success in the Market*', Kai Jakobs argues that the still widely held (especially by policy makers in Europe) perception that 'formal' standards bodies are somehow 'superior' to consortia is in urgent need of a revision. For those who want to set standards, the choice is not the least based on this characteristic. Rather, a standards body's characteristics need to be compatible with a company's strategy and its business model.

Chapter VII, '*How to Select the Best Platform for ICT Standards Development*', by Kai Jakobs and Jan Kritzner, aims to provide the information that potential standards-setters should consider when selecting a standards setting body (SSB). It proposes sets of attributes of both standards users and SSBs. The degree to which these attributes match can be taken as an indicator of an SSB's suitability for the task at hand.

So far, the chapters reported findings from the No-Rest project. The five chapters that make up **Section IV** '*Case Studies*', provide complementing case studies.

'*The Shaping of the IEEE 802.11 Standard: The Role of the Innovating Firm in the Case of Wi-Fi*' is the title of Chapter VIII, co-authored by W. Lemstra and V. Hayes. They explore and describe the role of the innovating firm in relation to the standards making process of WLANs. In particular, they focus of the link between NCR and its corporate successors in the creation of the IEEE 802.11 standard. Their focus is the leadership role assumed by NCR for initiation and creation of an open standard for Wireless-LANs.

Chapter IX is entitled '*The Evolution of e.Business: Can Technology Supply Meet the Full Business Demand?*' In this chapter, Tom McGuffog observes – form an industry perspective – that the supply of e-business technology has been outstripping the effective demand for such capability for some time. He notes that e-business messages are to a value chain partner has always been to trigger a specific reaction on time; the application of new electronic technologies must always support that demand by enhancing speed, certainty safety, security and low total cost.

Chapter X, by Mingzhi Li and Kai Reimers, is entitled '*China's Practice of Implementing a 3G Mobile Telecommunications Standard: A Transaction Costs Perspective*'. It analyses and evaluates the Chinese government's 3G policy of supporting the creation and implementation of the country's indigenous TD-SCDMA standard. On the supply side, the addition of a new standard has enriched choices available on the 3G mobile telecommunications market; however, on the demand side, the government had to force operators to adopt this standard due to their lack of interest in the new standard.

The purpose of Chapter XI, entitled '*International Collaborative Framework between European and Japanese Standard Consortia: The Case of Automotive LAN Protocol*', and written by Akio Tokuda, is to examine the collaborative framework for the standardisation of the automotive LAN protocol known as 'FlexRay'. This framework has been established between European and Japanese consortia in 2006. The chapter focuses on the contribution of the Japanese standards consortium to the drafting of the original conformance test specifications.

Chapter XII, by Tineke Egyedi, is entitled '*Between Supply and Demand: Coping with the Impact of Standards Change*'. Here, she argues that the occurrence of change in ICT/e-business standards is caused by an interplay of supply- and demand-side factors. On the latter side, we find, for example, evolving user requirements, new technological possibilities. Regarding the former, we may find that problems with the scope of a standard, and its implementation process, as contributing factors.

The one chapter of **Section V**, '*Policy Issues*' looks at some relations between governments' and standards. In Chapter XIII, '*Open Standards and Government Policy*', Mogens Kühn Pedersen, Vladislav V. Fomin, and Henk J. de Vries, find that today governments are disadvantaged participants in standardisation due to a range of factors. However, they argue that the powers of globalisation should motivate governments to opt for select positions and interventions in ICT/e-business standards setting.

Finally, we've also included four additional chapters in **Section VI**, '*Additional Readings*'. They discuss some interesting aspects complementing the major thrust of the book, thus giving the reader a fuller picture of what ICT standards research encompasses.

Chapter XIV, by Ioannis P. Chochliouros et al., entitled '*Developing Measures and Standards for the European Electronic Signatures Market*' examines the role of standards setting activities for the development of an 'open' European (virtual) market based on the effective usage of e-signatures.

Esther Ruiz Ben is the author of Chapter XV, entitled '*Quality Standardization Patterns in ICT' Offshore*'. This chapter give an overview of the development of quality standards related to offshore projects, focusing particularly on recent practices in Europe.

In Chapter XVI, Manuel Mora et al. give '*An Overview of Models and Standards of Processes in the SE, SwE, and IS Disciplines*'. They develop a descriptive-conceptual overview of the main models and standards of processes in the systems engineering, software engineering, and information systems disciplines.

The last, but hopefully not least, Chapter XVII is entitled '*E-Business Standardization in the Automotive Sector: Role and Situation of SMEs*'. Here, Martina Gerst and Kai Jakobs show how SMEs are facing a severe disadvantage in both sector-specific harmonisation and international, committee-based standardisation.

I hope that the various chapters, and indeed the book as a whole, will provide thought-provoking insights into the relations that exist, or may be assumed, between the supply of ICT/e-business standards and the demand for them. Perhaps some will even find new topics for their own future research here

Kai Jakobs
RWTH Aachen University, Germany

Section I
Introduction

Chapter I
An Integrated View of E–Business and the Underlying ICT Infrastructure

Martina Gerst
Innovation Space, Germany

Eric Iversen
NIFU-STEP, Norway

Kai Jakobs
RWTH Aachen University, Germany

ABSTRACT

The chapter argues that any distinction between "e-business" and "infrastructure" is artificial. It shows that the lower-level techncial standards that make up the ICT infrastructure exert a direct impact on the e-business standards and systems that are using it. Accordingly, any assessment of the effect of standards on e-business has to take into account all layers of standards.

1 INTRODUCTION

The analysis of standardisation in the ICT area is commonly segmented to study either demand or supply-side phenomena. Based on issues more often related to disciplinary interests (most often economics) than to current concerns of industry, studies tend to focus on either the initiation and elaboration of standards, or on conditions for their adoption and (much less often) their implementation. This book starts from the observation that this segmented focus significantly hampers the broader understanding of how standards interact with the networked organisations. The book therefore combines a study of supply and demand-side factors that affect the relevance and the quality of standards – and, thus, influence their impact – for networked organisations.

The market for electronic business solutions is vast and heterogeneous. E-business solutions have the potential both to affect the organisation of many existing markets but also have the scope to open up significant vistas for new economic activities (as the literature has been at pains to point out). In this setting it is therefore clear that characteristics rooted in the changing 'user environments' can prime demand for standards, can shape their relevance, and can therefore condition their potential impacts. It is equally clear that factors related to the way these standards are developed will affect their relevance and their ultimate impacts for existing markets as well as for emerging markets (perhaps unforeseen by the original sponsors of the individual standard).

In this context, this book addresses the dynamic between factors that condition demand and those that condition the supply for standard. The ultimate aim is to provide the basis on which to better understand how e-business standards might be better articulated to the changing needs of networked organisations. The book is concerned with the interaction of standards with their environments. In light of this interaction the focus is especially directed to the changing landscape of Standards Setting Bodies (SSBs), including their ability to adapt to, and potentially to influence these market environments.

1.1 Motivation

During the last 20 years, the business world has undergone significant changes. For some organisations, doing business globally has become critical to their survival, and others discover new opportunities by focusing their business in a local setting. In this process of change, Information and Communication Technologies (ICT) are playing a significant role both enabling and triggering the re-organisation of business activities. ICT became ubiquitous, invading all aspects of business domain.

The Internet has considerably accelerated the diffusion of inter-organisational networks, and has intensified the collaboration between organisations. Regardless of company size and type of business, today virtually all organisation's ICT systems are interconnected. In such an increasingly networked world, ICT and e-business standards aim to ensure interoperability between both different IT systems within and between organisations. As ICT-enabled collaboration has becomes a decisive tool in the struggle for competitive advantage, interoperability within and between organisations has become strategic necessity in all industries. To communicate and collaborate, interoperability is absolutely essential. However, seamless communication and integration of data and information is not possible in the absence of common standards – standards and the standardisation process have gained strategic significance.

Throughout the past twenty years there have also been considerable changes in the world of standards setting. Until the mid 80s, standardisation was virtually exclusively dominated by the formal Standards Developing Organisations (SDOs) such as ISO and CEN. However, in the late 1980s the slow and highly bureaucratic processes that then characterised formal SDOs was seen as inadequate to deal with the challenges that resulted from the increasingly shorter life cycles of ICT products. As a result, the number private standards consortia saw a massive increase during the 1990s, when in less than a decade more than 140 ICT standards consortia were created.

The emergence of such a huge number of SSBs, often with overlapping coverage, caused a fragmentation of the market for standards development. This fragmentation raised the problem of how to co-ordinate the organisations involved in the process. The economic literature has modelled extensively the co-ordination strategies of the players, which represent alternative forms of standards setting (i.e. market versus committee based standardisation). However, as a result of the supply fragmentation, this also needs to consider the organisations' choice between competing standards setting bodies.

Also, the ICT sector is subdivided into different industry categories, each of which has specific needs and requirements. Consequently, sector-specific standards are being developed and used, thus further contributing to the fragmentation of the market.

The process of standardisation is an integral part of the world of networked organisations, and for the evolution of the Information Society in Europe. Addressing standardisation issues requires a multi-disciplinary research approach to fully understand the economic, social and technical aspects of the process.

2 AN INTEGRATED VIEW OF E-BUSINESS AND THE UNDERLYING ICT INFRASTRUCTURE

Traditionally, a distinction has been made between 'applications' on the one hand, and 'infrastructure' on the other. Specifically, a variation on this theme has been used in the e-business domain – 'e-business' and 'ICT'. However, we would argue that this distinction is becoming increasingly blurred, and indeed artificial. Accordingly, throughout this book we have adopted the view that the infrastructure forms an integral part of any working e-business system. This section briefly outlines the motivation behind this,.

2.1 E-Business applications

Reflecting the wider deployment of Web technologies since the mid-90s, the older term e-commerce[1] was frequently re-defined along the lines of *"commerce enabled by Internet technologies"* (Seddon, 1997). It refers to the use of Web technologies both within and outside the organisational

borders (Riggins and Rhee, 1998), rather than the simple matter of buying and selling electronically. However, the distinction between e-commerce and e-business is extremely blurred; frequently, the terms are used interchangeably. Davydov (2000) for example defines e-business as *"an all-encompassing concept of enabling the exchange of information and automation of commercial transactions over the Internet"*.

Today, e-business is seen as a significant part of the strategy of most companies in their pursuit of cost reduction, efficiency and better performance (Amor, 2000.; Morath, 2000; van der Mandele, 2000; van Hooft and Stegwee, 2001; Venkatraman, 2000). Specifically, it is supposed to *"enable business process efficiencies in all aspects of enterprise activities"*. That is, e-business is one means of implementing business processes and thus, ultimately, business strategies.

Yet, e-business services are not provided by stand-alone artefacts. Rather, they are embedded in, and part of, a larger system, which also comprises the underlying ICT infrastructure. This is also reflected in the definition of e-business provided by Business W@tch[2]: *"E-business is ... about using technology to redefine your business. To succeed, you'll need an infrastructure flexible enough to absorb new technologies, maximize efficiency across your organization, and support business model changes"*.

2.2 ICT infrastructure

Over the past decades, the definition of the term infrastructure has been adapted to the technological developments. In an analogy to, for example, the road network, POTS[3] represented the communication infrastructure, to be complemented by packet-switched networks such as the various national X.25 networks in the seventies.

As late as 1992, the RACE project PALACE produced a survey of the requirements of the RACE Application Pilots on a communication infrastructure. In this survey, 'infrastructure' still only covered on the bottom three layers of the OSI/RM.

Eventually, the idea of 'infrastructure' broadened. Among others, Klingenstein (1999) and Hong & Landay (2001) included 'Middleware' into their idea of an infrastructure. That is, 'infrastructure' comprised the full seven-layer OSI stack; a considerable extension from the original view. More specific, elements of a middleware – and thus of an infrastructure – include (Eertink & Demchenko, 2000):

- Directories and public key infrastructure,
- Fixed-mobile integration and QoS management,
- Authorisation, access control, accounting & billing,
- Content descriptions and multimedia communication,
- Data management and data distribution in computational GRIDs,
- Active networks.

Along similar lines, agent-based systems are now considered part of an infrastructure (see e.g., (Bellissard et al., 1999)).

More recently, approaches may be observed that also include services like SOAP (Simple Object Access Protocol), WSDL (Web Services Definition Language), and UDDI (Universal Description, Discovery and Integration) in the infrastructure (see e.g., (Papazoglou, 2003), (Paolucci & Sycara, 2003). Web services are supposed to facilitate asynchronous communication between business processes by replacing proprietary interfaces and data formats with a standard web-messaging infrastructure.

2.3 Strategy, Applications, and ICT – Some Earlier Research

To quote Business W@tch once more: "*The use of ICT in business processes leads to e-business*[4]". In fact, in our view this sums up quite nicely the

extremely close links that exist between the ICT infrastructure and e-business applications.

Going one step further, Venkatraman (1991) identified inter-relation between business strategy and corporate ICT infrastructure. The categories he identified include

- 'Independent' no relation between ICT infrastructure and business strategy,
- 'Reactive' strategy shapes infrastructure,
- 'Interdependent' mutual shaping.

Recent research has extensively addressed the latter two categories, and the importance of adequate links between corporate ICT and e-business. For instance, Broadbent (1999) observe that "*... implementing process innovation requires an extensive set of infrastructure capabilities ...*". Even earlier research on IT/business strategy alignment has shown positive linkages among competitive strategy, information technology, and performance (Peteraf, 1993). Along similar lines, Wieringa (2004) locates a corporate 'communication architecture' at both the 'software applications' and the 'business processes' layers.

Industry as well has realised the importance of an alignment, and interlinkage, of ICT infrastructure and business strategy. Britt (2002) notes that "*A corporation's technology strategy should no longer be subordinate – developed after the business strategy is complete. The corporate technology strategy is woven throughout the business strategy*".

2.4 ICT Infrastructure Impact on E-business – Some Examples

Figure 1 shows the different levels of process integration across the stack of standards-based and e-business-related services.

While this hierarchy exists in most cases, in some important areas we may find examples of systems that clearly belong to the ICT infrastructure, but that at the same time exert a significant influence on e-business and business processes.

This holds especially for issues of scalability of e-business applications, which are closely linked to the underlying infrastructure. Issues like latency, scheduling or scalability may have considerable impact to the e-business application performance (Oudshoorn, 2003). The same applies for clearly ICT-related technologies like Grid-computing, which have enabling effects, with potentially enormous implications, on e-business (Silva & Senger, 2004).

Generally, technical standards play a crucial role in shaping not only the future form of the technology (Williams et al, 1993) but also nature and functioning of the organisation and the relationships between organisations (Tapscot, 1995). Consequently, the infrastructure standards affect the way in which organisations interact and do business electronically.

For example, whereas the standards for the new RFID products would be 'communication' standards (in Figure 1), they are essential in enabling organisations such as, e.g., WalMart and US DoD (Department of Defense) to integrate their global supply chains. In fact, this integration was triggered by the increased availability and maturity of RFID tags and readers. Here, elements of the ICT infrastructure, and the standards upon which they are based, have been instrumental for the design and implementation scalable e-business systems (Su et al, 2001).

Likewise, common network standards were critical to the success of the Cisco's 'global networked business model' (Kraemer and Dedrick, 2002.). This model was constructed based on the integration of all business relationships and the supporting communications within a 'networked fabric'. The global networked business model opened the corporate information infrastructure to all key constituencies, leveraging the network for competitive advantage. Infrastructure technology standards supported the creation of networks that linked Cisco with its trading partners and was at the core of the Cisco e-business strategy.

Network standards such as for wireless LANs (for example, the extension of the WirelessMAN Broadband Wireless Metropolitan Area Network Standard to support residential applications) affect the way in which business is conducted, hence shaping the evolution of e-business. The same holds for the role other standards for mobile communication enabled m-business.

3 IN CONCLUSION

From the aforementioned, we may conclude that not only the top-level standards (in Figure 1) have a direct impact on of e-business. Rather, the same holds for the technical standards at the lower levels of integration, the ICT infrastructure. Interoper-

Figure 1. Taxonomy of ICT standards

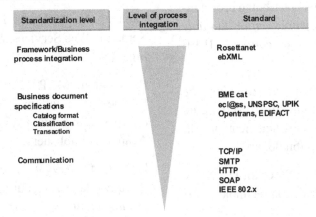

ability, which is key to e-business, can be – and in fact has to be – addressed at different layers. The standards of these three lower layers also determine the shape of e-business. Consequently, to assess the effect of standards on e-business, one has to take into account all layers of standards – including ICT standards.

Moreover, the notion of what exactly establishes an 'ICT infrastructure' changes; increasingly including higher layer protocols and services. In fact, this makes sense – ICT and e-business both serve to enable business making. Drawing a line between these two at some point in the protocol and service stack – with e-business services located above the line and ICT infrastructure below – would necessarily be arbitrary and thus not make much sense.

Once more, a quote from e-Business W@tch nicely puts it in a nutshell: "*The adoption and use of Information and Communication Technologies (ICT) by companies, often referred to as e-business, is widely seen as an important factor to improve the competitiveness of the European economy*".

4 REFERENCES

Amor, D. (2000). The E-business (R)Evolution. Living and Working in an Interconnected World. USA: Prentice Hall.

Bellissard, L., et al (1999). An Agent Platform for Reliable Asynchronous Distributed Programming. *Proc. 18th IEEE Symposium on Reliable Distributed Systems table of contents*. IEEE Computer Society.

Britt, F. F. (2002). *Multiplying business value: The fusion of business and technology*. IBM Institute for Business Value, http://managementconsult. profpages.nl/man_bib/rap/ibm06.pdf

Broadbent , M., Weill, P., & St. Clair, D. (1999). The implications of information technology in-frastructure for business process redesign. *MIS Quarterly. 23*(2).

Davydov, M. M. (2000). e-Commerce Solutions for Business and IT Managers. *Corporate Portals and e-business Integration*. New York, USA: McGrow Hill.

Eertink, H., & Demchenko, Y. (Eds.) (2000). Notes from the European Middleware Workshop (EMW2000). http://www.terena.nl/tech/projects/middleware/emw2000notes01.html

Hong, J. I., & Landay, J. A. (2001). An Infrastructure Approach to Context-Aware Computing. *Human-Computer Interaction, 16*(2, 3 & 4), 287-303.

Klingenstein, K. J. (1999). Middleware: The Second Level of IT Infrastructure. *Cause And Effect Journal, 22*(4), EduCause.

Kraemer, K., & Dedrick, J. (2002). Strategic use of the Internet and e-commerce: Cisco Systems. *Journal of Strategic Information Systems, 11*(1), 5-29.

Morath, P. (2000). *Success@E-Business. Profitable Internet Business & Commerce*. London: McGraw Hill.

Oudshoorn, M. (2003). Scheduling and Latency—Addressing the Bottleneck. In N. S. Shi & V. K. Murthy (Eds), *Architectural Issues of Web-Enabled Electronic Business*. Idea Group Publishing.

Paolucci, M., & Sycara, K. (2003). Autonomous Semantic Web Services. *IEEE Internet Computing, 7*(5).

Papazoglou, M. P. (2003). Web Services and Business Transactions. *World Wide Web: Internet and Web Information Systems, 6*, 49–91. Kluwer Academic Publishers.

Peteraf, M. A. (1993). The cornerstone of competitive advantage: A resource-based view. *Strategic Management Journal*, (pp. 179-191).

Riggins, F. J., & Rhee, H. (1998): Toward a Unified View of Electronic Commerce. *Communications of the ACM, 41*(10), 88-95.

Seddon, P. (1997). *Defining Electronic Commerce.* Department of Information Systems, University of Melborne, http://www.dis.unimelb.edu.au/staff/peter/research/InternetEra.htmlTapscott.

Silva, F., & Senger, H. (2004). Digital Communities in a Networked Society: e-Commerce, e-Business and e-Government. *Proc. Third IFIP Conference on e-Commerce, e-Business and e-Government.* Kluwer.

Su, S. Y. W., Lam, H., Lee, M., Bai, S., & Shen, Z. J. (2001). An Information Infrastructure and E-Services for Supporting Internet-Based Scalable E-Business Enterprises. *In Proceedings of the Fifth IEEE International Enterprise Distributed Object Computing Conference,* http://csdl.computer.org/comp/proceedings/edoc/2001/1345/00/13450002abs.htm

Tapscott, D. (2001). Rethinking Strategy in a Networked World. Strategy and Business. *Third Quarter* (24), 1-8.

van der Mandele, M. (2000). *E-Business and Strategy:* Arthur D. Little E-Business Center. http://www.netskill.de/ebusiness.nsf/7875A002F42DE041C125697E00562D54/$File/e-business_and_strategy.pdf. Acess date: April, 2005.

van Hooft, F. P. C., & Stegwee, R. A. (2001). E-business strategy: How to benefit from a hype. *Logistics Information Management, 14*(1/2), 44-53.

Venkatraman, N. (1991). IT-Induced Business Reconfiguration. In M. S. Scott Morton, (Ed), *The Corporation of the 1990s: Information Technology and Organizational Transformation.* Oxford University Press.

Wieringa, R., van Eck, P., & Blanken, H. (2004). *Architecture Alignment in a Large Government Organization: A Case Study.* CTIT Technical Report, http://wwwhome.cs.utwente.nl/~patveck/papers/wieringa_etal_caise04forum.pdf

Williams, R., Graham, I., & Spinardi, G. (1993). *The Social Shaping of EDI.* Paper presented at the Proceedings of the PICT/COST A4 International Research Workshop, Edinburgh.

ENDNOTES

[1] E-commerce may broadly be defined as *'Conducting business communications and transactions over networks and through computers'.* e-Business W@tch gives the following definition of e-commerce: "E-commerce refers to transactions between companies, private households and non-profit organisations (including government) via non proprietary networks that are established through an open standard setting process, and all activities needed to provide the necessary infrastructure to pursue these transactions."

[2] The European Commission has established e-Business W@tch as a market observatory which monitors and analyses the deployment of ICT in different sectors of the European economy.

[3] Plain Old Telephone System.

[4] http://www.ebusiness-watch.org/index.php?option=content&task=view&id=55&Itemid=67.

Section II
E–Business Standards and Business Models

Chapter II
The Demand for E–Government Standards

Knut Blind
Berlin University of Technology, Germany, Fraunhofer Institute for Systems and Innovation Research, Germany, & Erasmus University, Netherlands

Stephan Gauch
Berlin University of Technology, Germany

ABSTRACT

The chapter provides an overview and subsequent analysis of the demand for e-government standards in the EU. It describes the requirements for e-government standards in the EU, based on a number of ongoing national initiatives. A recently developed typology of service standards is used to structure the need for e-government standards demand in various dimensions. It turns out that the rather complex organisational structure of governmental organisations is the most important driving force for developing e-government standards.

1. INTRODUCTION

Like e-business, e-government covers an extremely wide range of topics, ranging from, e.g., electronic voting via e-taxation and geo-spatial data to e-education and e-health care. Also, the users are similarly diverse, including European, national, state and municipal authorities, and a host of specialised agencies. Many of these entities have already developed solutions for their individual tasks and problems, which are hardly ever compatible with anyone else's. In a sense, this situation is similar to the one that was observed in the e-business sector a couple of years ago. Priority aspects to be addressed include interconnectivity, data integration, access, and content management (Borras, 2003)[1]. These aspects are also crucial for e-businesses.

The different 'expressions' of e-government services are also similar to those in the e-business domain – functionality required for G2G[2] is roughly equivalent to B2B functionality, and G2C

Figure 1. The different expressions of e-government

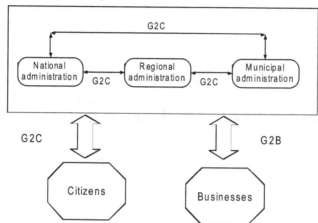

to B2C. G2B lies somewhere in between, but is closer related to B2C (see also Figure 1).

According to the Dutch Programme for Open Standards and Open Source Software in Government (OSSOS), benefits of open standards in e-government include (Werle, Iversen 2006):

- Reduction of dependence on external software suppliers and an increase in the range of choices;
- A way to combat monopolies in the software market in order to prevent abuse of dominant market positions;
- Enhancement of the quality of government information systems in terms of accessibility of information, transparency of action, security and future-proofness;
- Reduction of the cost of software implementations;
- Improvement of the exchange of data between government domains.

Some other aspects of e-government are also worth considering:

- Security aspects are extremely important, even more so than in e-business,
- There is considerable commitment to the use of standards (and open software; this holds despite the fact that many systems based on proprietary technology have already been implemented),
- Some national governments have implemented national 'standards' which are not necessarily open, and which do not necessarily provide for interoperability with European/international standards[3].

Overall, the majority of standards-related e-government activities focus on the identification of suitable existing standards, and to the provision of guidelines regarding their implementation and use. Also, these activities focus on the three lower layers of the interaction architecture (see Figure 2). So far, very little has been achieved in

Figure 2. An e-government layered interaction architecture

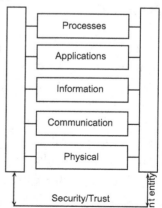

terms of standardisation for the two upper layers. Moreover, in Germany, for example, only some mandatory 'building blocks' have been identified which belong to the 'Application' layer (e.g., 'e-payment'; see (Lheureux et al. 2003)).

While many (e-business) standards may be deployed in the e-government context, dedicated e-government standards, and standards setting activities, are yet distinctly rare but the efforts towards them are increasing. This is true both for informal bodies, like the Organization for the Advancement of Structured Information Standards (OASIS) as well as formal bodies like the European Committee for Standardization (CEN).[4] OASIS, an informal standards body mostly active in developing Web Service and Markup Language standards, has formalized it's activities in e-government related standards by forming a OASIS eGovernment (eGov) Member Section in late 2007 with the specific aim to "assess interoperability frameworks of relevance to the public sector and promote more inclusive and citizen-centered e-government initiatives through the adoption and implementation of open standards". More precisely OASIS seeks to promote and develop standards relating to seven large areas of activity; election and voter services, identity management, tax, information access, emergency management, public procurement, and long-term archiving. Moreover it launched several Technical Committees (TC) in this context.[5] The purpose of those OASIS TCs is to provide a forum for governments to voice their needs and requirements with respect to XML (Extensible Markup Language) standards. These are then forwarded to appropriate other TCs. The XML.org Focus Area is supposed to serve as a central clearinghouse for information on XML and related standards for the public sector.

There is also substantial effort at the formal European level. Funded initially by industry and later by the EC, CEN/ISSS launched a Focus Group on e-Government and produced the "eGovernment Standards Roadmap" in early 2008

distinctly promoting a decentralized approach to e-government standardisation based on close cooperation between the European Commission and the informal consortia W3C and OASIS. This Focus Group is meanwhile discontinued as its purpose was limited mostly to establish said Roadmap. For the time being, subsequent activities are taken over by a CEN/ISSS Workshop entitled CEN/ISSS Workshop on Discovery of and Access to eGovernment Resources (WS/eGov Share). More specifically, one CEN/ISSS[6] Workshop looks at the related topic of a 'citizen card', another CEN Workshop is dedicated to defence procurement, and another one to Open XML interchange format for legal documents. Still, CEN Workshops are more or less created at random: with no underlying, overarching strategy – there is currently no coherent approach towards standardisation for e-government that would lead to a dedicated e-government CEN TC dealing with the different issues. Yet, as the following discussion will show, such an approach is badly needed but, due to the broad focus of e-government, may be hard to establish.

The problem becomes even more relevant when possible pressure from policy towards standards development in the area of e-government is taken into account. Both the i2010 eGovernment Action Plan (EC, 2006a) as well as the EC Communication on Interoperability for Pan-European eGovernment Services (EC, 2006b) highlight the relevance of standards and interoperability. Still, the focus in both documents is mostly aimed at the European Interoperability Framework (EIF) of which the second version is currently in its final stage of development. Only the EC Communication mentions the three formal standardisation bodies on the European level (CEN, CENELEC and ETSI).[7] There is another demand oriented factor on the European level that exerts pressure towards a unified framework in e-government. In 2006 the European Commission published the Services Directive (EC, 2006c) to establish an integrated framework for service provision between and within the member states of the European internal market. Three of the articles in this directive are of high relevance for the future provision of services in the context of e-government. Article 6 states that the member states shall ensure "points of single contact" (POSC), i.e. set up organisations or services that enable service providers to complete necessary formalities in context of the services providers area of service activity. In short, the member states are required to integrate all the relevant formalities and make them accessible via a single service or organisation. Article 7 takes this notion further and formulates a "right to information" that service providers have in relation to these POSCs and the formalities they integrate. Finally, Article 8 addresses the direct relation to e-government as these procedures have to be available by electronic means. The member states have to implement rules, regulations and administrative provisions before 28 December 2009. Standardisation is prominently mentioned in the light of quality of service. Based on the fact that the issue of standards and standardisation has become salient in recent policy documents, it is plausible to argue that demand for such standards will increase in foreseeable future.

2. CONCEPTUAL APPROACH

In order to give an overview and to analyse the demand for e-government standards in the EU, we apply the following approach. We take into account the data provided by the "IDABC eGovernment Observatory" (IDABC eGovernment Observatory 2005), the successor of the eGovernment Observatory "ePractice.eu", a European Commission service about eGovernment, eInclusion and eHealth, hosting regularly updated national fact sheets about national e-government related activities, as well as information from the "UN Global E-government Readiness Report 2005" (UN, 2005). The coverage of information refers to activities in the 27 Member States as well as

countries not part of the European Union. These sources provide us with a unique set of information and with valuable insight into e-government strategies, initiatives and projects in Europe presenting the situation and progress of e-government in each Member State of the European Union. They provide information on major past e-government developments, strategies, legal initiatives, key organisations involved in the e-government and key components of the infrastructure established to support the provision of services for citizens and businesses in each country.

Based on this source of information, we have identified only those initiatives and programmes that mention the need for the development of standards explicitly. Several activities require standards in one way or another. However, the focus on those activities that express an explicit need for standards, generates a much clearer picture of existing priorities.

Simple country-specific presentations of requirements for standards supporting e-government activities are likely to replicate common trends. Therefore, we have structured the trends in the demand for e-government standards according to a taxonomy of service standards. Governments on all levels provide different kinds of services ranging from national defence and internal security to simple administrative services like certification of marriage. Consequently, governmental bodies can be compared to service companies. In addition, more and more public services are outsourced to private service companies, e.g. waste collection or security services. However, it has to be noted that governmental institutions are often in a monopolistic position or in a compulsion to provide certain services. Furthermore, they are restricted by rather rigorous regulations, integrated in multiple organisation layers, but also able to rely on tax revenue in case of deficit spending or losses.

Whereas we can rely on a long tradition of standardisation and large stock of standards in the technical sector, standardisation related to services and service companies is just emerging. Furthermore, the simple transfer of typologies of standards approved for the manufacturing sector and physical products is not adequate. According to EN 45020, service standards are in general defined as standards that specify requirements to be fulfilled by a service to establish its fitness for purpose. Since this definition is very general, we rely on a services standards typology, which differentiate in more detail possible components of the service delivery process and the service result appropriate as objects for standardisation. Such classifications of standards, which are independent from specific service sectors, can be used to structure the demand for respective standards, but also to generate hypotheses about the demand and supply of standards.

The most recent and differentiated approach to set up a typology of service standards was developed by Vries (1999; 2001). According to his general definition, standards concern entities or relations between entities. Therefore, for a systematic approach to standards in the service sector, it is first necessary to define entities. Typical of services is the interaction between supplier and customer as the main entities. On the supply side, the organisation or the service company and service employees can be regarded as entities. Transferred to e-government, the various governmental levels, but also the institutions within one level are entities. Furthermore, both the service process and the service results can be considered as further entities, although often service process and result occur simultaneously. Finally, a distinction between delivery and final result has to be made. Based on these theoretical considerations, the following classification can be derived (see Table 1).

We will structure the demand for standards in e-government according to the categories in the left column in Table 1.[8] Based on the general and the country specific findings, we will derive some preliminary conclusions also addressing the supply side of standards regarding e-government standards.

3. THE NEED FOR E-GOVERNMENT STANDARDS IN VARIOUS DIMENSIONS

In our overview of the demand for standards in the various dimensions of e-government, we follow the categories of the taxonomy presented in Table 1. According to the information provided in IDABC (IDABC eGovernment Observatory 2005), there are no requirements for e-government standards for the quality, environmental or safety management of governmental institutions. There are no specific e-government standards for service employees, i.e. public officers, nor workrooms and physical objects supporting service delivery (without taking the ICT infrastructure into account, which will be mentioned separately in the context of internal and external communication processes). The lack of demand under these two categories is plausible, since the introduction of e-government activities does not change these very general types of standards necessary for running a service company and therefore also governmental institutions. However, it should be considered that public employees have to fulfil some minimum standards in order to be able to provide e-government based services effectively and efficiently. We also do not observe standard requirements and needs related to the specifications and the trustworthiness of service results, but also precautions, e.g. emergency measures and complaints handling. Although safety issues are addressed, which will be presented later, it could be discussed whether governments may introduce standards for in-time delivery of services not only in the context of e-government. The main question regarding the interaction between e-business and e-government standardisation is the comparability between such activities on the different dimensions. The best way to do this is to start with the main distinction between both concepts on an abstract level. While e-business is on the whole aimed at commercial aspects of ICT, e-government is aimed towards participatory

Table 1. Services standards typology

Standards for: Entities or relations between entities	...may concern:
Service organisation	Quality management, environmental management, occupational health and safety management. Solvency and other financial aspects. Crew, e.g., minimum number of staff and their educational level.
Service employee	Knowledge. Skills. Attitude. Ethical code (e.g., confidentiality).
Service delivery	Specification of activities. Trustworthiness. Privacy aspects. Safety aspects. Code of conduct.
Service result	Result specification. Trustworthiness.
Physical objects supporting service delivery	E.g., technical requirements for trains in public transport services.
Workroom	E.g., requirements for daylight access in offices.
Precautions	Emergency measures. Complaints handling. Guarantee.
Additional elements to the core service – delivery.	E.g. waiting facilities
Additional elements to the core service – results	
Communication between customer and service organisation (before, during and after providing the service)	Semantics (e.g., data elements to be used). Syntax (e.g., forms layout, syntax rules for electronic messages). Specification of Information and Communication Technology to be used. Protocols. Code of conduct. Approachability (e.g., hours of accessibility per telephone and average waiting time).
Communication within the service organisation or between this organisation and its suppliers	Semantics. Syntax. Specification of ICT to be used. Protocols. Code of conduct. Approachability.

(Source: Vries 2001)

aspects of ICT. The existence of such a focus can also be observed in the importance of accessibility standards that are a prominent factor in e-government interoperability (IDABC 2004). The implementation of recommendations of the Web Accessibility Initiative of the W3C concerning is still very low with more than 90% of French, German or U.K. sites not passing minimal accessibility checks of Web Content Accessibility Guidelines (WCAG) 1.0 Priority 1 tests (Marincu, McMullin 2004). Even though this phenomenon is not limited to government websites the role and actions of governments concerning accessibility standardisation can produce positive spill-overs into e-business standardisation. The participation focus does not exclude the relevance of G2B activities like e-procurement services, but highlights the primary objective that is both embedded in the institutional settings of either governments or companies and in their agenda and also leads to a difference in perception of the social roles of the demand side, namely individuals as customers or individuals as citizens. Comparability in this context can thereby broadly be distinguished by aspects of the demand side or target group of standardised services and the agenda of the supply side, namely governments or companies. Apart from rational reasons for standards that apply to both the economic and political realm (e.g. reduction of cost for service provision for either profit maximisation in business or cost-cutting on government side to manage their revenues) distinctions can mostly be made on the demand side. While companies aim to provide services for certain target groups, governments mostly have to provide services for the whole set of citizens. This might be the most striking difference between the rationales underlying both areas of standardisation. Even though it might be argued that in a due process of e-business standardisation activities standards are produced that reflect the needs of a large number of users this factor is of higher importance for e-government standardisation as in that case the access and thereby participation of all citizens is a primary objective.

3.1 Service Delivery

Under 'Service delivery', Vries mentions also privacy and safety aspects. Here, e-government activities generate additional requirements compared to traditional government activities. Consequently, Austria, but also Finland, France, Italy and Spain address explicitly the development of information security and data protection standards in their initiatives and strategies in order to guarantee the security of e-government products and services. The observation that not all Member States mention explicitly the need for security standards in the context of e-government can be explained by already existing international standards addressing information security, which can also be applied by governmental organisations.

3.2 Communication between Citizens and Governmental Organisations

The trend towards e-government is accompanied by an increasing pressure of governmental organisations to become more client oriented. In the light of standardisation this proves an important aspect, due to the heterogeneity of the demand side in question. This heterogeneity can be partly horizontal, and socially neutral aspects but might also include vertical heterogeneity, e.g. social stratification of society. Examples for such vertical heterogeneity effects might be the access of individuals in lower income classes to high performance computer equipment needed to access certain e-government services. This aspect is only of limited importance for e-business standardisation oriented to target groups but is a crucial factor for the government agenda to bridge potential political and participatory digital divides. We observe several initiatives to develop and implement standards that structure the interface between governmental organisations and citizens. The standardisation requirements range from harmonised web portals or gateways of governmental organisations, over standards for the exchange of documents, to e-signatures and electronic identity cards.

Since citizens are confronted not only with one governmental institution, but with several 'shops', standards are required in order to guarantee a unique layout for forms and structure of e-government portals or gateways.[9] This need is explicitly perceived in Austria, Poland and other countries. Consequently, Ireland is going to develop guidelines and standards for all public sector websites building on best practice in relation to design, search facilities and accessibility guidelines. The Netherlands recently announced to develop a meta-data standard for public sector websites in order to make it easier for citizens to find and access the information they need across the more than 1,200 separate government websites. In the Czech Republic, it is also stressed that e-government services have to be provided of comparable quality throughout the country based on open international standards (e.g. W3C). In Sweden, the goal of achieving a 24-hour Public Administration can only be realised by a minimum of binding rules and standards necessary for a well functioning electronic communication within the public administration and with its customers.

In the United Kingdom 'The Government Gateway' was already launched in 2001. It is a central registration and authentication engine enabling secure authenticated e-government transactions over the Internet. Citizens need to register with the Gateway in order to enrol for using online government services and subsequently transact securely with government departments. Built on open standards, the Gateway also enables the joined-up delivery of government services by allowing different systems in different departments to communicate with the Gateway and with each other. More explicitly, the exchange of documents requires standards. Belgium published recently a list of open standards to be used by public authorities aimed at facilitating the electronic exchange of information with citizens and businesses.

The efficient communication between the government and the citizens requires not only the effective exchange of documents. Since the private sector is a forerunner in use of digital signature we observe a close co-operation with the private sector.

Closely related to the issue of digital signature is the use of electronic ID cards and other forms of smart cards. Already in 1998, Sweden established an e-Identification infrastructure by approving standards regarding electronic ID. Following a framework agreement signed between the Swed-

ish Agency for Public Management and digital certificates suppliers, software-based electronic IDs (in particular the BankID developed by the largest Swedish banks) can also be used for certain e-government services. For the future, the Swedish government has plans to introduce an official electronic ID card containing biometric identifiers.

In 2003, the Italian Government signed an agreement with nine smart card providers to adopt a new unique standard ensuring interoperability of cards distributed across the whole Italian territory.

In Germany, the so called e-card strategy published in 2005 stated the importance of common standards for a number of e-government smart card initiatives in the areas of citizen identification, social security information and health insurance services to foster the development and take-up of transactional e-government services and maximise efficiency gains and cost savings. For example, a public-private e-signature alliance was formed in 2003 between the German Government and a number of private sector companies (banks, IT services companies, etc.) to establish e-signature standards based on current use of e-signatures in government and in the economy. In 2008 the specification for an eCard API framework was published by the Federal Office for Information Security. There have also been efforts by the DIN, the formal German standardisation body, to provide standards relating to e-government. In 2007 Focus ICT, a presidial committee of DIN formed to help implement the German standardisation strategy in ICT, made e-government an integral part of their overall strategy.[10]

Cyprus announced similar goals by pointing to the need for a European collaboration in order to put key pan-European services in place, such as cross-border company registration, electronic public procurement, job search and e-voting. In March of 2008 Cyprus initiated activities towards widespread implementation of eID cards in health services.

Ireland published a standard framework for Public Service Cards (PSC) in the year 2004. Public Service Cards are cards used to identify individuals using public services (i.e. medical card, social services card, etc.).

As already mentioned in the various initiatives outlined before, an electronic health insurance card is of major relevance for several countries. Besides the examples already mentioned, France also has developed new IAS (Identification, Authentication and Signature) standards for the health insurance card. This standard is implemented in the "Vitale 2" cards launched in 2007. Still, full coverage of this solution is to be expected in 2010 at best. The card will also be used to facilitate access to medical files and other personal medical-related information. Similarly, the Czech Republic aims to introduce smart cards compatible with EU standards for health insurance. As in France the process is still in development.

In Denmark, the Danish XML project, announced in 2001, aimed to define standards for exchange of data between government and the public. Data formats used by the individual authorities conform to a common, open, national standard. Moreover, a national agreement rendered the use of open standards mandatory in the public sector as of January 2008. The efforts undertaken relate mostly to exchange of information between citizens and the public authorities. Public Administrations are required to accept documents in ODF as well as OpenXML.

In Austria, the completion of the government-wide electronic record system (ELAK) in 2005 marks a key milestone of the Austrian e-government programme, leading to significant improvement in service delivery at the federal level. The electronic record is the original document; printouts are regarded only as copies. The digital handling of administrative procedures allows simultaneous processing, more efficient workflow, standardised working methods and cost savings in hardware procurement. The benefits for citizens and enterprises are faster administra-

tive procedures and the widespread delivery of electronic documents. In January 2008, Austria implemented the already mentioned eID cards to be used in health insurance. These cards carry a signature which is said to conform to European Standards. There is a considerable level of awareness in Austria as to the crucial role standards play in the overall context of e-Government.

In general all these e-government initiatives improve the workflow in government administration. We observe various initiatives of governments to standardise web portals, gateways, the exchange of documents, electronic signatures and identification cards, especially for e-health applications in order to optimise the interface between the e-government and the citizens. Although most e-government initiatives are restricted to the local or national territory, several initiatives highlight the need to recur on existing standards or to develop international or European standards.

3.3 Communication within the Governmental Organisation or Between Government and its Suppliers

Standards structuring the interface between e-government services and products and citizens are also relevant for the internal communication in governmental organisations or between the various governmental organisations at the different levels. In our overview we start with initiatives to develop and implement communication and interoperability standards required for e-government, then discuss the establishment of databases of software for governmental organisation and finally e-procurement standards.

For most of the countries, it is essential to establish standards for interfaces between governmental departments, institutions and various governmental levels that permit efficient and transparent communication. For example, the United Kingdom published already in the year 2000 the first version of the e-government Interoperability Framework (e-GIF), setting out the government's technical policies and standards for achieving interoperability and information systems integration across the public sector. In particular, it adopts XML as the primary standard for data integration and presentation on all public sector systems. Defining the essential pre-requisite for joined-up and web enabled government, the e-GIF is a cornerstone in the overall e-government strategy in the United Kingdom. The Danish XML project defines standards for the description of all relevant data in the public sector, so as to support easy and cheap access to and reuse of public data, and to enable data exchange and information systems interoperability across the public sector.

Finland started to develop methods for the integration of e-government systems and services by means of meta-data standardisation based on XML standards. In Sweden, the Government Interoperability Board was established in 2004 with the mandate to issue common standards and guidelines for electronic information exchange within government. The e-Government Interoperability Framework lists technical policies and specifications to guide IT decision-makers in their choices of IT systems to harmonise the use of technologies through out the Danish administration. Germany's e-government interoperability framework SAGA (Standards and Architecture for e-Government Applications) sets out the technical standards for the implementation of the e-government initiative BundOnline2005, the e-government initiative with its focus to determine the need for interoperability policies, technical standards and organisational requirements for online federal services. The Deutschland-Online strategy provides the framework for co-operation between all administration layers to interconnect Internet portals: The federal government, state governments and municipalities will create joint standards as well as data and process models for e-government. There has also been funding for strategic research projects like "Standards for an

integrated e-Government" in the activity "Innovation with Norms and Standards" funded by Federal Ministry for Economics and Technology. In 2007 a specific project has been established aimed at the standardisation of uniform data exchange which forms an integral part of the overall e-government related Deutschland-Online action plan. The plan is to develop semantic web standards and establish a set of XML based standards for the public sector under the acronym XÖV (XML in der öffentlichen Verwaltung/XML in the public services).

Besides these forerunners in Europe, especially the new Member States, e.g. Slovenia, try to comply with EU recommendations and orientations with regard to the European Interoperability Framework (IDABC 2004) for e-government services.

Managing documents electronically including finding consensus on how to organise digital or electronic signatures is a central challenge for the development of respective standards. The implementation of the EU directive on electronic signatures requires respective standards. Several Member States started to develop and implement respective standards. In Germany, general e-signature standards are developed based on current use of e-signatures in government and in the economy.

A central element within the interoperability initiatives is an agreement on common standards. Consequently, we observe in several countries attempts to reach commitments among governmental organisations to implement the same software and standards. For example, in Belgium, a list of open standards to be used by public authorities at all levels was recently published in order to support a better integration of federal back-offices, promoting the interoperability of their information systems. A central repository of information about data interchange standards, the so-called InfostructureBase was installed by the Danish government in 2003 not only addressing the public sector, but also the private sector. In the Netherlands, the 'e-Communes' project was launched in 2003 in order to encourage the exchange of best practices as well as the development of common local e-government standards and projects.

Besides the agreement on common standards, which promotes and guarantees interoperability between different organisations, cost effectiveness is another rationale to use the same, preferable open standards. Since we observe both, multi-level governance in all Member States and a huge number of governmental organisations at the local level, cost savings can be realised, if standards are either developed at the higher or highest level, which can then be transferred to the lower governmental levels. For example, the ME-DIA@Komm-Transfer project aims at identifying and developing transferable and standardised e-government solutions, including the standard for e-government data exchange OSCI (Online Services Computer Interface), for German local and regional authorities.

The German Government Site Builder is a new Content Management System (CMS) meant to become a government-wide standard. Austria established in 2004 a web-based plat-form providing Austrian municipalities with access to affordable and standardised e-government tools. The Spanish Government and the Federation of Municipalities and Provinces (FEMP) launched the 'PISTA-Administración Local' initiative, aimed at enabling small and medium-size municipalities to deliver services online. The project consists of the development of a standardised software application designed to enable the simple deployment of basic online information and services, which small local authorities will be able to use for free.

In the Netherlands, the open source software exchange platform enables public sector bodies to access, share and exchange open source software programs. It forms part of the programme for Open Standards and Open Source Software in Government (Verhoosel, Akkersdijk 2004), designed to stimulate the adoption and use of open source software in the Dutch public sector. In 2003, France established an open source content management system (AGORA) providing a quick and easy tool for managing internet, intranet or extranet sites at reduced cost. Its aim is to help rationalise content management and foster interoperability of web content and functionalities across government, while reducing website costs and building times, enabling web publication by non-technical staff, enabling content syndication across websites and organisations, and simplifying websites implementation through standardisation. Relying on open source software in establishing e-government services is especially a strategy for the New Member States to catch up quickly and cheaply with the more advanced countries in the EU. For example, in Slovakia the government is committed to building public administration information systems and using open software standards as cost-effective solutions.

In the previous section, we have collected initiatives of governments in the EU to improve the interface with its clients and customers, the citizens. However, we observe also activities to make the relationship with its suppliers more efficient by establishing e-procurement and in order to implement the new EU public procurement directives (2004/17/EC and 2004/18/EC). Following the activities at the European level, several Member states have fostered e-procurement in order to increase the efficiency of the procurement process, but also to save the costs and to increase the quality of the procured goods and services. These activities follow the efforts in the private sector.

Besides the implementation of European guidelines and standards (CEN 2005), which is of high priority in the new Member States[11], like in the Czech Republic or Estonia, to ensure interoperability of e-procurement systems across borders, we observe several progressive initiatives at the national level.

There has also been efforts to implement the Universal Business Language (UBL 2.0) developed by OASIS.[12] Denmark was the first to implement UBL as a standard for public sector e-procurement in 2004. Other Scandinavian countries including Sweden, Norway, Iceland and Finland have also implemented UBL. There have also been efforts to implement SAML, also developed by OASIS, as a framework for creating and exchanging security information.

The UK Government adopted also in 2004 a new common, open-standard IT language - dubbed UKGOV XML - to deliver interoperable e-procurement solutions to public institutions and their suppliers. In addition, a National e-Procurement Project has also been launched as part of the local e-government strategy to deliver standard e-procurement tools for councils. In 2005, Portugal launched the national e-procurement portal ('Portal de Compras'). Developed in the framework of the National e-Procurement Programme, the portal – which complies with the guidelines of W3C's Web Accessibility Initiative – aims to become the new standard for public procurement.

If we summarise the requirements of standards addressing internal communication within governmental organisations and with their suppliers, then we have to observe the general need to ensure interoperability of e-government systems, which is reinforced both by the heterogeneity of governmental organisations at one level and by the multilevel structure. Besides the use of standard IT language, common data formats for the exchange of documents, the use of common e-signature systems support the realisation of interoperable solutions. The various governmental levels with its numerous organisations down to single municipalities or local communities allow also the exploitation of economies of scale effects by the use of common standards, especially standard software. Besides using the same proprietary software in order to save licensing fees, the use of open source software also for the implementation of e-government solutions allows saving significant costs. The cost argument is also a driving

force for the introduction of standardised e-procurement solutions, which increase the market power of governmental organisations in order to procure goods and services at lower costs or at higher quality.

4. SUMMARY

The application of the taxonomy of service standards developed by Vries (2001) to structure and analyse the general requirements identified and activities already undertaken to establish e-government services in the EU based on the IDABC report on e-government (IDABC eGovernment Observatory 2005), the ePractice.eu country fact sheets and the UN Global E-government Readiness Report 2005 revealed the following patterns regarding the demand for standards. The rather complex and multi-level organisational structure of governmental organisations is the most important driving force for developing common standards in order to establish and ensure the internal interoperability of processes. This internal co-ordination process is still running and not all requirements for standards are already fulfilled despite significant progress and success especially in forerunner countries, like the United Kingdom and the Scandinavian countries. Due to several initiatives at the European level either via the publication of framework directives or first CEN workshop agreements, there is additional pressure, but also support, to promote the development of respective standards supporting the establishment and promotion of e-government. A good example for this pressure is the implementation plan regarding "Electronic IDentification Cards", the so-called "e-IDs". Some countries have already implemented an e-ID scheme like Spain, Italy, Portugal, Belgium, Sweden, Austria, Finland, Estonia, Norway and Iceland. Others like Germany, France, the Netherlands, Hungary, Bulgaria Latvia, Slovenia and Malta are in the process of implementation in 2008. Other countries like the

United Kingdom and Ireland, Poland, Slovakia, Romania and Lithuania are still in the development and planning phase. The plans to implement smart cards for identification are welcome and promoted by the European Commission. Still, there are considerable differences between countries both technically and also regarding the content that should be stored on those cards. Some implementations make use of European or international formal standards, other implementations do not conform to standards at all (IDABC, 2007). This challenge of integration of different regimes into a Pan-European e-ID system is a good example where standards on the European or international level could solve parts of the integration problem.[12]

Besides the requirement to ensure interoperable processes, it further has to be mentioned that the exploitation of economies of scale requires the use of common proprietary or de facto software standards in order to save licensing fees and promote also the use of open source software for the implementation of e-government solutions. The cost efficiency argument is also a driving force to implement standard-based e-procurement systems, which increase the market power of governmental organisations in relation to the suppliers of goods and services.

The use of standards in e-government solutions in order to improve the efficiency of communication between governmental organisations and their clients, the citizens, benefits also from the standards that are being implemented in the private sector in order to ensure internal interoperability, like standards for the exchange of documents or digital signatures. However, the need for further standards that increase the customer relation is yet to emerge. The restricted demand for this kind of standards, like structuring accessibility, or the reluctance to implement respective standards can be explained by the monopoly of governmental organisations to provide certain services. This special constellation explains the rather few standardisation activities being launched in order to

improve safety and privacy aspects in context of the provision of e-government services, although here solutions developed for the private sector can also be implemented.

REFERENCES

Blind, K. (2006). A Taxonomy of Standards in the Service Sector: Theoretical Discussion and Empirical Test. *The Service Industries Journal, 26*(4), 397-420.

Borras, J. (2003). *E-Government Challenges and Perspectives-the UK Perspective*. Office of the E-Envoy.

CEN (2005). *Analysis of standardization requirements and standardization gaps for eProcurement in Europe, CEN Workshop Agreement*, Brussels.

EC (2003). The Role of eGovernment for Europe's Future, COM(2003) 567, European Communities. European Communities, Brussels

EC (2006a). i2010 eGovernment Action Plan: Accelerating eGovernment in Europe for the Benefit of All, COM(2006) 173, European Communities Brussels.

EC (2006b). Interoperability for Pan-European eGovernment Services, COM(2006) 45, European Communities Brussels.

EC (2006c). Directive 2006/123/EC of the European Parliament and of the Council of 12 December 2006 on services in the internal market, Brussels.

IDABC (2004). European Interoperability Framework for Pan-European eGovernment Services - Version 1.0: Office for Official Publications of the European Communities.

IDABC eGovernment Observatory (2005). eGovernment in the Member States of the European Union, European Communities Brussels.

IDABC (2007) eID Interoperability for PEGS Analysis and Assessment of similarities and differences - Impact on eID interoperability, European Communities Brussels.

Marincu, C., & McMullin, B. (2004). A comparative assessment of Web accessibility and technical standards conformance in four EU states. *First Monday, 9*(7).

UN (2005). *UN Global E-government Readiness Report 2005: From E-government to E-inclusion*, UNPAN/2005/14, United Nations, New York

Verhoosel, J. P. C., & Akkersdijk, V. (2004). eGovernment for Businesses: Lessons learned from a trajectory of Standardization of Business Information. In P. Cunningham & M. Cunningham, (Eds.), *eAdoption and the Knowledge Economy: Issues, Applications, Case Studies* (pp. 604-610). Amsterdam: IOS Press.

Vries, H. J. (1999). *Standardization. A Business Approach to the Role of National Standardization Organizations*. Boston, Dordrecht, London: Kluwer Academic Publishers.

Vries, H. J. (2001). *Systematic services standardization from consumer's point of view*. Contribution to the ISO Workshop in Oslo May 2001, Oslo.

Werle, R., & Iversen, E. J. (2006). Promoting Legitimacy in Technical Standardization. *Science, Technology & Innovation Studies, 2*, 19-39.

ENDNOTES

[1] Consequently, OASIS, an SSB that is a major player in the e-business domain is also actively working in e-government standardisation. Within OASIS' Techncial Committee on e-government, projects are under way to cover Core Components, ebXML Registry, Harmonising Taxonomies, Naming and Design Rules, Semantic Interoperability, Records Management, Workflow, and Web Services.

[2] G2B = Government-to-Business, G2G Government-to-Government, G2C = Government-to-Citizen.

[3] The German government is a case in point; see e.g. [BundOnline, 2003]

[4] There are also considerable efforts that refer to standards but operate outside the standardisation system as such like IDABC which produced the European Interoperability Framework (EIF).

[5] These TCs reflect the large areas of activity addressed by eGov. The list includes the OASIS Election and Voter Services TC, the OASIS Emergency Management TC, the OASIS Tax XML TC as well as two TCs relating to legal documents (OASIS LegalXML Electronic Court Filing TC and OASIS LegalXML eNotarization TC).

[6] CEN Information Society Standardisation System, the 'ICT arm' of CEN.

[7] This is also true for an earlier EC Communication, the eGovernment Communication 2003, COM(2003) 567. There, interoperability is mentioned but the focus is more towards establishing interoperability by funding specific actions in the Sixth Framework Programme, Open Source activities and "open standards" in general. "Standards" are discussed as to their absence on European level and the fact that "different standards and the multiplicity of languages make it difficult to fully exploit the potential [of public-.sector information]" (EC, 2003).

[8] Blind (2006) performed an empirical test of the taxonomy by relying on survey data, which led to a further reduction of standards categories. For the sake of simplicity, we use the more differentiated version.

9   The European Services Directive does also react to this problem by asking for "one-stop-solutions".

10   The other two main areas of activity are: Security Systems and Transport telematics.

11   In Slovakia, the Office for Public Procurement has elaborated standard forms of public procurement notices, which will be sent by contracting authorities to the Office for Public Procurement electronically.

12   The European Commission has provided funding for such integration activities. STORK, a project in the ICT Policy Support Programme, seeks to tackle the issue of interoperability between the heterogeneous approaches. The European formal standardisation bodies as well as national standardisation bodies are not part of the project consortium.

Chapter III
A Taxonomy of Service Standards and a Modification for E–Business

Knut Blind

Berlin University of Technology, Germany, Fraunhofer Institute for Systems and Innovation Research, Germany, & Erasmus University, Netherlands

ABSTRACT

Against the background of theoretical typologies of service standards, a survey among European service companies addressed the question, in which service-related categories formal and informal standards are implemented. Relying on the assessment of the importance of the various service-related standardisation aspects, it was possible to identify a taxonomy of service standards containing five clusters of service standards "Service Management", "Service Employee", "Service Delivery", "Customer Interaction", and "Data Flows and Security", which correspond very closely to the ex ante applied typology derived from the literature. The analysis of the subsample of companies active in e-commerce reveals significant differences, which reflect their special needs caused by the distance to their customers.

1. INTRODUCTION

Since we are only at the beginning of service standardisation, a conceptual typology or an empirically founded taxonomy will be helpful to survey the upcoming standardisation activities regarding services, including e-business, to reduce the complexity of the different types of service standards, to identify similarities and differences, for comparative analyses and to shape future empirical investigations. A simple application or transfer of existing typologies of standards developed on the basis of the features of the manufacturing sector and material products is not adequate to tackle this challenge.

2. OBJECTIVES

The objective of the chapter is first to provide a review of existing typologies of service standards. In a second step, we compare the theoretical insights with the results of a survey among European service companies. This allows us to produce an empirically based taxonomy of service standards. Furthermore, one fifth of the sample is active in e-business activities, which allows us to compare the answers of this group with the rest of the sample. Based on these insights, we are able to determine the challenges of e-business for future standardisation activities.

3. METHODOLOGY

In order to achieve the objectives, the chapter is divided as follows. First, the state-of-the-art in service standards research will be apprehended by screening the relevant literature, including the very few existing empirical studies. Here, we focus especially on the few typologies of service standards. Based on this background, service companies were approached via a questionnaire in order to elucidate the importance and the current implementation of standards. The survey covered all Member States and the sample was distributed according to size and service sectors. The addressees were approached via e-mail and a link to an Internet-based questionnaire. More than 350 completed questionnaires are available to perform a test of the conceptual typology of standards in order to come to an empirically proved taxonomy of service standards. In addition, we are able to separate the answers of the one fifth of companies active in e-business. We focus on the estimation of the importance of various types of service standards and develop an empirically based taxonomy, applying a factor analysis approach.

4. RESULTS

In general, there is no broad literature on service standards and typologies. The most recent and differentiated approach to set up a typology of service standards was developed by De Vries (1999, 2001; see Table 1). According to his general definition, standards concern entities or relations between entities. Therefore, for a systematic approach to standards in the service sector, it is first necessary to define entities. Typical of services is the interaction between supplier and customer as the main entities. On the supply side, the organisation or the service company and service employees can be regarded as entities. Furthermore, both the service process and the service results can be considered as further entities, although often service process and result occur simultaneously. Finally, a distinction between delivery and final result has to be made. Based on these theoretical considerations, the following classification can be derived.

De Vries applied this classification successfully both to hair care service and to road transport service. These examples deliver indications about the appropriateness and the feasibility of this classification for use across all service sectors, which allows cross-sectional comparisons in the proposed empirical study and may help to identify also the need of cross-sectional service standards.

The major objective of this chapter is to test empirically this typology of service standards presented and to develop an empirically proved taxonomy. The qualitative and quantitative overview of service standardisation activities on the national, European and international level is not sufficient to detect clusters of closely linked types of standards, although they may be classified according to the ICS classification, which is still strongly influenced by technologies and the manufacturing sector. However, we follow another approach, which takes explicitly into account the views of service companies implementing service standards. We rely on the answers of a sample of European service companies to a questionnaire about the existing implementation of and future needs for service standards. In this chapter, we present first the characteristics of the sample, then the ranking of the importance of various types of service standards for the responding companies is presented. This assessment of the importance is the basis for a factor analysis, which allows us to test the typology of service standards discussed

in the literature and to develop an empirically based taxonomy.

Against the sound background of a literature review, a survey among European service companies addressed the question, in which service-related categories formal and informal standards are implemented. In total 364 European service companies responded to the on-line survey. Almost 60% of the sample has less than 250 employees. One third of the sample represents business services, one fifth education and social services, but also financial, transport and communication

Table 1. Services standards typology

Standards for: Entities or relations between entities	...may concern:
Service organisation	Quality management, environmental management, occupational health and safety management. Solvency and other financial aspects. Crew, e.g., minimum number of staff and their educational level.
Service employee	Knowledge. Skills. Attitude. Ethical code (e.g., confidentiality).
Service delivery	Specification of activities. Trustworthiness. Privacy aspects. Safety aspects. Code of conduct.
Service result	Result specification. Trustworthiness.
Physical objects supporting service delivery	E.g., technical requirements for trains in public transport services.
Workroom	E.g., requirements for daylight access in offices.
Precautions	Emergency measures. Complaints handling. Guarantee.
Additional elements to the core service – delivery.	E. g. waiting facilities
Additional elements to the core service – results	
Communication between customer and service organisation (before, during and after providing the service)	Semantics (e.g., data elements to be used). Syntax (e.g., forms layout, syntax rules for electronic messages). Specification of information and communication technology to be used. Protocols. Code of conduct. Approachability (e.g., hours of accessibility per telephone and average waiting time).
Communication within the service organisation or between this organisation and its suppliers	Semantics. Syntax. Specification of ICT to be used. Protocols. Code of conduct. Approachability.

Source: (de Vries, 2001)

service companies. Furthermore, around one fifth of the sample is already active in e-business.

In order to develop an empirically based taxonomy of service standards, we rely on the companies´ assessment of the importance of standards for service-related aspects. An alternative approach would be to use the answers on the actual use of different types of standards. However, the assessment of the importance differentiates between five levels (very low importance to very high importance), whereas the question for implementation just allows a "yes" or "no" option, which is too restrictive for more sophisticated statistical analyses.

First of all, we asked the service companies to assess the importance which standards have for 23 service-specific and standards-related aspects of their business. Figure 1 presents the ranking of the importance of standards for service related aspects. Standards are highly important for data security regarding customer interaction and internal data security. This is an issue which is very

closely related to information and communication technologies, which are also characterised by a high degree of standardisation. The same high importance of standards emerges for the issues of quality management[1] and customer satisfaction. Furthermore, standards for qualifications and skills of employees, standards regarding the evaluation of services by customers and standards for information systems and the service process are still of high importance. In contrast, standards for environmental management and ergonomics are at the bottom of the ranking and just over medium importance.[2]

In accordance with the existing typologies in the literature (de Vries, 2001), we have grouped the 23 aspects into the broader categories "service management", "service employee", "service delivery", "customer interaction", "internal interaction", and "general terminology" in the questionnaire. A factor analysis based on the assessment of the importance of the various issues confirmed this ex ante grouping, since we arrive at the fol-

Figure 1. Importance of standards for service-related aspects (3 = medium importance to 5 = very high importance)

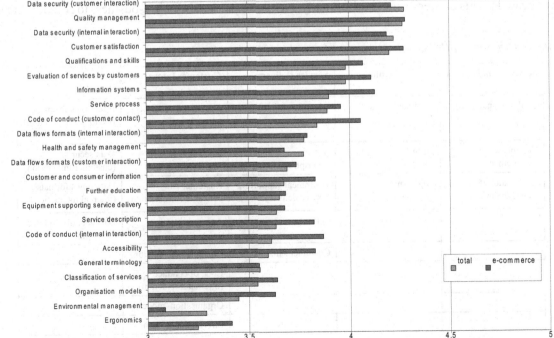

lowing clusters in Table 2. These clusters mean that we have five dimensions of service standards and each company is individually located in this five-dimensional space.

If we compare the empirically based taxonomy of the five types of standards for service-related aspects with the literature in more detail, we find – as already mentioned – a high similarity to De Vries' (2001) typology. The first group of standards for "Service Management" corresponds well to the standards De Vries lists under standards for service organisations. The second group of standards for the "Service Employee" covers the knowledge and skill aspect of De Vries' typology. Standards for "Service Delivery" covers standards for the classification and description of services, the equipment supporting service delivery, the service process and for customer satisfaction, whereas De Vries includes also trustworthiness, privacy, safety and code of conduct aspects. The latter aspect is included in our cluster of standards focusing on customer interaction, which contains also the evaluation of services by customers, customer information, the accessibility (e.g. hotlines), customer satisfaction. In addition, standards for organisational models and information systems are allocated in this cluster of standards. Finally,

we have an important cluster of standards concerning data flows and security, which is not explicitly mentioned by De Vries (2001), but is closely related to the mentioned trustworthiness and privacy aspects.

Concluding the comparison between the conceptual typologies of service standards and the empirically based taxonomy, we have to note the following main results. The conceptual approach of De Vries (2001) to understand standards as formal instruments to facilitate relations within or between entities reflects very well the empirical reality from the perspective of companies. However, the fine differentiation of different types of standards by De Vries cannot be confirmed by the empirical data. Furthermore, the flows of data and their security are a crucial aspect for the majority of service companies and constitute a single cluster of standards covering the internal and external dimension.

The companies active in e-business, a fifth of the total sample, address a higher importance – by comparison to the rest of the sample – to all those kinds of standards which try to standardise the interaction with the customers, e.g. the code of conduct with customers. This reflects the need of companies active in e-business to compensate for

Table 2. An Empirically-based taxonomy of standards for services[3]

Service Management	Service Employee	Service Delivery	Customer Interaction	Data Flows and Security
Quality management	Qualifications and skills	Classification of services	Evaluation of services by customers	Data flows formats (customer interaction)
Environmental management	Further education	Service description	Code of conduct (customer contact)	Data security (customer interaction)
Health and safety management	Ergonomics	Equipment supporting service delivery	Customer and consumer information	Data flows formats (internal interaction)
		Service process	Accessibility	Data security (internal interaction)
		Customer satisfaction	Customer satisfaction	
			Code of conduct (internal interaction)	
			Organisation models	
			Information systems	

the lost personal relationship to the customer by different kinds of standards, which allow a better satisfaction of the customer needs and to secure the quality of the services and goods delivered. The factor analysis based on the subsample of companies active in e-business leads to slightly different factors.

One the one hand we find a set of standards in the context of "Customer Interaction". Then standards for the environmental management and relevant for health and safety are combined into a second factor. A third factor deals with "Service Delivery". Finally, "Data Flows and Information Systems" represent a factor and "Data Security" a fifth separate cluster. These differences confirm that companies active in e-business have different needs for standards and for bundles of standards, especially regarding data security. Consequently, the general taxonomy of service standards has to be adjusted to the requirements of e-business companies.

5. CONCLUSION

Based on screening the state-of-the art in service standards research, we identified the peculiarities of services, which provide the background for the different typologies of service standards. Relying on the assessment of the importance of the various service-related standardisation aspects by a set of European service companies, it was possible to identify a taxonomy of service standards containing five clusters of service standards, which correspond very closely to the ex ante applied typology derived from the literature. In a next step, we checked whether this taxonomy emerges also for different service sectors and companies active in e-business, because they address a higher importance to all customer-related standards. Here, we find differences to the results of the factor analysis based on the total sample of companies.

In a next step of future research, one has to check whether this taxonomy is also valid for dif-

Table 3. An empirically-based taxonomy of standards for e-business[4]

Environmental, Health and Safety Management	Customer Interaction	Service Delivery	Data Flows and Information Systems	Data Security
Environmental management	Qualifications and skills	Quality management	Ergonomics	Data security (customer interaction)
Health and safety management	Further education	Classification of services	Data flows formats (customer interaction)	Data security (internal interaction)
	Customer satisfaction	Service description	Information systems	Data flows formats (internal interaction)
	Evaluation of services by customers	Equipment supporting service delivery	Data flows formats (internal interaction)	
	Code of conduct (customer contact)	Service process		
	Customer and consumer information			
	Accessibility			
	Code of conduct (internal interaction)			
	Organisation models			
	Information systems			

ferent service sectors and for service companies of different sizes or located in different countries. In a further step, the importance of the different types of service standards within the subcategories of the very heterogeneous service sector have to be determined, first on a conceptual, and second on an empirical basis. Furthermore, the ongoing standardisation activities have to be screened and categorised in order to test the usability of this taxonomy for practical reasons.

REFERENCES

de Vries, H. J. (1999). *Standardization*. A Business Approach to the Role of National Standardization Organizations. Kluwer Academic Publishers, Boston/Dordrecht/London.

de Vries, H. J. (2001). *Systematic services standardization from consumer's point of view*. Contribution to the ISO Workshop in Oslo.

Mörschel, I., & Schwengels, C. (2002). Standardisierungspotenziale für Dienstleistungen – Ergebnisse einer allgemeinen Bedarfserhebung. In DIN (Ed.), *Standardisierung in der deutschen Dienstleistungswirtschaft – Potenziale und Handlungsbedarf*, DIN-Fachbericht 116, Berlin et al.: Beuth Verlag GmbH, (pp. 51-65).

ENDNOTES

[1] Furthermore, in the open question, which standard is most important for the company, a significant number of respondents mentioned the series of ISO 9000 standards.

[2] These results do not confirm the results of a smaller survey in Germany, which asked for the general and not standard-related relevance of these aspects for service companies (Mörschel & Schwengels, 2002).

[3] We have not included "Terminology", since it applies to all companies and consequently all factors in the same intensity.

[4] We have not included "Terminology", since it applies to all companies and consequently all factors in the same intensity.

Chapter IV
Business Models and the Dynamics of Supply and Demand for Standards

Richard Hawkins
University of Calgary, Canada

ABSTRACT

With specific reference to information and communication technologies (ICT), this Chapter examines the structural relationship of various stakeholder groups to standardization, described both in terms of how different stakeholders demand and acquire standards and in terms of their corresponding motivations and/or capabilities to influence the standardization process. To this end, the Chapter will explore these dynamics in the context of 'business models', an emerging framework in the innovation context that describes commercial and organisational topologies for the supply and demand of goods and services from the perspective of how value is created and exchanged. Given the increasing synergy between many ICT standards and specific product and service environments, it will be shown how the business model is also potentially a useful device for understanding evolution in the supply and demand dynamics of standardization.

1. EVOLVING ANALYTICAL PERSPECTIVES ON SUPPLY AND DEMAND IN STANDARDIZATION RESEARCH

Social scientists have been studying standardization phenomena systematically for barely fifty years, the vast bulk of knowledge being produced only within the past twenty-five years. Much of the literature from before the mid-1980s now has the look of an 'old school', many of whose perspectives were still congruent with Whitworth's 19th Century definition of standards as technical specifications that created the greatest common good with the minimum possible means; i.e. specifications whose adoption would confer homogenous advantages upon a heterogeneous group of producers (Whitworth 1882).

At first, standards were discussed almost exclusively within a very instrumental framework as a form of public goods with high inherent social welfare characteristics stemming primarily from their role in reducing technological variety (Kindleberger 1983). This perception was largely the result of a narrow focus upon 'formal' standards as developed using quasi-juridical stakeholder consultation processes and published in the public domain by nationally or internationally accredited standards development organisations (SDOs). Accordingly, the overwhelming emphasis of the first phases of standardization analysis was upon organization and process. The context was often highly normative, focussed upon how to ensure greater procedural efficiency in standards development and application within the conventional SDO framework (e.g. Reck 1956; Woodward 1965; Verman 1973; Sullivan 1983; Wallenstein 1990). This emphasis persists to this day although in a much wider and more subtle variety of guises (e.g. compare Cargill & Bohlin 2007 with de Vries 1999).

However, it was recognized very early on that over and above their technical functions, standards also have strategic and competitive dimensions in a variety of contexts ranging from the industrial politics of supply chains to international trade (Thompson 1954; Middleton 1973; Crane 1978; Hemenway 1978). During the 1980s a 'new school' emerged, which preserved some of the earlier instrumental focus, but greatly expanded the analytical spectrum and took a much more critical and empirically rigorous stance regarding the organization, function and purpose of standardization. During this transformation, many new perspectives opened up on the question of how demand for standards is issued and fulfilled.

In the earlier 'instrumentalist' tradition, the supply-and-demand issue was relatively straightforward. Demand would emerge whenever enough producers recognized that proprietary solutions were more a source of costs than advantage. Supply was a coordination issue; either selecting an existing practice or otherwise developing a new practice collectively. The 'new school' challenged these rather simplistic premises, shifting attention to the strategic role of standards in coordinating markets as well as technology. In this framework, standardization decisions become much more closely connected analytically to business decisions and the supply and demand dynamics of standardization became linked with those of the actual products and services in which standards were embedded. Indeed, in much of the more recent literature, standards themselves have been treated as products in their own right, or otherwise so synonymous with specific product environments as makes no difference (Egyedi 2001; Bekkers 2001; West 2003).

Arguably, this transition between old and new schools was fuelled by at least two major developments. The first was the appearance of economic, social and political theories that proposed an active link between standardization and innovation. The traditional view was that standardization occurred late in the innovation process when technology was mature and the late stages of the product cycle were being reached (Vernon 1966). The new theory maintained that standards could (and typically did) influence the directions of technical change much earlier in the product cycle, mainly by building up positive returns to adoption and creating path dependencies, but also simply by defining key technological infrastructures and platforms upon which a variety of new products and services could be constructed (Katz & Shapiro 1985, 1986; Farrell & Saloner 1985; David 1985; Arthur 1989; David & Greenstein 1990; Tassey 1992, 2000).

From these beginnings, many social scientists began to investigate standardization over and above considerations of optimal technology selection (which was the focus of most economic theory). Many examined the public interest implications of standards and the strategic role that standardization could play in coordinating technologies and in organizing and regulating markets (Majone 1984; Breyer 1984; Salter 1988; Hawkins 1995; Graham *et al* 1995; Schmidt & Werle 1996; Krislov 1997). The impacts of such commercial and institutional alignments were further explored theoretically and empirically in terms of their potential effects on standardization decisions, in some cases right down to the committee level (Farrell & Saloner 1988; Weiss & Sirbu 1990; Economides & Flyer 1998). Bridges were built also between standardization and the regime of statistical indicators normally associated with innovation – like R&D investment, patenting, productivity and trade performance (Swann et al 1996; Blind 2004).

All of these new perspectives expanded the taxonomical framework of standardization, encouraged a much more critical view of its social welfare potential and focused in upon the strategic use of standards in furthering commercial agendas for innovation, although mainly as related to technology producer goods. In terms of supply and demand issues, however, this work brought standards squarely into the affray that surrounds one of the most perennially contentious issues in innovation studies; namely, whether innovation is driven primarily by supply or by demand (the classic 'push-pull' conundrum). Within the neo-Schumpeterian economic paradigm that has dominated innovation studies since the 1950s, scholars have waged a lively argument over this question. Many neo-Schumpeterians, and many others besides, have since maintained that innovation requires some form of interplay between supply and demand factors – a view that can be fleshed out to some extent in the business model context (more below) – or even that some types of innovation are mainly demand driven.[1]

This debate is by no means resolved, but it has moved decisively in the direction of recognizing that innovation involves more than technical change. There is now much more exploration of phenomena like 'co-invention' and 'consumers as innovators' (von Hippel 1988; Cowan et al 1991; Bresnahan et al 1996; McMeekin et al 2005). Also, much more attention is now being paid to the role in innovation of feedbacks and adaptive learning at the organizational level (Cohen & Levinthal 1990, Levinthal 1997; Kauffman *et al* 2000), how different institutional environments affect the likelihood that innovation will occur (Montalvo 2002) and how urban and regional environments can affect the pace of innovation (Cooke & Morgan 1998, Florida 2002).

Particularly important in the standardization context, many scholars now question the value of knowledge monopolies in innovation, stressing that innovation is produced by the combination of knowledge, implying a need for mechanisms (including standards) that facilitate knowledge coordination (Mazzolini & Nelson 1998, Chesbrough 2003, Macdonald 2004). Although these perspectives do not resolve the 'push-pull' conundrum, they have shed new light on what affects the ability of social groups to be receptive to innovation and to absorb its outcomes.

Arguably the other (and closely related) major development was the rapid diffusion of ICT which appeared to have an abundance of characteristics that challenged traditional views of standardization. In particular, the phenomenon of increasing returns to adoption was seen to have particularly strong and unique implications where electronic networks were concerned (David & Steinmueller 1990, Shapiro & Varian 2002). ICT standardization generated institutional challenges as well. Although early ICT standardization initiatives like OSI and ISDN were undertaken within established standards organizations, by the late 1980s significant centrifugal forces had begin to appear in the global structure of standardization institutions (Besen 1990; Besen & Farrell 1991; Hawkins 1992). By the late 1990s, spurred largely by the burgeoning Internet phenomenon, most of the significant standardization activity in computing and much of the telecom activity (especially in the higher value-added segments) was occurring in rapidly expanding array of independent consortia that were dominated by the major ICT vendors (Updegrove 1995; Hawkins 1999, Blind & Gauch 2005).

These developments prompted further investigation of standardization outside of traditional institutional contexts. The rapid accumulation of industry consortia in the ICT field was interpreted initially to be the result of asymmetry between the speed of technology development and the efficiency (or rather inefficiency) of the formal standards setting process – basically a time-to-market issue. However, no compelling evidence was ever produced that consortia actually accelerated the process. Moreover, the increasing complexity of the emerging standardization structure suggests strongly that the consortia phenomenon may have generated additional coordination costs and quality problems that may begin to induce stakeholders to prefer standards from more formal standardization venues (Cargill & Bohlin 2007; Blind et al 2007). As will be shown below, such institutional realignments are potentially significant in a business modelling context, where strong linkages are made between the success of a product and how various levels of value in that product are constructed in the market.

The outcome of was a general view that at least in areas like ICT, standardization and innovation were connected systemically. This suggested that competition between ICT standards – creating virtually a 'market' for standards in their own right – was now a normal feature of the standardization landscape. This would infer diverse motivations for creating and adopting standards among different groups of stakeholders and this generated many new questions about how demand for standards was actually generated and fulfilled within such a system. In particular it drew attention to the possibility that the impact of any particular standard could be expected to be quite different for each stakeholder group. The obvious concern was the

possibility that a standard might have a positive impact on technology vendors, but a negative impact on technology users, or *vice versa*.

The Producer-User Problem

Supply and demand relationships are usually characterized in terms of producers and consumers, or buyers and sellers. But for standards, such relationships are very difficult to define. In both old and new schools, the standardization process has been considered mainly from the perspective of technology producers who develop and apply standards directly to products that are sold on to users. That 'users' (variously defined as users of technology and/or standards) have a stake in standards is seldom at issue. But the problem has been cast more in terms of how to integrate non-producer constituencies more equitably and efficiently into what historically has been a vendor-dominated process (Jakobs et al 1996; de Vries 1999). Nevertheless, there remain serious questions about the capability, inclination or even wisdom of trying to influence these stakeholders to participate. Indeed, several studies of user participation in standardization indicate that structural barriers and transaction costs strongly bias standards outcomes towards producer agendas (Dankbar & van Tulder 1992; Evans et al 1993; Hawkins 1995).

Users of any particular technology or standard may form such a heterogeneous group that problems of awareness, aggregation, technical capabilities and coordination may be insurmountable (Foray 1996). Moreover, there are significant transaction and opportunity cost issues. Users almost always face the dilemma of whether the costs and risks of participating in standards development will be greater than any eventual disadvantage incurred by simply adopting standards that are developed by vendors (Liebowitz & Margolis 1995; Hawkins 1995). Moreover, in some cases, both producers and users can *adapt* standards: that many stakeholders choose this option is indicated by the high incidence of systems that are not fully compatible or interoperable even though nominally they conform to the same standards.[2]

The producer-user issue is especially important in the ICT standardization context because arguably the ICT producer goods sector is now neither the only nor perhaps even the most significant source of innovation in ICT. Increasingly, innovation lies less in the ICT producer sector itself, which is now typically oriented to commodity components, but in the many software-intensive applications and services, many of which are developed by industries, organisations or even by individual users outside of the ICT producer sector (Bresnahan et al 1996; Tassey 2004; Lipsey et al 2005). In other words, a diminishing amount of the added value is now marketed in the form of ICT producer goods and services, while an increasing amount is marketed in the form of ICT-enabled functions that are embedded in some other kind of good or service (Hawkins & Puissochet 2005).

These dynamics vastly increase the potential range of stakeholders in a given standard and call into question conventional distinctions between suppliers and users in the standardization literature. Thus, before we can explore these matters further, we must first set out a different basis for assessing the structural relationships of stakeholders to standards – a framework in which to organise knowledge about the relationships between stakeholders and about differences in stakeholder awareness, motivations and expectations. In particular concerning how demand for standards emerges, we must also examine how their value is determined by different stakeholders and on what basis this value is produced and exchanged. Then we can begin to envisage the connection between standards and business models and how the business modelling framework might shed new light on the supply and demand dynamics of standardization.

2. RE-EXAMINING STAKEHOLDER RELATIONSHIPS IN STANDARDIZATION

It is still common practice to divide standards stakeholders into two monolithic categories – technology 'producers' and technology 'users'. The old school would have regarded the formal standardization process as a way to balance producer and user interests. But this premise has been challenged by the studies of user participation (noted previously), many of which indicate that even if formal processes were to operate to maximum efficiency, there would remain two fundamental problems for stakeholder equity.

The first is that no set of 'neutral' negotiation rules can eliminate asymmetries of information. Vendors may have an incentive to restrict the amount of standards-relevant information that is placed in the public domain (especially where patents and copyrights come into the picture). This may place other stakeholders at a disadvantage in any negotiation process. On the other hand, there may be incentives for other stakeholders to monopolise information that is crucial for vendors; for example in the case of large institutional procurers of producer goods who may wish to impose proprietary specifications throughout a supply chain.

The second problem is that technology vendors are also users of standards, indeed, in many cases they are the only users who are aware of the standard. Most standards are acquired as already embedded in producer goods or services and thus transparent to most users. This may distance other types of standards users from the standardization process, but there is no guarantee that all vendor interests always will be represented either. ICT vendors use many standards but most cannot and do not play a significant role in developing all of the standards they use.

Various scenarios might be envisaged in which these complex stakeholder dynamics can be played out. In setting up these scenarios, three key sets of variables must be considered.

1. Relational Variables

One set of variables clearly must consider the relationship of various stakeholders to ICT itself – i.e. to the technology domain for which the standards are developed. Rather than thinking in linear terms of producers and users, we could consider instead an interactive **triad of ICT constituencies**:

- ICT **vendors** supply producer goods and services (branded ICT components, systems and software).
- ICT **appliers** procure components (hardware and/or software) from ICT vendors and then add value by configuring them for specific application environments. They also may perform R&D in order to produce ICT hardware and/or software 'in-house' that becomes added value in these environments.
- ICT **consumers** procure ICT producer goods and services from 'vendors' and/or ICT-enabled value-added goods and services from 'appliers', but they consume all of the accumulated value in these products and services. Some consumers (e.g. commercial end-users) may use these goods and services in order to create additional value, but they do not add further value to the ICT goods and services as such.

Each of these constituencies holds a distinctive and often different stake in standards. But under different circumstances with respect to different goods and services groups, a single stakeholder may hold positions in more than one constituency simultaneously. For example, if and when 'appliers' also market the hardware and/or software they develop (e.g. in the form of discrete products), they become ICT 'vendors' with respect to these products. Likewise vendors can elect to supply pre-configured items to both consumers and appliers, or to adapt at least some of their production facilities to meet applier specifications.

Consumers may acquire both 'vendor' (producer) and 'applier' goods or services (for example, a PC is a vendor good whereas a digital wrist watch is an applier good).

Thus, as illustrated in Figure 1, there is no linear relationship between the three constituencies, but rather many interdependencies and potential feedbacks. The space bounded by the constituencies is the **standardization arena** in which standards requirements are defined and in which the interests of stakeholders in each constituency are played out.

However, as illustrated in Figure 2, these interests may be pursued in a wide variety of institutional contexts. Figure 1 might infer a

Figure 1. The stakeholder triad

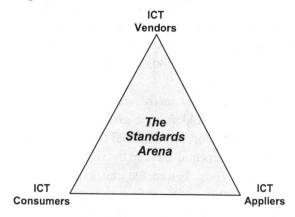

Figure 2. Intermediation of the standards arena

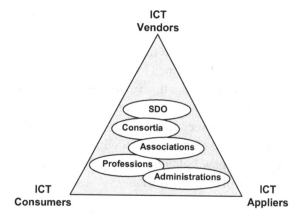

standardization outcome that is the result of spontaneous action by stakeholders to conform to one existing practice, which may occur through tacit agreement among stakeholders, or through the market. But as Figure 2 shows, the ICT standardization arena is now heavily intermediated by a range of institutions including formal SDOs, consortia, industry associations, professional organisations and public administrations in the form of various national and international regulatory bodies.

In this highly complex and increasingly interdependent environment, the distinction between informal standards and formal standards has in practice long since become completely blurred. Indeed, some of the most intriguing issues now concern the strategies of the various intermediary institutions. There are many questions about how and why different intermediaries act in concert with particular stakeholder constituencies, how intermediaries might compete with one other for the support of stakeholders, how and why different types of intermediaries might cooperate, or how intermediaries might engage in entrepreneurial behaviour to promote specific standards and standardization subject areas, or indeed how the business models of these intermediaries may become an issue.

2. Contextual Variables

A further set of variables relate to the technology development and innovation cycle. We could propose that there are at least three main *standards application contexts* in this cycle:

- *Direct application* occurs where standards are incorporated directly into new goods and services by vendors and/or appliers.
- *Indirect application* occurs where standards are acquired as already embedded in procured producer goods and services upon which further tiers of value are added by vendors and/or appliers.

- *End-use application* occurs where end-users acquire the standards-enabled functionalities of goods and services.

Mobile telephony is an example of how these application contexts might join up in a simple chain. Manufacturers engineer terminal, network and exchange equipment that conforms to the requirements of, for example, the GSM standard (direct application). The equipment is then applied by network operators and service providers who add value by configuring the functionalities provided by the GSM standard so as to offer commercially viable mobile services (intermediate application). The resulting features supported by the standard are then acquired by the consumer in the form of a conforming handset (end-use application).

3. Motivational Variables

The remaining set of variables concerns motivations for stakeholders to influence and/or contribute to the technical content of a standard. In principle, all constituencies can exert influence in the standardization arena. Even if they do not participate directly in the technical design of the standard, different constituents can shape its content through procurement decisions where one standard is preferred over another, or by prioritising certain characteristics and functionalities of the standard in specific application contexts. Thus, again we might suggest at least three types of roles which could be assumed in different instances by any of the stakeholder groups:

- *Controlling influence* is exerted in the form of substantial financial and technical contributions to the development of the standard.
- *Contributing influence* is exerted in the form of general support for the standards initiative including at least limited participation in developing, approving and/or applying the standard.

- ***External influence*** is exerted in the form of expressing standards preferences (explicitly or tacitly), mainly through procurement decisions and standards application practices.

3. STAKEHOLDER-CENTERED SCENARIOS FOR GENERATING STANDARDS DEMAND

From the aforementioned three sets of variables we can begin to construct scenarios that illustrate how stakeholders can interact in issuing and fulfilling demand for standards. Figure 3 illustrates a scenario in which the ICT *vendor* constituency plays both a significant role in the standardization process and is also the direct user of the standard. In this case, we could hypothesize that a relatively straightforward top-down application chain would develop. Certainly with proprietary standards, we could argue that this is a realistic scenario. We could hypothesize nevertheless that direct users will always have more incentive to take a controlling role in the standards process than indirect or end-users.

We could hypothesize also that if the locus of direct use were to change, the incentive to control

the standard would change. Accordingly, Figure 4 shows a contrasting scenario where the *applier* of ICT goods and services is the main instigator and direct user. An historical example is Electronic Data Interchange (EDI) whose standards were generated originally by various industry sectors independently of the ICT vendors (Graham et al 1995). In this case, we could hypothesize that vendors would assume an intermediate role, supplying components or systems to specifications issued by the applier. The consumer constituency retains a similar end-user relationship with the ICT applier to that shown in Figure 3, but in this case the vendor might also contribute to the end-user application, for example by providing specialised terminal equipment or software. However, we could hypothesise also that as the application environment became more mature, vendors would try to acquire a controlling role in the standard in order to integrate it with specific technology platforms.

Standards alliances between ICT vendors and appliers are now commonplace, as can be observed in the composition of many consortia whose principal members often include representatives of both constituencies. As shown in Figure 5, we could hypothesize that this would result in espe-

Figure 3. An ICT vendor scenario

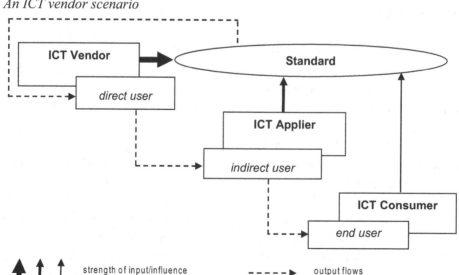

Figure 4. An ICT applier scenario

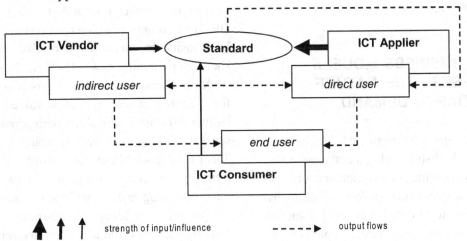

cially close linkage between direct and indirect use of the standards – essentially the application is designed to fit a specific producer platform. An example of this strategy would be the Digital Video Broadcasting (DVB) initiative where broadcasters (the indirect users of standards) collaborate actively to develop the set-top box platform with electronics companies (the direct users).

The aforementioned are only three of many scenarios that it would be possible to construct by juxtaposing relational, contextual and motivational variables in various circumstances. At some point, alliance scenarios that involve at least some types of consumers might be envisaged also. The Linux community is perhaps a prototype. The mechanism by which the Linux standard is developed technically is open also to individuals, in effect creating a community of 'expert consumers' – technically adept individuals (who may be ICT professionals in their own right)

Figure 5. An alliance scenario

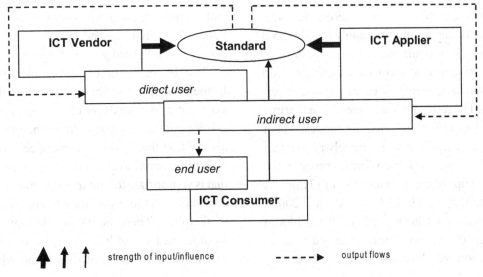

who participate with ICT producers and appliers in defining the standard.

4. USING BUSINESS MODELS TO RE-ASSESS THE NATURE OF STANDARDS DEMAND

As the technological environment for innovation in ICT is highly distributed and heterogeneous, typically involving the combination or coordination of technologies and knowledge from many sources in order to construct coherent product or service environments, standards become essential. But as noted at the beginning of this Chapter, innovation requires more than the coordination of technology; being also the product of social and organizational factors. Once we step into the complex dynamics of the stakeholder triad as described previously, we enter a world in which standardization processes are shaped visibly by the same forces that shape innovation in product and service environments. Thus, it can be expected that for many stakeholders, standards demand is not going to be expressed in terms specifically of demand for new or revised standards (which in any case are completely transparent to many stakeholders) but rather in terms of the complex vendor-applier-user relationships that result in innovations.

The business model concept presents an alternative way of describing the supply and demand dynamics of standardization in terms of how all of the aforementioned factors are motivated and coordinated in discrete product and service environments. The term 'business *model*' – as distinct from 'business *plan*' or '*financial* model' – is of relatively recent origin and is largely an artefact of rapid developments in on-line commerce and electronic supply chain management (Timmers 1998; Kraemer et al 2000; Afuah & Tucci 2002). Nevertheless, as Chesbrough & Rosenbloom (2002) point out, the activities normally discussed in connection with business models collectively

have many intellectual antecedents dating back to the observations of Chandler (1962), Penrose (1959) and others as to the relationship between how businesses structure themselves and their success in pursuing new lines of business.[3]

Most characterizations of business models focus upon their role in creating value by establishing various relationships with products and services that can generate revenues. Afuah & Tucci (2000) see these relationships simply in terms as how companies plan to "make money long-term using the Internet" (the key factor being "long-term" – building new businesses that are constructed to be sustainable in an electronic commerce environment). Mahadevan (2000) describes the business model more systemically, proposing that business models are defined in terms of the relationship between determinations of value, methods of extracting revenues based on that determination, and the structure of the various logistics and fulfilment systems required in order to capture this value for the seller (who may be a manufacturer, an intermediary, or a retailer).

The somewhat unique element that emerged from the business model debate is that *a relationship exists between how goods and services are exchanged and how their value is determined.* In other words, at least part of the value of an item is construed from the context in which it is exchanged. This context encompasses both the social relationships of production and consumption, but also the financial and market structures that pertain to any given group of goods or services.

The business model concept provides a framework for describing dynamics like these systematically. Analysis of a given product or service domain using this device begins with the assumption that in order to produce revenue, an enterprize must have developed a business model that is appropriate for the specific functionality of a specific asset (or system of assets) in a specific marketplace. These assets include capital investment in the form of ICT, the value of which can be enhanced and/or limited by standards.

From this perspective, specific variables emerge that may induce evolution and migration phenomena in the business models of various goods and services. This creates a dynamic framework within which to consider standardization demand. A direct linkage between business modelling and standardization can be established in that many of the relational, contextual and motivational variables that we see in the standardization process have analogues and complementarities in the business modelling process.

1. Relational Variables

In business modelling, we encounter three principal interactive stakeholder constituencies that are somewhat analogous to those in the standardization process:

- **Originators** produce branded goods and/or services.
- **Intermediaries** facilitate the distribution of goods and services through the provision of enabling technologies and transaction-related value-added services.
- **Consumers** use up all of the value created by originators and intermediaries.

As illustrated in Figure 6, these relationships are configured in a similar way around what we could call a **'business modelling arena'**. Current thinking about business models concentrates on the interactions between these stakeholder constituencies in establishing models in the market. The business modelling stakeholder triad as shown in Figure 6 is similar but not identical to the standardization triad as shown in Figure 1. The point of closest correspondence lies in the consumer constituency, which can be comprised of essentially the same types of stakeholders in both triads. Otherwise, the originators and intermediaries *may or may not* correspond respectively to the producers and appliers in the standardization triad.

If the business model is oriented to ICT producer goods (e.g. a model for retailing PCs or software), then the analogue is fairly exact. Relationships in the standardization arena can be expected to mirror directly those in the business modelling arena. However, as illustrated in Figure 7, where other types of producer goods are concerned, ICT producers and appliers *both* assume the role of intermediaries in the business modelling triad. This reflects the fundamental intermediate goods characteristics of ICT and implies that the vortex of ICT standardization activity lies in the intermediary domain. It can also imply either cooperation or conflict with the intermediation structure of specific *non-ICT* product/service environments.

The problem is that the interests of ICT producers and appliers may or may not be congruent with

Figure 6. Stakeholders in the business modelling arena

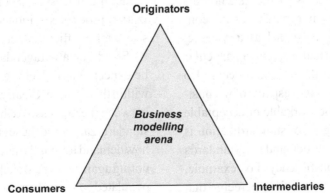

Figure 7. Juxtaposition of the standardization and business modelling stakeholder triads

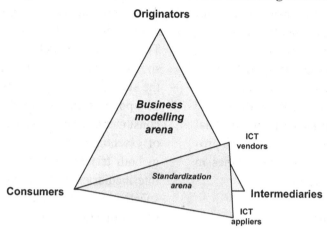

those of other intermediaries (or indeed originators), especially if they are oriented to exploiting the same value source. For example, both ICT producer firms and financial institutions could have divergent commercial interests in standards for internet banking platforms. ICT suppliers may see value in promoting as many informal standards possible in order to create favourable path dependencies and network externalities – i.e. to promote services platforms tied to their own proprietary technologies. The financial institutions, on the other hand, may wish to control the interface technology themselves, preferring to rely on formal standards to ensure basic connectivity, but otherwise leaving the interface open for the development of competitive service features.

Except under conditions of market power, business modelling typically involves various degrees of consensus formation between the stakeholders in the triad. Originators, intermediaries and consumers alike have to 'agree' (or at least acquiesce) in some formal or informal way that a particular model creates value for them. This process also may involve standards in that aspects of the business model may only be workable or acceptable to stakeholders if a degree of standardization is assured. This can create demand for standards by any stakeholder constituency. For example, if consumers of financial services perceive that

security standards for on-line banking are inadequate, or they are required to purchase additional technology to access each provider of these services, they could be expected to express a demand for standards by refusing to use the services. On the other hand, service originators who operate unique service environments behind proprietary standards may incur uncompetitive costs if they have to develop their own middleware rather than procure these services in the market. These are only two of many possible examples.

When we juxtapose the two triads (Figure 7), we see that wherever a product or service domain encounters the requirement to deploy ICT, the dynamics of business modelling intersect the dynamics of standardization in the ICT producer goods sector. But although the two stakeholder triads are linked, by no means will all business modelling processes be congruent with standardization processes – indeed there could be more scope for conflict than compromise.

Standardization agendas in the ICT domain can be expected to reflect the competitive pressures within this domain. Clearly, this can set up tensions between the processes of business modelling and standardization and these can have an impact upon how demand for standards is expressed. Moreover, noting again how the stakeholder triad typically is populated by several types of intermediary (Figure

2), it must be considered that the intermediation structure will be configured not only according to various stakeholder interests, but also to the emerging strategic and commercial interests of SDOs and consortia.

2. Contextual Variables

Contextual variables in the standardization process concern where and how the standards are applied. With business models, however, the application context is formed more by the asset characteristics of individual products and services and the relationships between various stakeholders in exploiting the value contained in these characteristics. Each different source of value becomes a separate context in which business modelling can occur.

Problematically, just how stakeholders interact in order to create value is as yet the least well developed part of the business model concept. Most current explanations centre on the 'value proposition', which unfortunately is yet another term of dubious provenance. Most commentators regard a value proposition as a 'statement of value' upon which both buyers and sellers can agree in a specific product and market context. The proposition need not be made only in terms of price. Aspects like transaction convenience and efficiency may complement or even outweigh price signals in buyer decisions.

The problem is that usually the originator is identified as the source of the value proposition, taking into account various demand signals in the market. But this possibility can be predicated only on the assumption of a high (and quite theoretical) degree of information symmetry between potential buyers and sellers.

Figure 8 illustrates the structure of a value proposition under the assumption of information symmetry. This construction is problematical where ICT is concerned in that so much ICT utility is undefined or latent. Appliers and consumers typically adapt the generic functionality of an ICT device or system according to their own specific needs or preferences, thus creating value-added applications. In turn, this action can create new markets for ICT producers as critical mass develops around specific user-developed functionalities. Thus, once the financial services and transport industries had pioneered EDI, telecom network operators began to exploit this new market with Value-Added Network services. Or, once enough consumers had 'discovered' the additional utility of SMS on their mobile telephones, this originally ancillary service became a major part of the service and revenue portfolios of GSM providers.

Clearly, in the ICT case at least, the value proposition works both ways in basically an asymmetrical and constantly evolving information environment. These dynamics are illustrated in Figure 9 which presents the seller/buyer relationship in terms of continuous interaction between the fixed value assumptions of producers and the evolving preferences of buyers.

Most producers cannot respond to user preferences on a completely dynamic basis for the

Figure 8. Abstract value proposition with information symmetry assumptions

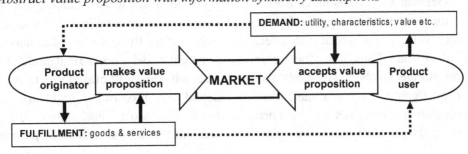

Figure 9. Value proposition with evolving information

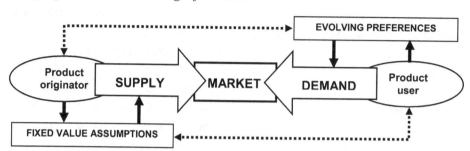

simple reason that they have a fixed asset base (made up of tangibles and intangibles) that cannot always be changed as rapidly as evolution in buyer preferences. Thus, producers have to assume that at least part of this sunk investment can be transformed into value for the buyer at any given time. Product and service strategies are planned accordingly. Thus, we can view market relationships in terms of tension between what buyers indicate they prefer at any given time and the degree to which producers are able or willing to respond. In situations of market power, there may well be no incentive to respond.

Moreover, investment in new or different business models can be highly strategic. Even though a model developed by one firm or organisation may be transferable – in some cases as a kind of public good with positive externalities – there can be considerable first-mover advantages in developing a new model. Similarly to process innovations, these advantages occur where technical control or influence is maintained over key interfaces and systems along with supporting standards.

We must also consider the value proposition from the standpoint of the institutional intermediaries that provide standards – SDOs and consortia. The business model concept is basically that the forms in which value is exchanged also affect determinations of value. Thus, it is conceivable that value propositions involving standards may be connected to different forms of intermediation. The value proposition of most SDOs is that open processes and quasi-juridical procedures yield

higher-value standards by maximizing consensus and increasing the potential for adoption. The value thus invested in these standards could be exploited by SDOs in a variety of ways, although heretofore most of them have linked value to publication or in some cases to certification and information services.

But new value propositions can be constructed around perceived inadequacies in this system. An obvious example is the longstanding issue of time-to-market. One of the original rationales for standards consortia to operate outside of the SDO system was that they could deliver the standards in a more timely fashion. The value proposition was that a standard had more value if delivered on a schedule that was linked to the actual progress of R&D and that specialised independent consortia could deliver this value better than SDOs. We know from subsequent investigations that this proposition was at best superficial – that consortia were not always more efficient or timely and that they increased coordination costs (Blind et al 2007).

But this begs the question of what the real value proposition was. The massive rise in consortia numbers would indicate that there must be such a proposition and that it is accepted by stakeholders. But as discussed earlier on, often the apparent model is not the real model. The task for research in a case like this is to determine what the actual value proposition is and how the business model relates to it. Thus, in the case of consortia, stakeholders may appear to be pursuing an 'efficiency' proposition but may actually be pursuing a 'strategic' proposition – developing standards to coordinate communities of users and producers of complementary products and services in specific business segments (Ballon 2007; Hawkins & Ballon 2007; Ballon & Hawkins 2008).

3. Motivational Variables

Although contexts may vary considerably, we can propose that in each case the motivations to develop and/or adopt a business model will depend upon the degrees of asset specificity and risk that apply to different stakeholders in a given commercial or public service enterprise. The asset contributions of originators and intermediaries (including ICT producers) consist of the various forms of capital investment, physical infrastructure and human resources that they contribute to any enterprise (basically the conventional economic factors of production).

In terms of the enterprise – i.e. the supply mechanism for goods and services (originators and intermediaries) – we can identify at least three basic types of assets:

- *Structural assets* are non-substitutable and specific to a particular enterprise. If any of these assets were withdrawn, the enterprise would fail. An obvious example would be the IPR in a crucial innovation.
- *Contributing assets* are specific to a particular enterprise, but may be substituted in that more than one source of these assets could be used, or one type of asset could be supplanted by another for the same function. For example, a retailer of insurance services can procure these from several underwriters.
- *Supporting assets* are entirely generic and available to any enterprise on equivalent terms. For example, all on-line services use essentially the same public switched telecommunication infrastructure.

All three types of assets are needed before a model can function, but likewise, various business models will operate within each of these asset profiles. Thus, an asset could play supporting or contributing roles in some enterprises, but structural roles in others. For example, the public switched telecommunication infrastructure is a supporting asset for most businesses, but a structural asset for the telecommunication operators. Their business models are geared to this asset and any change in these models incurs risk. Each individual business model must therefore be seen as part of an interactive configuration of models. We can propose that the viability of any given enterprise will depend upon the degree to which conflicts between the models can be managed.

But it is not only manufacturers and suppliers who must contribute assets to a business model. Consumers bring many assets to the marketplace as well. These are of two obvious types:

- *Disposable assets* in the form of the accumulated wealth that they exchange for goods and services.
- *Fixed assets* in the form of investments that contribute at least in part to the viability of various business models.

Similarly to firms, consumers also incur a type of transaction costs which, arguably, are significant (although not always sufficient) factors in determining what level of value consumers are willing to add to a product or service relative to what level they expect to be contained in that item at the time of purchase. A simple example is value added fresh food products. Some consumers are willing to purchase whole raw vegetables and preparing them for cooking themselves. Others are willing to pay more for vegetables that are already prepared. Even if this value added is not 'realised' (in that none of it is sold onwards), these types of decisions about where the value chain or system will terminate are critical elements in the consumer interaction with business models.

Equally important is consumer willingness to contribute fixed assets. For example, consumers must absorb the depreciation on a motor vehicle that they use to transport themselves to a point of sale and/or to transport purchased goods to their own premises. Individually, these costs may be small, but when aggregated they represent a major contribution to the ubiquitous cash-and-carry business model that underpins many retail enterprises. Without consumer willingness to participate in such a model by contributing these assets, the model would not be viable. It is part of the economic structure of the retailing model. Likewise, in order to do electronic transactions, the consumer must be willing to contribute a capital investment to electronic commerce models in the form of a computer and the required services that make it available for transaction purposes.

In principle, every asset holder can motivate business model evolution. However, in order to determine what motivates stakeholders to participate in a new or different business model, we have to consider all of the aforementioned asset contributions in terms of the degree of risk that a stakeholder would consider appropriate relative to an expectation of benefit. Clearly, the more structural these assets become, the higher the risk. Where product choice is limited and/or where key contributing and supporting assets are unavailable on a competitive basis, stakeholders may compelled to use a specific model. Otherwise, throughout the value chain (or value network) each purchaser has to be willing to incur the costs (and risks) of using a given business model.

5. USING BUSINESS MODELS TO DESCRIBE THE EMERGENCE OF STANDARDS DEMAND

The business model concept can be a useful device wherever it is necessary to examine the relationships of different actors to the same product or service. In order to function, a business model must to some extent be acceptable to all stakeholders, each of whom plays a role in the construction of value in the product or service to which the business model pertains. In this sense, business models could be seen to represent a kind of (at least tacit) consensus among these constituencies as to the commercial topology that will apply to a given product or service environment. Very typically, this topology maps onto a technological topology. Herein lies the pivot for using business models to illuminate how demand emerges for standardization.

If the characteristics of the relevant business models can be identified with respect to any product or service grouping, then so too can the forces that might generate changes in these models or shifts from one model to another. These same dynamics can also influence the emergence of demand for standards and can shape various aspects of the standardization process—in particular how and where standards are developed and the conditions under which they are made available to stakeholders. The business models of various ICT suppliers and intermediaries become relevant in this respect, but so do the models of SDOs, consortia and other relevant institutions. In any context, analysis of business models should reveal such characteristics as:

- Which actors are invested where and to what extent in a given enterprize;
- Enterprize structures and actor topologies;
- Market and financial structures;
- Revenue streams;
- Critical asset dependencies;
- Critical actor interdependencies and feedback mechanisms;
- Links between technological infrastructure and commercial or public service infrastructures;
- Stress points where new functionalities (and innovations) are likely to occur.

By mapping such variables in the business modelling arena with stakeholder dynamics in the standardization arena, it should be possible to identify relationships, interdependencies and feed-backs mechanisms. Comparative analysis of the business model contexts should indicate any asymmetries between standards requirements and the abilities of various standardization institutions to respond. Examining the standardization process from a business model perspective helps to explain the motivations of stakeholder communities to contribute to the process, or not, as the case may be.

In order to unpack the demand elements of this problem, value propositions would first have to be derived for a standard that corresponded to the value propositions underlying the products and services to which that standard applies. This would amount to a statement of why a specific standard, or a specific degree of standardization, or even the elimination of an existing standard would add value for each of the constituencies in the standardization arena with respect to that product or service.

REFERENCES

Afuah, A., & Tucci, C. (2001). *Internet Business Models and Strategies.* Boston: McGraw-Hill Irwin.

Arthur, B. (1989). Competing Technologies, Increasing Returns, and Lock-In by Historical Events. *Economic Journal, 99,* 116-131.

Ballon. P. (2007). Changing business models for Europe's mobile telecommunications industry: The impact of alternative wireless technologies. *Telematics and Informatics, 24*(3), 192-205.

Ballon, P., & Hawkins, R. (2008). Standardization and business models for platform competition: the case of mobile television. *International Journal of Information Technology Standards Research* (forthcoming).

Bekkers, R. (2001). *Mobile Telecommunication Standards: GSM, UMTS, TETRA and ERMES.* Boston: Artech House.

Besen, S. M. (1990). The European Telecommunications Standards Institute: A Preliminary Analysis. *Telecommunications Policy, 14*(6), 521-530.

Besen, S. M., & Farrell, J. (1991). The Role of the ITU in Standardization: Pre-eminence, Impotence or Rubber Stamp? *Telecommunications Policy, 15*(4), 311-321.

Beyer, S. (1982). *Regulation and its Reform.* Cambridge Mass: Harvard Univ. Press.

Blind, K. (2004). *The Economics of Standards - Theory, Evidence, Policy.* Cheltenham: Edward Elgar.

Blind, K., & Gauch, S. (2005). Trends in ICT Standards in European Standardization Bodies and Standards Consortia. *Proceedings of the 4th IEEE Conference on Standardization and Innovation in Information Technology,* (pp. 29-39).

Blind, K., Gauch, S., & Hawkins, R. (2007). How Stakeholders View the Impacts of International ICT Standards. *In the Proceedings of the 12th EURAS Workshop,* 16-17 May, Thessaloniki, Greece.

Bresnahan, T., Greenstein, S., Brownstone, D., & Flamm, K. (1996). Technical progress and co-invention in computing and in the uses of computers. *Brookings Papers on Economic Activity – Microeconomics,* (pp. 1-13).

Cargill, C. (1989). *Information Technology Standardization: Theory, Process, and Organizations.* Digital Press.

Cargill, C., & Bohlin, S. (2007). Standardization: A falling paradigm. In S. Greenstein & V. Stango (Eds.), *Standards and Public Policy.* Cambridge: Cambridge University Press, (pp. 296-328).

Chandler, A. (1962). *Strategy and Structure: Chapters in the History of American Industrial Enterprise*. Cambridge MA: MIT Press.

Chesbrough, H., & Rosenbloom, R. S. (2002). The role of the business model in capturing value from innovation: Evidence From Xerox corporation's technology spin off companies. *Industrial and Corporate Change, 11*(3), 529-555.

Chesbrough, H. (2003). *Open innovation: The new imperative for creating and profiting from technology*. Cambridge: Harvard University Press.

Cooke, P., & Morgan, K. (1998). *The Associational Economy*. Oxford: Oxford University Press.

Cowan, R., Cowan, W., & Swann, P. (1997). A model of demand with interactions among consumers. *International Journal of Industrial Organization, 15*(6), 711-33.

Cohen, W., & Levinthal, D. (1990). Absorptive Capacity: A New Perspective On Learning And Innovation. *Administrative Science Quarterly;* March, *35*(1), 128-152.

Crane, R. J. (1978). Communication Standards and the Politics of Protectionism. *Telecommunications Policy, 2*(4), 267-281.

Dankbaar, B., & van Tulder, R. (1992). The Influence of Users in Standardization: the Case of MAP. In M. Dierkes & U. Hoffmann (Eds.), *New Technology at the Outset: Social Forces in the Shaping of Technological Innovations*. Frankfurt and New York: Campus Verlag, (pp. 327-349).

David, P. A. (1985). Clio and the Economics of QWERTY. *American Economic Review, 75*(2), 332-337.

David, P. A., & Greenstein, S. (1990). The Economics of Compatibility Standards: An Introduction to Recent Research. *Economics of Innovation and New Technology, 1*(1) 3-41.

David. P. A., & Steinmueller, E. (1990). The ISDN Bandwagon is Coming, But Who Will Be There

To Climb Aboard?: Quandaries in the Economics of Data Communication Networks. *Economics of Innovation and New Technology, 1*(1), 43-62.

de Vries, H. J. (1999). *Standardization: A Business Approach to the Role of National Standardization Organizations*. Dordrecht: Kluwer.

Economides, N., & Flyer, F. (1998). Technical Standards Coalitions for Network Goods. *Annales d'Economie et de Statistique, 49/50*, 361-380.

Egyedi, T. (2001). Why JavaTM was not standardized twice. *Computer Standards & Interfaces, 23*(4), 253-265.

Evans, C. D., Meek, B. L., & Walker, R. S. (Eds.) (1993). *User Needs in Information Technology Standards*. Oxford: Butterworth-Heinemann

Farrell, J., & Saloner, G. (1985). Standardization, Compatibility and Innovation. *Rand Journal of Economics, 16*(1), 70-83.

Farrell, J., & Saloner, G. (1988). Coordination through Committees and Markets. *Rand Journal of Economics, 19*(2), 235-251.

Florida, R. (2002). *The Rise of the Creative Class*. New York: Basic Books.

Foray D. (1995). Coalitions and committees: How users get involved in information technology standards. In R. W. Hawkins, R. Mansell, & J. Skea (Eds.), *Standards, Innovation and Competitiveness: The Politics and Economics of Standards in Natural and Technical Environments*. Cheltenham: Edward Elgar.

Fox, M. (2004). E-commerce Business Models for the Music Industry. *Popular Music and Society, 27*(2), 201-220.

Freeman, C. (1994) Critical survey: The economics of Technical change. *Cambridge Journal of Economics, 18*, 463-514.

Graham, I., Spinardi, G., Williams, R., & Webster, J. (1995). The Dynamics of EDI Standards

Development. *Technology Analysis & Strategic Management, 7*(1), 3-21.

Hawkins, R. (1992). The Doctrine of Regionalism: A New Dimension for International Standardization in Telecommunication. *Telecommunications Policy, 16*(4), May/June, 339-353.

Hawkins, R. (1995). Standards-Making as Technological Diplomacy: Assessing Objectives and Methodologies in Standards Institutions. In R. Hawkins, R. Mansell, & J. Skea (Eds.), *Standards, Innovation and Competitiveness: the Politics and Economics of Standards in Natural and Technical Environments*. Cheltenham: Edward Elgar, (pp. 147-158).

Hawkins, R. (1995). Enhancing the User Role in the Development of Technical Standards for Telecommunication. *Technology Analysis & Strategic Management, 7*(1), 21-40.

Hawkins, R. (1999). The Rise of Consortia in the Information and Communication Technology Industries: Emerging Implications for Policy. *Telecommunications Policy, 23*(2), 159-173.

Hawkins, R. (2003). Looking beyond the .com bubble: exploring the form and function of business models in the electronic marketplace. In H. Bouwman, B. Preissl, & C. Steinfield, (Eds.), *E-Life after the dot-com Bust*. Hamburg: Springer/Physica, (pp. 65-81).

Hawkins, R., & Puissochet, A. (2005) Estimating Software activity in European Industry, paper prepared for the FISTERA consortium in the European Union Sixth Framework (IST-2001-37627).

Hawkins, R. & P. Ballon (2007). When standards become business models: reinterpreting 'failure' in the standardization paradigm, *Info – the Journal of Policy, Regulation and Strategy for Telecommunications, Information and Media, 9*(5), 20-30.

Hemenway, D. (1975). *Industrywide Voluntary Product Standards*. Cambridge: Ballinger.

Jakobs K., Procter, R., & Williams, R. (1996). Users and standardization: Worlds apart? The example of electronic mail. *StandardView, 4*(4), 183-191.

Katz, M. L., & Shapiro, C. (1985). Network Externalities, Competition, and Compatibility. *American Economic Review, 75*, 424-440.

Katz, M. L., & Shapiro, C. (1986). Technology Adoption in the Presence of Network Externalities. *Journal of Political Economy, 94*, 882-841.

Kauffman, S., Lobo, J., & Macready, W. G. (2000). Optimal search on a technology landscape. *Journal of Economic Behavior & Organization, 43*, 141–166.

Kindleberger, C. P. (1983). Standards as Public, Collective, and Private Goods. *Kyklos, 36*(3), 377-396.

Kraemer, K. L., Dedrick, J., & Yamashiro, S. (2000). Redefining and extending the Business Model with Information Technology: Dell Computer Corporation. *The Information Society, 16*(1), 5-21.

Lane, R. E. (1991). *The Market Experience*. Cambridge: Cambridge University Press.

Levinthal, D. (1997). Adaptation on rugged landscapes. *Management Science, 43*(7), 934-950.

Liebowitz, S. J. & Margolis, S. E. (1995). Path Dependence, Lock-In and History. *Journal of Law, Economics and Organization, 11*(1), 205-226.

Lipsey, R., Carlaw, K., & Bekar, C. (2005). *Economic Transformations: General Purpose Technologies and Long Term Economic Growth*. Oxford: Oxford University Press.

Macdonald, S. (2004). When means become ends: considering the impact of patent strategy on innovation. *Information Economics and Policy, 16*, 135-158.

Mahadevan, B. (2000). Business Models for Internet-Based E-Commerce: An Anatomy. *California Management Review, 42*(4), 55-69.

Majone, G. (1984). Science and Trans-Science in Standard Setting. *Science, Technology and Human Values, 9*(1), 15-22.

Mazzoleni, R., & Nelson, R. (1998). Economic theories about the benefits and costs of patents. *Journal of Economic Issues, 32*(4), 1031-1052.

McMeekin, A., Green, K., Tomlinson, M., & Walsh, V. (2002). *Innovation by Demand: An Interdisciplinary Approach to the Study of Demand and its Role in Innovation.* Cheltenham: Edward Elgar.

Middleton, R. W. (1973). Standardization and International Economic Co-operation. *Journal of World Trade Law, 7*(5), 500-510.

Montalvo, C. (2002). *Environmental policy and technological innovation: Why do firms adopt or reject new technologies?* Cheltenham: Edward Elgar.

Mowery, D. C., & Rosenberg, N. (1979). The influence of market demand upon innovation: a critical review of some recent empirical studies. *Research Policy, 8*, 102-53.

Penrose, E. (1959). *The Theory of the Growth of the Firm.* London: Blackwell.

Reck, D. (Ed.) (1956). *National Standards in a Modern Economy.* New York: Harper & Brothers.

Salter, L. (1988). *Mandated Science: Science and Scientists in the Making of Standards.* Dordrecht: Kluwer.

Schmookler, J. (1966). *Invention and Economic Growth.* Cambridge, Harvard University Press.

Schumpeter, J. A. (1912). *Die Theorie der Wirtschaftlichen Entwicklung.* Duncker & Humblot: Leipzig

Schumpeter, J. A. (1939). Business Cycles: A Theoretical, Historical and Statistical Analysis of the Capitalist Process (Volume 1 and 2). McGraw Hill: New York.

Schumpeter, J. A. (1942). *Capitalism, Socialism and Democracy.* George Allen and Unwin: New York.

Setterfield, M. (2002). *The Economics of Demand-Led Growth: Challenging the Supply-Side Vision of the Long Run.* Cheltenham: Edward Elgar.

Shapiro, C., & Varian, H. (2002). The art of standards wars. In R. Garud, A. Kumaraswamy, & R. Langlois (Eds.), *Managing in the Modular Age: Architectures, Networks, and Organizations.* Oxford: Blackwell, (pp. 247-315).

Sullivan, C. D. (1983). *Standards and Standardization: Basic Principles and Applications.* New York: Marcel Dekker Inc.

Swann, G. M. P. (1993). User Needs for Standards: How Can We Ensure that User Votes are Counted? In B. Meek et al (Eds.), *User Needs in Information Technology Standards.* Butterworth/Heinemann.

Swann, G. M. P., Temple, P., & Shurmer, M. (1996). Standards and Trade Performance: The British Experience. *Economic Journal, 106*, 1297-1313.

Swann G. M. P. (1999). Marshall's Consumer as an Innovator. In S. C. Dow & P. E. Earl (Eds.), *Economic Organisation and Economic Knowledge: Essays in Honour of Brian Loasby.* Cheltenham: Edward Elgar Publishers.

Tassey G. (1992). *Technology Infrastructure and Competitive Position.* Norwell MA: Kluwer

Tassey, G. (2000). Standardisation in technology-based markets. *Research Policy, 29*(4/5), 587-602.

Tassey, G. (2004). Policy Issues for R&D Investment in a Knowledge-Based Economy. *Journal of Technology Transfer, 29*(2), 153-184.

Thompson, G. V. (1954). Intercompany Technical Standardization in the Early American Automobile Industry. *Journal of Economic History, 14*(1), 1-20.

Timmers, P. (1998). Business Models for Electronic Markets. *Electronic Markets, 8*(2), 3-8.

Towill, D. R. (1997). The seamless supply chain - the predator's strategic advantage. *International Journal of Technology Management, 13*(1), 37-56.

Updegrove, A. (1995). Consortia and the role of government in standard setting. In B. Kahin & J. Abbate, J. (Eds.), *Standards policy for information infrastructure*. Cambridge, MA: MIT Press.

Von Hippel, E. (1988). *The Sources of Innovation*. Oxford and New York: Oxford University Press.

Verman, L. C. (1973). *Standardization: A New Discipline*. Hamden: Archon Books.

Vernon, R. (1966). International Investment and International Trade in the Product Cycle. *Quarterly Journal of Economics, 80*(2), 190-207.

Wallenstein, G. (1990). *Setting Global Telecommunications Standards: the Stakes, the Players and the Process*. Dedham: Artech House.

Weiss, M. B. H., & Sirbu, M. (1990). Technological Choice in Voluntary Standards Committees: and Empirical Analysis. *Economics of Innovation and New Technology, 1*(1), 111-133.

West, J. (2003). How open is open enough? Melding proprietary and open source platform strategies. *Research Policy, 32*(7), 1259-1285.

Whitworth, J. (1882). *Papers on Mechanical Subjects. Part I. True Planes, Screw Threads, and Standard Measures*. London: E. F. & N. Spon.

Woodward, C. D. (Ed.) (1965). *Standards for Industry*. London: Heinemann.

ENDNOTES

[1] Over time, Schumpeter's own conception of the innovation process evolved considerably (Schumpeter 1912, 1939, 1950), but he remained steadfastly dismissive of demand factors (especially consumer demand) as drivers of innovation, focussing instead upon the function of entrepreneurship in stimulating the supply-side. See Schmookler (1966), Mowery & Rosenberg (1979) and Freeman (1996) for an overview of the historical debate about the role of demand in innovation, and Setterfield (2002) for an overview of current opinion on demand led growth in a broadly neo-Schumpeterian framework. For an overview of the 'pre-Schumpeterian' history of this issue, see Swann (1999).

[2] Egyedi & Hudson (2005) discuss this issue in relation to the problem of how to ensure the 'integrity' of standards (particularly informal standards) in the face of interoperability problems as might occur between different applications that are nominally compliant to the same standard.

[3] These arguments are obliquely related to boundary-of-the-firm debates, but differ in that they are not concerned with why firms limit their size and operational scope (e.g. due to transaction costs), but rather with how firms grow new business areas.

Section III
Successful Standards Development

Chapter V
Emergence of Standardisation Processes:
Linkage with Users

Ian Graham
University of Edinburgh, UK

Raluca Bunduchi
University of Aberdeen, UK

Martina Gerst
University of Edinburgh, UK

Robin Williams
University of Edinburgh, UK

ABSTRACT

For RFID technology (radio frequency identification), the forms of the standardisation processes are co-evolving with the technology and are being shaped by the technology itself and by the needs of users. However, the engagement of the large majority of end-users in standards development is at best limited. Based on semi-structured interviews with key actors in the automotive industry, the chapter discusses the role that RFID standards play in shaping the adoption of RFID systems in the automotive supply chain.

1. INTRODUCTION

The growing importance of standardisation in the development and implementation of innovative information technologies has been matched by a growing complexity of the processes within which these technologies are developed. This complexity is seen in the institutional diversity of processes, including varying membership rules, decision-making procedures and policies towards intellectual property, and also in the emergence of overlapping bodies with interests in emerging technologies. Whereas the conventional model of standardisation was based on national recognised standards organisations, for example BSI (British Standards Institution) in the United Kingdom, developing national standards or feeding requirements into international bodies, most obviously ISO (international Organization for Standardization), we now see actors, both individual and commercial, coming together to establish consortia. This chapter will look at one emerging technology, RFID (radio frequency identification), to argue that the form of the standardisation processes are co-evolving with the technology and are being shaped by the technology itself and by the needs of users.

De Vries (1999) has argued that the primary reason for the flowering of consortia has been the ability of consortia to develop standards more quickly than the traditional standards development processes. Krechmer (2000) argued that the reasons for the growth of standardisation consortia have been more complex, with consortia benefiting from being able to draw on funding from commercially motivated participant firms, being able to locate themselves as the most significant locus for standardisation in their area, having the freedom to negotiate the incorporation of proprietary intellectual property and being able to market themselves as a brand. Krechmer argued that the traditional standardisation processes still enjoyed benefits from being state sponsored, but that the rise of consortia was reducing state involvement in standardisation. Egyedi (2006) argues that this move to consortia, especially where there is an open membership and transparent decision-making, does not lead to a reduction in democratic accountability. However, one effect of the splintering of information technology standardisation is that it presents potential users with an array of standards processes that they can choose to engage with.

This chapter examines the role that standardisation is playing in shaping the adoption of RFID technology and the extent to which the institutional context of standardisation is hampering the technology's adoption, focusing on the automotive industry, where there is an expectation of RFID having significant impacts but with a low level of engagement with standardisation bodies. The study is based on a qualitative methodology, using semi-structured interviews with key actors to collect the data. The respondents are listed in Appendix 1. The analysis is structured in two parts: we first introduce RFID technologies and standards, and then discuss the role that RFID standards plays in shaping the adoption of RFID systems in the automotive supply chain.

2. RFID: AN EMERGING TECHNOLOGY

RFID is an automatic identification technology that uses radio to read and write data from and to tags attached to items. An RFID system consists of readers and the tags that can be read, supported by computers the handling the interaction between tags and readers and usually interfacing with wider enterprise systems. The antenna within the reader emits radio signals to activate the tag and reads and/or writes data to it. When an RFID tag passes through the electromagnetic zone, it detects the reader's activation signal. The decoder within the reader decodes the data encoded in the tag's integrated circuit and the data is passed to the host computer for processing. A tag contains a microchip where the data regarding a particular item is stored. There are three types of RFID operating within different radio frequency ranges: low frequency RFID systems most commonly used in security access, asset tracking, and animal identification applications; high-frequency systems used in applications such as ID cards and electronic tickets; and ultra-high frequency systems which are commonly used in applications such as railway wagon tracking and automated toll collection. The latter offer longer read ranges and higher reading speeds, but they are generally more expensive than low and high frequency systems (Rees, 2004).

The focus of this chapter is on RFID applications used in the supply chain for item tracking and tracing, which are generally low frequency systems. In supply chain applications, RFID systems have a number of technical advantages over the use of barcodes, the dominant established technology. RFID has the potential to simplify the process of tracking items, without any need for line-of-sight visibility and with multiple tags detected simultaneously. RFID tags can be read through a variety of substances, are less susceptible to damage than barcodes and have a write capability which is a significant advantage in interactive applications such as work in process or maintenance tracking. As such, RFID systems are a useful tool in improving the visibility in the supply chain relative to the barcode based optical technology, hence reducing time and costs, significantly lowering transport and operating cost, reducing capital, and the incidence of misplaced packaging during transport when moved between suppliers. Such claimed benefits have led organisations managing complex supply-chains to militate for the adoption of RFID.

Some of the earliest RFID supporters were large retailers such as Wal-Mart, Metro and Tesco, and governmental agencies such as the US Department of Defense, whose decision to mandate all its suppliers to adopt RFID by 2005 as a logistics and inventory management tool significantly accelerated the pace of RFID deployment during the beginning of this century (Leaver, 2004; McGinity, 2004). Most of the large IT vendors such as Sun, IBM, Oracle and Microsoft have been extending their application development and middleware technology to accommodate RFID. Application vendors, such as SAP, have begun to offer RFID enabled software. Integration specialists such

as TIBCO have added RFID specific features to their existing integration broker technology, whereas a number of RFID pure players such as ConnecTerra and OATSystems have offered RFID hardware products (Leaver, 2004). At the same time, early studies of RFID adoption were predicting a fast diffusion. For instance, an Allied Business Intelligence Inc. study was predicting a jump in the RFID market from \$1.4 billion per annum in 2003 to \$3.8 billion in 2008, while an International Data Corp. study was forecasting an growth in spending on RFID for tracking and tracing in retail supply chains to nearly \$1.3 billion in 2008 (KPMG, 2004).

However, despite such early optimism, the rapid adoption of RFID in supply chain on a global scale has been slower than expected (Wu et al, 2006). A study of RFID adoption identified the lack of standards as being one of the barriers inhibiting the uptake of RFID (Wu et al, 2006). Despite the technical merits of RFID, the strong mandates from large customers, and the promotional efforts of the IT vendors many companies are reluctant to embark on large RFID projects. Most of current RFID users deploy RFID in the form of small-scale projects, usually within organizational borders. These users have raised a number of concerns including the high costs of tags, the poor reliability of technology and the lack of pervasive and unified RFID standards (Jakovljevic, 2005; Wu et al, 2006). The lack of a unified RFID standards and the lack of consistent UHF spectrum allocation across the globe for RFID partially explain the reluctance of users to invest in current RFID systems and hampers the growth of RFID systems in the world market (Wu et al, 2006). Many of the organisations that are implementing RFID are global multinationals who have an interest in pushing for a global RFID standard, in particular for the air interface frequency protocols that enable the same tag to operate in all parts of the world. However, the regulation of radio frequencies forces tags to operate on different frequencies between Europe and the United States.

3. RFID STANDARDS

The RFID standardisation landscape is complex with overlapping regional and sectoral initiatives (Straube et al, 2007), but globally can be characterised by two competing standardisation initiatives, one within the formal procedures of ISO and one coordinated by a consortium, EPC-global, developers of the Electronic Product Code (EPC) standards, complemented by a plethora of industry-specific RFID standardisation efforts, such as the American Trucking Association in the transport industry, the Near Field Communication forum in consumer electronics, mobile devices and computer industry or the Automotive Industry Action Group in the automotive industry.

ISO RFID standardisation activities began in 1995, when a joint ISO IEC JTC1 committee, SC31, was set up within ISO to focus on standardisation of automatic identification techniques. SC31 membership is dominated by RFID manufacturers such as Internet Corporation and Paxar in the US delegation, or Texas Instruments in the French (http://usnet03.uc-council.org/SC31/member_directory). RFID ISO standards are generic, being able to be supported by any system and in any context, irrespective of the data that is being carried. ISO standards cover 4 different areas:

- Technology - ISO 18000 (SC31)
- Data content - ISO 15418, 15434, 15459, 24721, 15961, 15962
- Conformance and performance - ISO 18046, and ISO 18047
- Application standards - ISO 10374, ISO 18185, 11785

ISO 18000 is the ISO standard defining air interfaces for tags frequencies, specifying how the RFID tag communicates with the tag reader. The ISO 18000 includes five ranges of frequencies ISO 18000-2 for <135KHz, ISO 18000-3 for 13.56MHZ, ISO 18000-4 for 2.45 GHz, ISO 18000-6 A/B for 860-960MHz and ISO 18000-7

for 433MHZ (active), The ISO standards are defined at a very high level, focusing on the interface rather than on the data which is transported.

In parallel with the ISO standardisation efforts, MIT and UCC together with a number of industrial partners, including Procter & Gamble, Gillette and Wal-Mart, set up the Auto-ID consortium in 1999 to research RFID technologies and standards which in 2003 delegated the standardisation responsibilities to a new organisation, EPC. EPC members included end users, primarily from consumer packaged goods, large retailers and solution providers, including hardware and software providers and consultants. In contrast with ISO standards, EPC standards describe the tag and the air interface depending on the data being carried. EPC standards are developed around EPC's RFID system that includes the EPC coding structure, the Object Naming Service, the EPC tag and the EPC air interface. Consequently, EPC standards prescribe the physical implementation of the tags and readers, rather then specifying their generic characteristics. The EPC standards include five categories of standards:

- EPC tag data standards: include standards for the assignment and encoding of identities for physical objects, locations, loads, assets, etc., and most of them are based on the existing EAN UCC standards, developed for barcode applications;
- Air interface frequency standards: standardise the interface between tag to reader and is the counterpart of ISO 18000 series. There are three variations of this standards: class 0 (read-only); class 1 (read/write) and UHF Generation 2 (read/write). The later improves upon existing Class 0 and Class 1 standards by allowing worldwide operation and improved performance;
- RFID reader specifications: reader protocol (defines a standard "wire" protocol for reader to host communication) & reader management (defines a standard interface for managing readers);

- Software standards: Object Naming Service standard (solves the problem of locating EPCIS and other services that provide data about EPC), and Application Level Events standard (which is a declarative query language allowing filtered, aggregated EPC data from multiple real-time sources);
- EPC Information System (EPCIS): is a server that provides information on objects and products thus allowing the exchange of business-level EPC data, at business process level and within/across the enterprise.

The EPC standards cover both the software and the hardware, so are broader in scope than the ISO standards that focus on hardware standards. However, whereas the ISO standards allow for any data to be carried between the tag and the reader, EPC hardware standards are more limited than ISO standards being data specific and mainly operating within the UHF band between 860-930MHz, with one standard for 13.56MHz.

ISO and EPC RFID standards can be seen as complementary, even more so when one considers that the only direct competition between their areas of standardisation is the standard for air interface frequencies, specifically between the ISO 18000-6 A/B standard for 860-960MHz and the EPC class 0, 1. For both EPC and ISO supporters having a single, global standard is attractive. The benefits coming from standardization would be lost if in different parts of the globe, multinationals have to invest in different technologies for RFID. As explained by a respondent: *"The important thing from the supply chain's point of view is that when a manufacturer sticks a tag on his product, he doesn't know where that's going to end up, it could be in any country, it could potentially be in any supply chain in any industry sector. So it's very important for him that when he puts the tag on, that tag will be readable wherever he goes, otherwise he has to have different inventories, different SKUs for different places, he needs to keep these track where it's going to go to make*

sure that the right thing is on it, so that causes him a huge amount of cost and problems and means that different products can't cross over in different boundaries. So it's very important that we end up with one tag that works across the world and in every sector." (EPCUK)

Such pressures from their members forced ISO and EPC to attempt a reconciliation of their activities, for example through the ratification of EPC standards within ISO. As one of the respondents commented: *"Many of the people on the ISO side will have already had intimate dealings with the EPC Global generation 2 specification, so the hope is that that will move forward fairly fast and we'll end up with an 18006 part C or an EPC Global, whatever you want to call it, specification which is the same and we end up, which is where everybody wants to be, with an RFID standard."* (EPCUK). The institutional evolution of RFID standards development is therefore following a similar path to that seen earlier with electronic data interchange (EDI) standards: ostensibly competing institutions defining complementary areas of interest rather than fighting over the same ground in a "standards war" (Graham et al, 1995).

4. RFID ADOPTION IN THE AUTOMOTIVE INDUSTRY

The automotive industry is an excellent example to illustrate the application of RFID technologies to solve current business issues, such as supply chain process control, asset management, counterfeit detection or spare-part tracking. The following section provides a brief overview of the automotive environment and the challenges faced by automotive companies. Some of the challenging issues that have to be solved in this sector are ideal application areas for RFID. The next section discusses the role that the standards have played in shaping the adoption of RFID within the automotive industry.

4.1. The Adoption of RFID in the Automotive Industry: A Snapshot

The automotive industry faces a number of challenges. First, there is strong global competition and an increasing number of different models which forces both car makers and their suppliers to find new ways to collaborate effectively. Second, sales figures are stagnant in the triad markets (US, Europe & Japan) in the past years forcing organisation to find new way to achieve cost reduction, for example by re-organising their supply chains. In addition, external pressures increase the constraints on the industry, for example recently the EU Commission has released the End-of-Life Vehicle Directive which regulates the take-back and recycling of old cars. Such challenges increase the demand for real-time information and accurate data (e.g. distinct identification) throughout the industry's entire supply chain. RFID is one solution to address such demand and increase the supply chains transparency and therewith the supply chain efficiency.

Despite the potential of RFID, currently, RFID applications within the automotive industry are limited to in-house supply chain controls and asset management. In-house supply chain control applications, the so-called "closed loop scenarios", have been used particularly to streamline logistic processes in order to gain efficiencies in operations, including tracking parts or providing control over inventory management. Asset management applications involve the use of RFID to ensure the visibility, identification and location of pallets, containers or other movable assets.

One of our respondents, representing a car manufacturer, had been using RFID for two years in a "closed loop scenario" *as a tool to manage, operate and control the logistic flow of [vehicle] bodies. The logistic information where exactly the body in the plant is situated goes straight in the production logistics of the manufacturing control system.* (CM). Through enabling better control over the movement of the bodies within the

organization, the RFID investment was expected to lead to better logistic information. Nevertheless, the RFID implementation proved to be a very challenging process, failing to deliver many of its expected benefits. First, the technology delivered by the vendor was expensive, technically unreliable and failed to meet the expected levels of performance. However, while costs and poor reliability hampered adoption, standardisation issues between system elements also emerged as a significant barrier to investing in RFID supply chain applications on a larger scale.

4.2. The Role of Standards in Shaping RFID Adoption in the Automotive Industry

A survey of the automotive industry found that while 75% of the respondents had problems with the current process and tracking capabilities of the entire supply chain, 41% of the survey respondents had no plans to deploy RFID (Reale, 2006). This section discusses the role that RFID standards play in inhibiting the automotive industry's adoption of RFID technologies.

An analysis of the RFID standardisation process in 2005 suggested that there are a number of standard-related barriers to RFID adoption (Gerst & Bunduchi, 2005). First, the lack of a common, global standard has led to a congested RFID market, with a large number of different, and generally proprietary, products and services. Second, due to the interaction of standards, RFID technologies cannot offer an off-the-shelf turnkey solution. Thirdly, due to the fragmented and congested market, the total costs of RFID implementation are not transparent. And finally, RFID technologies require a huge effort in terms of standardisation. RFID standards are a major issue in securing the high investments in RFID technology on different levels (e.g. interface protocol, data structure, etc.). Not only different standards co-exist in parallel, but also different actors with sometimes divergent interests influence the standardisation life cycle.

While in-house, closed-loop scenarios do not require an open and global standard, aftermarket applications building interoperability between business partners on a global scale cannot be implemented in the absence of a global RFID standard. Even in the case of closed-loop scenarios, lack of standards is acknowledged as adding to deployment cost, and was cited as the main barrier to deployment by 18% of respondents (Reale, 2006). The interviews with consultants in the automotive industry confirmed that the willingness of potential users to implement RFID was affected by the lack of relevant standards. One of the consultants operating in the automotive industry has explained that *"standardisation is extremely important in the area of RFID. The situation as it is could be characterised by a very split market, many vendors on the hard and software side, few technology standards which will see the light very slowly, whereupon this will not be yield to standardisation bodies but will be driven by individual applications in an industry as a quasi de-facto standard. We think that this will emerge in the automotive area but in a time scale of 2 to 3 years"* (C1).

Standardisation bodies such as EPCglobal and ISO are recognised as being significant providers of RFID standards, but the users argued that industry-specific private consortia and initiatives should be playing a more significant role. According to C1: *"As long as standardisation will be driven by hardware and software vendors no real industry standard will be established. This means, it has to be driven from the user side, in our case from OEM side. They have to agree on certain national, European or global standards. Otherwise, there are many meetings and working groups of standardisation bodies that are engaged but which are not able to produce binding standards due to a lack of commitment of the user side. The user commitment only will come then when a real proof of benefit, real business cases, can be shown"* (C1). Users of the technology are caught in a dilemma between remaining outside the standards development process because participation is not a strategic priority, but concerned that the emergence of proprietary standards may lead to future costs: *"For us, the important point is that technology has to fit our needs and works properly. Therefore, we are not involved in any standardisation activity. But we have an eye on the technology market and are very well aware of any kind of monopolistic behaviour that is normally translated directly into the price. Often, once a standard product is developed, the vendor aims for unreasonably high prices."* (CM).

The evolution of EPCglobal was welcomed as it forced the established standardisation bodies such as ISO to be more active in RFID standardisation. They also see standardisation efforts in a more practical light: *"Auto-ID has been driven by EANCOM and industry-specific organisations. EPC is working on the 2.0 standard with focus on retailing and consumer goods but all other industries have a close look on it. They are not really ready, therefore I expect a lot of adaptation in the near future. Standards bring RFID a step further ahead. Integration will be much easier, because similar applications allow for a better and more seamless integration. On the other hand, there are not that many standards that became accepted. Big corporations often start a de-facto standard such as VW with its KLT[1]...that got adopted by VDA[2] and is today a VDA-KLT: there are other examples"* (C2). The engagement in standardisation organisations from a user perspective seems to depend to a large extent on the motivation of a company. If a company has a real need and some pressure as well as a clear idea about what they want to realise with RFID technologies in the next five years, then it makes sense to participate and influence the work of standardisation bodies. *"But this requires a strategy which certainly does not get formulated in the IT or logistics department, where actually most of the RFID projects start. An RFID strategy must be linked with an overall business strategy...if on the board of management level, goals have been formulated, with a clear focus on RFID, then it make sense to be engaged in standardisation bodies".* (C1)

The existence of diverse standards acts as a barrier to adoption by firms who are waiting to see which standards become dominant and forces early adopters to accommodate multiple standards. This led a consultant interviewee to take a pragmatic attitude to the dangers of waiting for a global standard to emerge, whilst accepting implicitly that this would increase costs for users: *"The big corporations are already working on a global basis. So, these companies will not perceive this game US vs. Europe in standardisation. If no global standard occurs, only a US one, a European one and an Asian one, then the companies will take it as it is because in other areas of business, there is also a lack of global standards. But this requires a decision at some point of time that the companies have to deal with three or more standards...because then the technology can be adapted to it. To wait if there will be in some time a global standard might be dangerous for a company and is a kind of utopia. From a company perspective, the only requirements are the basic conditions. And dependent on the markets where companies are working with, they will adopt different standards".* (C1)

In a sector like the automotive industry, dominated by global corporations, there are strong pressures to move towards a unified global standard. In interviews all respondents agreed that the only workable long-term solution was for a convergence of EPCglobal and ISO standards. However the relative low level of engagement by user firms in standards bodies implies that, other than through their implementation decisions, users were doing little to bring this about.

CONCLUSION

Earlier studies have found that technology standards development tends to be driven by IT vendors (Jakobs, 2000), whereas data and business process standards tend to emerge as a result of direct end-user involvement (Markus, 2003). In a similar way, whereas the former tend to be generic, the later are industry specific (Markus, 2003). Such a distinction is reflected in RFID standardisation, which occurs today within two distinct and yet overlapping processes, ISO and the EPCglobal. Whereas ISO RFID standards are driven by component manufacturers and focus on high level, generic technology interoperability, EPC was founded by and focused on the needs of large retailers, in concert with RFID system vendors and addresses data specific standards.

The engagement of the large majority of end users in RFID standards development is limited. Their major concern is to avoid lock-in to a particular hardware or software vendor, which explains why they consider RFID standards development as important, in principle. However, their general attitude towards standardisation can be characterised as a "wait and see position". There are three reasons for this. First, RFID technology is still an immature technology. The majority of existing RFID projects are implemented in-house and as such there is no need to integrate external parties. Consequently, there is no urgency for end-users to become involved in standardisation activity. Second, most of the prospective RFID users are too small to consider themselves as being able to influence standardisation. Consequently, most potential RFID users do not include standardisation in their business strategy and no budget is available to participate in RFID standardisation. Finally, RFID technologies are not used as a commonplace technology to support every day business. The major current concern for end-users is that the technology *"just has to work".* Until the basic economic, social and technological issues surrounding RFID development are solved, standardisation will be only a remote concern for end-users. For users remote from the processes of standardisation both ISO and EPC are seen as legitimate bodies developing standards, with the two processes so remote that worrying about the validity of a hierarchical process versus a process embedded within a consortium is not a significant issue. However, driven by the need to reduce cost and gain supply chain visibility, RFID applications are becoming more widespread, pushing standardisation into a more prominent position. However, as has been shown in the automotive industry, collaboration between users and standardisation bodies still facilitates the success of standards development, and further, supports adoption, where it does take place.

REFERENCES

AIM, Radio Frequency Identification – RFID. A basic primer, AIM White Paper, 1.11, September 28th, (1999), http://www.aimglobal.org, Access Date: January, 2005

Andel, T. (1998). Managing supply chain relationships. *Transportation & Distribution, 39*(10), SCF10-SCF14.

Barrat, M. (2004). Understanding the meaning of collaboration in the supply chain. *Supply Chain Management: An International Journal, 9*(1), 30-42.

Bearing Point, Beyond compliance: the Future promise of RFID. White Paper: communications, consumer, industrial & technology.

Borders, A. L., Johnston, W. J., & Rigdon, E. E. (2001). Beyond the Dyad: Electronic Commerce and Network Perspectives in Industrial Marketing Management. *Industrial Marketing Management, 30*(4), 343-358.

De Vries, H. (1999). *Standardization: A Business Approach to the Role of National Standardization Organizations*. Springer.

Egyedi, T. (2006). Beyond Consortia, Beyond Standardization? In K. Jakobs (Eds.), *Advanced Topics in Information Technology Standards and Standardization Research, 1*. Idea Group Publishing.

Fleisch, E. et al. (2004b). *From operations to strategy: The potential of RFID for the automotive industry*. Study of the M-Lab St. Gallen/Zurich with Booz Allen Hamilton, April 2004.

Gerst, M., & Bunduchi, R. (2005). *Challenges in the adoption of RFID standards, published by the European Commission, Strengthening Competitiveness through Production Networks – A perspective from European ICT research project in the field of 'Enterprise Networking'*. pp. (pp. 81-90).

Graham, I., Spinardi, G., Williams, R., & Webster, J. (1995). *Technology Analysis & Strategic Management, 7*(1), 3–20.

Gulati, R., Nohria, N., & Zaheer, A. (2000). Strategic Networks. *Strategic Management Journal, Special Issue: Strategic Networks, 21*(3), 203-215.

Harrington, L. H. (1998). Software tools to revamp your supply chain. *Transportation & Distribution, 39*(11), 59-70.

Hill, S. Jr, (2002). True supply chain management. *Manufacturing Systems, 20*(2), 48-49.

Hogart-Scott, S. (1999). Retailer-supplier partnerships: hostages to fortune or the way forward for the millennium? *British Food Journal, 101*(9), 668-682.

Howgego, C. (2002). Maximising competitiveness through the supply chain. *International Journal of Retail & Distribution, 30*(12), 603-605.

Jakovljevic, P. J. (2004). RFID – A new technology set to explode? *TechnologyEvaluation.Com*, (12th of April 2004), http://www.technology-evaluation,com/Research/ResearchHighlights/Scm/2004/04/research_notes/TU_SC_PJ_04_22_04_1.asp, Access Date: February.

Knospe, H., & Pohl, H. (2004). RFID Security. Information Security *Technical Report, 9*(4), 39-50.

KPMG (2004). KPMG's Auto Executive Survey 2004 – Client Preview.

Krechmer, K. (2000). Market Driven Standardization: Everyone Can win. *Standards Engineering, 52(4)*, 15–19.

Leaver, S. (2004, August). Evaluating RFID Middleware. *Forrester*, (pp. 1-21).

McGinity, M. (2004). Staying Connected. *Communications of the ACM, 47*(1), 15-18.

McKinney, J., & Barraclough, G. (2003). Radio Frequency Identification Technology Overview. *Pharmatech*, (pp. 110-112).

Morgan, R. M., & Hunt, S. D. (1994). The Commitment-Trust Theory of Relationships Marketing. *Journal of Marketing, 58*(3), 20-38.

Raza, N., Bradshaw, V., & Hague, M. (1999, October). Applications of RFID technology. *IEEE Colloquium on RFID Technology*. London.

Reale, K. (2006). *RFID continues to take Back Seat in Automotive*. AMR Research Report.

AMR Research (2005). *The Auto Industry and RFID*.

Ruppel, C. (2004). An information systems perspective of supply chain tool compatibility: The roles of technology fit and relationships. *Business Process Management Journal, 10*(3), 311-324.

Sarma, S. E., Weis, S. A., & Engels, D. W. (2005). RFID Systems and Security and Privacy Implications. *Workshop on Cryptographic Hardware and Embedded Systems*, (pp. 454-470), http://citeseer.ist.psu.edu/sarma02rfid.html, Access Date March, 2005.

Schindler, E. (2003). Location, Location, Location. *netWorker, 7*(2), 11-14.

Schmitt, P., Michahelles, F., & Fleisch, E. (2006). *An Adoption Strategy for an Open RFID Standard - Potentials for RFID in the Automotive Aftermarket*. Auto-ID Labs White Paper WP-BIZAPP-024.

Straube, F., Bensel, P., & Vogeler, S. (2007). RFID Standardisierungslandkarte. *PPS Management, 12*(4), 20–23.

Tompkins, J. A. (1998). Time to rise above supply chain management. *Transportation & Distribution, 39*(10), SCF16-SCF18.

Tyndall, G., Gopal, C., Partsch, W., & Kamauff, J. (1998). Supercharging Supply Chains: New Ways to Increase Value through Global Operational Excellence. New York: Wiley.

Whitfield, K. (2002). Looking both ways. *Automotive Design & Production, 11*(4), 36.

WEB SITES

http://adams1.com/pub/russadam/history.html, Access date: April, 2005.

http://www.afeindustries.com/rfid_faq.htm#18, Access date: May 2005.

http://www.aimglobal.org/technologies/rfid/what_is_rfid.asp, Access date: February 2005.

http://www.aimglobal.org/technologies/rfid/common_applications_rfid.asp, Access date: March, 2005.

http://www.belgravium.com/Technologies/html/barcode_rfid_glossary_a-c.html, Access data: April, 2005.

http://www.belgravium.com/Technologies/html/what_are_bar_codes_and_how_do_.htm, Access date: April, 2005.

http://www.epcglobalinc.org, Access date: February, 2005.

http://www.hightechaid.com/stdsupdate/stds_update1.htm, Access date: April, 2005.

http://www.manufacturing.net Access date: of 09/11/04.

http://rfdesign.com/mag/radio_accelerating_ adoption_radiofrequency/, Access date: May, 2005.

http://www.rfidinc.com/r3tags.html, Access date: March, 2005.

http://www.rfidjournal.com, Access date: March, 2005.

http://www.spychips.com/, Access date: April, 2005.

http://usnet03.uc-council.org/sc31/, Access date: April, 2005

ENDNOTES

[1]   KLT: Kleinladungstraeger: special form of transport unit in the automotive industry.

[2]   VDA: Verband Deutscher Automobilindustrie: German national automotive association.

APPENDIX: LIST OF INTERVIEWEES

Interviewee	Code
a representative serving on the ISO RFID committee	ISO
two representatives of the EPCglobal process, one from the United States and one from the UK	EPCA & EPCUK
a representative from the Auto-ID Centre that spawned the EPC initiative	AID
two RFID user representatives, one from a car manufacturer, and one from a supplier of RFID components that also uses RFID within some of its own supply chain applications	CM & CS
representatives of technology vendors	SV1 & SV2
representatives from two consultancies that provide RFID services	C1 & C2

Chapter VI
Perceived Relation between ICT Standards' Sources and their Success in the Market

Kai Jakobs
RWTH Aachen University, Germany

ABSTRACT

This chapter briefly outlines a study that looked at potential links between ICT / e-business standards' origins and their subsequent success in the market (or lack thereof). The outcome of the study suggests that companies who need to either implement or set standards do not distinguish between 'formal' standards setting bodies (SSBs) and consortia. Rather, specifics of the individual bodies are of interets, including, among others, their processes, IPR rules, and membership.

1 INTRODUCTION

Standards emerge from very different sources, ranging from sufficiently powerful individual companies to voluntary global standards developing organisations. Each of these entities has its own rules and bylaws, works in a specific environment, attracts a certain group of stakeholders, and can be described by a unique set of attribute types and values.

It could be hypothesised that stakeholders select a specific Standards Setting Body[1] (SSB) for (some of) their future standardisation activities based on best matches between an SSBs characteristics and their own business models, strategies, and/or technical needs. Likewise, it could be assumed that a stakeholder's selection of a specific standard (out of a set of competing ones) will be based on similarly objective criteria (such as, for instance, functionality, technical fit, performance, etc).

On the other hand, one could also suspect that other, less tangible reasons may also play a role in such selection processes. For example, aspects like individual preferences and prejudices of working group members, reputations of a technology's source, technologies that are considered 'hot', even media hype, may have considerable impact.

One typical example here is the common wisdom that the outcome of the formal Standards Developing Organisations' (SDO) process is of 'higher value' than the outcome of an industry standards consortium (recently, the number of those who subscribe to the opposed view has been increasing, though (see, for example, [Cargill, 2005], [Kamlani, 2005], [Krechmer, 2003]).

In this chapter, the impact of an SSB's perceived 'credibility', or reputation, on the success of its products in the market will be studied. That is, the more 'intangible' factors that may have an impact in the process of selecting either a platform for standards setting, or a standard for implementation, will be analysed.

2 SOME BACKGROUND

According to [Cash et al., 2002], *"Legitimacy refers to whether an actor perceives the process in a system as unbiased and meeting standards of political and procedural fairness."* Along similar lines, [Orlikowski & Robey, 1991] note that *"... human action is guided by cultural notions of legitimacy, ..."*. Obviously, (perceived) 'legitimacy' also plays a role in the selection of an SSB, or of one of its products.

For SSBs, this implies that they need to establish an adequate level of legitimacy to become (or remain) relevant. At least for formal SDOs, this is typically based on government endorsement which, in turn, requires that a *"... voluntary consensus standards body is defined by the following attributes: (i) Openness; (ii) Balance of interest; (iii) Due process; (vi) An appeals process.; (v) Consensus, ..."* (Office of Management and Budget Circular A-119; quoted in [Bukowski, 2003]).

Somewhat strangely, the 'old' international SDOs, i.e., ISO and IEC[2], did not enjoy any governmental endorsement when they were founded[3]. Even today, an 'authoritative' source of their legitimacy (i.e., why they are referred to

as 'formal') seems to be missing[4]. A widely held belief is that this status was 'earned' basically by tradition – i.e., by having done beneficial standardisation work over decades[5]. People now seem to trust these institutions (which may be to a lesser degree the case in the ICT sector, which is comparably young and where many SDOs were not really fully fit for the job at hand).

Typically, consortia do not enjoy the benefit of government endorsement. Thus, they need to explore other routes towards legitimacy. Van Wegberg notes that popular means to establish an SSB's legitimacy include (among others; see [van Wegberg, 1999]).

- Participation of key players.
- A track record in a certain field.
- IPR assets.
- Co-operation with other SSBs.

Once established, there is obviously the possibility that SSBs, especially formal SDOs, eventually undermine their legitimacy. This may, for instance, be achieved by allowing members to incorporate company standards into international, regional or national standards [Grebe, 1997]. Likewise, an excess of unresolved disputes and disagreements undermine the legitimacy of the standards setting process, both in the opinion of its members and in the eyes of the rest of the world [Freeman, 1996].

Not only SSBs need to achieve an adequate level of legitimacy. Also, both organisations and individuals participating in the standards setting process need such legitimacy, or reputation, in order to be able to push their ideas and views, and to influence the process accordingly.

Recent studies have shown that in standards setting an individual's reputation is frequently more important than that of the respective employer. This holds at least for the working level, i.e., for the technical work that is done within an SSB's committees or working groups. Here, influence rather more depends on an individual's technical knowledge and experience. Yet, even at this level in many cases influence is apparently related to market power. At higher, decision-making level, the market power of a company is playing a decisive role [Jakobs et al., 2003].

At working level, one way to gain legitimacy and reputation would be through technical sophistication, which is frequently combined with assuming a leading role in the group (e.g., editor, rapporteur, etc), and with generally taking over some responsibility. It has frequently been observed [(e.g., by Spring et al., 1995]) that almost all working groups are driven by a small group of individuals; usually ten percent or fewer. Much in line with this observation [Jakobs et al., 2001] found that aspects like 'strong sense of purpose', and even such trivial things like 'being present at meetings' have a considerable impact on an individual's performance and reputation.

In an attempt to improve reputation and legitimacy, companies aiming to actively influence standardisation, and with a shortage of suitable employees, frequently resort to hiring people with the right expertise. [Heywood et al, 1997] report that large companies hire people who have gained influence and reputations in official standard setting organisations. Complementing that, they are also sending more and more people to committee meetings, to lend more weight to their proposals.

3 THE STUDY

3.1 Background and Motivation

By now, the web of standards setting bodies has become an enormously complex environment, with a very large number of players with almost incomprehensible interrelations and overlapping work areas.

About thirty years ago, there was a clear distinction between the then 'quais-monopolist' CCITT[6] on the one hand, and the world of IT standards on the other. Through CCITT, the various national PTTs[7] (or equivalent organisations) were developing standards for the telecommunication sector. ISO was in charge of almost all other IT-related standardisation activities. The various national SDOs developed their own specific standards, but also contributed to the work of ISO (see Figure 1).

Over time, five trends contributed to an increasingly complex standardisation environment in the area of information and communication technologies (ICT).

- The increasingly shorter technology life cycles in the ICT sector,
- The growing importance of ICT for business,
- The 'discovery' of the Internet for commercial purposes,

Figure 1. The ICT standardisation universe in the seventies (excerpt; see [Jakobs, 2008])

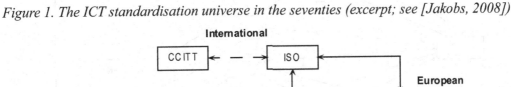

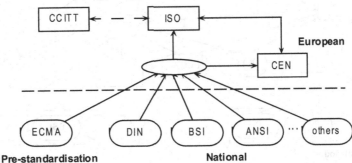

- The de-regulation of the telecommunication sector,
- The globalisation of markets.

The emergence of standards consortia was one result of these trends (especially, but not exclusively of the first one; see, e.g., [Besen, 1995], [Cargill, 1995]). They represented an 'external' competition for the SDOs, and managed to marginalise them in many fields ((Wireless) Local Area Networks, (W)LANS, and electronic business being prominent examples). Well-known examples of highly successful consortia today include, for instance, the W3C (the World Wide Web Consortium), OASIS (the Organization for the Advancement of Structured Information Standards), or OMG (the Object Management Group).

In parallel, the economic importance of standards grew. It is safe to assume that a technology or system standardised by an respected SSB will be supported by this SSB's members, subsequently also by their customers or business partners and perhaps, ultimately, by the whole sector. This holds the promise of huge financial gains for its proponents. Likewise, backing a loosing system implies both severe monetary losses and a severely reduced market share for its supporters. In such a case, and in an attempt to save the day, a new consortium could be established to standardise the loosing system. Obviously, this approach increased the number of consortia and led to an even higher complexity of the standards setting environment (see also Figure 2).

As a result, today many companies are forced to participate in a large number of SSBs to make sure that they do not miss a potentially relevant development. This holds especially for large manufacturers and service providers, but also for large users (see e.g., [Updegrove, 2003] and [IBM, 2008]))

Likewise, it is becoming more and more important for companies to select the 'right' body for a planned standards activities – the choice of an SSB is an important contributor to the success – or failure – of a standards setting activity.

In addition to hard, auditable facts it may be hypothesised that other, more intangible reasons exist for the selection of a specific SSB (good reputation, recent press coverage, previous experiences, etc). Specifically, the outcome of the study

Figure 2. The ICT standardisation universe today (excerpt; source: [Jakobs, 2008])

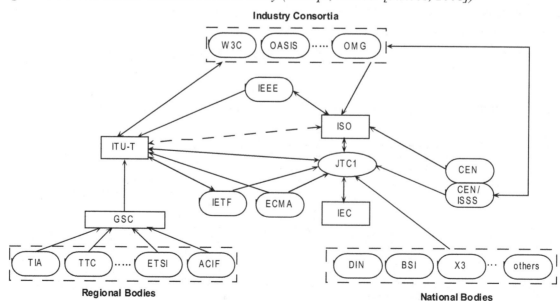

presented should provide some insight into any possibly more intangible reasoning behind the selection of an SSB.

As George Paolini, JavaSoft's Director of Corporate Marketing acknowledged (cf. ([Garud et el., 2002]). *'In today's world, it's really about first creating mindshare and awareness about a technology, and then driving that technology to reality. That's really what Java has been about.'*

3.1 Some Technicalities

A questionnaire, comprising 22 open-ended questions was developed. These questions were subdivided into four sections, entitled

- 'General background information.'
- 'Knowledge and perceptions of standards setting bodies.'
- 'Selecting standards.' Here, respondents were asked to assume they had to select one out of a number of competing standards offering similar functionality for implementation either locally within their organisation, or for integration into a product/service their organisation is planning to sell.
- 'Actively contributing to standards setting.' Here, respondents were asked to assume they had to select the most suitable SSB for a standards setting activity that is crucially important for their organisation.

The questionnaire was sent to

- A selection of individuals from industry who could safely be assumed to be knowledgeable,
- Two distribution lists the subscribers to which are primarily standards researchers and/or active in standards setting,
- Selected members of relevant professional organisations (eema, an independent trade association for e-Business; SES, the Standards Engineering Society; and IFAN, the International Federation of Standards Users).

In total, 19 responses were used as the basis for the analysis of organisations' reasons for selecting a specific SSB. Out of these 19 respondents, 6 came from universities, 5 from industry, 2 from SDOs, 2 from contract researches, 2 represented industry associations and 1 a regulator[8].

3.1 Hypotheses: Discussion

(H1): International/regional SSBs are considered more important than national ones.

A large majority of the respondents stated that international (global) bodies are the most influential ones (specifically in the e-business and telecommunications sectors). While this view was expressed across the board, it was particularly stressed by respondents from industry.

I subscribe to the view on standardisation: do it once, do it internationally. Formal international standards are the first choice, then national standards. (industry representative 2)

However, at the same time respondents were cautious not to generalise

Huge differences, but difficult to generalize. As an international company we focus on globally recognized SDOs. (industry representative 5).

This caution would seem to suggest that even in the inherently global areas of e-business and telecommunications industry sees a role for national or regional standards. This, however, would be in stark contrast to the view (also expressed by some) that regional standards bodies are not really desirable.

... If the goal is to increase European economic success, ETSI is doing well. If the goal is to support world-wide compatibility, ETSI is more of a problem, than a solution. (consultant)

I regard regional standards, en CEN, CENELEC, as an unfortunate temporary phase. (industry representative 2)

Yet, the same respondent qualified this statement, observing that

... there are areas where international standards are not appropriate because of cultural, climatic or other differences between countries. International standards which try to cover such areas frequently end up so bland as to be useless or contain so many options to cover all eventualities as to be totally confusing for the general user. (industry representative 2)

Likewise, national bodies are said to be hardly in a position to contribute meaningfully:

National bodies like DIN, AFNOR, NIST... have a great difficulty in having a good international view of what is happening in the standards field, where all the big decisions are now taken .... (SDO representative 2)

One explanation for the continuing importance of national bodies, and for the motivation that led to the establishment of regional bodies, would be that:

... Governments will perceive national and/or regional standards as tools for regulation and policy setting, ... (industry representative 1)

Yet, smaller companies (i.e., SMEs) will have major problems following, let alone contributing, to international standardisation. For them, a narrower geographic scope is of benefit.

ESOs are the major driving force for us; nationals come after. World bodies are difficult to follow and to influence .... (association representative 2)

Another respondent from industry associated the geographical scope of an SSB with the size of the potential market for a standard.

Standards arising from international SDOs have the potential to create massive network externalities. This is limited in the case of regional SDOs. (industry representative 7)

Along similar lines, another one suggested that the origin of a standard may not be as important as its envisaged usage. The level of acceptance is said to be key.

That would probably depend on the particular usage for which a standard is intended. Industries tend to give more value to standards that are more likely to gain widespread acceptance, wherever they might come from, and, in certain cases, will fight to promote consortia or even proprietary specs that best fit their strategies. (industry representative 3)

This aspect will come up again, and will be further discussed as follows. [Blind, 2004] shows in his studies the more positive impact of international standards at least on trade.

(H2) Formal SDOs are seen as being more 'trustworthy' than consortia.

Extending the analysis from formal SDOs to also include standards consortia, common wisdom has it that the standards produced by formal, accredited SDOs are of a higher value than those produced by organisations outside the system of formal national, regional, and international SDOs. This holds for consortia as well as for industry fora or any other form of alliance.

Respondents' comments indicate rather mixed perceptions. Indeed, most respondents from the research domain subscribe to the popular perception that consortia are able to move quicker, are market-driven and more responsive to market needs. However, there seems to be a little confusion about the term 'consortium' – one respondent considered the W3C as a formal body and compares it to a 'newcomer' on the scene, who is working on topics also covered by the W3C – the 'Web Services Interoperability Organization'.

Yes, in my view, industrial consortia are more dynamic and quick in response, and they are more indicated for integrating advances and innovations ..... Another example is that of the WS-I consortia, that was much more dynamic than the W3C in setting up detailed implementation specifications for Web Services. (university representative 5)

Following up on this perception might be interesting – it indicates the view that some long-standing, well-known consortia are hardly distinguishable from formal SDOs. An analysis of the processes and IPR regimes suggests that this view is not too far off the mark, at least in this respect.

Along similar lines, two responses from practitioners suggest that the process adopted by an SSB is the decisive point. In this respect, both see advantages on the side of the formal SDOs:

.... formal SDOs can be expected to offer full guaranty for due process and fairness, which is reflected in the IPR policy and all other operational rules. This fundamental difference is reflected in the recognition provided by respected international organizations such as the UN, the WTO and the European Commission based on conformance to stringent requirements of openness, transparency, consensus and global relevance. (SDO representative 2)

'Formal SDOs are preferable to consortia if they are available. Consortia with open membership and transparency like DVB are preferable to ad-hoc consortia with closed membership. (regulator representative)

It is quite telling that the latter comment was made by a representative of a regulatory body.

Related to the aforementioned, it was noted that the products that result from the different processes may have different characteristics, specifically in terms of IPR.

Standards are in the public domain or owned by consortia. (association representative 1)

Overall, the views expressed by the practitioners are a little more differentiated; no prevailing perceptions (or prejudices) can be identified. Here as well some respondents stress that consortia are quicker and more flexible, but market relevance and also maintenance of standards are considered important.

... for voluntary standards the main criterion is acceptance by the market ... (industry representative 5)

Speed, though, may well be important. However, in the opinion of another respondent from industry, not only the speed of standardisation should be considered, but also the speed of adoption of a standard. Here, he sees an advantage for the SDOs.

Consortia standard bodies come out with standards at a much shorter time than formal SDOs, owing to industry backing. However, the presence of splinter consortia bodies may affect the adoption of standards. Formal SDO, take a longer time to come out with standards, but once the standards are formed, the adoption is faster. (industry representative 7)

Obviously, once the use (or non-use) of standards has legal implications, SDOs' products enjoy a clear advantage.

The issue of standards maintenance came up several times. On the one hand, this assumes a reasonable longevity of a standard, and also its originator's capability to adapt it to new (technical) developments. Here, it may assumed that formal SDOs have a certain edge, as many consortia a comparably short-lived, and only few care about standards maintenance.

... However, they [consortia] do not have a long life so there is a problem with respect the maintenance of the specifications. (industry representative 4)

A number of respondents, again all from an industry background, also point at the links that exists between consortia and SDOs.

Consortia are a little bit faster because they use the work of formal SDOs in specific problems. (industry representative 4)

This is certainly true for some cases (the example of XML, which is based on SGML, developed by ISO in the mid/late eighties, comes to mind). However, the 'typical' course of events is the other way round – specifications developed by consortia are passed to formal SDOs for approval.

Consortia have an important role in DEVELOP-ING standards but the end product should be published by an SDO... (industry representative 2)

A recent prominent, albeit eventually unsuccessful, example of this a approach would be SUN's activities to get JAVA standardised by JTC1 (see e.g. [Egyedi, 2001]). This, however, carries the risk that SDOs will degenerate to 'rubberstamping entities':

I sometimes hear comments in SDOs from people that fear that the body will ultimately be converted

into a 'rubberstamping' agency for standards developed elsewhere .... (industry representative 2)

Indeed, the PAS-process may be interpreted as a means for JTC1 to stay relevant in an environment that is largely populated by consortia.

(H3) Perceptions of an SSB differ for different technologies.

In addition to, and complementing, the aspects discussed before experience seems to indicate that several SSBs are 'specialists' in certain areas, and not really relevant in others. For example, IEEE are *the* force behind the development of local area networks (both cable-based and wireless), but are of hardly any importance at all in other sectors of mobile communication.

Obviously, some SSBs were founded with a very specific scope:

ATM forum is for ATM only. Frame relay forum is for frame relay only. (industry representative 4)

Yet, several other more general cases were also noted by the respondents, where SSBs proved particular competence in certain areas. Two examples:

... JTC1 had to rely on ECMA for its standards on magnetic and optical memory units, W3C is probably more relevant presently for XML than any other SSB, MPEG had a dominant contribution of consortia (e.g. DAVIC), etc. (the list could probably go on indefinitely). (industry representative 1)

CEN/ISSS and UN/CEFACT for B2B .... (research representative 1)

Similarly, a division of labour may occur between co-operating bodies. This may, for instance, be based on perceived specific competencies.

... Even when there is cooperation (like JTC1 with ITU-T, for example), you can always find a division of work: JTC1 had the leadership in OSI, while (the old) CCITT SG 7 leaded in MHS. (industry representative 1).

Some respondents also identified certain SSBs as poor performers in some domains:

Take the IETF. High respect concerning some of their protocols like SIP, but less for issues like OAM or MPLS (here they are promoting company specific proposals and do not listen to the requirements of operators). (industry representative 5)

One observed that SSBs may also move into areas where standardisation is considered inappropriate:

CEN has produced good standards but has ventured into areas where national guidance is appropriate rather than standards .... (industry representative 2)

(H4) The origin of a standard is important for its success in the market.

If charged with the task of selecting one out of a number of competing standards offering similar functionality (either for implementation locally within an organisation, or for integration into a product/service to be sold) most respondents would, first and foremost, want to have information about the degree of global recognition of a standard and, particularly, about its level of acceptance in the market (critical mass of users). In fact, the latter aspect is crucially important; one respondent from telecommunications industry even stated that he

... may have to recommend a standard that I don't believe in because everybody is using it. (industry representative 4)

Related to the aforementioned, information about the standards incorporated in both competing and complementing products would be of interest, as well as information about potentially relevant legal requirements in major target markets.

Somewhat surprisingly, 'standards maintenance' was mentioned by only one respondent.

Various criteria would be applied during this selection process. Overall, the fit of the standard into the envisaged environment within which it would be applied would be important. This includes several aspects. For one, existence of competing standards (both existing and emerging) would be important. Also, the degree to which requirements are met would be important, including the standard's ability to interoperate with existing applications and standards, as well as its fit into the implementer's existing product/service portfolio. Suitability for certain types of customers (e.g., SMEs) might also be an issue (depending on the type of standard). Moreover, IPR aspects (no proprietary elements, no licensing fees) play a role as well.

Respondents expressed a slight preference for international standards, but this doesn't seem to be a hard requirement. A representative response was:

The source is of less relevance, as long as certain criteria are fulfilled: e.g. market acceptance, IPR policy. (industry representative 5)

Characteristics of the originating SSB (previous track record and its 'respectability') were also mentioned, albeit only by some.

a track record is relevant, but limited. It may also be beneficial, to start a consortium. (industry representative 5)

Asked to list the criteria they would apply for the selection of the most suitable SSB for a standards setting activity crucially important for their respective organisation respondents identified three broad sets of such criteria:

- The SSB's process' characteristics – efficiency, speed, consensus, IPR policy, scope (geographical, sectoral).

  Overall, however, none of the aspects one would expect to be considered important seems to play a significant role for a majority of respondents. An SSB's IPR policy was mentioned by many, but even this does not quite seem to have the overriding importance one would have thought. Likewise, speed does not seem to be such an important issue for the respondents either (with one exception). The fact that an SSB's process is well defined and that the body is capable of actually managing this process appears to be as important as the individual characteristics of said process.

- Market aspects, including factors such as, for instance, user requirements, characteristics of complementing/competing products, differentiation form competition, etc.

  Standard body supporting the standard. Role of industry leading players and their stance regarding the standard. Presence of complementary/ competing standards. Level of adoption of the standard. Presence/absence of communities of practice. (industry representative 7)

- Compatibility between an organisation's strategy (or underlying policy) and an SSB's characteristics.

Judging by the number of respondents who listed this aspect it seems to be much more important than the process' characteristics.

... I would probably try to develop in the SSB that best fitted my strategy. ... (industry representative 1)

It is important that [we] can bring in the principles behind [our country's] regulatory policy (ie. promotion of competition, ensuring interoperability, maximising benefits to endusers, protection of consumers) into the standards debate. (regulator representative)

Some respondents also mentioned preferences with respect to the geographical/ sectoral scope of an SSB, a preference for European standards available in different languages was also mentioned (by the representative of an SME umbrella organisation).

Opinions were equally split with respect to the importance to be associated with earlier successful standards produced by an SSB (its 'track record'). Comments ranged from

Generally, I do not see a direct relation between the previous track record of an SSB and its ability to successfully handle a new work item. (industry representative 1).

to

ISO TC184/SC4 has one [a track record]. It is very important. (university representative 2)

However, it also emerged that information about track records (or lack thereof) are not as widely disseminated as one might expect, and not necessarily, albeit frequently, considered important.

Rather than looking in the past (for a track record) the expected future level of adoption of a standard is also considered important.

We judge the standards based on their adoption, especially by the major product vendors. We also analyse standards from the point of view of their potential. Values vary based on the participation and support of industry leading players, which play a key role in their adoption. (industry representative 7)

Along similar lines, one respondent also observed that rather than looking for a track record it might be worthwhile considering the option of forming a new SSB (which would, obviously, not have any such track record per-se).

The scope of a standard is another distinguishing factor. Here, both applicability (i.e., sector-specific vs general) and the level of detail (specific vs generic) were identified as sources for differing values of standards. In the former case, sector-specific standard are associated with a lower value, as many SSBs are said to not attempt to make their standards compatible with those from other sectors.

... too many purely sectoral standards that don't look at what is being done in other industrial sectors; ... (SDO representative 1)

On the other hand, standards that are too generic because they follow the 'one size fits all' approach are also considered rather worthless. A similar argument was put forward in relation to international standards (see H1).

... IEEE LOM is a 'least common denominator' standard, reluctant to including advanced capabilities, since it targets 'the whole population'' of practitioners. ... (university representative 5)

Finally, asked if the type of an SSB would make a difference (for active participation), two camps emerged. One group of respondents made it very clear that they would normally prefer a formal SDO for such endeavours.

With very few exceptions preference for formal SDOs. (regulator representative)

The other group stated that the type of SSB would not be that important; rather, the characteristics of an SSB , as well as other aspects, which are unique to each case and cannot really be predetermined would have to be considered.

... depending on the type of intended usage, the status of development of the associated artifacts, and many other circumstances, a particular SSB might emerge as preferred. (industry representative 1)

Quite surprisingly, only one respondent (from a university) expressed a preference for consortia, because of the perceived slowness of formal SDOs.

Looking at the 'true' origin of standards (i.e., at working group level), various comments stressed the impact of individuals on the outcome of the process. This is particularly troublesome for the selection of a suitable SSB, as it adds another dimension which is extremely hard to take into account adequately. Some sample quotes:

It depends on many factors. E.g., in the same committee, depending on the project leader or convenors, the results can be of very different value. (industry representative 2)

ISO work is impacted strongly by the approach of each committee's chair. (consultant)

CEN is dependent on the quality of the people managing projects; ... (SDO representative 1)

Related to this, one respondent also pointed out some typical differences in membership between individual SSBs.

The ITU is more formal .... ISO work is impacted strongly by the approach of each committee's chair. ETSI work is greatly improved by the advantages of hiring technical experts to address technical areas. Committee T1 is dominated by telco operators and vendors who have become more myopic as their industry changes. IEEE, as an individual membership organization, attracts a younger and more technically driven set of experts. IETF has the huge advantage of some ground breaking past work and an ability to attract young and bright engineers .... (consultant)

4 SUMMARY AND CONCLUSION

4.1 Summary

A number of hypotheses have been derived (largely) from the literature study. The most relevant of these were used as the basis for the development of the questionnaire. These will be discussed as follows.

Especially in the ICT sector, European and international standards have long played a crucial role. Most national bodies adopted relevant ISO or CEN standards as national ones; just adding a national foreword and possibly a translation of the most important technical terms used in the document. Accordingly, the importance of national standards in this sector has diminished over quite a number of years.

Also, for many formal SDOs still have some sort of competitive edge over consortia and other SSBs. This is partly due to their importance in (government) procurement activities, but also to the widely held perception of fairer and more open processes adopted by SDOs. These observation led to the following hypothesis:

- (H1) International/regional SSBs are considered more important than national ones.
- (H2) Formal SDOs are seen as being more 'trustworthy' than consortia.
- (H3) Perceptions of an SSB differ for different technologies.
- (H4) The origin of a standard is important for its success in the market.

They will be discussed in the following.

(H1): International/regional SSBs are considered more important than national ones.

The responses here were fairly homogeneous overall. National SDOs are considered by most as being of rather little relevance in the e-business and telecommunications sectors. Likewise, the potential market size may be larger for international standards. Possibly a bit surprising, regional (e.g., European) SDOs were also not regarded too favourably by several respondents. This is understandable given the inherently global nature of the sectors in question.

That is, (H1) seems to be only partially correct; over-estimating the role of regional bodies by equating their importance with that of international bodies.

On the other hand, and considering the importance attributed to the adequate participation of SMEs in standards setting (see e.g. [EC, 2001], [EC, 2004]), particularly NSOs may enjoy a renaissance. They may well become the channel through which the needs and requirements of those stakeholders which cannot realistically participate in standards setting at the global level (due to, for example, lack of expertise, but also because of such rather more mundane reasons as lack of adequate financial resources) can be fed into the global standards processes.

(H2): Formal SDOs are seen as being more relevant than consortia.

Perhaps somewhat surprisingly, perceptions of SDOs and consortia differ only marginally. A slight edge is conceded to the former in terms of acceptance and adoption of their products, for the latter, in terms of speed of the standards setting process. Neither aspect is considered crucially important, though. Accordingly, (H2) must be considered as wrong.

That is, a general preference for either SDOs or consortia cannot be concluded. While certain constituencies do seem to have specific preferences (regulatory bodies for international/European SDOs, European SMEs for European/national SDOs), especially practitioners from industry point at the different, yet complementing roles of consortia and SDOs.

(H3): Perceptions of an SSB differ for different technologies.

This seems to be definitely the case. Several reasons may be identified for this. For one, certain SSBs were founded with a very specific purpose, and never ventured beyond that. In other cases SDOs rely on the specific expertise of other bodies for the production of international standards. It may also happen that the type of membership of an SSB (as opposed to the SSB per se) is considered more appropriate for a given task. This was the case for the standardisation of an electronic messaging system. Here, the national PTTs were seen by many as the most suitable institutions to ensure the widest possible implementation of the standard (and as the guarantor of interoperability of the implementations). Accordingly, CCITT was the standards body of choice.

(H3) may thus be considered correct.

On the other hand, it also seems that an SSB should not regard widely recognised previous successes as a license to also adopt other areas for standardisation.

(H4): The origin of a standard is important for its success in the market.

Selection of a standard for local implementation, or for integration into commercial products or services, hardly seems to depend on its institutional origin per se (i.e., whether it originated from a formal SDO or a consortium). IPR issues are the one exception in this context.

Rather, more practical aspects seem to be important, most notably a standard's fit into the environment within which it will have to operate, the fit into the product portfolio in case of a manufacturer or a service provider, as well as its likely future adoption by the market.

Somewhat in contrast to this, the characteristics of an SSB's process seem to play a role for the selection of an SSB for pro-active standards setting. However, here as well they are not as-signed the importance one would expect. On the other hand, this lack of perceived importance is in line with the responses regarding the relevance of different types of SSBs.

The most important aspect to be considered for potential standards-setting activities is the match between an SSB's characteristics and the proposer's strategy. That is, any platform for standardisation activities would need to be able, and flexible enough, to accommodate potentially very different strategies. These might require, for example, to focus on technical details, or on the emergence of a new standard. Likewise, various degrees of influence are likely to be required, also depending on the underlying corporate strategy.

All in all, the requirements listed form a very mixed bag – no single dominant demand can be identified.

The 'track record' of an SSB appears to play a more important role for a company assuming the role of a potential active contributor to standardisation than it would if the role of a user were assumed. While by no means agreed upon by all, the importance of such a track record was mentioned far more frequently for standards setting than it was for standards deployment.

Here again, the type of SSB is considered not relevant by many. While some (notably regulator and SME association) expressed a preference for SDOs, many others stated that this would (have to) be a case-by-case decision.

Finally, it was observed by many that the impact individuals (most notably, chair persons) may have on the process must not be under-estimated. A consequence of this observation would be that aspects such as, for example, the individual make-up of a working group, and the previous track-record of the convenor/chairman (or absence of it), and possibly even the make-up of the committee will have to be taken into account if the suitability of a particular SSB for a new standards initiative is to be evaluated.

It follows that (H4) cannot be considered correct.

4.2 Conclusions

The one conclusion that immediately suggests itself is that companies who need to either implement or set standards are not that much interested in issues like 'consortium vs SDO'. In fact, it seems that this distinction is hardly valid any more. This is further re-enforced by the fact that several respondents mixed up formal SDOs and consortia. This is understandable if one considers that the rules and regulations of several (of the long established) consortia (such as, e.g., OASIS or W3C) can hardly be distinguished from SDOs. Likewise, within ETSI a company's number of votes depends on the membership fee it is paying.

Rather, considerable importance is assigned to the processes adopted by an SSB. Here, IPR aspects seem to play the most important role. More generally, an SSB's characteristics need to be compatible with a company's strategy and its business model. Accordingly, preferences will frequently depend on the characteristics of the individual case; there's hardly any general 'SSB of choice' (with the possible exception of 'specialist' SSBs, which are – at least temporarily – the sole occupants of a market segment (e.g., the ATM Forum)). Obviously, SDOs may enjoy a competitive advantage in cases where regulatory requirements call for 'formal' standards. However, given the aforementioned, this increasingly artificial distinction may need to be revisited.

5 REFERENCES

Besen, F. M. (1995). The standards process in telecommunication and information technology. In R. W. Hawkins, et al. (Eds.), *Standards, Innovation and Competitiveness*. Edward Elgar Publishers.

Blind, K., Thumm, N., Bierhals, R., Hossein, K., Iversen, E., van Reekum, R., & Rixius, B. (2002). *Study on the Interaction between Standardisation and Intellectual Property Rights*. Final Report to the DG Research of the European Commission (EC Contract No G6MA-CT-2000-02001), Karlsruhe.

Blind, K. (2004). *The Economics Of Standards - Theory, Evidence, Policy*. Edward Elgar, ISBN 1 84376 793 7.

Bukowski, R. W. (2003). The Role of Standards in a Performance-based Building Regulatory System. http://fire.nist.gov/bfrlpubs/fire02/PDF/f02032.pdf.

Cargill, C. F. (1995). *Open Systems Standardization – A Busienss Approach*. Prentice Hall.

Cargill, C. (2002). Uncommon Commonality – A Qust for Unitiy in Standardization. In S. Bolin, (Ed.), The Standards Edge.

Cargill, C. (2005). Open Source, Open Standards, Open Issues: Structuring a Busienss perspective. In S. Bolin, (Ed.), *Standards Edge – Open Season*.

Cash, D., Clark, W., Alcock, F., Dickson, N., Eckley, N., & Jäger, J. (2002). *Salience, Credibility, Legitimacy and Boundaries: Linking Research, Assessment and Decision Making*. John F. Kennedy School of Government Faculty Research Working Paper RWP02-046. John F. Kennedy School of Government, Harvard University.

Egyedi, T. M. (2001). Why Java™ was -not-standardized twice. *Computer Standards & Interfaces, 23*(4).

European Commission (2001). On Actions Taken Following the Resolutions on European Standardisation Adopted by the Council and the European Parliament in 1999. *COM*(2001) 527 final.

European Commission (2004). The role of European standardisation in the framework of European policies and legislation. Communication from the Commission to the European Parliament and the Council. *COM*(2004) 674. http://europa.eu.int/comm/enterprise/standards_policy/role_of_standardisation/doc/communication_en.pdf.

Freeman, R. (1996). *Developing Standards: A Market-Driven Approach.* http://www.peostri.army.mil/E-DIR/ED/SEI/documents/013.pdf.

Garud, R., Jain, S., & Kumarasawamy, A. (2002). Institutional entrepreneurship in the sponsorship of common technological standards: The case of Sun Microsystems and Java. *Academy of Management Journal, 45*(1).

Grebe, A. (1997). *Standards: Today's Trade Barriers Are Tomorrow's Global Markets.* http://www.ses-standards.org/displaycommon.cfm?an=1&subarticlenbr=56.

Heywood, P., Jander, M., Roberts, E., & Saunders, S. (1997). Standards, The Inside Story: Do Vendors have too much Influence on the Way Industry Specs are Written and Ratified? *Data Communications,* March, (pp. 59-72).

IBM (2008). *IBM Announces New I.T. Standards Policy.* http://www-03.ibm.com/press/us/en/pressrelease/25186.wss.

Jakobs, K., Procter, R., & Williams, R. (2001). The Making of Standards. *IEEE Communications Magazine, 39*(4).

Jakobs, K., Egyedi, T., & Monteito, E. (2003). *Helping SDOs to Reach Users. – Final Report.* http://www-i4.informatik.rwth-aachen.de/~jakobs/grant/FinalReport.pdf.

Jakobs, K. (2004). (E-Business & ICT) Standardisation and SME Users – Mutually Exclusive? *Proc. Multi-Conference on Business Information Systems, Track 'E-Business – Standardisierung und Integration*, Cuviller Verlag, Göttingen.

Jakobs, K., & Mora, M. (2008). Co-ordinating Rule Setters – Co-operation in ICT Standards Setting.

Proc. 2008 International Conference on Information Resources Management (Conf-IRM).

Kamlani, D. (2005). ICT Standards and the New Arms Race – The Rule of 3 (+N). In S. Bolin, (Ed.), *Standards Edge, Future Generation.*

Krechmer, K. (2003). Face the FACS. *Proc. 3rd. Int. Conf. On Standardization and Innovation in IT.* IEEE Press.

Orlikowski, W. J., & Robey, D. (n.d.). Information technology and the structuring of organizations. *Information Systems Research, 2*(2).

Spring, M. B., Grisham, C., O'Donnell, J., Skogseid, I., Snow, A., Tarr, G., & Wang, P. (1995). Improving the Standardization Process: Working with Bulldogs an Turtles. In B. Kahin & J. Abbate, (Eds.), *Standards Policy for Information Infrastructure.* MIT Press.

Updegrove, A. (2003). *Major Standards Players Tell How They Evaluate Standard Setting Organizations.* http://www.consortiuminfo.org/bulletins/jun03.php.

van Wegberg, M. (1999). *The Design of Standardisation Processes in ICT: An evolutionary transaction cost approach.* http://www-edocs.unimaas.nl/files/nib99001.pdf

ENDNOTES

[1] This term is used to cover both 'formal' bodies like ISO and ITU, industry consortia like OASIS and W3C, as well as others (like, e.g., the IETF).

[2] The International Electrotechnical Commission.

[3] The third one, CCITT (ITU) is a UN treaty organisation.

[4] The European bodies are 'legitimised' by an EC Directive.

5   See also the discussion on http://mail-i4.informatik.rwth-aachen.de/mailman/private/siit/2005-February/thread.html

6   International Telegraph and Telephone Consultative Committee, the predecessor of the ITU-T.

7   Post, Telephone and Telegraphy administration.

8   This is hardly a representative sample, as all addressees are very knowledgeable about standards and standardisation processes. However, the selection was largely dictated by practical issues.

Chapter VII
How to Select the Best Platform for ICT Standards Development

Kai Jakobs
RWTH Aachen University, Germany

Jan Kritzner
RWTH Aachen University, Germany

ABSTRACT

The chapter tries to provide the information that potential standards-setters should consider when selecting a standards setting body (SSB). It proposes classifications of both standards users and SSBs. The former focuses on users' strategies and business models, the latter describes SSBs' characteristics in different categories. The SSB that yields the best match should be given some preference, as it is likely to offer the most successful platform for the envisaged standardisation activity.

1 BACKGROUND AND MOTIVATION

These days, a web of SDOs (Standards Developing Organisations) operate at various geographical level. These include, for example, ISO[1] and ITU[2] at the global level, ETSI[3] and PASC[4] at regional level, and ANSI[5] and BSI[6] at the national level issue what is commonly referred to as 'de-jure' standards – although none of their standards have any regulatory power[7]. Likewise, a plethora of industry fora and consortia (a recent survey found more than 270 [ISSS 2008]), such as, e.g., the World Wide Web Consortium (W3C), the Organization for the Advancement of Structured Information Standards (OASIS), or the Open Group, to name but a few of the longer standing ones, produce so-called 'de-facto' standards.

In addition, one may also distinguish between voluntary, regulatory, pro-active, reactive, public, industry, and proprietary standards; this list is by no means exhaustive.

As a result, there exists an almost impenetrable maze of what is generally referred to as 'standards', ranging from company specific rules, over regional and national regulations, up to globally accepted norms. As Andrew Tanenbaum put it:

"The nice thing about standards is that there are so many to choose from."

This highly complex structure implies that organisations wishing to become active in standards setting (for whichever reason) need to consider their options very carefully. For one, pros and cons of joining the standardisation bandwagon vs trying to push a proprietary solution need to be taken into account. Standards based products or services may imply price wars and lower revenues, but may also open new markets and widen the customer base. Offering a proprietary solution may yield (or keep, rather) a loyal customer base, but may also result in a technological lock-in and, eventually, marginalisation.

Once having decided to go for a standard, a firm normally (though not necessarily; sadly, trying to prevent the emergence of a standard may well be a motive, too) wants to make sure that the 'right' standard emerges. Yet, what exactly characterises the 'right', or at least a 'good' standard is far from being clear. Indeed, different companies may well have very different views here, largely depending on factors such as, e.g., their respective own technological base, corporate strategies, business models, etc. These determine the level of involvement in standards setting (an organisation wishing to create a new market in a certain domain is likely to adopt a different approach to standards setting than a company which only needs to gather advance intelligence for its business), and also the best platform for doing so (that is, the selected standards setting body's characteristics should be compatible with the company's goals). Standardisation may thus be seen as an interface between technical and non-technical (e.g. economic, organisational and even social) factors. Standards are not only rooted in technical deliberations, but also result from a process of social interactions between the stakeholders and also, probably most notably, reflect the economic interests of the major players.

The remainder of the chapter is organised as follows: The market for standards is discussed in chapter 2, introducing the web of SSBs, and looking at the characteristics of the different types of standards users. Subsequently, chapter 3 introduces an approach towards a classification of SSBs. A more detailed discussion on the attributes of the different user categories is given in chapter 4. Finally, chapter 5 provides some concluding remarks

2 THE MARKET FOR STANDARDS

The setting of standards is based on supply and demand. The 'supply side' of standards, the Standards Setting Bodies[8] (SSBs), tries to meet the requirements of the 'demand side', i.e., the standards users or, more generally, the market[9].

As the requirements of the market change over time, the 'supply side' needs to dynamically adapt to these changing requirements. Such adaptations manifest themselves in various ways. Most prominently over the last couple of years, new forms of SSBs as well as new SSBs have emerged at a sometimes alarming speed (see e.g., [Cargill, 1995]). Likewise, the individual bodies have adapted (had to adapt) the products and services they offer, to accommodate the market needs. These adaptations will be discussed in the following sections.

2.1 The Network of Standards Setting Bodies

Over the last three decades, the proliferation of SSBs has lead to an extremely complex situation in the market for standards in the ICT [10] sector. Figures 1 and 2 give an impression of the situation in the seventies and today, respectively (both are not complete, though).

In addition to the new formal, and largely regional, SDOs (such as, e.g., ETSI, TTC, etc.) which have been established over the last decades, a considerable number of industry fora and consortia have been founded as well.

Figure 1. The ICT standardisation universe in the seventies (excerpt)

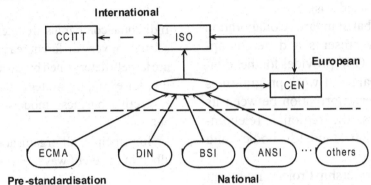

Figure 2: The ICT standardisation universe today (excerpt; adapted from [Jakobs, 2000])[11]

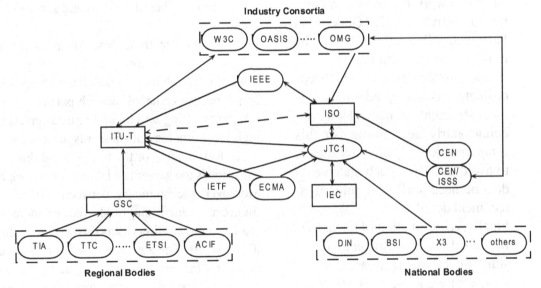

Two major aspects of today's standardisation are a direct result of this highly complex structure.

- **Fragmentation and overlap:** With few exceptions (cordless telephony would be an example) there is no such thing as a one-stop-shop for a new standards-setting activity. Typically, several SSBs are active in similar and overlapping domains. As a result, there may well be competition either generally between SSBs covering similar

ground (RosettaNet and ebXML would be an example here), or temporarily between SSBs working on similar projects (e.g., the IEEE 802.11a/b/g standards and ETSI's HIPERLAN/2). Consequently, there is an urgent

- **Need for co-ordination:** Given the diverse nature of the individual SSBs, this is extremely difficult to achieve.
  o A high level of co-ordination exists for the SDOs (ISO, CEN, national bodies; to avoid inconsistencies and contradic-

tions between international/regional/national standards).

o The Global Standards Collaboration (GSC) represents a different approach – GSC provides for the regular exchange of work programmes and other information between its members, the regional Telecommunication standards bodies and the ITU.

o ETSI Partnership Projects represent a related approach to co-ordination. Covering both SDOs and consortia, such projects co-ordinate a group of regional SDOs and industry consortia working towards a common objective. The '3rd Generation Partnership Project' (3GPP) is the most prominent example.

o In most other cases in which co-ordination is attempted a liaison is the instrument of choice. However, being a fairly loose mechanism this is not a particularly effective means to avoid overlap – such statements do not necessarily go into great technical detail.

o Finally, co-ordination of the activities of different consortia active in similar/overlapping areas is not always desired; some consortia were primarily established in the market to compete with others.

2.2 The Users of Standards

Individual companies are interested in standards setting for very different reasons. Their interests are largely determined by various factors, including, for example, strategic technological needs, respective business models, market positions, etc.

In principle, all organisations use standards, albeit in different ways.

- *Direct* users of standards incorporate standards into the ICT systems they are building and selling, or into the services they offer.
- *Indirect* users of standards then use these standards-based systems and services.

In addition to these types of users we find growing group of 'mediators'; typically represented by consultancies who sell their knowledge and expertise gathered through participation in standards setting activities[12]. Figure 3 depicts this high-level typology of standards 'users'.

Unfortunately, for the task at hand this classification is too general and thus not very helpful. Moreover, the boundary between 'direct' and 'indirect' is increasingly blurred, as more and more formerly indirect users turn towards selling ICT systems. The automotive industry is a case in point – modern cars are equipped with fairly complex electronic systems communicating via 'Car Area Networks'.

For a more helpful classification of standards users we need to look at the stakeholders' motiva-

Figure 3. A high-level typology of standards 'users'

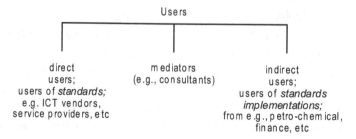

tions for an active participation in the standards setting process in order to be able to analyse SSBs' capability to cater for actual market needs. This motivation is not necessarily related to an organisation's status as a direct or an indirect user of standards.

In most cases the respective level of interest of companies wishing to get involved in a new standards setting activity will differ widely. For some, the nature of a standard, or even the fact that a new standard will materialise, may be a matter of life or death. For others, an emerging new standard may be of rather more academic interest.

Still at a fairly general level, prospective participants in a standardisation activity may be subdivided into three categories – 'Leader', 'Adopter', and 'Observer', respectively[13]. The motivation to actively participate in standards setting, and for joining – or maybe even establishing – an SSB will be very different for members of each individual category, and may be summarised as follows:

- **Leaders:** These are companies for which participation in a certain standards-setting activity is critical. They may even create a new consortium to establish a platform for the standardisation work they consider crucial. They are prepared to make a large investment in such an activity. For these companies, the strategic price of not participating in a given standards effort can far outweigh its costs. 'Leaders' aim to control the strategy and direction of a SSB, rather than to merely participate in its activities. Large vendors, manufacturers, and service providers are typical representatives of this class.
- **Adopters:** Such companies less interested in influencing strategic direction and goals of the SSB. Adopters are more interested in participation than influence (although they may want to influence individual standards).

Large users, SME vendors and manufacturers are typically found here.
- **Observers:** Such companies (and individuals) main motivation for participation is intelligence gathering; they don't want to invest any significant resources in the effort. Typically, this group comprises, for instance, academics, consultants and system integrators.

See section 4 for a more detailed discussion of the characteristics of these different categories.

3 CLASSIFYING STANDARDS SETTING BODIES

SSBs can be categorised according to very different criteria. The most popular, albeit not particularly helpful distinction is between formal SDOs and consortia. Typically, the former are said to be slow, compromise-laden, and in most cases not able to deliver on time what the market really needs. In fact, originally the formation of consortia was seen as one way of avoiding the allegedly cumbersome processes of the SDOs, and to deliver much needed standards on time and on budget. Consortia have been widely perceived as being more adaptable to a changing environment, able to enlist highly motivated and thus effective staff, and to have leaner and more efficient processes. Accordingly, attributes associated with SDOs include, for example, 'slow', 'consensus', and 'compromise-laden', consortia are typically associated with 'speed', 'short time to market', and 'meets real market needs'.

However, it is safe to say that this classification, including the over-simplifying associated attributes, are not particularly helpful for organisations who want to get a better idea of what the market for standards has to offer. This holds all the more as an organisation's requirements on an SSB very much depend on a combination of factors specific to this particular organisation.

Accordingly, a more flexible approach towards classification was adopted. Rather than pre-defining certain categories, a set of attributes has been identified that can be applied to describe SSBs. This description can than be matched onto an organisation's requirements on SSBs, thus allowing companies to identify those SSBs that best meet their specific needs.

These attributes fall into four categories adapted from [Updegrove, 2005]:

* General
* Membership
* Standards setting process
* Output

The attributes associated with each of these categories will be discussed as follows.

3.1 'General' Attributes

These attributes serve to provide some high-level information about the working environment an SSB has defined for itself. The form of governance chosen, for instance, provides information about which body, and who, is making the ultimate decisions, which in turn may help reveal the level of transparency in the SSB's decision making process. This is also of interest to those who wish to exert a certain level of influence.

Finance and staffing are important for an evaluation of an SSB's ability to survive. These are also valuable indicators for the commitment of the SSB's (leading) members – if they are prepared to invest (heavily) into its activities they are also likely to try and make sure that the objectives are met.

The IPR policy adopted may have significant impact on the attractiveness of an SSB to holders of relevant IPR. An SSB needs to find a reasonable balance here – the policy must neither deter IPR holders (who may be afraid of loosing valuable assets) nor potential users (who may be afraid of implementing a standard with high licensing fees

attached to it). Thus, this policy may also have implications on the level of openness envisaged by the SSB.

The latter also holds for the number and types of an SSB's liaisons. They are a good indicator of an SSB's openness towards relevant work done elsewhere. Moreover, liaisons are one means of co-ordination, thus at least somewhat reducing the risk of standardising on a technology that is at odds with other standards.

The level of competition an SSB faces indicates one aspect of the risk to be associated with going for its standards, with a high level suggesting a high risk of eventually being stranded with a loosing technology. Conversely, a 'monopoly' situation may indicate a reasonably safe bet.

Along similar lines, a good reputation of an SSB (albeit possibly somewhat hard to quantify) may suggest higher chances of its output to succeed in the market (see chapter 5 for a more detailed discussion relating to this aspect).

3.2 'Membership' Attributes

Information on the membership base of an SSB are relevant with respect to the level of its openness, and its decision making process (both formal and informal). A small number of hand-picked members, for instance, or membership levels with very different associated fees and rights suggest the idea of a rather more closed group of decision-makers (possibly despite a huge overall membership base). Likewise, it may reveal an SSB's support of the needs of a specific clientele (e.g., large manufacturers).

The overall number of members serves as a very rough first indication of the success factors of an SSB's output. A broad membership base may provide valuable support for a standard.

More important than the number of members, however, is the 'quality' of the membership. That is, an SSB's chances of being successful in the market are much better if large potential users and major vendors/manufacturers or service providers are among its members, and thus likely to support its output.

In addition , the level of membership of these companies is of interest – it indicates whether they are only interested in e.g., intelligence gathering, or if they want to play an active role in the standardisation process, and in the SSB in general.

Who is actually working actively in an SSB is probably even more important. A company's active participation in an SSB's standards setting process is a very good indicator of this company's support of the SSB's standards setting activities.

Finally, the individual member representatives may be supposed to act as corporate representatives, or in an individual capacity. In the latter case the points listed previously may become slightly less relevant, as it is not necessarily ensured that WG members actually represent the corporate goals of their respective employers.

3.3 'Standards Setting Process' Attributes

An SSB's standards setting process not only reflects its ability to quickly adapt to a changing environment and newly emerging requirements, to meet a window of opportunity, or to support real-world implementations. It also shows the level of 'democracy' considered desirable by the SSB, and again, whether or not certain stakeholders are more equal than others. A high a level of 'democracy', in turn, may be attractive for some stakeholders, but a deterrent for others.

'Time' is a crucial factor for many standards setting initiatives. That is, in most cases standardisation should be at least in sync with the technical development[14], maybe even ahead of it. Certainly, lagging behind for too long will make a standard irrelevant for most purposes. In fact, 'shorter time to market' has always been one of the major arguments in favour of consortia. Also, meeting a window of opportunity is a crucial success factor for a potential standard. Accordingly, the time it takes from submission of a proposal

to form a working group to address a specific topic until the final acceptance of the standard is an important factor. This time span, in turn, comprises three elements:

- The time it takes to establish a working group,
- The time it takes this WG to do the work, and
- The time for the final ballot.

Obviously, this depends very much on, for example, the level of consensus sought, and on the decision mechanisms adopted by the respective SSB.

That is, there are other aspects of an SSB's standards setting process that may be of interest to potential proposers, which may have a negative impact on a process' duration, and which need to be addressed as well. Particularly, these include the degree of openness of a standards setting process, its transparency, the required level of consensus, and the observation of due process.

Basically, these attributes describe the level of 'democracy' observed by a standards setting process. Are the elements of the process, the decisions taken, and the reasons for these decisions well documented and available? Does everyone have the right to speak, and to be listened to? Is there a way to appeal against a decision, and how does it work? Which level of consensus is required (e.g., at working group level, at membership level)? In many cases, it will be necessary to balance the requirement for speed and the need for a broad consensus.

In many instances a standards setting process should not stop once a standard has been described on paper. Other aspects may at least be as important as a base standard. Most prominently, these include the availability of interoperable implementations of a standard, and proof of an implementation's conformance with the standard. Whether or not an SSB's process requires the former, or if the SSB provides for the latter, may well be important aspects to be considered.

3.4 'Output' Attributes

Finally, the types of deliverables produced also give an indication about an SSB's flexibility. For instance, full-blown formal standards indicate a lengthy, democratic, consensus-based process, whereas technical reports or similar types of deliverables suggest a faster, more adaptable process with a lower level of consensus. Information about the number of implementations shows the relative 'importance' of an SSB, as does, to a certain level, the fact that it is accepted PAS submitter to ISO. The latter also indicates an SSB's willingness to meet the associated requirements on its process. A standard that is maintained, and possibly developed, over time suggests that it is envisaged to be long-lived, and also says something about the SSB's willingness to adapt its deliverables to changing environments.

In order to improve a standard's chances of success in the market it will help if it originated from a well accepted source. The number of implementations of other standards from an SSB may serve as one indicator of this SSB's 'credibility'. Also, the free availability of a standard's specification may help disseminate it more widely.

In some instances, especially for a more long-term planning, it may be of interest whether of not an SSB maintains its standards, or whether it has adopted a 'fire and forget' approach. A standard's maintenance will need to cover, for example, the addition of technical corrigenda, of addenda covering additional functionality, and maybe eventually the release of a follow-up version of a standard. In each of these cases, backward-compatibility has to be ensured. A well-managed maintenance process is extremely helpful if longevity and adaptability of a standard are or concern.

Along similar lines – an SSB should make sure that a new standard does not contradict other, established ones. At the least it should have a mechanism in place to ensure consistency of its own standards, ideally this should extend to all standards (although this will be next to impossible to achieve).

Last, but not least, an SSB might want to consider the impact a standard might have. While hard to do, this might be a worthwhile exercise that may well safe serious money which might otherwise be wasted on a standard with little or no chances of success in the market.

Table 1. SSB descriptors

General	Description
Internal	
overall goals business models	These provide some general background information. 'Business models' should be helpful for matching with 'demand side's', well, demands.
governance	'Governance' is important for those who wish to influence the goals and activities.
finances staffing	'Finances' and 'staffing' are important to evaluate the chances of an SSB's long-term survival.
IPR policy	IPR policy should not deter any stakeholders.
External	
reputation	Joining an SSB with a poor reputation, or with a poor record, will not make too much sense in many cases.
competition	Do competing SSBs exist, or are they likely to emerge in the near future?

continued on the following page

Table 1. continued

liaisons	Is the SSB prepared to co-operate with other entities?
Membership	**Description**
Quantitative: • overall # of members • membership levels • membership fees	Provides some information about the relevance of the SSB. In many cases, some are more equal than others. Who decides, who does the work, and are these the same? May also help to determine a prospective new member's chances of active contribution and decision.
Qualitative: • key players involved? • 'active' members • individuals' capacity	Are those organisations important in the specific sector on board? Which are missing? Which members are prepared to invest resources into activities like e.g. editing documents, leading WGs, etc? Is there a 'corporate whip', or do reps decide independently? What are the SSB's rules?
Standards setting processes	**Description**
Timing: • time for TC/WG establishment, • average time until finalisation	Indicates the effort/time required to finalise a new standards project. Helps to determine whether or not a (perceived) window of opportunity can be met.
Process characteristics: • openness • transparency • required level of consensus • observation of due process • decision mechanism	Basically to determine how fair the process is? Do I have a say, or do the big guys determine? Can I complain, and to whom? Etc.
Beyond standardisation: • implementations required? • proof of interoperability required • conformance testing	Indicate a more 'praxis-oriented' approach; crucial if products/services are to hit the market pretty soon.
Output	**Description**
Types of 'products'	Do an SSB's deliverables suit my needs? I do not always need a full blown standard, and may be prepared to swap consensus for speed.
Quantitative aspects: • standards output • # of implementations	Do they actually produce standards, and are they implemented on an adequate basis? Indicates importance of output; if nobody implements the stuff it's hardly worth the effort.
Dissemination: • PAS submitter? • specs for free?	Related to 'liaisons' above. Is an SSB prepared to bring its specs into the public domain? And are they prepared to do it for free?
Follow-up activities: • standards maintenance • impact considered? • consistency checks in place?	How does an SSBs react to changes in technology/requirements? And to errors/inaccuracies? Do they reflect on what they are doing? Are standards checked for consistency with others?

The individual descriptors discussed previously are summarised in Table 1.

3.1 APPLYING THE CRITERIA TO SOME RELEVANT SSBS

The critaria identified previously are applied (in Table 2) to a number of SSBs which are of importance in the e-business / ICT sector.

3.2 Coping With Changes in the Market

The aforementioned list of attributes may also be used to establish whether or not an SSB is likely to be able to cope with changes in the market, or to actually trigger them.

In order to (actively) trigger changes in the market, an SSB's membership is the most impor-

Table 2. The characteristics of the SSBs

	OASIS	OMG	W3C	CEN/ ISSS	ETSI	JTC1
IPR policy	RF[15] (members) RAND[16] (others)	RF	RF	RAND	RAND	RAND
Liaisons	Numerous (including e.g. ISO, JTC1, ISSS, W3C)	Cross-membership (OASIS, W3C, NIST)	Numerous (including e.g. ETSI, IETF, ITU, JTC1)	On WS basis (e.g., ISO, ITC1, OASIS)	Numerous (including e.g. ISO, JTC1, ITU, national/ regional SDOs many consortia)	Numerous
Overall # of members	Ca. 400 organisations Ca. 200 individuals	Ca. 800	Ca. 360	N/a (varies considerably between WSs	600+	67 (member states at JTC1 level)
Key players involved?	Yes	Yes	Yes	Often	Yes	Yes
Membership levels	3: Sponsors, Contributors, Individual (may not vote)	5 (three main): Contributing Domain Platform Influencing Residual: Test and Analyst	2: Full, Affiliate (both have same rights)	1	4: Full, Associate, (may vote) Observer, Counsellor	2: (P)articipating (may vote) (O)bserving
Membership fees	Sponsors: 13,500 USD Contributors 5,750 USD (not-for-profit: 1,000 USD) Individual 250 USD annually	Contributors: $10K-70K (based on revenue) Domain and Platform: $5K-35K Influencing: $2.5K-20k	Full: 172,500 USD Affiliate: 17,250 USD (for first three years)	Very little, possibly free	Based on turnover; 6,000 euros for SMEs	Based on GNP
Individuals' capacity	member representative (but individual vote at TC level)	member representative	WG: member representative; AB: individual	member representative	(member representative)	individual
To establish new activity	3 'eligible persons[17]'; business plan; decision after 15 days, BoD[18] may veto	RFP: initiated in TC (also SIG), TF elaborate RFP, approved by AB. Accepted by TC (vote). RFC: bypasses RFP.	Initiated by W3C staff, general review at least 4 weeks; decided upon by Director	Business plan	4 supporting Members prepared to contribute; decision after one month	No time frame specified
Average time until finalisation	16 – 24 months	12-15 months from RFP: shorter for RFC	Typically around 24 months	Varies; typically 1-2 years.	Around 4 years for a European Norm	Up to 48 months; ca. 12 months for PAS process
Openness technical activities	Every 'eligible person' may participate,	Eligible members may submit proposed solutions , also with support of non-members. Information (RFI) may be invited from outside	Open to all members,	Open to everyone	Open to Full and Assoc. ETSI members; external experts for STF[19]	Individual WG members must be authorised by national SDO.

continued on next page

Table 2. continued

	OASIS	OMG	W3C	CEN/ISSS	ETSI	JTC1
Trans-parency	description of process and voting procedure publicly available	Ability to track the adoption process. Finalized documents are publicly available	info on process and outcome publicly available; public may comment; TRs undergo public review	Comments phase recommended, but not mandatory	Limited (largely to members) transparency	Limited (largely to members) transparency
Required level of consensus	Balloting mechanism at TC and OASIS level; BoD may keep proposal from balloting	2/3 majority of eligible voters on finalized submission. Submitted to BoD for final decision.	Consensus based, at both technical and W3C level, but W3C director's approval is always required	Consensus based at WS level.	At TB level: consensus/ voting At ETSI level: consensus/ weighted individual voting by members	Balloting should only take place once consensus has been achieved; P-members cast votes.
Observation of due process	Yes	n/a	Yes	Yes (albeit somewhat limited)	Yes	Yes
Implemen-tations required?	Yes (three inter-operable imple-mentations)	A precondition. Non-implemented can be 'retired'	Yes (one implementation)	No	No	No
Types of 'products'	Committee Drafts Standards	OMG specification ('adopted technology')	Working Notes	CWAs[20]	ETSI Standard, ES European Standard, EN ETSI Technical Specification ETSI Technical Report, TR ETSI Guide, EG Special Report, SR	ISO Standard ISO/PAS ISO/TS Technical Specification ISO/TR Technical Report International Workshop Agreement (IWA)
Number of implemen-tations	?	Return to this	?	?	?	?
Output	15 standards (since 2002); 17 Committee Drafts (excluding ebXML specifications prior to 2002)	130+ in total http://www.omg.org/technology/documents/spec_catalog.htm	80	73 CWAs (many of which are multi-part) plus 21 withdrawn CWAs (since 1999)	Ca. 1,800 deliverables in 2003, 14% standards	120+ Technical Standards in 2002
Specs for free	Yes	Yes	Yes	Yes (almost all)	Yes	No

continued on next page

Table 2. continued

	OASIS	OMG	W3C	CEN/ISSS	ETSI	JTC1
Standards mainte-nance	No official mechanism, but new versions are produced relatively frequently	Codified revision process, including bug page.	Error tracking is part of the process; dedicated 'errata page'; approval of new version follows same procedures as for new TRs	CWA revision/withdrawal after 3 years	No official procedure for most deliverables; reaction to comments; approval of new version follows same procedures as new deliverables	Regular reviews every 5 years (3 years for PAS submissions); Amendments are also used
PAS submitter	No	?	No	No	No	N/a
Impact considered	?	Viability is reviewed.	?	?	?	?

tant aspect. If a sector's key players participate in a standards setting activity its impact may be expected to be much higher than in a case where a standard has been put together be a group of 'nobodies' (i.e., without the sector's 'Leaders').

To attract the group of participants necessary to enable a future standard to be successful in the market, a number of pre-requisites need to be fulfilled. Here, an SSB's IPR policy is one of the most important single factors – it must not deter IPR holders to participate, nor put off users because of a fear of license fees attached to the deployment of the standard. [Blind & Thumm, 2004] find evidence that companies with strong patent portfolios are more likely to stay away from formal standardisation processes. The type of deliverable offered by the SSB is also important here, a point that is closely related to the speed of the process and thus also to the decision making process applied. Moreover, liaisons are an important criterion – if an SSB is co-operating with others, and willing to align its output with the (emerging) standards developed elsewhere, the chances of success will improve considerably. Accordingly, the following subset of SSB descriptors may be used to evaluate an SSB's ability to trigger change (see also Table 3).

(Passively) adapting to changes requires different but related capabilities. Here, the ability to attract new or emerging key players is of primary importance. To be able to do so, the overall characteristics of an SSB need to be in line with the business models of these companies. Again, its IPR policy will be important, as well as sound finances, an adequate staffing, and membership levels providing for companies' desired level of influence.

An SSB's previous track record in adaptability to changes would also be of interest here.

Table 3. Descriptors and values indicating an SSB's ability to influence

Descriptor	Value
IPR policy	Must not deter any important stakeholders.
liaisons	Co-operation with other SSBs is important.
overall # of members membership levels key players involved? 'active' members	A critical mass is helpful. A levels to guarantee strong influence should be available. Important actors need to be on board, competition should be limited. Important members need to be prepared to invest resources
decision mechanism	Does the process provide adequate influence for the 'leaders'
Types of 'products'	The process must be able to meet a window of opportunity

A major, yet simple indicator here would be the lifespan of the SSB – one that has been around for decades may be expected to be able to adapt to changes; otherwise, it would already have gone out of business.

4 MORE ON STANDARDS USERS

A categorisation of standards users into 'Leaders', 'Adopters', and 'Observers' has been introduced in sect. 2.2. The characteristics of the members of each respective category will now be elaborated in terms of how their strategic goals relate to typical requirements on SSBs.

4.1 Leaders

When deciding about joining an existing SDO or consortium (the latter preferably as a founding member; in most cases founding members have a greater say concerning the goals and strategies of a consortium), as opposed to founding one, Leaders specifically need to analyse an SSB's governance – does it provide for the level of influence they want to exercise? Or is a strong group with incompatible goals already well established, and likely to block any new activities? Also, the IPR policy is of crucial importance – with too lenient a policy many important players may be hesitant to join, a too restrictive policy may prevent users from adopting any standards of this SSB.

In addition, Leaders will need to carefully analyse several characteristics of an SSB they are considering to join, and match them to their strategic goals. The most important of these characteristics are summarised in Table 4.

In addition to the 'positive' goals identified previously, the analogous 'negative' goals may also be observed. I.e., to prevent the creation of

Table 4. Leaders' criteria

Strategic Goals	Most important SSB characteristics
To create a market	**Governance**: Does it provide for strong influence of interested players? Or is it rather more 'egalitarian'? **Finance**: Are finances sound? Will the SSB have the stamina to survive the process? Does it depend heavily on individual entities/contributors? **IPR policy**: Is the IPR policy adequate? Will it eventually put-off users who are afraid of high licensing fees? Will it deter holders of important IPR from joining? **Reputation**: Is the SSB well respected in the area in question? Related to that – are its standards widely implemented? **Competition**: Are there competing consortia? Are competitors likely to emerge, or are all relevant players members? **Membership levels**: does the highest membership level available guarantee the necessary level of influence? Who else is at this level? Are leading users represented in the 'upper' levels? **Key players involved?**: Who are the active players, and which roles do their representatives assume (individual capacity / company rep)? Are the 'right' companies represented? Are all relevant stakeholders represented? Are leading users on board? Are any key players missing? Is the combined market power adequate? **Timing**: Will I be able to meet a window of opportunity?
To create a (successful) standard	**Governance**: Does it provide for strong influence of interested players? Or is it rather more 'egalitarian'? **Finance**: Are finances sound? Will the SSB have the stamina to survive the process? Does it depend heavily on individual entities/contributors? **IPR policy**: Is the IPR available inside the SSB adequate, or is licensing of third-party IPR necessary? **Reputation**: Is the SSB well respected in the area in question? **Membership**: Are there potential allies/ opponents? Is adequate technical expertise available, at both corporate and individual level? **Key players involved?**: Is the combined market power adequate? Are relevant stakeholders represented? Are important stakeholders absent? **Timing**: How long will it take to develop a standard? Will the window of opportunity be met? **Process characteristics**: Can the process be used against me; e.g., to delay the standard? For how long? What are the decision mechanisms? **Products**: Does the SSB offer an appropriate type of deliverable? **Dissemination**: Will the specifications (and possibly reference implementations) be available for free?

a new market, or of a successful standard, may also be strategic goals of an organisation. In both cases, the considerations concerning the important characteristics of an SSB remain the same. The same applies for the considerations to follow.

4.2 Adopters

Most companies will be in this category. Their goals will be rather more tactical than strategic. Accordingly, they will rather more aim at technically influencing the actual standard rather than the market, and would like the new standard to be in line with their own developments. In addition, they will want to gather specific intelligence early on, and maybe adopt their developments accordingly. Another motivation for adopters to actively participate in standards setting may be the desire to share development cost by moving part of this work into the standards body (see also Table 5).

Given the aforementioned goals, companies in this group tend to go for full rights of participation in all technical activities, but may be less interested in influencing the strategic direction of the efforts and goals of the SSB.

4.3 Observers

Many companies and individuals will have a need to know what an SSB is working on but will not be interested – or will not have the means – to actively participate in any form. That is, their main interest lies in the gathering of general knowledge (Table 6; important, for instance, for consultants).

5 SUMMARY AND CONCLUSION

This chapter's aim was to provide some guidance for companies wishing to become active in

Table 5. Adopters' criteria

Adopters – Strategic Goals	Most important SSB characteristics
To influence standard development	**Governance**: does it provide for strong influence of interested players? Or is it rather more 'egalitarian'?
	Membership: Is a membership level available that provides for adequate influence? Who else is at this level? Who are the 'active' members?
	Key players involved?: Are the important players on board? Who are potential strong opponents or allies?
	Individuals' capacity: Do I need to know the individual reps and their views, and the roles they are likely to assume?
	Required level of consensus: Is it possible to exploit the consensus requirement in order to delay the process or to cripple the outcome?
To share development costs	**Membership**: Are enough (important) members with similar interests on board, at an adequate membership level (to indicate sufficient interest)?
To gather specific early intelligence	**Membership**: Is a level available that offers a good RoI; i.e. one that does gives access to all relevant information without costing a fortune

Table 6. Observes' criteria

Observers – Strategic Goals	Most important SSB characteristics
To gather general (early) intelligence	**Membership**: Is a level available that offers a good RoI; i.e. one that does gives access to all relevant information without costing a fortune?

ICT / e-business standards setting. To this end, a method has been developed to describe SSBs in such a way that its suitability as platform for a new standards-setting becomes immediately apparent. That is, this method can be applied by a potential standards-setter to identify the SSB that will be most suitable for its current needs.

Obviously, the result of this exercise will heavily depend on the strategic goals of a company in a given sector. Therefore, a classification scheme for standards users has also been proposed. This scheme takes into account the overall goals of a company, its business model, and its strategies with respect to the sector in question. Taken together, these may require to

- Strategically influence the market through standardisation,
- Exert tactical influence on a standard,
- Observe.

The interpretation of the description of an SSB heavily depends on these goals. For each of the aforementioned, a subset of the initial criteria was identified and described. It should be noted here that depending on the goal of a company a criterion may have to be addressed differently. Fort instance, for a company aiming to influence the market through a new standard – without any specific interest in its technical nuts and bolts – a group of influential key players (i.e., 'Leaders') who would also support this standard is essential. On the other hand, for a company wishing to influence the technical content of a standard it will be important not to have any strong potential opponents.

Thus, in order to optimise its standardisation activities a company needs to know its own goals, identify the key players in the sector in question, and apply the described method. This should at east lead to a reasonably good initial idea of which SSB to select for the required standards setting activities.

6 REFERENCES

Blind, K., & Thumm, N. (2004). Interrelation between patenting and standardisation strategies: empirical evidence and policy implications. *Research Policy, 33*(10), 1583-1598.

Cargill, C. F. (1995). A Five-Segment Model for Standardization. In B. Kahin & J. Abbate (Eds.), *Standards Policy for Information Infrastructure.* MIT Press.

CEN/ISSS (2008). *ICT Standards Consortia survey,* 14th edition. http://www.cenorm.be/cenorm/businessdomains/businessdomains/isss/consortia/index.asp.

Jakobs, K. (2000). *User Participation in Standardisation Processes - Impact, Problems and Benefits.* Vieweg Publishers.

Jakobs, K. (2003). *Information Technology Standards, Standards Setting and Standards Research: Mapping the Universe.* Presented at: Stanhope Center's Roundtable on systematic barriers to the inclusion of a public interest voice in the design of Information and Communications Technologies. http://www.stanhopecentre.org/cotswolds/papers.htm.

Sherif, M. H. (2003). When is standardization slow? *Int. J. on IT Standards & Standardisation-Research, 1*(1).

Updegrove, A. (2005). *Evaluating Whether to Join a Consortium.* http://www.consortiuminfo.org/evaluating/.

ENDNOTES

[1] The International Organization for Standardization.
[2] The International Telecommunication Union.

[3] European Telecommunications Standards Institute.

[4] Pacific Area Standards Congress.

[5] American National Standards Institute.

[6] British Standards Institution.

[7] It should be noted, however, that references to standards in EU Directioves, for example, well may give them quasi-regulatory status.

[8] This term refers to both formal SDOs as well as industry consortia and fora.

[9] Please note that this also holds for those standards 'pro-actively' specified by SSBs.

[10] Information and Communication Technologies.

[11] Please note that neither does this figure show all relevant SSBs, nor all links that exist between individual SSBs (which may change over time anyway).

[12] In the following this group will not be considered.

[13] Adapted from [Updegrove, 2005].

[14] This does not necessarily hold for infrastructural technologies (such as, e.g., ISDN), where getting everything right the first time is more important than speed (see e.g., [Sherif, 2003], [Jakobs, 2003]).

[15] Royalty Free.

[16] Reasonable and Non-Discriminatory.

[17] Employees of member organisations or individual members

[18] Board of Directors

[19] Specialist Task Force; a group of external experts hired for rapid specification development.

[20] CEN Workshop Agreements.

Section IV
Case Studies

Chapter VIII
The Shaping of the IEEE 802.11 Standard:
The Role of the Innovating Firm in the Case of Wi-Fi

W. Lemstra
Delft University of Technology, The Netherlands

V. Hayes
Delft University of Technology, The Netherlands

ABSTRACT

In this chapter the authors explore and describe the role of the innovating firm in relation to the standards making process of Wireless-Local Area Networks, and in particular the link between NCR and its corporate successors in the creation of the IEEE 802.11 standard, which is at the basis of the global success of Wi-Fi. Their focus is the leadership role assumed by NCR c.s. responsible for the initiation and creation of an open standard for Wireless-LANs.

1 INTRODUCTION

In integrating the various perspectives on the process of standardisation, we place the entrepreneur at the centre stage, as the entrepreneur decides whether or not to use an existing standard or to develop a new standard by engaging a standards developing organisation to realise the business objectives. For an entrepreneur the participation

in standards activities represents a decision of strategic importance. In following an existing standard the strategic option chosen is typically one of adaptation to the 'rules of the game' prevailing in an industry. In an environment that is dominated by one or a few powerful players this can make a lot of sense. In the 1970s, NCR, a leading manufacturer of point of sale terminals, had to acknowledge that most of its terminals would have to be connected to back-office systems provided by IBM. Hence, to become successful in the market its products had to be provided with interfaces and protocols compatible with IBM mainframe computers. This placed NCR in a follower position, being dependent on functionality that IBM protocols would support. Moreover, it was always confronted with a delayed product introduction relative to its main rival in the business – IBM – as new protocols first needed to be examined and subsequently emulated. IBM was not very forthcoming with interface and protocol information ahead of its own product launch. NCR was faced with interfaces that were proprietary, and would become a *de facto* closed standard through IBM's market dominance.

The alternative and opposite strategic option that was in principle available to NCR was to create competitive advantage by establishing new rules and introducing a new competitive game. De Wit and Meyer observe that a firm wishing to break the rules and intending to establish a leadership position based on a new set of rules must: "…move beyond a compelling vision, and work out a new competitive business model. If this new model is put into operation and seems to offer a competitive advantage, this can attract sufficient customers and support to gain 'critical mass' and break through as a viable alternative to the older business model. To shape the industry, the firm will also need to develop the new competences and standards required to make the new business model function properly." (2004). In hindsight we may conclude that this is what NCR did in relation to developing a new wireless Local Area Networking product to connect point of sale terminals to back-office computer systems, thereby creating the foundation for what would become the global success of Wi-Fi, to be based on an open standard known as IEEE 802.11.

In practice, successful strategies are often much more the result of a process of incrementally finding the right path forward, rather than of bold declarations of intent. The contours of a successful strategy tend to unfold over time as the firm shapes its position in interaction with its environment, while expanding its capabilities in a particular direction.[1] For the onlooker strategy can hence be considered as: "a pattern in a series of important decisions." In this Chapter, our intent is to unravel the historic developments related to the standardization of Wireless Local Area Networks (WLANs) and discover this pattern by exploring and describing the central role of NCR. The firm that has assumed a leading role in exploiting the standards making process, in what appears to be a two-prong approach in achieving its objectives: connecting the process of standardisation to the processes of product development and market introduction. Thereby we acknowledge that a standard derives its success from its adoption in the market.

Our detailed account starts in 1980. The Ethernet, which would become the standard for wired-LANs, was still subject of a major standardization battle within the standards developing organisation IEEE. Moreover, recall that the Apple II had been launched in 1977, while the IBM PC would be introduced in 1981. Mobile computing equipment like laptops and notebooks still had to be introduced.

To place the development of a wireless-LAN standard in context, we will explore, in summary form, the main events in the developments of wired-LANs, thereby recognizing the central role the IEEE as a standards developing organization (SDO) has played in the development of both the wired and wireless LAN standards,. It should be noted that NCR had initiated the development of a wired-LAN based on Ethernet technology to link its point of sale terminals to the back-office computer at the client premises. This had resulted in the MIRLAN product. The LAN developments are of course directly linked to the developments in computing, and it is interesting to note the recurring linkages to the development of the Internet.

2 THE PRECEDING DEVELOPMENT OF WIRED LOCAL AREA NETWORKS

From the early days computers had operated in stand-alone mode serving a single site. An early example of a central computer being part of a large-scale data network was the SAGE system (Semi Automated Ground Environment) installed by the US Air Force in 1958. This system used telephone lines to link radar stations and other devices across the USA to mainframe computers to provide centralized command and control. One of the first civilian wide area networks installed in 1964 by American Airlines was the SABRE system (Semi-Automatic Business-Related Environment) to coordinate airline seat reservations. It connected over 1,200 terminals to the mainframe computer via 12,000 miles of telephone lines, making it a large-scale Wide Area Network (WAN) application (Von Burg, 2001).

The sharing of supercomputer power as part of the US Defense ARPA program led to the development of the ARPANET, which created the first wide area computer-to-computer network, using leased telephone lines. In 1970 the first five nodes would be connected, primarily supercomputers at university research centres, using packet switching. In contrast to circuit switching as used in telephony whereby a two-way connection is established for the duration of the call, in the case of packet switching the information to be transmitted is divided in messages of fixed length to which an address is added, thereby forming the packet that is subsequently transmitted on a store-and-forward basis through the network. The ARPANET would evolve to the current day Internet (Abbate, 1999; Lemstra, 2006; Von Burg, 2001).

The introduction of the minicomputer in the late 1960s meant that it was becoming cost effective for research departments within universities to own their computers rather than time sharing a mainframe. At the University of California,

Irvine, Farber became interested in linking these minicomputers to create a local distributed computing system. The local area network he built became known as the UC Irvine Ring, In 1971 this first LAN became operational and by 1975 it connected computers, terminals, printers and a magnetic tape unit. The network operated on twisted-pair and on coaxial cable, at speeds of up to 2.3 Mbit/s. The stations were connected in a ring topology and to manage the communication flow a token, a specific bit pattern, was transmitted continuously in one direction around the ring. If a station wished to transmit information it would 'seize' the token, change the bit pattern to 'busy' and add a destination address as well as the information to be transferred. At the destination the information would be retrieved and the token would be returned to the sender station to be set 'free' again (Von Burg, 2001).

In a parallel development, the ARPA program had also set-off research into the use of packet switching in land-based radio and satellite radio applications. As the noisy telephone lines on Hawaii appeared ill suited for data transmission, Abrahamson at the University of Hawaii decided to try packet radio as an alternative for wire-based local area networking across the seven campuses and many research institutes. The resulting Alohanet used two radio channels, one channel to broadcast packets from the computer center to the user stations and one channel from the user stations to the computer centre. The second channel would be subject to interference if two or more stations would send information at the same time. Rather than trying to prevent collision, the designers made sure the system could recover if a collision would occur, relying on the acknowledgement by the computer station of the packets being received in good order. If the user station did not receive an acknowledgment it would resend the information. To avoid the collision of two terminals and potential endless retransmissions, the Aloha protocol specified that the stations should use different waiting times before retransmitting: at random, but within a specified range (Abbate, 1999).

The Aloha wireless-LAN would play an unexpected role in the development of the wired-LAN. As a graduate student at Harvard University, Robert Metcalfe was completing a PhD on packet switching networks. He had been drawn into the ARPANET developments through participation in the MAC Project at Massachusetts Institute of Technology (MIT). In pursuing the theoretical contribution of his PhD he was introduced to the Aloha network protocol for which he would devise a new waiting algorithm that would radically improve the throughput of the network under heavy load conditions.[2] In 1972, while still working on his PhD, Metcalfe accepted a job at Xerox Palo Alto Research Centre and was asked to design a system to connect the newly developed Alto workstations. The requirements set out by Xerox for the local area network were: (1) to be capable of connecting hundreds of computers over hundreds of meters; (2) to operate at very high speed; (3) to be using coax cable to meet the transmission requirements; and (4) had to cost no more than five percent of the cost of the personal computers it would connect. Based on his dissertation work Metcalfe created a random-access broadcast system dubbed the Alto Aloha network, soon to be renamed Ethernet. In this wired implementation, a station would 'listen to the wire' and when it found the wire to be silent it would initiate transmission. The principle applied became known as Carrier Sense Multiple Access with Collision Detection (CSMA/CD). The first version of Ethernet introduced in 1973 would cover a distance of 1 kilometer, connect a maximum of 256 stations and operate at a speed of 2.94 Mbit/s (Abbate, 1999; Von Burg, 2001).

Following the inventions by Farber and Metcalfe a few firms started to commercialise proprietary LAN technologies. For instance Network Systems established in 1974 would pursue a mainframe LAN business addressing interconnectivity problems at fast growing data centres.

Zilog, established by Intel alumni in 1974, applied a strategy of forward integration based on its successful communication chip. Nestar, founded in 1978 by researchers from IBM and Carnegie Mellon University, focused from the outset on linking Apple II microcomputers and introduced in 1980 Cluster/One. Note that the Apple II had been introduced by Jobs and Wozniak in 1977. Datapoint, established in 1968 as a third-party manufacturer of computer terminals, introduced a network-based distributed computing system called ARC. This system would become a direct competitor to the early Ethernet. The products of the other companies would flounder in an early and rapidly changing market. As Von Burg concludes: "The commercialization efforts by the four pioneers... ...initiated the pre-dominant-design period. By 1980, they had created a small market but not yet an entire industry – nor had they set the standard." (Von Burg, 2001).

2.1 The Three IEEE 802 Wired LAN Standards

In 1979 DEC, Intel and Xerox formed the DIX alliance with the goal of establishing an industry-wide *de facto* LAN standard. DEC needed to link its new VAX computers to create a distributed computing environment. DEC liked the Ethernet solution as it seemed possible to increase its throughput and Metcalfe had suggested to contact Xerox to license the technology. The alliance opted for an open standard as this would increase the adoption of their LAN systems and increase the overall market. Moreover, the partners saw opportunities for augmenting the sale of other products. Furthermore, Xerox and DEC were pursuing an open strategy to attract third-party supplier of Ethernet components. In particular IC manufacturers, Intel being their first supplier. According to Von Burg the three firms complemented each other very nicely: "Xerox had the technology; DEC provided market clout, credibility, and some Ethernet components; and

Intel brought the chips, so vital in achieving steep price reductions" (Von Burg, 2001).

One of the earlier network standards established under the leadership of Loughry at HP was approved in 1974 as IEEE 488, and was aimed at the remote control of programmable instruments in industrial processes. Recognizing the distance limitations of this standard Graube at Tektronix started pushing for a new standard and submitted in 1979 a project authorization request to the IEEE, which would be approved and the first meeting of IEEE 802 would be convened in 1980. Participants were computer manufacturers, vendors of office automation products, vendors of factory automation systems and LAN start-ups, e.g. 3Com – established by Metcalfe in 1979, and Ungermann-Basss – a 1979 spin-off of Zilog. The various participants were pursuing different objectives and could not agree on one single standard. Hence, the IEEE Standards Activities Board would ultimately approve three standards: in 1985 the IEEE 802.3 for Ethernet, primarily supported by the DIX alliance, HP, Data General, 3Com and Ungermann-Bass; in 1985 the IEEE 802.4 for Token Bus, supported by the vendors of factory automation systems; and in 1986 the IEEE 802.5 for Token Ring, with IBM as its main proponent. In 1987 HP initiated an extension effort to standardize a 10 Mbit/s version of Ethernet, which would use telephone wire rather than coax. In 1990 this so-called 10Base-T standard would be approved by the IEEE Standards Board (Von Burg, 2001). Figure 1 provides a time line of the developments of wired-LANs with an indication of the number

Figure 1. Developments in wired-LANs

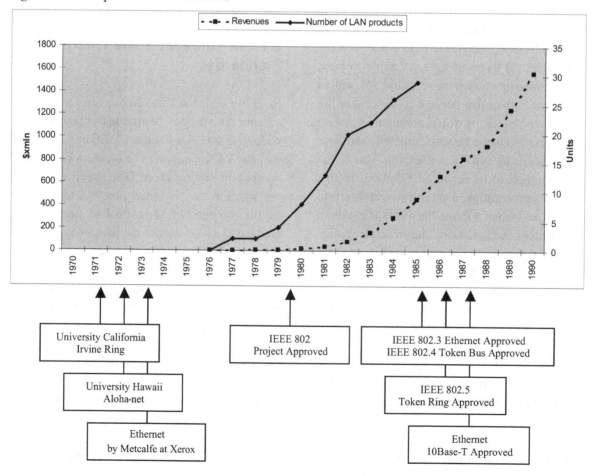

of competing products. Reflected are the LAN products being introduced and the revenues of the major LAN companies involved.[3]

The chart reflects a time lag between the invention of the LAN and the start of the standardisation process of 8 years. The interval between the start of the standardisation process and the publication of the first official specification is 6 years. It should be noted that the objective of the DIX alliance was to standardise an existing technology and product, i.e. Ethernet.

Interesting in this account of the wired-LAN developments is the role of the Aloha network; it implies that the wired-LAN was taken to the air by Abrahamson, to return to the wire by Metcalfe, and to be taken to the air again by Tuch of NCR.

3 THE NEED FOR A WIRELESS LOCAL AREA NETWORK[4]

In creating a wireless-LAN NCR solved first and foremost a product-market issue: the lack of 'mobility' in the cash register product portfolio had become a serious shortcoming. Retail department stores, one of the main client groups of NCR, reconfigured the sales floor on a regular basis and the cost of rewiring the transaction terminals was considered a significant expense.

To address this issue NCR had conducted a study into the use of infrared light technology, but, quickly recognized that radio technology would be a much better option: "…if it was permitted, if we could make it work, and if we could turn it into affordable products", as Johnson at the NCR Corporate R&D Division summarized the challenges (Johnson, 2007).

3.1 A Different Medium: A New Institutional Player

Unlike the coax cable, and later twisted-pair copper wire, as used in the case of the Ethernet LANs, one can not simply start using radio-communication to create a wireless-LAN. Radio-communication involves the use of electro-magnetic (EM) waves.[5] These waves are generated by the radio-transmitter and are intended to be detected by the radio-receiver. However, if more than one transmitter uses the same frequency within the receiving range of the receiver the intended communication may be distorted or not anymore intelligible. This is referred to as interference, the effect of unwanted energy. Interference is being considered harmful if it endangers the functioning of a radio-navigation service or other safety services, or seriously degrades, obstructs, or repeatedly interrupts a radio-communication service. To avoid harmful interference the 'disturbing' transmitter could reduce its signal strength or use another frequency, if it was aware of its disturbing effect, and if it would be inclined to avoid the disturbance. In the early days of ship-to-shore communication this is exactly what the radio operators did. However, with increasing traffic and with increasing distances being covered by radio this self-regulatory human-based model for managing the use of an open-access resource was not sustainable. Hence, given the importance of good quality radio communications, which was clearly underscored during the Titanic disaster in 1912, governments have assumed the role of regulator to control the use of the radio frequency spectrum (ITU, 1965). The spectrum management paradigm that has emerged since the first international coordination meeting in Berlin in 1906 replaced the open-access regime by a regulated-access regime essentially dividing the available radio frequency (RF) spectrum in bands designated for particular applications. The major considerations in this allocation are the propagation characteristics of the particular RF-band and the capacity required for the application. At the national level these allocations are translated into assignments to users, whereby the assignment is typically granted on an exclusive basis, and with a set of specifications for the (type of) equipment to be used; all intended to guarantee the proper operation and to avoid harmful interference, within and outside the assigned band.

The allocation of RF spectrum to users has traditionally been done on a first-come first-served basis, whereby applicants have to convince the regulator that the allocation would be justified on economical grounds or on the basis of public interest. Stimulated by the political climate set by the Carter Administration, Chairman Ferris of the US Federal Communications Commission (FCC)[6] intended to extend the deregulation spirit to the radio frequency spectrum. He would like to end the practice whereby numerous requests for spectrum would be brought forward, based on special cases of technology application. The adagio was 'let us unrestrict the restricted technologies' (Marcus, 2007). Dr. Steve Lukasik, the Chief Scientist of the FCC, was requested to identify new communications technologies that were being blocked by anachronistic rules. It was Marcus, employed at the Institute of Defense

Analysis, who suggested that spread spectrum was such a technology and as a consequence he was invited to join the FCC to follow up on the idea.[7] In December 1979 the MITRE Corporation was invited to investigate the potential civil usage of spread spectrum. Their report of 1980 started the public consultation process on the use of spread spectrum technology. In the Notice of Inquiry the FCC proposed the civil use of spread spectrum (FCC, 1981). Until 1981 this technique had remained officially classified as military technology (Mock, 2005). In the Report and Order of May 9, 1985 the FCC authorized the license-exempt use of spread spectrum in the three bands designated for Industrial, Scientific, and Medical (ISM) applications: the 902-926 MHz, the 2400-2483.5 MHz and the 5725-5850 MHz bands (FCC, 1985). This authorization provided NCR and many other firms with the opportunity to use the RF spectrum as a new medium and apply wireless technologies in data communications applications.[8]

Figure 2. IEEE 802.11 standards mapped to the OSI reference model

Reprinted from "Network modernization in the telecom sector: The case of Wi-Fi" in *The Governance of Network Industries* (2009) edited by Künneke, Groenewegen and Auger, with permission from Edward Elgar.

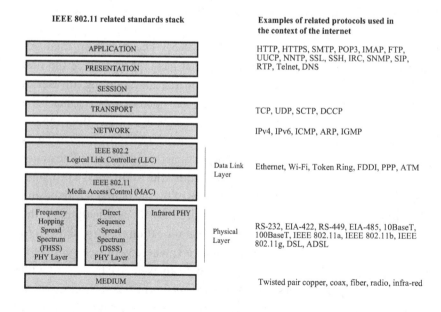

3.2 A Layered Approach to Problem Solving

Following the FCC Report & Order, NCR Corporate initiated in 1986 a feasibility study into the use of a wireless technology in local area networking, which was assigned to the Engineering centre in Utrecht, the Netherlands. Copper wires, coax and (shielded) twisted pair, differ from radio frequency spectrum in their transmission properties and in the way the medium can be accessed. In terms of the Open System Interconnection (OSI) model this implied that new designs were required at the physical layer (PHY) and at the medium access layer (MAC), see also Figure 2 which shows the layers of the OSI protocol stack in relation to examples of current day protocols used in the context of Ethernet and the Internet (Based on Ohrtman & Roeder, 2003). Any possible further impact on the higher layers of the stack (network through application) would also have to be assessed.

The first part of the feasibility project was to determine what power levels were needed and under what rules such products could be certified by the FCC. One of the issues was the so called "processing gain" requirement. This was the factor that had to be used in a direct sequence spread spectrum system to "expand" the bandwidth above the bandwidth you would "normally" need just to get your information data signal transmitted. The logic here is that the more "spread" or processing gain the system has, the more the signal looks like "noise" to others – the more capable the system is in rejecting other signals, so more coexistence would be possible in an unlicensed band (Tuch, 2007)[9]. Of course there is a trade off between the data rates to be achieved and the complexity of the total system and thus the costs. Interactions with the FCC suggested that a signal with a code sequence of length 10 or greater was required. This information implied that a WLAN could be realized operating at 1Mbit/s or more. The team set

to work to get the processing gain parameters set, and to established a code which had a length of 11 with the required properties that were determined from indoor propagation studies.[10] The feasibility study resulted in a Wireless-LAN Demo unit and a set of related product specifications.

After the feasibility study, including the creation of modem models, a prototype of the radio frequency system and indoor propagation measurements, had ended with positive results, the development team in Utrecht convinced the Retail Systems Division that product development was also best carried out by the same team. In the fall of 1988 the team set out to create a Wireless Network Interface Card (Wireless-NIC) to build a Wireless-LAN with an over-the-air data rate of 1-2Mbit/s, to be used in the retail markets that NCR was serving. The NIC would have to operate in the 902-928 MHz band, the lower ISM band as specified by the FCC. This lower band was selected to provide the maximum possible range, as opposed to the ISM bands at 2.4 and 5 GHz which have higher levels of attenuation, and would lead to higher cost of the electronics involved.

The creation of a new Medium Access Control (MAC) protocol became the focus of the product development effort. To limit costs and to reduce the development time the team intended to leverage as much as possible existing MAC designs and to make use of existing protocol standards where possible. Finding a related MAC was in essence a search for a MAC protocol already being implemented using a wireless medium, or to find a MAC implemented for another medium, such as twisted pair copper or coax cable, that could be adapted to wireless use. This search led to the Alohanet, which had morphed into IEEE 802.3 Ethernet, and to the MAC used in the Token Bus standard, which was very recently approved as IEEE 802.4. It became clear that the standards development organisation to focus on was IEEE and in particular the "802" committee.

4 PURSUING AN OPEN STANDARD

In considering the options the firm has at its disposal with respect to the type of standards to pursue, Von Burg distinguishes between two types of standards: proprietary and open, and three types of related technological communities: proprietary, sponsored and open. The proprietary community forms around a completely proprietary technology and related standard, and as the proprietor refrains from licensing its technology, this community comprises only the proprietary firm and its practitioners as well as any resellers and supplier of its technology. Resellers will only form weak ties to the community because they forgo asset-specific investments and can easily switch to a rival's product. In this case the proprietor remains solely responsible for maintaining and upgrading the technology. However, the reliance on a single firm can constitute a bottleneck in the innovation process and a severe handicap in a modular system requiring a great diversity of (complementary) capabilities. In the sponsor community that forms around an "open-but-owned" standard, the sponsor licenses its technology, hence, the community includes the licensees, who may simply resell the technology, but may also engage in manufacturing or make other asset-specific investments in the technology. In the latter case they will develop strong ties with the sponsor. The maximum degree of openness is represented by the open technological community, which forms around *de jure* standards. As this community lacks a controlling proprietor, it is less hierarchically structured, and encompasses innovators that can operate on equal terms and are independent of each other. This implies that communal interactions and a division of labour can extend over several firms. Moreover, participants are protected from unilateral manipulations as the changes in the technical specifications are subject of a democratic decision making process (Von Burg, 2001).

Within NCR *de facto* standards had been a curse rather than a blessing, as they were of a proprietary nature. Although the company was a leading provider of point-of-sale terminals, most of the time these terminals had to be connected to a back office computing system, mostly supplied by the leading mainframe provider IBM. Having a dominant position in this market IBM used proprietary protocols to connect terminal equipment to its mainframes and mini-computers. As a result much of the protocol expertise of the Utrecht development team originated from the analysis and subsequent emulation of IBM protocols. Where NCR had the opportunity it would promote the use of open standards and participate in sponsored and open technological communities.[11] Moreover, NCR recognized that a lack of a standard could result in chaos in the application of the newly released spectrum. Hence, in their WLAN product development efforts they were poised to pursue an open standard and create a community around a shared technology.

The development team recognized that having an already established group within IEEE 802 to sponsor a new physical layer was a much faster process than trying to start a new standard from scratch. The IEEE 802.4l Task Group was already working on a wireless variant driven by General Motors, but it seemed it was "losing steam".[12] The Chair of the 802.4l Task Group did not attend anymore, but the Executive Secretary was available and willing to convene on request of NCR a meeting in July 1988.

The lack of activity in the Task Group represented an opportunity for NCR to take the lead and drive the process towards results. Considering the importance it attached to developing standards-based technology it accepted the consequences of having to fund the chairperson. In the following meeting in November Hayes was elected to take over the chair of this Task Group. However, as Tuch observed: "Making the 802.4 protocol fit with the wireless medium was like trying to use a boat to get across a swamp instead of a hovercraft." (2007). Having concluded that the Token Bus MAC protocol was not suitable for the purpose, the MAC used as part of the IEEE 802.3 Ethernet standard still might be adapted. One of the key issues was how to get "collision detect" implemented using a wireless medium. A solution developed by NCR and Inland Steel was presented to the IEEE 802.3 Ethernet standards group, to solicit interest to start a new wireless working group (Tuch & Masleid, 1991). The group was apparently too busy with the evolution of the Ethernet standard towards higher speeds to support this initiative. With a negative vote for the proposal the political stage was set to "start from scratch" with a new Wireless MAC standard. Under the leadership of Tuch of NCR, the companies interested in establishing a wireless local area network standard quickly generated the necessary paperwork for the establishment of a new standardization project within IEEE. At the July Plenary meeting, the IEEE 802 Executive Committee approved the request, and with the subsequent approval by the Standards Activities Board the new "802.11" Working Group was born and Hayes was appointed as the interim chairperson.

4.1 NCR Taking the Lead in IEEE 802.11

September of 1990, at the first meeting of the 802.11 Working Group Vic Hayes was elected as the Chair.[13] At the November 1991 meeting of the Work Group the MAC and PHY subgroups were established. The subgroups set the rules for the information the proponents had to submit for the "802.11" membership to make a well informed decision. Once the proposals would be available, the two groups had the task of selecting the appropriate technology for the project. In most of the cases the sub groups used a process of selection whereby in each round of voting the proposal with the lowest number of supporting votes would be removed from the list, until a proposal would reach

majority support. The proposal reaching majority support would be submitted to the Working Group for approval as the technological basis for the draft standard.

4.2 Centralized vs. Decentralized Architecture

The first point of contention emerging in the MAC Task Group was about the principle to be used in assigning channel capacity to a terminal based on the shared use of the radio spectrum. A similar issue in the Wired-LAN arena had split the industry and led to three different incompatible standards having been approved by the IEEE. For WLAN IBM proposed a centralized approach while NCR together with Symbol technologies and Xircom submitted a proposal that supported a decentralized mechanism. The merits of the two proposals were intensely debated.[14] In the end the proposal for a decentralized approach won the vote; one of the reasons being that this protocol would support "ad hoc" networking, whereby a terminal would be able to independently coordinate communications with another terminal.

4.3 Resolving the Options Introduced by the FCC

In its 1985 Report & Order the FCC had specified two different spread spectrum modulation techniques that could be used: Frequency Hopping (FHSS) and Direct Sequence (DSSS). When put to a vote in the PHY group neither of the two modulation techniques obtained the required 75% level of support. Proponents of FHSS claimed it was easier to implement, while DSSS had the promise of a more robust system with a higher data rate. The individuals in the FHSS camp feared that the required investment in silicon would be significant, while the DSSS camp tried to refute the argument based on their experience in the implementation of pilot versions. As neither of the two groups could get the required level of support, both modulation technologies were included in the standard; ultimately the market would have to decide.

4.4 Different Perceptions on User Needs

The applications of WLAN that NCR had in mind were data-only, as was the case with many other participating vendors involved in mobile data capturing applications. However, a group of participants considered the support of isochronous services, i.e. voice, to be important to capture the market of home users. Based on an initiative by Proxim an industry consortium was established, the so-called HomeRF Working Group (Negus, Stephens, & Lansford, 2000).[15] The consortium chose the Frequency Hopping method as the basis for their standard.[16] The HomeRF protocol combined elements of the 802.11 Frequency Hopping standard *in statua cendi*, and TDMA-based voice support from the DECT standard.[17] The FH method adopted by the group supported a data rate of 1.6 Mbit/s. HomeRF was positioned as a low cost solution having a relaxed PHY specification.

When the IEEE adopted the "802.11b" project for an 11 Mbit/s WLAN, the consortium announced a second release of the specification for speeds of 6Mbit/s up to 10 Mbit/s (Negus et al., 2000). Therefore, they filed a letter at the FCC asking for a change of the Frequency Hopping in the form of an interpretation of the existing rules to widen the channel width from 1 MHz to 3 and 5 MHz. However, the FCC disagreed and started a rules change procedure with a Notice of Proposed Rules Change (FCC, 1999). On August 31, 2000, the FCC released the Report and Order, changing the Frequency Hopping rules (FCC, 2000).

The HomeRF battle against the 802.11 Working Group was fierce. Despite the support of major players in the industry the HomeRF initiative failed. According to Lansford the reasons for the failure were twofold (2007)[18]:

1. Because none of the consortium members were developing PHY silicon, they were forced to abandon a PHY that was similar to 802.11FH and switch to the OpenAir PHY developed by Proxim. Many companies in the HomeRF working group felt this made the standard a proprietary system, and

2. The adoption of 802.11b in 1999 and its support by several silicon vendors (Harris, Lucent Technologies[19], etc.) drove down prices relatively quickly compared to the single silicon source for HomeRF. The HomeRF consortium had assumed that FH products would always be cheaper than DS products, but market competition invalidated that assumption.

4.5 Approval of the IEEE 802.11 Standard

At the meeting of November 1993 the foundation technology of the MAC was selected. The first Letter Ballot on the draft standard was started at the November 1994 meeting. In total four ballots were needed to reach the required level of 75 % support. The Sponsor Letter Ballot was issued on August 1996 and after two recirculation ballots the draft standard was submitted to the Standards Activities Board (SAB) in August 1997, to be approved at their September meeting and to be published on December 10, 1997 as IEEE 802.11 – 1997 edition, covering Frequency Hopping at a data rate of 1 Mbit/s and Direct Sequence at 2Mbit/s.[20]

5 INPUT FROM THE MARKET: THE NEED FOR INCREASED DATA RATES

Following the approval of the 100 Mbit/s Ethernet standard in 1993, high speed wired-LAN products had been introduced in the market and during the final editing of the IEEE 802.11-1997 specification it was becoming clear to everybody in the "802.11" community that also higher data rate Wireless-LANs would be required. The goal set was to extend the performance and the range of applications in the 2.4 GHz band, and specify a higher speed wireless access technology suitable for data, voice and image information services in the lower 5 GHz band.

The least contentious was the 802.11a variant in the 5 GHz band. There were two main proposals, one from Breezecom (later Alvarion) and NEC on a single carrier modulation method and one from Lucent Technologies and NTT, based on OFDM.[21] The voting was won by the Lucent Technologies and NTT combination, leading to a 54 Mbit/s based standard.

The voting for the IEEE 802.11b PHY was very contentious and an example how different positions in technological advancements are equalized in a standards making process. The main contenders were Harris and Lucent Technologies, and a proposal from an outsider Micrilor, a start-up company with very good radio knowledge. There was a degree of truth in a 3Com statement that most of the Lucent Technologies supporters had decided to side with Micrilor in the voting to avoid that Harris and their supporters would have an unfair advantage in the market, as they already had progressed substantially in their development efforts. As the voting stalled, in the same week representatives of Lucent Technologies and Harris sat together and acknowledged a compromise was needed. Subsequently they worked out a new radio transmission scheme, different from anything that had been proposed before, called Complementary Code Keying (CCK). Because this proposal gave no advantage to any party the joint proposal was accepted in the next meeting of the Working Group six weeks later, resulting in the IEEE 802.11b standard.

5.1 Approval of the First Extensions IEEE 802.11a and 11b

Project IEEE 802.11a and Project 802.11b f were balloted at Working Group level in November 1998 and re-circulated twice to start the Sponsor ballot in April 1999. After 2 recirculation ballots, both were submitted to the SAB in August 1999. IEEE 802.11a was officially published on December 30, 1999 and covered data rates up to 54 Mbit/s in the 5 GHz band. IEEE 802.11b was published on January 20, 2000, covering a 11 Mbit/s data rate in the 2.4 GHz band.

In parallel the group undertook to revise the IEEE 802.11-1997 standard, to lead it through the ISO/IEC process to become adopted as an International Standard. After carefully synchronizing the processes within the two organisations, the revision of IEEE Std 802.11, 1997 edition was published on August 10, 1999 designated ISO/IEC 8802-11:1999. The IEEE 802.11a resp. 11b version were ratified by ISO in late 1999 resp. 2000.

6 COMPETING ACTIVITIES IN THE EUROPEAN STANDARDS ARENA

Following the decision making by the FCC, an ad-hoc group on Radio-LANs within the CEPT, the body responsible for the harmonization of spectrum use in Europe, recommended that the 2.4 GHz band destined for ISM applications to be opened for the license-exempt use of RadioLAN devices, and it requested ETSI, the body responsible for the development of telecommunication standards in Europe, to develop the necessary standard to define the technical characteristics and the measurement method (ETSI, 1993).[22] In 1991 the European Radio Commission assigns the 2.4 GHz ISM band for WLAN use; on a non-protective and non-interference basis, without the need for an end-user license (CEPT, 1991). This paved the way towards a global allocation of spectrum for Wireless-LANs. This represented great news for the equipment vendors as it would allow for expansion of scale in manufacturing.

The ad-hoc group subsequently allocated the 5150-5300 MHz and an optional extension to 5350 MHz for RLANs (CEPT, 1992). As often happens in Europe, this allocation of the spectrum was tied to devices adhering to a specific standard, in this case the standard tagged HIPERLAN (High Performance Local Area Networks), yet to be developed. HIPERLAN was aimed at providing high speed (24 Mbit/s typical data rate) radio local area network communications in the 5 GHz band compatible with wired-LANs based on Ethernet and Token ring standards. HIPERLAN was aimed to cover a range of 50 m and to support asynchronous and synchronous applications.

Following the establishment of the IEEE 802.11 Working Group for wireless local area networks in July 1990, Hayes had been invited to participate as an industry representative in the ad-hoc RLAN committee of CEPT, and in the Technical Committee ETSI-RES 10. This provided the NCR Team, and upon the 1991 acquisition the AT&T Team in Utrecht with a rather unique position to leverage its activities in IEEE and ETSI, and to align as far as (politically) possible the activities in the two standard setting bodies. Again the company volunteered to provide the chair person; Kruys became the second chair of ETSI-RES 3. The Committee published its first technical specification HIPERLAN/1 in 1997.

A second version HIPERLAN/2 was developed as part of the ETSI-BRAN Broadband Radio Access Networks project to provide much higher speeds (up to 54 Mbit/s data rate) for communication in the 5 GHz band between portable computing devices and broadband ATM and IP networks. This version supported multi-media applications, with emphasis on quality of service (QoS) aspects.[23]

Neither the HIPERLAN/1 nor the HIPERLAN/2 standard completed in 2004 have become

a success. Also HIPERLAN had to compete with a much more matured IEEE 802.11 standard for which devices had been developed that had already reached a price point too low to compete with effectively.

7 MAKING THE STANDARD A MARKET SUCCESS

The decision by NCR to exploit the new business opportunity through the development of an open standard in cooperation with others was an important step in realizing its WLAN vision. While manufacturing partners can be aligned through the standardization process, real products are required to convince potential customers of the benefits that Wireless LANs can provide. Market research initiated by NCR to establish the right product positioning strategy indicated that LAN (re-)wiring was cumbersome and expensive, estimated at US$ 200-1500 per 'drop'. Also the lack of expertise was mentioned as an issue; the connection of PC adaptors to the coax cable and localizing faults in the early Ethernet systems was know to be cumbersome. Lower overall cost was identified as the key feature of Wireless-LANs.

Ahead of a formal standards approval, NCR launched its first WaveLAN product for the US market at Networld in Dallas, in September of 1990. The product operated at 915 MHz and used one communication channel providing a dats rate of 2 Mbit/s. It was a desktop PC plug-in board, essentially a radio based Network Interface Card (NIC), and required an external antenna. The general product release was in May 1991 Prospective customers appeared to be fascinated by the technology, but the benefits were perceived as marginal and the price as too high. At the product launch the price was set at US$ 1,390 per card. In comparison an ARCNet card was sold at US$ 300, an Ethernet card at $ 495, and a Token Ring card at $ 645. However, giving the difference in implementation only a Total Cost of Ownership calculation would provide for a fair comparison. Although this improved the business case significantly, within short NCR would lower the price of the PC plug-in to $ 995.

In the course of 1991 it became clear that the product was incomplete in the view of prospective customers. Multiple Access Points (AP) would be needed to cover larger buildings, to be connected to the wired-LAN infrastructure; plus the capability of roaming (also called hand-off) between the APs. The implementation looked relatively easy as the client stations, PC/laptop, could keep track of the signal strength of each AP within reach and switch the connection to the AP with the best transmission performance. However, the R&D efforts increased significantly when the system had to be 'scaled-up', and became comparable to the efforts involved in the development of the NIC.

7.1 Getting the Product: Market Combination Right

To improve the results of their sales efforts the NCR team emphasized the Total Cost of Ownership of WaveLAN in replacing cable. But many prospects did not accept the proposition because of the significant upfront investment required. The case could be argued more successfully if the WLAN would support mobile applications, but early products were too bulky and required too much power to be feasible for mobile devices. Getting the product right was further complicated by the different computing environments that prospective customers had. And to complicate matters further IBM introduced a new hardware interface, the Microchannel bus, to replace the AT bus.

The good news was that that the market did show price elasticity: lower prices did lead to an increase in volume. However, volumes remained low as most deals involved 10-20 cards, with contracts for 1000 cards being the exception. The combination of WaveLAN and outdoor commu-

nications continued to be very compelling. The reach of the card was extended by using 'power amplifiers', which boosted the output power well beyond the maximum prescribed by the FCC. The FCC did attempt to reinforce compliance with the regulation by prescribing a special antenna connector for these applications, only available through recognized outlets.

Packaged solutions, sometime in combination with other NCR products, was another way of going to market that was being pursued. In the banking sector attempts were more successful with the so-called 'replicated branch', which included a central staging and testing of the computer system of a bank branch office. The system would subsequently be trucked to the site and be installed overnight.

7.2 Global vs. Local Products

The differences between the early successes in the 915 MHz US market and the 'international' market adopting 2.4 GHz raised the strategic question within NCR whether a global product or localized products should be pursued. The 915 MHz lower frequency range had the advantage of a larger reach, as attenuation of radio waves increases with frequency. However, in the 2.4 GHz band more spectrum had been assigned and hence more channels could be accommodated and used simultaneously, increasing the systems performance. While on the one hand a global product would be more cost effective, product costs at 2.4 GHz would be higher than at 915 MHz. Moreover, as the products would provide the same functionality, it would be difficult to differentiate in pricing.

The decision was essentially determined by market forces. Competitors who were only marketing products in the 2.4 GHz band pushed the advantage of more channels, which gave the customers the impression that the 2.4 GHz product was providing a higher data rate. With the illusion of higher speed the issue of a shorter range became a mute point. In 1993 AT&T would release the 2.4 GHz WaveLAN PC adaptor for the global market. It operated at a data transfer rate of 2 Mbit/s and provided 13 different channels that could be preselected within the assigned band.[24] The card was connected to an external antenna. Also in 1993 the form factor of the 915 MHz US product was improved through the release of a PCMCIA card version. In 1995 followed the 2.4 GHz version of the card for the global market.

Moreover, in 1993 AT&T was successful in closing the first contract for large scale deployment of WaveLAN at Carnegie Mellon University (CMU) in Pittsburgh, Pennsylvania. The project involved the deployment of Access Points to serve 10,000 students, faculty and staff moving about the university campus (Hills, 1999; Hills & Johnson, 1996). The acquisition of CMU as a client would provide a perfect test-bed for a large scale deployment of WLANs.

7.3 Security Concerns

As it is much easier to eavesdrop on a wireless system than on a wired system the level of security provided by WLANs raised doubts in the minds of prospective customers, which in turn frustrated its adoption. From the outset WaveLAN included as an option a Data Encryption Security chip. This chip was used until the IEEE standard was implemented, which included the so-called Wired Equivalent Privacy (WEP) algorithm, providing a basic authentication and encryption method.[25]

7.4 Crossing the Chasm

Summarizing the situation in early 1997 Links concludes: "While the early product development period 1987-1991 had been cumbersome, the period 1991-1994, involving the general availability of the WaveLAN product and a major marketing and sales effort, had not been much better. We had essentially 'doubled our bets' with adding a 2.4 GHz product, but there were no real profits

in sight. After the first period we had a Wireless LAN card, after the second period we had a Wireless LAN system. Hence, we could bridge into a wired environment, and we could roam through buildings while staying connected. After the first period we had a US-only product, after the second we had a worldwide product. This was all encouraging in terms of progress. However, the market acceptance of Wireless-LANs was still very low. There were serious concerns raised about the lack of a standard. All companies, the major ones Proxim, Aironet and now AT&T and the many smaller ones including Breezecom, WaveAccess, Xircom, all had different products. All of them were telling the prospects why they were the best and what was wrong with the technology of the competitor. The consequence of this all was that prospective customers did not trust anybody – "data was precious, and waves were weird" – so the prevailing attitude was "wait and see". It was clear that we needed standards, higher data rates, and lower costs.

By then we had all read the books by Geoffrey Moore, "Crossing the Chasm" and "Inside the Tornado". If there was one case of technology driven innovation that was clearly showing the difficulty of 'Crossing the Chasm' it had to be Wireless LAN. I would conclude that we had explored all possible market segments that could have become our 'beach head'. Albeit, so far we had failed to deliver in full on the 'whole product' concept. But… by 1997 we finally had a standard-based product available."(Links, 2007). [26]

In the course of 1998 the Lucent Technology senior management started questioning the results of the Wireless LAN project. This was after only two years of involvement and with limited visibility of what had been spent in the preceding decade. Slowly but surely resources were moved to other more promising radio projects, such as Wireless Local Loop (WLL). Nonetheless, the sales team kept pushing WaveLAN. The fortune of WaveLAN and for that matter WLANs would take a turn for the better following an unexpected call from Apple Headquarters, simply stating: "Steve Jobs wants to have a meeting with Rich McGinn about wireless LANs." Apparently Steve Jobs, who had returned to Apple as 'interim CEO' to reinvigorate the company, had decided that Wireless-LAN had to be the key differentiating feature for the iBook which was scheduled to be launched in 1999. The meeting in the Apple Boardroom was an interesting one, with Steve Jobs concluding the meeting with: "We need the radio card for $50, and I want to sell at $99." Then Steve apologizes, he has to leave – stands up, says "Hi!" and goes. The room falls silent (Links, 2007).

For Steve Jobs the job was done, for Lucent Technologies the work started. The target was audacious, because early 1998 the cost level of the cards was still above US$ 100. The chipsets for the next round of cost reductions had been designed, but it was not clear whether the target set by Apple could be met by spring of 1999. In the following months several rounds of negotiations took place to obtain agreement on the product definition. Apple wanted a special interface, moreover, they wanted three versions of the Access Point. Also the price was subject of some tough negotiations and a complicating matter was that the initial agreement had been based on the existing 2 Mbit/s product. The standards making process had advanced substantially and the 11 Mbit/s product version was expected to become available in 1999. Apple wanted to go directly to the 11 Mbit/s, but did not want to accept a higher price. It became an all or nothing negotiation. The product was launched as the Apple Airport in the summer of 1999, with the PC card priced at US$ 99 and the Access Point at $ 299. At this price level the 11 Mbit/s Wireless LANs could compete effectively with the 10 Mbit/s wired Ethernet. The industry was shocked. Links recalls: "We were accused of "buying" the market and that we were losing money on every card sold. But we were not. The mechanism we used was to 'forward' price the product. With the volume going up quickly

the costs would also come down quickly, and the market share gained would bring in the margin. That is the theory – well, it worked in practice, and it worked very well as would turn out in the following years." (Links, 2007).

Dell was the first PC vendor to follow the trend set by Apple. However, the cooperation with Dell had an additional complicating factor: they used the Microsoft Operating System. As a consequence Lucent was faced with another hurdle to overcome. As Microsoft had become overloaded with requests to resolve interface issues, they had installed a new certification procedure called Wireless Hardware Quality Labs. Unfortunately some requirements in the certification program were incompatible with the operation of Wireless-LANs. This required Lucent to work closely with Microsoft to resolve these issues. Initially some compromises were made and waivers obtained to expedite market deployment. Eventually the cooperation involved creating new software to support Wireless-LANs proper, to be included in the release of XP in 2001.

With this effort done, the two world leading PC operating systems had in-built features to support Wireless-LANs, and hence another dimension of the "whole product" concept had been resolved. The Apple Airport had become the beachhead, or in the terminology of Geoffrey Moore: the head pin on the bowling alley (1995). With the success of the Apple Airport the "chasm" had been crossed effectively, the company was entering the "tornado zone". Within a year all other PC vendors had followed the example set by Apple. Agere Systems, had almost a clean sweep of the Wireless-LAN market for PCs.[27] This success replaced the business user, as the main target of WLAN applications, by the home user.

This new period posed new challenges. Ramping up volume in manufacturing became the key challenge, which implied lead time reduction, improving inventory management, optimizing test capabilities. In the early days the radio part of the card had about 15 test points and involved manual calibration. Now, the cards are fully tested through software. The early cards had about 300 components, which has come down to 30 and would go down further to 10. All the result of moving from a production level of 100 cards per week in 1991 to 100,000 cards per week in 2001 (Tuch, 2007).

7.5 The Wi-Fi Alliance

With the approval of the IEEE 802.11 standard two major implementation variants were allowed, a consequence of the FCC Report & Order that included the two spread spectrum variants: frequency hopping and direct sequence. This could in practice lead to two companies claiming to be compliant while the products would be incompatible. This situation forced the leading Wireless LAN companies to collaborate and they initiated the Wireless Ethernet Compatibility Alliance (WECA) in 1999, as a non-profit organisation driving the adoption of a single DSSS-based world-wide standard for high-speed wireless local area networking. Governed by a small Board WECA quickly established an interoperability testing procedure and a seal of compliance, the Wi-Fi (Wireless Fidelity) logo. In 2002 it changed its name to the Wi-Fi Alliance to acknowledge the power of the Wi-Fi brand. As of July 2007 the organisation had certified the interoperability of over 3,500 products (Wi-Fi Alliance, 2007).

7.6 The Ultimate Success

By early 2001 Agere Systems, as a spin-off of Lucent Technologies, had reached the summit as supplier of Wi-Fi products with an approximately 50% market share, inclusive of the OEM channel. By that time the market had grown to an US$ 1 billion annual level. By the end of 2001 it became clear that the industry was moving into another phase. With the broad acceptance of Wi-Fi it was clear that the Wireless-LAN functionality would be progressively integrated into the various com-

puter and networking products. The competition would shift from the plug-ins toward the chipsets, as was confirmed by the moves of e.g. Intersil, Broadcom, Infineon, and AMD. As a consequence the ORiNOCO brand (as successor to WaveLAN) and the related infrastructure products, Access Points, Residential gateways and Outdoor Routers, were separated organisationally from the chip activities. In 2002 Agere sold the ORiNOCO business unit to Proxim in a friendly take-over valued at US$ 65 mln. Agere Systems continued to develop the Wireless LAN technology and turned it into new chipsets. They also sold the technology to other chipset providers to allow the integration with other I/O technologies.

Meanwhile Intel had expanded its WLAN expertise by acquiring Xircom in 1999. In 2003 Intel launched the Centrino chipset with built-in Wi-Fi functionality for mobile computers. This launch was supported with a US$ 300 mln marketing campaign, essentially moving the success of the "Intel inside" campaign to an "Wi-Fi inside" campaign. This marks the ultimate success of Wi-Fi, having moved from PC adaptors, through plug-ins and integrated chipsets, to functionality that has become part of the hardware core of laptop computers. This also moved the industry into another era and ends the period of the specialty suppliers. As a result Agere Systems discontinued its Wireless LAN activities in 2004. The remaining WLAN expertise transitioned 'in person' to other firms, in particular to Motorola, a company active in the field of WiMAX, another member of the Wi-Family.

8 NEW STANDARDS REQUIREMENTS EMERGING FROM WI-FI DEPLOYMENT

While the initial application of WLANs had been targeted by the manufacturers to be in the corporate domain, Apple had opened up the home networking market. The massive adoption by the users shaped the emerging market. This triggered another set of entrepreneurs, including telecom operators, to use Wi-Fi to provide (semi) public access to the Internet at "hotspots". It has been the Starbucks initiative to provide wireless access to the Internet in their coffee shops that has set off Wi-Fi as the preferred means of accessing the Internet in public areas in general. For Starbucks it was the prospect of attracting more customers and keeping them longer in the coffeehouse, in particular after the rush hour, that made investments in the new service an interesting proposition.[28]

Next to these commercially oriented organisations, groups of volunteers have emerged that are providing Internet access for free or at very low cost. The shared Internet access and often also direct communications among community members is provided based on Wi-Fi Access Points being interconnected forming a wireless Neighbourhood Area Network (WNAN). These communities of volunteers are mostly motivated by their enthusiasm to explore the possibilities of new technologies and their wish to demonstrate their technological savvy. A typical example of a Wi-Fi community in the Netherlands is 'Wireless Leiden', a group of volunteers that started in the year 2001 and has built a WNAN that includes 60 nodes, is covering most of the Leiden city, and is being linked to neighbouring towns covering an area of about 500 km[2] (Vijn & Mourits, 2005). One of the first technical challenges the group was facing in building the network was that Wi-Fi had been designed as a network access solution and not as a network node. In home applications Wi-Fi access points (APs) are typically connected via ADSL or a Cable Modem to provide connectivity with the 'public' network, in particular the Internet. Through the functionality of an in-built router an AP can support multiple computers. Hence, in this way family members can share the access provided. Depending on how the AP is configured, any Wi-Fi compatible computer

within the coverage range of the AP may use the AP to access the Internet. This may include house guests, neighbours or passers-by.[29] This is the so-called infrastructure or managed mode of the IEEE 802.11 standard. However, Wi-Fi stations can also communicate directly with each other, i.e. without an AP, in the so-called peer-to-peer or ad-hoc mode.[30] The distance that can be covered is limited, typically 50 meters, depending on the propagation of the radio signals.[31] In this mode each Wi-Fi equipped PC can be considered a Wi-Fi island. If more than two of these islands could be connected a Wi-Fi based Neighbourhood Area Network can be created. However, the 802.11 standard does not provide an automatic means to communicate through intermediary stations. An alternative approach is using the so-called 'repeater mode' whereby APs are interconnected using radio links rather than cables. This mode is used for example in the case of the 'Wireless Leiden' NAN. Each network node is thereby equipped with three Wi-Fi cards, one using an omni-directional antenna to serve nearby Wi-Fi stations, and two cards with an unidirectional antennas to provide a link to two neighboring nodes (Wireless Leiden, 2006a). The network node is a PC equipped with special software to provide the network function, which includes the issuance of IP addresses (DHCP function), the directory function for relating the name to IP address (DNS function), the routing function (OSPF), and the remote maintenance functionality (based on SSH). Recognizing that the reliability of the network depends on the proper functioning of the nodes, which are often located at places that are difficult to access, e.g. rooftops and church towers, the procedure to create a node has been standardized in the form of a "Node Factory".[32] The software upon which the first nodes were built appeared to fail with growing network size, this forced the volunteers to develop and deploy their own dynamic routing software.

8.1 Municipal Networks

Wireless municipal broadband access has become a major item in the USA with highly visible initiatives in e.g. Philadelphia, San Francisco (involving Google) and Silicon Valley.[33] Reasons that are being stated for municipalities to pursue the opportunity to enter the market for wireless broadband service provision include: (1) opportunity to fill the gap in available and affordable (wired) broadband access, where private firms fail to provide service or offer services at a price considered to be too high; (2) to create a 'third pipe" next to DSL and cable to improve competition; (3) making the city more competitive in attracting business; (4) improving intra- and intergovernmental communications, improving quality of work life for employees; (5) the opportunity to offer services at lower costs of deployment e.g. through ownership of rights-of-way, the use of municipal premises and leveraging internal use of the network (Hudson, 2006; Tapia et al., 2005; Weiss & Huang, 2007).

8.2 Forward Momentum in IEEE 802.11

Although NCR, or its corporate successors, is not involved any more, the innovation journey of Wi-Fi continues unabated, exemplified by the vendor community pursuing extensions to the existing IEEE 802.11a/b standards to cater for, e.g., operation of Wi-Fi in different regulatory domains (IEEE 802.11d), the improvement of quality of service functionality (11e), and enhancements of security (11i). Moreover Task Groups were approved to increase the data rate to 600 Mbit/s range using MIMO (11n), to support fast roaming (11r), mesh type networking (11s), and improve the inter-working with external networks (11u).

9 SUMMARY AND REFLECTIONS

The current day success of Wi-Fi can be traced back to a change in government policy intended to simplify the rules for the use of radio frequency spectrum and the idea to allow public use of spread spectrum technology. The 1985 decision of the FCC to allow spread spectrum based radio communication in the three bands designated for Industrial, Scientific and Medical applications triggered communication firms to innovate and develop new short range data communication products. NCR recognized the need to leverage existing standardized communication protocols and became the driving force in the development and adoption of a Wireless-LAN standard – IEEE 802.11, as were its corporate successors AT&T, Lucent Technologies, and Agere Systems. In contracting with Apple and subsequently cooperating with Microsoft the product reached the

Figure 3. Relationship between Wi-Fi related innovation avenues

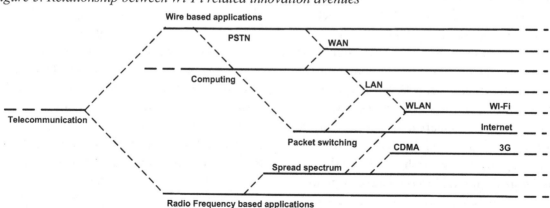

mass market. In the process the product moved from its intended use as WLAN in the corporate environment to application in the home. Subsequently the home and business use was extended through Internet access services being provided at 'hotspots', 'hotzones', and more recently through 'municipal' networks. The low-threshold technology resulted also in networks being created by communities of volunteers in developed as well as developing countries to provide alternative network access.

In the process Wi-Fi moved from functionality that was being added to a PC or laptop by way of an external plug-in, to functionality that is being built into every laptop, based on an integrated chipset.

9.1 Reflections from a Theoretical Perspective

The Wi-Fi case is a good example of an 'innovation journey' (Van de Ven, Polley, Garud, & Venkataraman, 1999) and it illustrates how a new 'innovation avenue' (Sahal, 1981, 1985) emerges as a fusion of two existing avenues: LANs and Spread spectrum; see Figure 3.

It is also a good illustration of the different sources of innovation that play a role in the shaping of a product or service as argued by Von Hippel (1988; 2005). In our case the emphasis has shifted from the more traditional role of the manufacturer, to the operator as supplier of a service, to the users building Wi-Fi based community networks.

In the Wi-Fi case we can also recognise the notions of evolutionary theory, i.e. novelty generation, transmission and selection, as well as retention. The Wi-Fi development can be related to Nelson and Winter (1977; 1982) who argue that technical advance is an evolutionary process in which new technological alternatives compete with each other and with prevailing practice, whereby *ex-post* selection is determining the winners and losers, usually with considerable *ex-ante* uncertainty regarding the outcome. Thereby we recognise the Lamarckian metaphor of economic evolution which allows acquired characteristics based on learning to be passed on and which acknowledges purposeful intention with respect to changing behaviour. This is in contrast to the Darwinian metaphor whereby change can only take place through mutations at birth and which is considered to be random (Lemstra, Hayes, & Van der Steen, 2009).[34]

The development of Wi-Fi was triggered by a major shift in the institutional arrangements: the assignment by the FCC of unlicensed radio frequency spectrum for communication purposes. The technology to be applied had been developed in the military domain and was now prescribed for use in the private domain. This can be characterised as a change in the institutional selection environment. Although the FCC ruling prescribed a certain type of technology, firms generated a broad variety of initial products using proprietary protocols. From a theoretical perspective, the FCC opened the possibility for novelty generation. The incompatibility resulted in a fragmented product market, increasing the risk for the users with respect to future developments. Through NCR taking a leadership role in establishing a coalition the novelty generation in the product market moved to the selection mechanism of the standardization process. The standardization process has been a process of retention and learning of the various firms involved in the development of Wi-Fi. A strong contribution to the development of the content of the standard, a high degree of participation, as well as skillful negotiation and maneuvering are the major ingredients determining the outcome of this process. A process being facilitated through well established formal procedures within the IEEE.[35] Wi-Fi emerged as the winner of the battle against HomeRF and HIPERLAN. This connects to the economic literature describing how a dominant design emerges (Abernathy & Utterback, 1978; Murmann & Frenken, 2006). Once resources come to be largely focused on the leading technology

Figure 4. Wi-Fi standards and NCR products

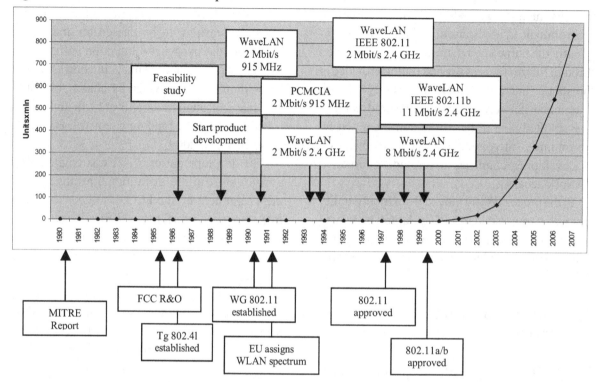

further improvements may soon make it and its further developments the only economic way to proceed because competing design are left so far behind (Dosi, 1982; Nelson & Winter, 1977; 1982). Implicitly the case shows the importance of software platforms in forging the successful adoption of this hardware oriented product (Gawer & Cusumano, 2002).

The product life cycle of Wi-Fi reflects a long gestation period of almost 15 years, followed by a rapid take off in the last 5-6 years, see Figure 4 reflecting the milestones related to the standards process and to the product introductions by NCR c.s. against the Wi-Fi chipsets shipped (based on: Instat, 2007). In comparison to the standardization of wired LANs the intervals are comparable but appear to be somewhat longer, which can easily be explained from the fact that the product development took place in parallel with the standardization process. From the establishment of WG 802.11 it took 7 years until the first

specification was published. The interval between product initiation and the market inflection point has been much longer, approx. 14 years.

The aspect of retention can best be illustrated by characterizing the Wi-Fi based ecosystem that has emerged and is evolving (based on: De Leeuw, 2006, 2007; Kamp, 2005): In the third quarter of 2007 over 43 million WLAN NICs were shipped from Taiwan, 37% more than the previous year; a market scan in 2007 identified 180 end-product vendors, providing 3289 different products; client devices with Wi-Fi functionality include: notebooks, PDAs, mobile phones, streaming music and video players, digital camera's, printers, video beamers, gaming devices, and home audio-systems; hotspots worldwide are well in excess of 206,000 in 135 countries; in the USA over 400 cities and counties are reported with operational municipal networks, networks under deployment, or plans issued for Wi-Fi networks.[36]

Figure 5. Overview of contributions to 802.11

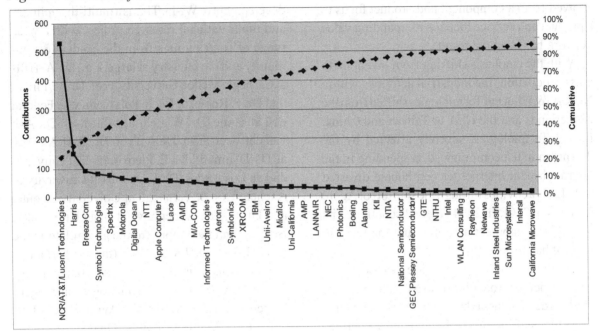

9.2 Reflecting on Firm Strategy and Standards

The case story of Wi-Fi is a good example of how the processes of standardization, product development, and market introduction are interlinked. It shows the linkage to firm strategy. The extensive period required for the standardization illustrates the commitment, the tenacity and the resources required from an emerging industry leader involved in 'rule breaking' (De Wit & Meyer, 2004). Figure 5 illustrates the leadership commitment by NCR and subsequently AT&T and Lucent Technologies: with 531 contributions for the period 1990-1999, representing 23% of the total and almost four times as many as the next company in the sequence.[37] The case also shows the importance of relationships and collaboration at the various junctures in the standardization process to achieve the desired outcome.

Moreover, the case shows the importance of institutions in technology and product development. For examples, the FCC as national regulatory agency in providing the governance of the radio

spectrum; the IEEE providing the ICT-industry with a platform to develop standards.

The activities of NCR can be connected to a role of the entrepreneur as in the view of Casson: "an entrepreneur is someone who specializes in taking judgmental decisions about the coordination of scarce resources" (as quoted in Ricketts, 2002). A particular challenge for the entrepreneur is to move the business beyond the early adopter phase into the mass market phase, i.e. from selling successfully to the technology enthusiast and visionaries to selling to the pragmatists. In the terms of Moore, the 'chasm' was crossed in 1999 through a strategic cooperation of Lucent Technologies with Apple and subsequently Microsoft. While Wi-Fi started as a technological innovation, its development became characterized by subsequent releases of the IEEE 802.11 standard. These standards were translated into chipsets which became incorporated in products, which in turn became part of communications systems. In our case-study, we observe that first these WLAN systems were applied in the corporate domain, subsequently in the private domain, followed by the public domain. As a result the industry evolved from a component and product focus to a product and service focus. An expanding value network has been the result.

With the emphasis shifting from invention to mass production, the industrial activities within NCR/AT&T/Lucent Technologies shifted from the Netherlands and the USA to Taiwan and China. Lucent Technologies, severely affected by the downturn in telecommunication spending in the aftermath of the Internet/telecom bubble, divested its WLAN activities through the spin-off of Agere Systems in 2001. In 2004 Agere discontinued its WLAN development activities and the team in Utrecht has been dissolved.

However, as the original radio expertise moved with the people from Philips to NCR, the success of Wi-Fi developments has triggered new start-ups by former staff of Lucent Technologies, continuing the innovation process. For instance through Airgo, established in 2001 and recently acquired by Qualcom, continued to lead developments in the Wi-Fi space, in particular with high data rate MIMO (multiple inputs multiple outputs). Airgo designed chips which have resulted in the first ever MIMO consumer products being introduced in the market by a number of suppliers. Following in the footsteps of NCR, Airgo is contributing extensively to IEEE 802.11 Task Group 'n', aimed at achieving high throughput extension (Van Nee, 2006).

Next to knowledge diffusion through start-ups, former Agere staff has moved to other (leading) companies in the wireless industry including Motorola, and they continue to push the envelope in terms of innovation and standardization in wireless communications.

ACKNOWLEDGMENT

This chapter draws upon a research project executed within the Faculty Technology, Policy and Management at the Delft University of Technology (TUDelft) aimed at documenting the genesis and development of Wi-Fi. This is a multi-disciplinary and multi-national research project with a wide range of contributions from the academic community and the industry at large, e.g., Dr. A. Hills at Carnegie Mellon University, Prof. Dr. M. Finger and Dr. P. Rossel at Ecole Polytechnique Fédéral de Lausanne, Dr. W. Lehr at MIT, Prof. Dr. A-J. van der Veen at TUDelft, Prof. Dr. W.H. Melody at TU-Denmark, Dr. E. Pietrosemoli at Universidad de Los Andes, Dr. K. Jakobs at University of Aachen, Drs. S. Verhaegh at University-Twente, and Dr. L. Van Audenhove at Vrije Universiteit Brussel; and field input from e.g. regulators: the FCC (USA), OPTA and AT (the Netherlands); various firms within the communication industry e.g. NCR/AT&T/Lucent Technologies, and Agere Systems, Aruba Networks, Avinity, Gandalf, GreenPeak, Motorola, Philips, Qualcom, SonyEricsson; from standardization organizations: e.g. IEEE and ETSI; from operators: e.g. Casema, KPN, Swisscom, T-Mobile; and from wireless community founders e.g. Wireless Leiden, Djürsland, AirJaldi.

TRADEMARKS

REFERENCES

Abbate, J. (1999). *Inventing the internet.* Cambridge, MA: MIT Press.

Abernathy, W. J., & Utterback, J. M. (1978). Patterns of industrial innovation. *Technology Review, 80*(7), 40-47.

Borisov, N., Goldberg, I., & Wagner, D. (1999). *802.11 Security.* Retrieved 2007-01-30, from http://www.isaac.cs.berkeley.edu/isaac/wep-faq.html

CEPT. (1991). *Recommendation T/R 10-01 (Oslo 1991, revised in Madrid 1992), Wide band data transmission systems using spread-spectrum technology in the 2.5 GHz band. Superseded by T/R 70-03.*

CEPT. (1992). *Recommendation T/R 22-06 (Madrid 1992, revised at Nicosia 1994), Harmonised radio frequency bands for high performance radio local area networks (HIPERLANs) in the 5 GHz and 17 GHz frequency range. Superseded by T/R 70-03.*

Crane, M. (2007). *Stealing Starbuck's Wi-Fi customers.* Retrieved 2007-08-28, from http://www.forbes.com/2007/02/23/fonbucks-wifi-starbucks-ent_cx_mc_0226fonbucks_print.html

De Leeuw, G. J. (2006). *Wi-Fi in the Netherlands.* Paper presented at the 9th Annual International Conference Economics of Infrastructure, Delft, the Netherlands.

De Leeuw, G. J. (2007). *A snapshot of the Wi-Fi world in 2007.* Delft, the Netherlands: TUDelft.

De Wit, B., & Meyer, R. (2004). *Strategy: process, content, context - An international perspective.* London: Thomson.

Dosi, G. (1982). Technological paradigms and technological trajectories - A suggested interpretation of the determinants and directions of technical change. *Research Policy, 11,* p147-162.

ETSI. (1993). *ETS 300 328 Radio Equipment and Systems (RES); Wideband transmission systems; Technical characteristics and test conditions for data transmission equipment operating in the 2,4 GHz ISM band and using spread spectrum modulation techniques.*

FCC. (1981). *GEN Docket 81-413, Authorization of spread spectrum and other wideband emissions not presently provided for in the FCC rules and regulations. Notice of Inquiry, June 30, 1981.* Retrieved 2008-01-30, from http://www.marcus-spectrum.com/documents/SpreadSpectrumNOI.pdf

FCC. (1985). *GEN Docket 81-413 Report and Order in the matter of: Authorization of spread spectrum.* Washington, D.C.: Federal Communications Commission.

FCC. (1999). *ET Docket 99-231, Amendment of Part 15 of the Commission's rules regarding spread spectrum devices. Notice of Proposed Rulemaking, released June 24, 1999.* Retrieved 2008-02-08, from http://www.fcc.gov/searchtools.html

FCC. (2000). *ET Docket 99-231, Amendment of Part 15 of the Commission's rules regarding spread spectrum devices. First report and order, released August 31, 2000.* Retrieved 2008-02-08, from http://www.fcc.gov/searchtools.html

FCC. (2007). *About the FCC.* Retrieved 2007-01-05, from http://www.fcc.gov/aboutus.html

FON. (2007). *What's Fon?* Retrieved 2007-08-30, from http://www.fon.com/en/info/whatsFon

Gawer, A., & Cusumano, M. A. (2002). *Platform leadership: How Intel, Microsoft and Cisco drive industry innovation.* Boston: Harvard Business School Press.

Hills, A. (1999). Wireless Andrew. *IEEE Spectrum, 36*(6), p49-53.

Hills, A., & Johnson, D. B. (1996). A wireless data network infrastructure at Carnegie Mellon University. *IEEE Personal Communications, 3*(1), 56-63.

Hudson, H. E. (2006). *Municipal wireless broadband: Lessons from San Francisco.* San Francisco: University of San Francisco.

Instat. (2007). Personal communication.

ITU. (1965). *From semaphore to satellite.* Geneva: International Telecommunication Union.

Jakobs, K., Hayes, V., Tuch, B., Links, C., & Lemstra, W. (Forthcoming). Towards a wireless LAN standard. In W. Lemstra & J. P. M. Groenewegen (Eds.), *The genesis of Wi-Fi and the road toward global success.*

Johnson, D. B. (2007). Personal communication.

Kamp, D. (2005). *Analysis of the emergence of Wi-Fi.* Delft: TUDelft.

Lansford, J. (1999). HomeRF: Bringing wireless connectivity home: Intel.

Lansford, J. (2007). Personal communication.

Lemstra, W. (2006). *The Internet bubble and the impact on the development path of the telecommunication sector.* TUDelft, Delft, The Netherlands.

Lemstra, W., & Hayes, V. (2009). License exempt: Wi-Fi complement to 3G. *Telematics & Informatics.*

Lemstra, W., Hayes, V., & Van der Steen, M. (2009). Network modernization in the telecom sector - The case of Wi-Fi. In R. W. Künneke (Ed.), *The governance of network industries: Redefining rules and responsibilities.* Cheltenham, UK: Edward Elgar.

Links, C. (2007). Personal communication.

Marcus, M. (2000). *Commercial spread spectrum.* Retrieved 2007-06-28, from http://www.marcus-spectrum.com/documents/Orlando_000.ppt

Marcus, M. (2007). Personal communication.

Mock, D. (2005). *The Qualcomm equation.* New York: AMACOM.

Moore, G. A. (1995). *Inside the tornado.* New York: Harper Business.

Murmann, J. P., & Frenken, K. (2006). Toward a systematic framework for research on dominant designs, technological innovations, and industrial change. *Research Policy, 35,* 925-952.

Negus, K. J., Stephens, A. P., & Lansford, J. (2000). HomeRF: Wireless networking for the connected home. *IEEE Personal Communications, Feb.*

Nelson, R. R., & Winter, S. G. (1977). In search of a useful theory of innovation. *Research Policy, 6,* 36-76.

Nelson, R. R., & Winter, S. G. (1982). *An evolutionary theory of economic change.* Cambridge, MA: The Belknap Press of Harvard University Press.

Ohrtman, F., & Roeder, K. (2003). *Wi-Fi Handbook - Building 802.11b wireless networks.* New York: McGraw-Hill.

Palo Wireless. (2003). *HomeRF overview and market positioning.* Retrieved 2007-08-07, from http://www.palowireless.com/homerf/homerf8.asp

Ricketts, M. (2002). *The economics of business enterprise - An introduction to economic organisation and the theory of the firm.* Cheltenham, UK: Edward Elgar Publishing.

Roberts, H. M. (2000). *Robert's rules of order - Newly revised.* Cambridge MA: DaCapo Press.

Sahal, D. (1981). *Patterns of technological innovation.* Reading, MA: Addison-Wesley.

Sahal, D. (1985). Technology guideposts and innovation avenues. *Research Policy, 14,* 61-82.

Schwartz, M. (1987). *Telecommunication networks: Protocols, modelling and analysis.* Reading, MA: Addison-Wesley.

Tanenbaum, A. S. (1996). *Computer networks* (Third Edition ed.). Upper Saddle River, NJ: Prentice-Hall.

Tapia, A., Stone, M., & Maitland, C. F. (2005). *Public-private partnerships and the role of state and federal legislation in wireless municipal networks.* Paper presented at the Telecommunications Policy Research Conference.

Tuch, B. T. (2007). Personal communication.

Tuch, B. T., & Masleid, M. A. (1991). Wireless information transmission system. USA: US Patent and Trade Mark Office.

Updegrove, A. (2005). Participating In Standard Setting Organizations: Value Propositions, Roles And Strategies. *Consortum Standards Bulletin, vol. 5*(no. 9).

Van de Ven, A. H., Polley, D. E., Garud, R., & Venkataraman, S. (1999). *The innovation journey.* Oxford, UK: Oxford University Press.

Van Nee, R. (2006). *Current status of Wi-Fi standardization.* Paper presented at the 9th Annual International Conference Economics of Infrastructures, Delft, the Netherlands.

Vijn, M., & Mourits, G. (2005). Wireless netwerk dekt Leiden. *Informatie, Okt.*

Von Burg, U. (2001). *The triumph of Ethernet.* Stanford, CA: Stanford University Press.

Von Hippel, E. (1988). *The sources of innovation.* Oxford, UK: Oxford University Press.

Von Hippel, E. (2005). *Democratizing innovation.* Cambridge, MA: MIT Press.

Walker, J. (2000). *Unsafe at Any Key Size: An Analysis of the WEP Encapsulation*: Intel.

Weiss, M. B. H., & Huang, K. C. (2007). *To be or not to be: A comparative study of city-wide municipal Wi-Fi in the US.* Paper presented at the Telecommunications Policy Research Conference.

Wi-Fi Alliance. (2007). *Get to know the alliance.* Retrieved 2007-08-16, from http://www.wi-fi.org

Wireless Leiden. (2006a). *Techniek.* Retrieved 2006-06, from http://www.wirelessleiden.nl/techniek/

Wireless Leiden. (2006b). *Wi-Fi.* Retrieved 2006-06, from http://wiki.wirelessleiden.nl/wcl/cgi-bin/moin.cgi/WiFi

ENDNOTES

[1] In relation to participation in the standards making process a more nuanced classification can be made in observers, adopters, contributors, and leaders, as well as opponents (based on: Jakobs, Hayes, Tuch, Links, & Lemstra, Forthcoming; Updegrove, 2005).

[2] Metcalfe proposed to increase the re-transmission intervals with increasing traffic loads. For a more extensive discussion of the technical features see Chapter 8 on Polling and random access in data networks in Schwartz (1987p403-47) and Chapter 4 the Medium access sublayer in Tanenbaum (1996p243-335).

[3] Included are the revenues from: 3Com, Bridge Communications, Cabletron, Chipcom, Corvus, Excelan, Gateway, Interlan, Nestar, Network Systems, Novell, Proteon, SynOptics, Sytek, Ungermann-Bass and Vitalink. Excluded are companies such as Apple, Datapoint, DEC, IBM, Intel, Wang and Xerox as no separate LAN revenues could be obtained. The product introductions are approximate (Von Burg, 2001p101, 218-9).

[4] The case history of Wi-Fi has first been summarized by Lemstra and Hayes, and published in the Journal *Competition and Regulation in Network Industries* Volume 9, No. 2, June 2008, pp 135-173.

[5] In 1873 Maxwell positioned the theoretical concept of electro-magnetic waves; in 1888 Herz was able to create, detect and measure

EM-waves; in 1894 Marconi used EM-waves to demonstrate the wireless telegraph.

6   The Federal Communications Commission is an United States government agency, directly responsible to Congress. The FCC was established by the Communications Act of 1934 and is charged with regulating interstate and international communications by radio, television, wire, satellite and cable. The FCC's jurisdiction covers the 50 states, the District of Columbia, and U.S. possessions (FCC, 2007).

7   The invention of spread spectrum, in the form of frequency hopping, dates back to 1942 when a patent was granted to actress Hedy Lamarr and composer George Antheil: U.S. Patent # 2,292,387, issued on August 11, under the title: "*Secret Communications System*" (Mock, 2005).

8   In 1988 the first real civil applications of spread spectrum appeared in the form of a Local Area Networks, e.g. the Gambatte MIDI LAN, which became very popular with top rock musicians. A derivative was used in nuclear power plants, under the name of Midistar – Pro. From 1990 onward the number of equipment authorizations by the FCC expanded significantly, see Marcus (2000).

9   At the time, Tuch was leading the wireless R&D efforts of the Utrecht Engineering centre.

10   The code's property: The periodic and aperiodic autocorrelation function of this 11 length code is "bounded" by one. Actually it turned out that this was a "known code" called the Barker Sequence used in Radar Systems that was "rediscovered".

11   An example is the participation of NCR in the Unix community for the development of their line of computers.

12   According to the PAR this taskgroup is denoted 802.4c which through a transcription error became 802.4l.

13   Hayes would serve as Chairperson of the IEEE 802.11 Working Group for 10 years, the maximum period allowed.

14   To reach agreement within the IEEE Working Groups and Task Groups individuals opposing a proposal in a vote have to explain the reasons for their opposition. By making these reasons explicit the group as a collective is invited to find ways to resolve the issue and if successful it has broadened the support for the resulting proposal.

15   Companies that were involved in HomeRF development included: Butterfly Communications, Compaq, HP, IBM, Intel, iReady, Microsoft, Motorola, Proxim, OTC Telecom, RF Monolithics, Samsung and Symbionics (Lansford, 1999).

16   According to Marcus, a consideration for choosing FH might have been that the 11 chip PN code defined in IEEE 802.11 Direct Sequence was questioned by some members of the FCC Office of Engineering and Technology to be in full compliance with the FCC rules.

17   Digital Enhanced Cordless Telecommunication; originally: Digital European Cordless Telephone.

18   Lansford has been Co-Chair of the Technical Committee for the HomeRF Industry Working Group and wireless system architect with Intel Corporation.

19   With the 1996 tri-vestiture of AT&T, the WLAN activities moved to Lucent Technologies.

20   Soon after the SAB approval, conforming products with either 1 Mbit/s FH and 2 Mbit/s DS appeared on the market. The third option, based on infrared, never made it into products.

21   Orthogonal Frequency Division Multiplexing.

22   Note that in Europe the 900 MHz band is used for GSM.

23 A HIPERLAN2 Global Forum was established to support its deployment, supported by e.g. Bosch, Dell, Ericsson, Nokia, Telia and TI (Palo Wireless, 2003).

24 The 13 channels were partly overlapping; only 3 channels were non-overlapping.

25 The security of Wireless LANs has remained an ongoing concern. With the approval of the IEEE 802.11-1997 standard the Wired Equivalent Privacy (WEP) algorithm was introduced, providing a basic authentication and encryption method. WEP was designed in the 1990s and was purposely weak, to remain within the confines of existing export requirements (Ohrtman & Roeder, 2003p61-85). In late 1999 and early 2000, initial attacks on WEP were identified and made public, just at the time when WLAN technology was becoming popular, and thus a fertile area of investigation for security researchers and an attractive target for hackers. Papers by Borisov, Goldberg, and Wagner (1999), and Walker (2000) discussed the vulnerabilities of WEP. While some businesses deployed WLAN technology in combination with Virtual Private Network and proprietary security solutions, the response by the industry was the development of an IEEE 802.11 standard-based solution, with interoperability certification developed by the WECA – later Wi-Fi Alliance.

26 At the time Links was Product Line Manager of WaveLAN.

27 Note that in another episode of corporate transformation Agere Systems had been incorporated in 2000 as subsidiary of Lucent Technologies, assuming the activities of the former Micro-Electronics Division, and including WaveLAN.

28 Between the use of Wi-Fi for-free in the home and for-a-fee in hotspots a new model has been introduced by Varsavsky in 2006 as FON. The business model of FON is aimed at opening up privately owned hotspots. The revenue from the FON Access Point is split 50/50 between the FON organisation and the "Fonera" owner (Crane, 2007; FON, 2007).

29 Sharing of Internet access is by (most) operators considered as an unintended use of the fixed network access facilities. Many operators have adjusted their supply contracts to make access sharing illegal. However, enforcement is a totally different matter.

30 See for details of the IEEE 802.11 architecture descriptions e.g. Orhtman and Roeder (2003).

31 Trials executed by the 'Wireless Leiden' organisation using appropriate antennas have demonstrated connectivity over 9 km with throughput of up to 500 kbyte/s (Wireless Leiden, 2006b). Applications in e.g. Tibet and the Andes have shown that Wi-Fi is very suitable for the realization of much longer point-to-point connections.

32 The 'master' machine of the "Node Factory" runs on FreeBSD 5.0 operating system. The version management is based on Subversion, an open source application that runs over the Web and that allows for 'anonymous' users. On this platform specific 'Wireless Leiden' functionality (Webweaving) has been added, as well as a configuration database (Genesis).

33 Tapia indicates that in 2005 over 100 cities have announced plans for municipal wireless (Tapia, Stone, & Maitland, 2005).

34 For a comparison of the two distinctly different development trajectories of Wi-Fi and cellular communications see Lemstra and Hayes (2009).

35 The IEEE for instance use the Robert's Rules of Order (Roberts, 2000).

36 In terms of the evolution metaphor Wi-Fi is being considered primarily within the product class of Wireless-LANs. When the role of Wi-Fi is considered as a public network

access solution it should also be considered in the class of network access products, and thereby to be compared with wireless access technologies, including Wi-MAX. Albeit, the two areas represent distinctly different design paradigms (Lemstra & Hayes, Forthcoming).

[37] The chart shows the number of contributions from each company having submitted 10 or more papers from the start of IEEE 802.11 in the period 1990 till the end of 1999. This count includes the documents provided for administrative purposes, such as meeting minutes, agendas, and ballot results.

Chapter IX
The Evolution of e.Business:
Can Technology Supply meet the Full Business Demand?

Tom McGuffog
UKP.eb, UK

ABSTRACT

In this chapter, the evolution of e.business is described. The ever-changing balance between demand and supply is outlined. The conclusion is reached that, while technology provides many solutions to long-standing issues, along with great opportunities to create and meet new demands, some fundamental business needs for cost-effective processes and security of communication have yet to be met. Furthermore, value chain management re-development is an essential pre-requisite of the successful application of e.business. Proposals for improvements are therefore also made.

INTRODUCTION

In the 1970s there was a growing demand to communicate trading messages electronically between customers and suppliers, in order to reduce costs and to improve customer service. However, the existing supply of technology did not then support this demand. Indeed, technology alone can never meet the communications requirements of business and administration. E.business only fulfils its potential when each business message unfailingly results in the recipient actioning precisely what the sender has asked for. Clearly, it takes more than technology alone to achieve this. Therefore, electronic technology and value chain management improvements need to develop in a mutually supportive manner[1].

A Value Chain is the overall combination of internal and external resources – human, physical, financial and data – which require to be marshalled and managed, directly and indirectly, in order to achieve the objectives of any organisation, and especially to optimise its net value and benefit to each participant. This is achieved through enhancing performance, speed, certainty, safety and security of service at low operational, capital and through life costs. In turn, these means can be optimised through the judicious employment of e.business, provided that more simple and standard business processes and data are also used by the value chain participants.

For example, until, in the later 1970s and early 1980s, when some more standard value chain processes and business messages were agreed, supported by standard item coding, along with the development of cost-effective communication networks for electronic data interchange (EDI), e.business supply could not begin to meet well key customer demands.

Since then, the demand for e.business has continued to grow rapidly. But, the supply of technological solutions has grown faster than the ability or willingness of many organisations to utilise these fully and economically. The advent of the Internet has provided many beneficial developments, such as e.mail, e.exchanges, e.catalogues, e.collaboration and other data files, along with the facility to communicate directly with most people and places. Nevertheless, the many technical enhancements have not obviated the need for organisations to simplify and standardise their internal and external value chain processes and data if they are to derive the full potential cost-effective benefits of collaborating electronically. Too often, both public and private organisations are unwilling to alter long-standing ways of doing business in order to gain the benefits from more simple, standard, speedy, certain and low cost value chain processes. Indeed, sometimes they unwisely believe that that the introduction of e.technology will of itself improve the quality of their processes and data.

Organisations rarely demand technology. They demand real benefits which the supply of technology can help to support, provided that the appropriate process and data architectures are in place in both senders and recipients of electronic messages. Sound organisations rarely wish to exchange every type of message with everyone. Certainty, security and well specified, sound communication frameworks are as equally important as speed and universality. In this chapter, the evolution of e.business is described. The ever-changing balance between demand and supply is outlined. The conclusion is reached that, while technology provides many solutions to long-standing issues, along with great opportunities to create and meet new demands, some fundamental business needs for cost-effective processes and security of communication have yet to be met. Furthermore, value chain management re-development is an essential pre-requisite of the successful application of e.business. Proposals for improvements are therefore also made.

THE EARLY HISTORY OF e.BUSINESS

I first became involved with e.business around 1970 when my company, Rowntree Mackintosh of York, UK (confectionery and food), was examining ways to reduce the costs and to improve the accuracy of invoicing customers, and thereby to improve the speed of payment. We considered the use of magnetic tapes delivered via couriers, but there was not a widely used standard for such tapes at that time, nor an agreed standard for most paper, let alone electronic, invoices. Thus, Supply could not meet Demand.

Nine track phase encoded magnetic tape had started to become more widely used, but there were many different and incompatible electronic media (tapes, cassettes, disks etc) either being re-developed, or becoming short-lived. Even within companies, point-to-point electronic communication was difficult, despite them being all 'IBM Blue' or devoted uniquely to another computer supplier.

Although the technical ability of electronic media to communicate directly with each other improved substantially in the 1970s, e.business did not begin to advance greatly until both business message standards and also standard product coding were introduced. The key industries involved in the earliest development of e.business were the finance and motor industries (using agreed message standards unique to each industry and even to each country, particularly the USA), and also the grocery and fast moving consumer goods (FMCG) industries – manufacturing, wholesaling and retailing – which first developed standard product coding, and then messages, in both the USA and UK. Parallel developments followed in Scandinavia, Germany and France.

FMCG product coding began in the USA via the Universal Product Code (UPC) system, and later developed globally via the European/International Article Number System (EAN – now Global Standards 1 - GS1). This enabled all firms to identify each consumer and traded unit in a standard way at the point of sale (via scannable symbols), across the value chain, and also within orders and invoices. This is a fundamental pre-requisite for the automatic processing and actioning of messages, aligned with the physical handling of stock items. The early alternative in e.messages was to describe items within Registered Text fields; but this was very susceptible to error.

In the USA, the American National Standards Institute (ANSI X12) standards for electronic data exchange became the main message standards. In the UK, the Article Number Association (ANA), which was responsible for product bar coding, set up an Electronic Data Interchange (EDI) standards group in 1979, which I chaired for many years. We called this the Trading Data Communications Standards Group (TRADACOMS), and it was instituted because many ad hoc electronic messages were being introduced by individual firms. Each dominant retailer, for example, was introducing its own standards for electronic invoicing as a result of which the cost and complexity of suppliers meeting these demands were growing rapidly.

We based the TRADACOMS standards on the United Nations Trade Data Interchange (UNTDI) syntax, which I found being developed and used (under the leadership of Don Trafford) by the UK Simpler Trade Procedures Board (SITPRO) to structure fax messages which facilitated international trade. The use of this standard, global syntax (or electronic grammar) was a key breakthrough, since, up to that point, e.message developments in Europe and North America were often hard-coded, and therefore difficult to develop, use and evolve.

Initially we provided standards for e.invoices, but soon thereafter for orders and two dozen other messages, including master data files which provided structured data on traded items and on value chain participants. The EAN codes provided sound linkages from the e.messages (which could therefore be a simple stream of codes and quantities) to the master data files (which provided the detailed descriptions of the products and traders). Even at that early stage we believed that master data files ought to be synchronised between customers and suppliers in advance of exchanging electronic messages in order to minimise subsequent errors and delays.

Major retailers wanted to reduce their costs of clearing suppliers' paper invoices, which most often had different formats and contents. Fortunately they recognised that a common standard was much preferable to those ad hoc approaches which individual companies had already introduced. Demand was leading Supply again.

THE MESSAGE STANDARDS

The TRADACOMS EDI Message Standards were developed and tested in 1980 and 1981 and published in five volumes in 1982[2]. These included all the main trading messages and master data together with compatible standard paper documentation. The Standards covered the then available main technologies - magnetic tapes, disks and some point-to-point communication. In parallel, Brian Doouss of Unilever and Donald Harris of Tesco were largely instrumental in persuading the UK government that electronic invoicing was legally acceptable via the 1980 Finance Act – some major countries have yet to achieve this.

We established at an early stage that the message standards had not only to be based on standard Data Elements (such as locations, consumer and traded units, quantities, prices, discounts), but also on agreed business Processes. The most fundamental of these is the Order Process[3]. An Order is (should be) for the delivery of one or more Items to one Location at one Date/Time. This is because a physical Delivery (and hence Delivery and Receipt Notes) can only be for one or more Items to one location at one Date/Time. Then the Invoice will match to the Delivery and back to the Order. In this way, both internal and external business processes AND computer systems will be most compatible and least prone to error.

While we persuaded most companies and FMCG industries to accept these principles, we had a number of battles to fight. For example, the tobacco industry at that time had different ways of specifying quantities across orders, invoices, consumer data and logistical data – dozens, hundreds, cases, etc. We insisted that they conform to the EAN standards for consumer units and traded (logistical handling) units for e.business purposes. On the other hand, Marks & Spencer would not budge from specifying their orders to suppliers in terms of all the items for all their receiving locations for a series of dates. Therefore we also specified an Order Picking/Complex Order message to meet their requirements, which were sub-optimal in terms of overall value chain effectiveness.

Thus, at that time, there was a relatively widespread and growing demand for e.business, which in turn required new, (mainly) standard business process and data architectures. However, their application was limited by the lack of cost-effective technologies, as well as by the inertia of some individual firms and industries.

ENCOURAGING SUPPLY TO MEET DEMAND

Having published tried and tested message standards in 1982, it soon became evident that there were severe practical and economic limitations to the exchange of e.messages by magnetic tape, or by point-to-point transmissions using the computing standards of the day (such as the two dozen versions of IBM's 2780 'standard').

We examined US experience of EDI networks, which tended to be relatively high cost and restrictive in their capability and availability, since they employed spare off-peak capacities in central mainframes across the world.

Therefore the TRADACOMS Group at the ANA specified a 'store and call forward' EDI network (TRADANET) which would employ the TRADACOMS standards. Only agreed standard messages would be sent from and to specified customers and suppliers. A sender would batch together all messages of one type (e.g. all orders prepared that day) and send them to the network, which would sort them by recipient and store them until they were called forward, along with all other such messages, by the specified recipient. A business could not receive a non-agreed or non-standard message from a non-agreed trader. Therefore, this network would be radically different, more cost-effective and secure, as well as more resilient, than the existing EDI facilities. The telecommunications links to and from TRADANET also had a relatively high degree of security. Thus, these early EDI developments offered a substantially greater degree of comprehensive security than many subsequent Internet developments.

Our standards development group had neither the capability nor the funds to develop and operate such a network. Therefore we specified and published an Invitation to Tender, hoping that at least a few companies would respond. In the event seventeen did so from across the world. We ran a 'beauty parade' over several days and eventually selected BARIC/ICL to work with us because they displayed both the commitment and the capability to build the network which we wanted, rather than merely to enhance what they already had. The charges for providing these new EDI services had to be substantially lower (e.g. one tenth) than any then available in order to make the facility economic for all types and sizes of business. That is, each business had to be able to use the one facility to communicate with all of its trading partners of any size. Thus we created a new definition of the demand for e.business facilities which had then to be supplied afresh.

Interestingly, the leader of the ICL team at that time was Chris Gent, who went on to head Vodaphone. One could argue that it, along with other mobile telephony companies, radically increased a limited consumer demand through imaginative technological development aided by skilful marketing. Supply started to lead demand in that market place, as it often does with a rapid pace of technological development. However, demand cannot lag too far behind or there will be 'boom-bust'.

One of my most memorable days took place towards the end of 1984 when the first trial of the TRADANET network took place. A number of manufacturers and retailers (including Rowntree Mackintosh, Cadbury, Unilever, Tesco, and Boots) each sent TRADACOMS orders and invoices to each other and called them forward for successful processing. Unlike most internal, let alone external, computer projects, this worked well first time due to the capability, enthusiasm and dedication of all the participants, including, of course, ICL.

The national launch of TRADANET then took place in April 1985, and its use expanded rapidly thereafter, not only in the UK but also abroad (e.g. Southern Africa and the Far East), since this supply model well met the pent-up demand.

Other industries, such as vehicles, pharmaceuticals and insurance, developed similar or equivalent networks and standards around the same period[4].

Of course, there had been electronic exchanges for financial transactions for several years. These mainly employed the SWIFT Standards[5]. As ever, financial organisations would rarely take account of other industries' standards, and they would often offer to their clients the electronic facilities they used themselves in order to 'lock' them in and to enhance their own revenues.

Then matters started to become (even) more complicated.

DEFINING REAL DEMAND AND KEEPING UP WITH SUPPLY

In the 1980s, as today, both computer users and governments were increasingly concerned about the market power of the large computer and software suppliers. Would a few companies become too dominant, and exploit their oligopolistic powers? Would technological development be stifled if proprietary standards were imposed on both computer users and small suppliers?

One response to these concerns was public and private sponsorship of Open Systems Interconnection Standards (OSI). It was believed by some that all would be well (or at least better) if all computer hardware and software could be developed to commonly agreed standards. Then users could buy equipment and software in the confidence that all subsequent developments and communications would be compatible. Some of us believed that, however worthy the objectives, this task was too complex, large and costly for the available (or indeed any) resources, and also that there are substantial limits to the ability, and the desirability, of official standardisation of technology to control market forces.

I well remember being berated in public at a Computer Aided Trade conference in the mid 1980s by a European Union official for daring to promote EDI instead of OSI, even although EDI was available and being used cost effectively by all sizes and shapes of firms in order to get round the problems of using different hardware and software.

Clearly there is an ongoing danger with proprietory standards, however imaginative they are. One firm's technological breakthrough can become another's barrier to market entry. Furthermore, people with practical experience in business and government are finding it increasingly difficult to spend the required time in standards committees. These may then be dominated by ICT companies (seeking not only to protect their own product offerings but also sometimes to disadvantage their competitors), by consultants, or by 'professional' standards makers. There always should be a balanced and business-experienced involvement in standards development, particularly because value chain management understanding is at least as important as e.competence.

EDIFACT

A not dissimilar issue arose in relation to the fact that the Americans were continuing to use ANSI X12 syntax for their EDI messages and many other countries were using UNTDI. It was naturally felt that it would be better if all countries used the same syntax and message standards, particularly for international trade. Since neither the USA nor the Europeans were willing to compromise, and since it was felt that further improvements could be made to both syntax and messages, a new standard began to be developed in agreement with some key ANSI and UNTDI users under the auspices of the part of the United Nations Economic Commission for Europe which dealt with trade facilitation (UN ECE CEFACT). A key driving force behind these developments, known as EDIFACT standards[6], was Ray Walker, the Chief Executive of SITPRO.

Rapid progress was made in developing the EDIFACT standards across the globe. They have many merits and continue to be widely used. As ever, a fundamental problem is how to define real,

ongoing user demand for each business process and data, and thereby for each standard data element and message. It has always been difficult to persuade different industries, and dominant firms and governments, that their needs are the same as others in terms of processes and data. EDIFACT has many merits and is widely used. However, the principal resulting problem is that, in order to gain widespread agreement to the EDIFACT standards, many options were included from which each user or group could choose what suited it best.

When business and administrative processes and their associated data are not defined and delimited in a rigorous way, standards are in danger of not being multilateral but rather bilateral. That is, each pair of users, or at least each industrial group, had now to pre-define in detail how the standards should be applied in practice by them. Consequently, some user groups tried to delimit the choices within EDIFACT to suit their business needs. For example, EAN International developed a version of EDIFACT called EANCOM[7]. This work was led by key e.business figures such as Peter Jordan, Andrew Osborne, and Pierre Georget. There are other similar partial standards. Multilateral international e.trading thereby did not become sufficiently easier. Within the USA ANSI X12, and within the UK TRADACOMS, continue to be used well and cost-effectively to this day for communicating the key value chain messages (orders, invoices, etc), because they have worked cost-effectively and securely, because it is time-consuming and costly to re-test message standards with all trading partner combinations, and also because, I believe, there is not yet an integrated business and e.business standard which offers sufficient attractions to encourage many businesses, governments, industries and institutions to adopt more simple and standard internal and external business processes and data across the principal value chains of the world.

This applies equally to the many attempts to persuade people to adopt common standards for e.business across the Internet. Defining a sound and committed demand is never easy in e.business, and even imaginative supply never guarantees demand, particularly if this involves making substantial internal changes in order to standardise systems and data. Far too often, it has been argued that organisations should build cross-reference tables which link their data definitions to each of their trading partners' own definitions. This is a potentially error-prone and expensive approach.

It is to be hoped that the Core Components work of UN CEFACT, in conjunction with ISO, ITU and IETC, will lead to an agreed universal data element dictionary. Great care needs to be taken that a data element, and messages with the same function, are not defined differently simply because various industries or governments wish this, and are not willing to compromise wisely. Furthermore, standard data definitions must be accompanied by standard value chain processes. For example, too many public sector organisations find it very difficult to recognise that the process by which they should be placing an order with a supplier should be exactly the same as for the private sector, particularly since most suppliers support both sectors.

SIMPL.e.BUSINESS

The fundamental principles which should govern the design and use of e.business standards were enshrined by my colleagues (Nigel Fenton, Nick Wadsley, Robin Kidd) and me within a framework which we called Simpl.e.business[8]. I asked for and received the approval of UN.CEFACT for this direction in 1998 and again in 2000[9]. In summary, the principles are – E.business messages should be based on agreed, simple, standard business Processes, such as - ' an Order should be for the delivery (or actioning) of one or more items (products or services) to one place at one date/time'.

Therefore a standard Order would indicate Order Type (delivery, movement, production, payment, treatment, etc) : unique Order Number : Customer (location code) : Supplier (location code) : Date/Time Required : Items (product or service codes) : Quantities and Totals. The syntax, data elements and messages should be independent of particular technologies, and thereby not susceptible to perpetual change. All descriptive data should be held within defined Master Data files which are accessed via standard codes. Master Data relate to – Traded Items (Products and Services, also their Prices/Costs, and also their Technical Specifications) : Value Chain Participants (Customers, Suppliers, Agents, Authorities, and Individuals) : Procedures (Processing Rules, Recipes, Treatments) : Ongoing, semi-permanent Value Chain Assets. Master Data should be pre-aligned among value chain Participants prior to the exchange of electronic messages in order to minimise errors and delays. For example, an order could be from a Doctor (Customer) to a Radiology Department (Supplier) to treat a specific Patient (Individual) employing a defined Procedure using a certain Machine (Asset). Actioning such a message should also involve automatically confirming, through scanning or radio frequency identification (RFID), that the correct treatment is being applied to the correct patient by the correct clinician.

In my General Theory of Value Chain Management Data[10], Dynamic Data files are also defined. These allow data on actions, events and outcomes to be compared with plans, budgets and expectations in order to measure performance.

In summary, this approach to structuring value chain management data is defined as- 'Optimum value, speed, certainty, safety, security and low total cost can only be achieved via agreed Objectives, standard Processes, Messages, Data, Identities, Auto Identities, Master Data and Dynamic Data.' This sequence of decision-taking must be followed before investments are made in computer networks and software.

THE WORLD WIDE WEB AND E.BUSINESS

The World Wide Web has enormous potential for quickly linking all people and organisations electronically. The Internet languages have been structured in such a way as to make screen images relatively easy to build and to use. Therefore, it takes many more coded instructions to construct an Internet message than an equivalent EDI message. In turn, an EDIFACT message contains more lines of code than an EANCOM message, which is longer than a TRADACOMS message. The more standard the processes and data, and the fewer the choices that have to be made by trading partners, in addition to the natures of the various languages and syntaxes, the shorter can be the messages and the easier they can be to interpret and to action.

Clearly, if all organisations and individuals possess Web-enabled facilities, and these are at a compatible level of development, the potential for universal e.business is immense. That potential is currently most often realised when the users are individuals sitting at screens and sending data to other individuals or systems. Therefore, the data often needs to be interpreted or corrected. The ultimate goal is for all businesses to be able to send, receive, process AND action ALL e.business messages (whether via the Internet or via other electronic means) AUTOMATICALLY. I define this ideal as Automated Data Interchange (ADI),which in turn depends on more simple and standard process and data architectures across all value chains wherever this is practicable and cost-beneficial.

There are many occasions when data needs to be received and processed in real time – for example for tracking and tracing valuable shipments or for valuing financial balances. Equally there are numerous situations in business and government when the receiving organisation is only going to process their messages when all the orders or invoices, for example, have been received from all their trading partners – once an hour, or once per picking, packing or production shift, or once per day or week depending on the nature of the business being done. Vast sums of money have been wasted developing on-line real time systems using the latest Internet technologies when a much simpler EDI-type approach (such as store and call forward, using a Value Added Network, or Virtual Private Network via the Internet) would have sufficed and would have been much cheaper. Thus technology availability, or its potential arrival, can sometimes distort the true nature of what is needed, by unwisely claiming that changing internal and/or external processes is unnecessary, or that understanding the true nature of your value chain is not that important, or that consistent coding and data standardisation can be avoided.

This is not the place to describe the many interesting developments in Internet software and systems, nor to predict what will be most valuable in the future. It is certainly true that such developments tend to run ahead of the abilities of most organisations to make sound and economic use of them. Few key decision-makers (and many of their advisers) understand what each new development should mean for their organisations, how well tested and stable each is, what might soon replace it, and therefore when and how much they should invest in it. Many businesses and governments have been, and continue to be, badly burned by investing too much too early in major Internet and other IT systems. Sound, clear and consistent objectives are vital, supported by well designed process and data architectures. Evolutionary prototyping of IT and e.business systems is infinitely preferable to the 'big bang' approach which is so often followed by disappointing consequences.

Nevertheless, great potential remains. The various Web Mark-up languages continue to evolve – HTML and SGML into XML, and via OASIS (Organisation for the Advancement of Structured Information Standards[11]) into e.business XML

(ISO 15000), and then UBL (Universal Business Language). There is also a Universal Modelling Language (UML) which can describe and document a process and automatically turn it into code; but, understandably, cannot tell you how good the process is nor optimise it. Such benefits depend on developments being made via Value Chain Management and elsewhere .

It is not many years since Web Services was announced as the latest solution to e.business which would allow all organisations to structure their messages in such a way that not only would all recipients be able to receive them, but also that these messages would be able to seek out the required systems and data within the recipients' networks and thereby automatically process the transaction. This is an amazing new technology, which, however, represents a potential nightmare for most recipients of external electronic messages, who have installed complex security systems and firewalls to prevent such incursions. As was stated by the inventor of the World Wide Web, Tim Berners-Lee – "The Web was originally conceived as a tool for researchers who trusted one another implicitly; strong models of security were not built in. We have been living with the consequence ever since."[12].

It is early days to comment on Web 2.0, let alone Web 3.0. Similarly, with Adaptive Intelligent Agents, and with the Semantic Web[13] and its structure of the Resource Development Framework (RDF Data Language), Ontology Languages and Inference Engines. They will offer much that is new, and also valuable, particularly in aiding the search for related data across many data files. However, it is to be doubted whether they can ever obviate the need for agreed, standard value chain processes and data. Indeed, it can be justifiably argued that technological specifications do not 'care' whether a process (or data) is 'good' or 'bad'. Computer technology aims to automate any process of any merit. Technical developments tend to be 'agnostic' about business process improvement. Thus, the supply of technology continues to race ahead of sound demand for certain, accurate and timely communications.

e.EXCHANGES

With the widespread use of Internet connectivity, many electronic exchanges were set up. Clearly, these have for long been of major benefit in certain industries, such as banking, finance, share dealing, foreign exchange, commodities, and aerospace. In other industries, such as FMCG and logistics, some of the early promise has not been fulfilled, sometimes because major companies would refuse to take part in an e.exchange used by their main competitors. Corralling competing businesses in some industries is like 'herding cats', and therefore expensive and unprofitable. This has been particularly true in relation to maintaining accurate, standard master data files for products and prices, on which e.exchanges depend.

One of the facilities offered by e.exchanges which has achieved most success has been e.auctions which allowed customers to invite bids from suppliers for well-defined and widely traded products.

International banking transactions are relatively easily conducted using the SWIFT standards and related networks and exchanges. One could not effectively buy and sell shares or foreign currency without electronic exchanges. Nevertheless, the technical ability to undertake such transactions must not encourage the users to ignore the risks and limitations. Wild swings in market prices, for example, have been made more extreme through the use of automatic buy/sell algorithms linked into electronic exchanges. Computerised mathematical models do not obviate the need of people to understand what is actually happening in the 'real world', and to mitigate their risks. A 'junk' bond is equally junk (or sub-prime) even when it is electronically traded, especially when it metamorphoses across the globe.

E.CATALOGUES

A sound alternative to e.exchanges for the purpose of accessing accurate data on products and prices is an electronic catalogue which is held on a supplier's computer. This most often applies to 'indirect' items, rather than the principal ingredients, components and packaging which are combined into finished products. This can be used for generating orders not only on the customer's computer, but also on the supplier's system. Such orders are then automatically and accurately turned into picking documents and delivery notes. Electronic invoicing may then be done in batches once per week or per month. Once more, an agreed sound business process can quickly and reliably become electronic reality.

ALIGNING MASTER DATA AMONG VALUE CHAIN PARTICIPANTS

Some exchanges have specialised in the pre-alignment, or synchronisation, of master data among trading partners. Much remains to be done in this arena. A key issue has been that 'silos' not only exist between firms, industries and governments, but also within each of these. For example, saying that Company X has agreed to support the standard electronic alignment of master data may only mean that its Logistics and Finance functions have agreed to do so, while its Buying function continues to insist on receiving product and price data to its own formats. Similarly, although many valiant attempts have been made to persuade governments to develop a Single Electronic Window by which businesses would identify themselves once to all government departments, departmental 'silos' too often insist on their own separate systems which are not thereby 'joined-up' for the user.

UN e.DOCS FOR INTERNATIONAL TRADING AT SITPRO

David Turner and I recognised that even with the global availability of the Internet, products still have to cross international boundaries at Customs Posts where there may not be a computer terminal, or a screen picture may not be accepted. Even where an up-to-date facility exists, paper documents may be essential. Therefore an e.business system called Web ElecTra was developed, which was then accepted by UN.CEFACT and named UN e.docs[14]. This allows standard international trade documentation to be sent and received electronically anywhere in the world, and then made available in the most appropriate form for each outpost.

S.T.E.P. STANDARDS FOR ENGINEERING

Good progress has been made in the development of standards to support computer aided design and manufacturing (CAD CAM) and the exchange of product model data. This includes those engineering developments which require separate organisations across the world to collaborate in the design, testing, manufacturing and lifetime support of complex equipment, including embedded software (which may account for a quarter of the total cost). For example, when an aeroplane and its engines require local maintenance or enhancement throughout their lives, this can take place safely and economically through secure electronic access of the required records held by the original manufacturers and others. The key standards here are STEP (Standard for the Exchange of Product Model Data - ISO 10303 – maintained by the TC 184 Committee[15]), for which a key figure in their development has been Howard Mason. These advances are good examples of where the demand for immediate, worldwide, and secure access to up-to-date and accurate data has progressively been delivered not just by technological advances, but also, importantly, by agreement among the key industrial and governmental players that they should and would agree to certain standard processes and data.

COLLABORATIVE EVENT MANAGEMENT (CEM)

There are many examples of e.business tools to support the management of Value chain operations or events, such as the development and launch of new products. As with the STEP standards, pre-agreed standard business processes and data are vital. In the 1990s, when I was Director of Planning and Logistics for Nestle UK, we found that many new product launches and promotional events were not taking place as agreed with retailers because quantities, dates and prices were being changed unilaterally, or because plans agreed at head office level were not known at shop or warehouse levels.

Therefore with supply chain and buying colleagues in Sainsbury, our sales, marketing and supply chain colleagues agreed a new well structured process for defining and managing product launches and promotions. This involved deciding who needed to know, to agree, and to communicate which information in sequence. I define this as a Role Model[16]. This process was then quickly converted into an Internet supported system by EQOS Ltd[17] (– Similar procedures were agreed in the US for Collaborative Planning Forecasting and Replenishment – CPFR[18]). Each participant in the CEM process was able to access appropriate computer screens showing data exactly the same data relevant to their roles, and indicating which information was provisional and which was 'final' – that is sufficiently stable to allow production, supply and distribution to

commence. Thus the buyer and the salesman would sit together and reach initial agreement on a promotion. This would be sent automatically to senior management for their agreement, and also to both supply chain departments to determine production and distribution dates and detailed quantity plans. All subsequent changes would be seen by all relevant staff in both companies. Final agreed data were then automatically communicated to each company's computer systems for onward distribution to all functions involved. In this way the scope for error and delay was minimised.

So successful was this EQOS Collaborative Event Management System that Sainsbury and Nestle were awarded the BT Prize for Innovation in e.business in 1998. Given a soundly defined process, it was not difficult for the available technology to support it. Hard work was then involved in ensuring that all staff in each function did what was required of them on time.

CONCLUSION

The Supply of e.Business technology has been outstripping the effective Demand for such capability for some time. In the 1970s and 1980s, much effort was put into agreeing standard processes and data for various industries, and then into developing electronic means of supply to meet this demand. Particularly with the advance of the Internet through the 1990s, technological developments have tended to race ahead of the ability and willingness of public and private organisations to implement these cost- effectively. This looks likely to continue, as a result of both Moore's Law and of electronic inventiveness. It is difficult, although vital, for businesses and governments to simplify and standardise their business processes and data architectures. There is always the tendency for management to make the processes (and hence the data) in any value chain more complex and more diverse than is necessary or wise. Furthermore, ICT suppliers have a vested interest in promoting proprietary standards and solutions, and business consultants rarely promote standard low-cost solutions. Competition is too often easier to employ than sound, and legal, collaboration with key value chain partners. Electronic technology R&D is not sufficiently driven by what business and government are capable of digesting. Politicians and chief executives still remain remarkably ignorant about the limitations of technology. Indeed, some still believe that outsourcing their IT and e.business will relieve them of the responsibility of addressing these vital business and economic issues.

The reason for sending a message to a value chain partner has always been to have it actioned in full and on time. The application of new electronic technology must always support that demand by enhancing speed, certainty safety, security and low total cost. When faced with a new technology, management must always ask themselves whether there is a real cost- effective opportunity, after fulfilling all the pre-requisites for success defined previously, and after mitigating the risks involved, to run a more valuable business with it or without it.

REFERENCES

Collaborative Planning Forecasting and Replenishment (CPFR), operated by VICS USA www.vics.org

Core Components – developed by UN/CEFACT with ISO, ITU and IETC. To be used, hopefully, by EDIFACT, ebXML, OASIS, and 'all' of e.business. – 2001-08. See also UNe.docs. www.unece.org/cefact

'D.I.A.M.O.N.D.– a General Theory of Value Chain Management Data – adding strength and sparkle to your value chain ' Tom McGuffog. UK Partners for electronic business. London, 2004.

EANCOM Standards supported by GS1 - www.gs1.org

EQOS Ltd. For details see www.equos.com

For details about OASIS see - www.oasis-open.org

Pharmanet served the pharmaceutical industry; Istel and Motornet served the vehicle industry, which tended to use the Odette standards; Limnet served the London insurance market .

SWIFT e.message standards serve the banking industry – www.swift.com

EDIFACT EDI Standards – United Nations Economic Commission for Europe, Standards for Administration, Commerce and Transport – version D.08A. Geneva, 2008

Simpl.e.business – paper by Tom McGuffog, Nigel Fenton and Nick Wadsley - e.centre.uk : b. 'B.e.e. Business enabled electronically, the future for e.business' – Tom McGuffog. UK Partners for electronic business. London, 2002.

Simpl.e.business – proposals from UK Delegation to plenary of UN/ECE.CEFACT. Papers in 1997/CRP10; 1998/4; 2000/24; 2002/32

For STEP standards, see - www.steptools.com . See also – www.ukceb.org.uk

'Web Science Emerges'. Nigel Shadbolt & Tim Berners-Lee. Scientific American Vol 299 No 4, October 2008

'Semantic Web'. L. Feigenbaum, I. Herman, T. Hongsermeir, E. Neumann, S. Stephens. Scientific American Vol 297 No 6, December 2007

The Fundamental Value Chain Process – from Plan to Payment – Tom McGuffog –British Standards Institution ICT4 Paper. London, 2007 www.bsi-global.com

The TRADACOMS Electronic Data Interchange Message Standards – The Article Number Association (then e.centre.uk, now GS1 UK). London, 1982 - www.gs1uk.org. See also www.gs1.org

The Value Chain Forum of the Chartered Institute of Logistics and Transport – www.ciltuk.org.uk - to be published in Spring 2009

ENDNOTES

1   The Value Chain Forum of the Chartered Institute of Logistics and Transport – www.ciltuk.org.uk - to be published in Spring 2009

2   The TRADACOMS Electronic Data Interchange Message Standards – The Article Number Association (then e.centre.uk, now GS1 UK). London, 1982 - www.gs1uk.org. See also www.gs1.org

3   The Fundamental Value Chain Process – from Plan to Payment – Tom McGuffog –British Standards Institution ICT4 Paper. London, 2007 www.bsi-global.com

4   Pharmanet served the pharmaceutical industry; Istel and Motornet served the vehicle industry, which tended to use the Odette standards; Limnet served the London insurance market .

5   SWIFT e.message standards serve the banking industry – www.swift.com

6   EDIFACT EDI Standards – United Nations Economic Commission for Europe, Standards for Administration, Commerce and Transport – version D.08A. Geneva, 2008

7   EANCOM Standards supported by GS1 - www.gs1.org

8   Simpl.e.business – paper by Tom McGuffog, Nigel Fenton and Nick Wadsley - e.centre.uk.

9   Simpl.e.business – proposals from UK Delegation to plenary of UN/ECE.CEFACT. Papers in 1997/CRP10; 1998/4; 2000/24; 2002/32

10   'D.I.A.M.O.N.D.– a General Theory of Value Chain Management Data – adding strength and sparkle to your value chain ' Tom McGuffog. UK Partners for electronic business. London, 2004.

11   For details about OASIS see - www.oasis-open.org

12   'Web Science Emerges'. Nigel Shadbolt & Tim Berners-Lee. Scientific American Vol 299 No 4, October 2008

13   'Semantic Web'. L. Feigenbaum, I. Herman, T. Hongsermeir, E. Neumann, S. Stephens. Scientific American Vol 297 No 6, December 2007

14   Core Components – developed by UN/CEFACT with ISO, ITU and IETC. To be used, hopefully, by EDIFACT, ebXML, OASIS, and 'all' of e.business. – 2001-08. See also UNe.docs. www.unece.org/cefact

15   For STEP standards, see - www.steptools.com . See also – www.ukceb.org.uk

16   'B.e.e. Business enabled electronically, the future for e.business' – Tom McGuffog. UK Partners for electronic business. London, 2002.

17   EQOS Ltd. For details see www.equos.com

18   Collaborative Planning Forecasting and Replenishment (CPFR), operated by VICS USA www.vics.org

Chapter X
China's Practice of Implementing a 3G Mobile Telecommunications Standard:
A Transaction Costs Perspective

Mingzhi Li
Tsinghua University, China

Kai Reimers
RWTH Aachen University, Germany

ABSTRACT

This chapter analyses and evaluates the Chinese government's 3G policy of supporting the creation and implementation of the country's indigenous TD-SCDMA standard. On the supply side, the addition of a new standard has enriched choices available on the 3G mobile telecommunications market; however, on the demand side, the government had to force operators to adopt this standard due to their lack of interest in the new standard. Building on insights gained from North's theory on the transaction costs of politics, the authors explain this standardization process as a result of interaction between the political market and the economic market which has ultimately been driven by ideology shifts that took place on multiple levels of China's society in recent years. They contribute to the standardization literature by demonstrating how North's theory can be used for integrating political and economic aspects in the analysis of standardization processes.

But it is political markets in non-democratic polities that urgently need ... transaction costs analysis. The far greater imperfections of such markets in communist and Third World countries are the root of their poor economic performance since it is polities that devise and enforce the property rights that are the incentive structure of economies. Douglas North, a Transaction Cost Theory of Politics, 1990

The exceptions in the modern world to the representative polity as a prerequisite to economic growth suggest the high pay-off from modeling the political process in third word countries.
Douglass North, Institutions and Credible Commitment, 1993

I INTRODUCTION

Generally speaking, there are three mechanisms in coordinating industry standards selection and standardization processes: (1) the committee approach, including trade associations and standards developing organizations (SDOs); (2) the market leadership approach, either led by a single dominant market player or through consortia and alliances; (3) by government fiat. While the first two approaches may be categorized as "voluntary" and are gaining more and more dominance in mature economies, recently a renewed interest in initiating and facilitating IT standardization processes by the state can be observed, especially in the EU (Anonymous, 2008).

In line with this trend, the Chinese government has been strengthening its involvement in the development and implementation of standards in the ICT industry in recent years, which provides a good case study for studying government behavior in the ICT standards setting and standardization process. With rapid globalization of the ICT markets, it is foreseeable that battles over control of industry standards will become more and more fierce. Lessons learned from the China case will have implications not only for the national strategy of emerging economies in similar stages of economic development as that of China; rather, firms and governments in more developed economies can also gain insights regarding how to better penetrate emerging ICT markets in this ever more integrated business world.

As summarized in Suttmeimer and Yao (2004), the Chinese government's strong support for developing its domestic ICT industry standards comprises: China's 3G mobile phone standard "TD-SCDMA"; an alternative to the Windows operating system standard through the promotion of Linux; its own successor to DVD's, the "EVD" (Enhanced Versatile Disc) standard; a new digital audio standard (AVS—Audio, Video Coding Standard) for MPEG (Moving Picture Experts Group); a Chinese-developed standard IGRS (Intelligent Grouping and Resources Sharing) for communicating among digital devices; and standards concerning radio frequency identification tagging (RFID). The introduction of a new security standard for wireless devices, the WLAN Authentication and Privacy Infrastructure (WAPI) standard, has received international attention and become a major issue in U.S.-China trade relations. Most recently, the central government's Standardization Administration has decided to integrate two domestic digital TV transmission technologies, developed by Tsinghua University and Shanghai Jiaotong University respectively, to form the national standard for digital broadcasting in place of the previously adopted European standards.

While the most cited rationale for developing and adopting domestic ICT standards has been the hope for eliminating or reducing royalty payments to foreign intellectual property (IP) holders, the cost of this practice has been obvious and significant. After years of efforts directed at developing the industry value chain based on the TD-SCDMA standard, China's 3G mobile networks have still not been put in place; while the government had announced that the digital TV broadcasting standard would be implemented by August 2007, the implementation date has been delayed indefinitely. Almost all the efforts spent on the other ICT standards initiatives are encountering significant obstacles as well.

Motivated by the policy acts aforementioned, this chapter attempts to build a transaction cost perspective for explaining government behavior in a country's information technology standards development and implementation process, especially for an emerging country such as China which is a latecomer in the game of IT standards setting but has ambitious goals of catching up with world leaders. We particularly single out China's indigenous 3G mobile telecommunication standards, TD-SCDMA, as our main focus for the following reasons: the telecommunications industry is one where both markets and committees play a role in standards setting and where the interaction of firms and governments are not well understood (Funk and Methe, 2001; Besen and Saloner, 1988); among all the IT standards promotion efforts in China, TD-SCDMA is the most prominent one which has been used by the government as a showcase for its efforts of building an innovative society which reflects a shift of ideology on multiple levels of the society in recent years, which can help better understand events in similar cases. On the theoretical front, this chapter makes a contribution to the literature by applying insights from the transaction costs theory of politics proposed by North in an effort of explaining government behavior in the IT standards creation and diffusion process in situations where economic and political markets are not clearly separated, as is typically the case for developing countries and emerging economies. In particular, we try to test whether North's ideas about the role of ideology and organizations in shaping the political process can provide valid explanations for the interplay between the economic market and the political market for the case of IT standardization processes.

The chapter is organized as follows: Section II reviews relevant literature on the role of government in the creation and diffusion of mobile telecommunications standards; in Section III we build a transaction cost perspective for analyzing government behavior in IT standards setting, especially for the case of a developing country, based on North's theory on the transaction costs of politics; Section IV gives a detailed account of the development process of China's TD-SCDMA 3G standards; in Section V we apply the theory developed in Section III to the analysis of the China case, and Section VI concludes the chapter.

II LITERATURE REVIEW: THE ROLE OF GOVERNMENT IN THE CREATION AND DIFFUSION OF MOBILE TELECOMMUNICATIONS STANDARDS

Government's involvement in ICT industry standards and standardization processes has always been a controversial issue, both from an academic and from a practical perspective. While more and more people believe that issues related to ICT standards ought to be settled by market forces rooted in beliefs in the principle of the "survival of the fittest", there are also strong voices calling for the active involvement of the government: "If standards are an impure public good (as we believe they are), then the government has not only the right but the duty to intervene when the private sector fails. We believe that the beginnings of the failure—as evinced by either chaos or monopoly—are beginning to be seen." (Cargill and Bolin, 2007)

Interestingly, a book edited by Steinbock and Noam (2003) contains arguments both in favor of and against heavy government involvement in the processes of mobile telecommunications standardization. For example, Sugrue (2003), former head of the FCC Wireless Bureau, argues that the advantages of having the market set the standards for mobile telecommunications systems outweigh those of government-sponsored universal standards, even if no single standard emerges, as was the case in the USA. Conversely, Economides (2003) in the same book claims that the failure of the government to ensure the development of a single standard for mobile communications is one of the main factors accounting for the falling behind of the USA in this technology.

There are also some reconciliatory views toward the role governments should play in the mobile telecommunications standards setting processes. For example, Funk and Methe (2001) show that both governments and firms had a strong effect on the creation of global standards in the mobile communication industry through a hybrid system of committees and markets, and that governments can and did influence forecasted installed base and thus had a strong effect on the demand and the number of standards as well as on their degree of openness.

The policy issues related with China's information technology industry standards setting and standardization processes has also caught attention in the information systems literature in recent years. Gao (2007) investigates China's experience of developing and deploying wireless local area network (WLAN) and analyzes the social, institutional and technological elements that influence the process of WLAN standardization. Reimers and Li (2007) propose a transaction cost perspective on evaluating the government's policy of creating an indigenous 3G standard and argue that introducing this new standard will likely increase transaction costs on both the user and the supplier sides. The current paper builds on these previous efforts of analyzing China's standardization policies; specifically, it documents more recent developments concerning TD-SCDMA and it provides more details of the whole process of the standard creation and implementation process; the paper contributes to the standardization literature by demonstrating how, through application of North's transaction cost theory, the interaction of economic and political markets typical for standardization processes in developing countries can be addressed and understood.

III A TRANSACTION COST PERSPECTIVE OF UNDERSTANDING GOVERNMENT'S ROLE IN IT STANDARDS CREATION AND DIFFUSION BASED ON NORTH'S TRANSACTION COST THEORY OF POLITICS

As summarized in Section II, most of the academic literature on government's involvement in IT standards has been following the neoclassical methodology and did not take the transaction costs of standardization processes into consideration. In addition, the IT standards literature has been biased toward the experiences of global leaders in this industry, including the US, Europe, Japan and Korea. The experiences of emerging economies such as China and India who are playing the catch up game have been largely neglected (however, cf. Reimers and Li, 2007, and Gao, 2007).

In the case of mobile communications standards, almost every country's government has played some role in the selection of standards and their subsequent adoption process. How to rationalize differences and commonalities in such engagement has become an interesting question from both academic and practical perspectives. We believe insights from transaction cost theories can substantially complement this line of research and help build an integrated view of the government's role in shaping IT standards creation and diffusion. While the concepts of transaction costs have been successfully utilized in the analysis of a variety of industries, North extends the idea of transaction costs into the analysis of political markets, where transactions are interpreted as *"vote trading"* or *"log rolling"* in order to understand how agreements are achieved in the political market (North, 1990).

In North's (1990) framework forms of governance are treated as behavior of organizations on economic markets which is influenced by formal and informal institutions through affecting levels of transaction costs (organizations are the players, institutions are the rules of the game). Some organizations engage in the production of new knowledge which, if incorporated into products, becomes technical change on economic markets. In addition, some organizations also engage in activity on political markets in order to affect institutions (and thus the rules of the game played on economic markets). Whether such political activity results in transaction cost reducing or increasing changes of the institutional framework largely depends on ideology (which thus becomes a major force in explaining rise and decline of whole societies). The influence of ideologies increases as uncertainty regarding outcomes of political transactions increases. In analogy to the entrepreneur who drives technical progress on economic markets, North (1981) also introduces the political entrepreneur who drives change on political markets (whose activity is in addition to the political activity of organizations). As for whether the tools of transaction costs can be applied to the analysis of situations in developing countries where the political markets are qualitatively different from those of democratic societies, he argues that "It is political markets in non-democratic polities that urgently need such transaction costs analysis. The far greater imperfections of such markets in communist and Third World countries are the root of their poor economic performance since it is polities that devise and enforce the property rights that are the incentive structure of economies." (North 1990, page 364). As will be shown in Section IV and V, in developing countries like China, the boundary between the economic market and the political market is usually blurred, and ideology in the disguise of national pride drives entrepreneurs to initiate changes in the institutional environment, which then directly or indirectly shapes the governance of transactions. Understanding the mechanism through which these forces engage

in interaction remains a daunting task, and cases like the efforts and conflicts in the promotion of indigenous information technology standards can help accumulate empirical evidence and to formulate promising research directions.

IV CASE DESCRIPTION: DEVELOPMENT AND IMPLEMENTATION OF TD-SCDMA[1]

Origin of the Standards

The major figure driving the creation of the TD-SCDMA (Time Division-Synchronous Code Division Multiple Access) standard was Mr. Li Shihe, a chief engineer at a research institute affiliated with the former Ministry of Postal and Telecommunications, which was later divided into two separate ministries, the Ministry of Post and the Ministry of Information Technology Industry. Mr. Li was among the first group of intellectuals who were selected to study in the west after China's economic reform and open door policy was implemented in the late 1970s. After getting his doctoral degree from the University de Montreal, Canada, Mr. Li returned to his research institute and became fascinated by the development of the world's emerging mobile communication technology. While the markets for both mobile communication exchange equipment and terminal devices were then dominated by foreign companies, Mr. Li was instrumental in initiating China's first mobile communications network design and the selection of equipment in 1985. He also helped the city of Jiangyin in developing mobile analogue services and devices.

The reality and prospect of China's economic development and his accumulated experience stimulated Mr. Li's ambition. He started to shift his attention from developing products based on existing standards to setting up China's indigenous standards, arising out of his consistent belief that there is not much difference among the different

3G mobile technologies from a technological perspective and that it is ultimately a game of distributing economic wealth as a result of creating artificial intellectual property protection.

In 1993, while Qualcomm developed the CDMA (Code Division Multiple Access) technology, Mr. Li was also doing similar research and trying to figure out how to outplay Qualcomm. Soon after, he was promoted to the position of the Vice Director of the Ministry of Post and Telecommunications' Institute of Research on Telecommunications Science and Technology and got to know two key figures who were also critical to the design of the TD-SCDMA standards, Mr. Chen Wei and Mr. Xu Guanghan. Mr. Chen was a project manager at Motorola's semiconductor division and Mr. Xu was an Assistant Professor at the University of Texas at Austin. Mr. Chen and Mr. Xu were trying to design a solution compatible with CDMA, but they were not able to reach a deal with Qualcomm regarding patent rights and therefore decided to shift to a new design, SCDMA (Synchronous Code Division Multiple Access). In June of 1994 the three of them talked for three days behind closed doors and decided to adopt TD (Time Division) as the key element.

In Spring 1995, the then Head of the Bureau of Science of the Ministry of Post, Mr. Zhou Huan, had a meeting with the three people in a classroom at the University of Texas at Austin. After talks which lasted for four days, they came up with a prototypical design called TDS. In 1995 a joint venture named Xinwei Communications Technology Co Limited was created, with investments from the Ministry of Post and Telecommunications' Institute of Research on Telecommunications Science and Technology and another private Company.

Becoming One of the Three International 3G Standards: Playing the National Card

Even today, Mr. Li Shihe believes that "the advantage of TD-SCDMA lies in its playing of the national card" and that there is a clear economic rationale for this strategy since "the investment on upgrading or replacing the current 2G networks will be in the range of several hundred millions of dollars".

In 1997 the Ministry of Post and Telecommunications held a meeting, discussing whether to submit the TDS design to the Institute of Telecommunications Union (ITU). Most participants in this meeting objected to the idea of joining the game which had always been played by foreigners. Mr. Zhou and another high ranking official supported the idea and insisted that "there has to be the first time and it is worthwhile to have a try."

In November 1998, the ITU Study Group 8 (SG 8) - Mobile, radiodetermination, amateur and related satellite services - held its 15th conference in London and decided to eliminate some of the 10 proposals put forward by Japan, South Korean, Europe, China and the US. At that moment the US-backed CDMA 2000 and the EU-backed WCDMA were engaged in a fierce battle and they were strongly against the TD-SCDMA standards proposed by China. After Mr. Zhou Huan appealed to the Ministry of Information Technology of China for help, the Ministry issued a letter to the relevant multinational companies' Chinese divisions, warning them of the consequences of killing TDS. "Mr. Zhou has been helping us stand the pressures from all the directions", said Mr. Li Shihe, "Without his support, TDS wouldn't have survived till today."

Finally, in May 2000, on the ITU conference held in Turkey, the TDS standards proposal put forward by China's Datang Group (the former Institute of Research on Telecommunications Science and Technology of the Ministry of Information Technologies with Mr. Zhou Huan as Chairman of the Board of Director) was named one of the three 3G standards, together with Europe's WCDMA and the Qualcomm's CDMA2000.

Formation of the TD-SCDMA Industry Alliance: Government Support of the Standard

The government has always been relentlessly supporting the development of the TD-SCDMA standards. In October 2000, the State Planning Committee, the Ministry of Science and Technology and the Ministry of Information Technology jointly pushed the major mobile communications organizations including Datang, Huawei (a major competitor of Cisco in the equipment manufacturing market) and Zhongxing (the number two communication devices manufacturer in China) to form the TD-SCDMA Industry Alliance. At that time, Siemens, the only international supporter of TD-SCDMA which had already gradually lost its confidence in the technology, decided to enlarge its R&D support for development of the standard in view of China's strong backing of it.

In fact, before the formation of the alliance, the major firms such as Zhongxing, Huawei and Putian (a major state-owned information products manufacturer in China) had all put a high stake in the development of products based on the WCDMA and CDMA2000 standards. Except for Datang, all these firms and the major telecom operators had some difficulty in understanding why China wanted to foster a new standard, given the fact that the two mature standards had already been commercialized in other countries.

In December 2003, the then Chairman of China Mobile's Board of Directors, Mr. Wang Xiaochu, openly declared the company's desire to adopt WCDMA as its standard, only supplemented by TDS. He said, "Let alone the fact that the equipment manufacturers for TD-SCDMA don't have the sufficient capability, it is a difficult choice per se for the operators to choose TD."

Since the formation of the alliance, Datang has opened many patents to the firms in the alliance urged by government pressure. Initially Mr. Li Shihe and Mr. Zhou Huan both had difficulty accepting this order, but later on they convinced themselves that they were doing this for the interest of the nation. Mr. Li Shihe questioned the attitude of the domestic firms and operators: "when we see the possibility of success, shouldn't we have some sentiments for our own technology?", "In Japan and Europe, it was the government who decided which standards their operators needed to adopt. Telecommunication is a special industry which cannot fully depend on the market force. It must be decided by the government regarding what systems and what technologies to be adopted by the operators.", "What we are doing is beyond the scope of firm behavior, it is a national behavior."

Process of Commercializing the Standards

In 2000, the Institute of Science and Technology of the Ministry of Information Technology where Mr. Li Shihe worked was transformed into the Datang Telecommunications Science and Technology Development Corporation, with Mr. Zhou Huan as the Chairman of the Board of Directors and the President as well. In September, Mr. Li indicated that China's telecom operators would be able to run their networks based on the TD-SCDMA standards, and the major mission of Datang would be to ensure the technology was mature and to commercialize it.

But when it came to the year of 2001, there had not been a single TDS-based phone being put into use. At that time, 3G technology was already in use internationally which put great pressure on Mr. Li and his colleagues. Out of their commercial interest, the international equipment companies vehemently lobbied the Chinese government and urged the issue of 3G licenses. TDS and Datang faced the danger of being abandoned by the market. In this difficult moment, the Ministry of Information Technology organized a 3G technology test of all the three standards and reached the conclusion in April 2002 that WCDMA and CDMA2000 were not ready for commercial use.

In the first half of 2003, the European Union once again urged China to adopt WCDMA, and in the autumn of that year, executives of multinational communications equipment companies also sped up their efforts of trying to open the China market by persuading the Chinese government to issue 3G licenses. However, in order to give sufficient time for the TD-SCDMA standards to mature, the government didn't issue a single 3G license until 2008, despite all the continuous lobbying and public speculation about the timing of issuing the licenses.

After several small scale trials in some cities in April 2008, partly in anticipation of the demands from the Beijing Olympics, a large-scale test and commercialization project was initiated in eight large cities including Beijing, Shanghai, Guangzhou, Shenzhen etc., in which 60,000 TD-SCDMA based 3G device terminals were put into usage. However the results were far from fulfilling the expectations, problems such as insufficient amounts of base stations, instable signals, low transmission rates, and blurred image were exposed.

Forced Carrier of the TD-SCDMA Standards: China Mobile

Up to the year 2008, in China's mobile telecommunications markets there were two firms competing, China Mobile and China Unicom. China Mobile had been in the dominant position. In 2007, China Mobile's net profits were even greater than the total revenue of China Unicom. The ongoing telecom restructuring will most likely force China Mobile to adopt the TD-SCDMA standard in order to leverage the company's sound financial situation for the further nourishing of the standards. However, from the beginning China Mobile preferred to adopt WCDMA as its 3G standards since the transition from its 2G GSM standards would be much smoother.

As early as 2003, Mr. Yang Zhiqiang, vice director of the Technological Division of China Mobile, pointed out at the "2003 TD-SCDMA International Forum" that WCDMA is most suitable for the evolution of GSM which will realize the most scale economies and make the consumers enjoy 3G services at the lowest costs. In mid-2005, Vice President of China Mobile, Mr. Lu Xiangdong, indicated that China Mobile had already provided WCDMA services and hoped to get a WCDMA license. In early 2006, the President of China Mobile, Mr. Wang Jianzhou, declared that China Mobile would like to go directly to HSDPA(3.5G). Soon after, China Mobile started to build its EDGE network.

In February 2006, China Mobile's plan of a national test of WCDMA was called off by the government and it was ordered to start building TD-SCDMA pilot networks. Following the order of the Ministry of Information Technology, some already existing parts in the WCDMA pilot networks were demolished and the building of the data supporting facility was stopped.

One of the reasons why China Mobile was hesitant about adopting the TD-SCDMA standards was that it had no confidence in the standards developer, Datang. Datang initiated development of the TD-SCDMA standards in 1999, however, since 2006 with ever escalating demands for capital, it could only operate on loans. The reason why the government assigned the task of developing the TD-SCDMA standards to Datang was related to its government connection. "After some contacts with Datang Mobile, I gradually felt that it did not look like a R&D corporation, but rather a research institute run by the state. You can find all the problems of a SOE and a state-run research institute. I was starting to question its capability and whether it could really push TD-SCDMA to the market, " said Mr. Shi Wei, director of the Market and Industry Division of the Economic Reform and Management Institute affiliated with the State Committee on Development and Reform, "In 2006, I got to know that Datang was short in financing its R&D on TD-SCDMA and did not have many channels to obtain new funding.

At that time I thought that it would be better to have Huawei to be the R&D conductor of TD-SCDMA ". (The Troubled Commercial Test of TD-SCDMA, *IT Times Weekly*, April 28, 2008, in Chinese, Translated.)

Compared with those of WCDMA and CDMA2000, the R&D investment in TD-SCDMA was quite smallish. In theory, the investment on TD should come from several channels including government's subsidy, investment from the capital market, industry research funds and companies' own investment. However, up to 2006, the support from the government to Datang directly and indirectly was only several hundred million RMB, and some funds specified by the government for the purpose of supporting the TD pilot were not in place. Datang suffered losses in every year and therefore had quite limited funds to spend on R&D.

Value Chain Created by the TD-SCDMA Standards

The economic benefits envisioned by the TD-SCDMA advocates consist of the billions of dollars in the industry value chain to be created based on the standard; in addition, the standard is believed to enable reductions in royalty payments to international patent holders such as Qualcomm. Also, it was hoped to create more market opportunities for China's firms in the equipment manufacturing industry.

However, since China Mobile started to test the technology in eight cities, the results have been less than stellar. BDA China, a consulting and market research firm focusing on the telecom, media and technology sectors (TMT) in China and other emerging markets, said in a report that its analysts tested some TD-SCDMA phones and found problems including "erratic service quality, expensive and immature handsets, weak transmission signal and limited coverage." (WSJ, June 30, 2008)

Currently TD lags behind WCDMA by about 5 to 10 years, and WiMAX has already become another 3G standard and will compete directly with TD-SCDMA since both standards use the same frequency.

In addition to the problem of inadequate network coverage, the immaturity in handsets is another major setback. Compared with the several hundred types of handsets available for WCDMA, TD-SCDMA only had six. It is anticipated that once TD-SCDMA is put into large scale commercial use, it will be plagued by an insufficient amount of handsets of poor quality if support from first class manufacturers cannot be secured.

In fact, the drawbacks in handsets availability reflect the problem of the bottleneck in microprocessors. The firms supplying microprocessor chips for TD-SCDMA don't have enough experience and cannot be expected to catch up with the more mature technology in a short period of time. Since TD is not a mainstream 3G technology, most international handsets firms put their major investment on WCDMA, and only several domestic firms are working on development of TD-SCDMA based 3G handsets.

V CASE ANALYSIS: INTERACTION OF POLITICAL AND ECONOMIC MARKETS DRIVEN BY IDEOLOGY

Among all the efforts of promoting indigenous information technology standards, the case of TD-SCDMA has been deemed the most successful in China. Despite all the difficulties it has encountered, it is most likely the TD-SCDMA standards will survive and prevail for some time in the Chinese market with the strong support from the government. North's theory of the interaction between the economic market and the political market and the idea that economic policies are shaped by ideology and political and economic entrepreneurs can help elucidate the logics therein.

Ideology Shift: From Attracting FDI to Building an Innovative Society

Suttmeier and Yao (2004) coined the term *"New Techno-Nationalism"* to describe China's efforts of promoting its indigenous IT standards, which has caused some fierce rebuttals from the Chinese IT community claiming that China's practice should be called *"New Globalism"* rather than *"New Techno-Nationalism"*.

While *"New Techno-Nationalism"* refers to the case that "technological development in support of national economic and security interests is pursued through leveraging the opportunities presented by globalization for national advantage" (Suttmeier and Yao, 2004, page 1), the core ideas behind *"New Globalism"* call for "the late coming nations and firms to join the game of standard setting, to overcome the inefficiency in the global community through elimination of the monopoly power in the standards setting procedure" (New Globalism: A Research Report on China's High Technology Standards Strategy, ChinaLabs, 2004.)

Regardless of the terms being used, this controversy indeed reflects the Chinese society's rethinking on its strategy of "exchanging" markets for technology which has been believed to be a success story in the world, as reflected in a high-ranking government official's following remarks.

The TD-SCDMA standard is our nation's first complete communications system standard which has been accredited by the international community. It will be of great significance for changing of our country's backward situation in mobile telecommunications industry and for improving our capability of autonomous innovation and our core competence. The industrialization of TD-SCDMA is an important breakthrough in autonomous innovation of our country's high technology field, and has accumulated precious experiences for speeding up the upgrading of our country's industry structure, and for building an innovative society. — Mr. Lou Qinjian, Vice Minster of the Ministry of the Information Technology Industry

A popular argument circulating in the Chinese business and government circles also shows the eagerness of their efforts to catch up in the battle for controlling standards,

Third class companies make products; second class companies develop technology, and first class companies set standards. (Quoted in Suttmeier and Yao, 2004, page 1)

It is in this changing environment shaped by the society's ideological shift that political and economic entrepreneurs such as Mr. Li Shihe and Mr. Zhou Huan have been able to acquire relevant knowledge and successfully lobby the government to support creating the organization for developing and diffusing the TD-SCDMA standard.

The Blurred Boundary Between Political and Economic Markets

Dixit (1996) extends North's ideas and develops the notion that economic policy making is a dynamic process and concludes that "A policy rule and institution created for one purpose can gradually acquire its own life and get transformed for quite different purposes." "There are similar aspects of dynamic inconsistency within the political process itself, but more important, these also interact with the performance of the economy." While in any country there is an intimate linkage between economic market and political market, in a transition economy such as China it is typical that the political market situation has a more important leverage on the economic outcome. In the China TD-SCDMA case, we may see the result of "Politicians with specific assets (in locations, industries, etc.) and their pivotal supporters with economic specific investments (human or physical capital specific to an industry) may together conspire to cause a lock-in of policy." (Dixit, 1996, page 57)

From the perspective of North's (1990) concept of political markets, the question arises how such a market functions in a non-democratic society as North has developed this concept in view of democracies while also insisting, as pointed out before, that applying transaction cost analysis to non-democratic societies would be a fruitful and urgently needed exercise. In democracies, politicians can trade votes, i.e. a clearly defined "political commodity" that exists and has value only in political markets. However, this clearly only applies to political systems based on voting as their main collective decision making process. What then is the political commodity that can be traded in non-democratic societies?

If 'pure' political commodities do not exist, politicians need to use commodities that have value only in economic markets. This is clearly true for the TD-SCMA case were politicians control parts of the economy and thus can hand out lucrative resources, including top-management positions in large state-owned companies. This, then, creates the interdependence or 'lock-in' that Dixit refers to in the aforementioned quotation and which, from the perspective of North's concept of political market, results in a blurring of the boundary between political and economic markets. This has severely constrained the ability of the leaders of the large operators to implement their strategies regarding upgrading mobile networks, to the detriment of their companies' business.

VI CONCLUSION

In the global telecommunications market, WCDMA and CDMA 2000 have already staked out their claims; as a latecomer, China's TD-SCDMA isn't expected to gain prominent international presence. Despite the enthusiasm of the standards' promoters, the future of the standard is still uncertain.

Even if the government can enforce the standard's adoption by some telecom operators such as China Mobile, the operators can still figure out smart ways to abandon the standard. The experience of the Chinese government's effort can be regarded a case study of ideology-driven interactive game of economics and politics.

In this chapter, we have contributed to the literature by providing an integrated analysis of the involvement of political and economic markets in standardization processes based on North's transaction cost theory. We have also applied North's transaction cost theory to the case of a developing country which as was suggested by North. We demonstrated that in a society lacking a stable institutional framework, ideology plays a relatively larger role enabling political entrepreneurs to play the 'national card' in pushing for an indigenous standard in spite of massive resistance from economic markets. In addition, the blurred boundary between political and economic markets contributed to the desire of politicians to draw on economic markets in order to promote political goals. Thus, North's framework helps to understand the TD-SCMA standardization process which, from a purely economic perspective, would not be explicable.

REFERENCES

Anonymous (2008). The Way Forward. *Discussion document for the Open Meeting of the Conference. European ICT Standardization Policy at a Crossroads: A New Direction for Global Success.* organized by the European Commission - Directorate-General for Enterprise and Industry, Brussels, 12 February 2008.

Besen, S., & Saloner, G. (1988). Compatibility Standards and the Market for Telecommunication Services. In R. W. Crandall & K. Flemm, (Eds.), *Changing Rules: Technological Change, International Competition and Regulation in*

Telecommunications. Brookings Institution, Washington, DC.

Cargill, C., & Bolin, S. (2007). Standardization: A Failing Paradigm, Standards and Public Policy. In S. Greenstein & V. Stango (Eds.), *Standards and Public Policy*. Cambridge University Press. (pp. 296-328).

ChinaLabs (2004, July). *New Globalism: A Research Report on China's High Technology Standards Strategy*. Beijing.

Dixit, A. (1996). *The Making of Economic Policy: A Transaction-Cost Politics Perspective*. The MIT Press.

Economides, N. (2003). Wireless Services and Network Economics. In: D. Steinbock and Eli M. Noam (eds.): *Competition for the Mobile Internet*. Boston et al.: Kluwer Academic, pp. 121-128.

Funk, J., & Methe, D. (2001). Market- and Committee-Based Mechanism in the Creation and Diffusion of Global Industry Standards: the Case of Mobile Communication. *Research Policy 30*, 589-610.

Gao, P. (2007). Counter-Networks in Standardization: a Perspective of Developing Countries. *Information Systems Journal, 17*, 391-420.

North, D. C. (1981). *Structure and Change in Economic History*. New York: Norton.

North, D. C. (1990). *Institutions, Institutional Change, and Economic Performance*. Cambridge: Cambridge University Press.

North, D. (1990). A Transaction Cost Theory of Politics. *Journal of Theoretical Politics, 2*(4), 355-367.

North, D. C. (1993). Institutions and Credible Commitment. *Journal of Institutional and Theoretical Economics, 149*(1), 11-23.

Reimers, K., & Mingzhi, L. (2007). Effectiveness of the International 3G standardization Process and Implications for China's 3G Policy. *International Journal of Public Policy, 2*(1/2), 124-139.

Steinbock, D., & Noam, E. (2003). *Competition for the Mobile Internet*. Kluwer Academic Publishers.

Sugrue, T.J. (2003). Spectrum Policy and the Development of Advanced Wireless Services. In: D. Steinbock and Eli M. Noam (eds.): *Competition for the Mobile Internet*. Boston et al.: Kluwer Academic, pp. 15-19.

Suttmeier, R., & Yao, X. (2004). China's Post-WTO Technology Policy: Standards, Software, and Changing Nature of Techno-Nationalism. *the National Bureau of Asian Research Special Report*.

ENDNOTE

[1]   The information in this section is compiled from materials published in Chinese news media and the website of the TD-SCDMA Industry Alliance, http://www.tdscdma-alliance.org/ (in Chinese). If not specified otherwise, all the direct quotations come from, "The Father of TD-SCDMA on the past and future of the Standard", *Nandu Weekly*, May 30, 2008, in Chinese, translated).

Chapter XI
International Framework for Collaboration between European and Japanese Standard Consortia:
The Case of the Automotive LAN Protocol

Akio Tokuda
Ritsumeikan University, Japan

ABSTRACT

To develop automobiles that fulfill the criteria of "environment-friendliness" "advanced safety", and "riding comfort", coordination between ECUs (electronic control units) is indispensable. Since one or a number of functions is carried by the coordination of separate ECUs, it is important to standardize automotive LAN protocols to ensure reliable interoperability. In parallel with standardization, conformance test specifications for the protocols have played an increasingly important role in securing the interoperability of the complex LAN bus system. The present chapter, whose purpose is to examine the international collaborative framework which has been established between European and Japanese consortia since 2006 for the standardization of the automotive LAN protocol known as "FlexRay", will focus on the contribution of the Japanese standard consortium to the drafting of the original conformance test specifications. The FlexRay protocol is expected to become the de facto standard in the automotive high-speed safety protocol market.

INTRODUCTION

Quantity in the Ancient Regime was bound up in ritual and custom. This meant that measurement standards were potentially open to dispute, negotiation, and change — albeit with the consent of the local community. (Ken Alder, 2002)

This chapter examines the international framework for collaboration between European and Japanese standard consortia in the standardization of the automotive LAN protocol known as FlexRay and focuses on the contribution of the Japanese standard consortium in drafting the original conformance test specifications. The FlexRay is seen as the most promising candidate as *de facto* standard for the next-generation automotive high-speed LAN bus system. In the course of the analysis, our focus will be on the Germany-based FlexRay Consortium (hereafter FRC) and the Japan-based JasPar (Japan Automotive Software Platform and Architecture).

In the case of the automotive LAN protocol studied here, as in the other standard-setting processes of the standard consortia, we reaffirm that there is no pre-determined optimal solution available to serve as the standard (Doz, Olk, Ring, 2000; Ring, Doz, Olk, 2005). In the standard-setting process, the 'strategic intents' of the players active in the consortia are at work. Accordingly, the solution arrived at is the result of a compromise between the intents of the players involved. Analyzing who the players are and what kinds of strategic intent are behind their actions, and responding proactively to these actions, is the *modus operandi* of the world of standardization. Whether to make an exit from the process, or to raise your voice in the process, or to just indicate your loyalty toward the process (Hirschman, 1970): whichever of these options is chosen, players who do not have a clear strategy can easily be forced into a disadvantageous position right from the pre-competitive stage (Kurihara, 2006; Tokuda, 2007). The players involved in FRC and

JasPar, and these standard consortia themselves, are no exception to this rule.

A case study taken from the FlexRay standardization process provides suitable material for an examination of the strategic process (or political decision-making process) which is at work both within and between the consortia. The standardized specifications adopted as a result are no more than the 'product of a compromise' worked out on the basis of the normative judgments made by the standard consortia after reconciling the interests of the various players involved. If only to avoid 'compromise results' damaging to the interests of the Japanese automotive industry, JasPar should respond to FRC's normative judgments with a consistent strategy embracing options for bargaining.

The present chapter attempts to understand the strategic intent of JasPar's contribution vis-à-vis FRC under the collaborative framework. In doing so, we will first trace back the process of standardization of automotive LAN protocols, which used to be centered on the individual protocols of the different manufacturers (Section 1); we will then examine some of the distinctive features of the collaborative framework with particular reference to the division of labour between the consortia (Section 2); finally we will investigate the reason why JasPar decided to draft the corresponding conformance test specifications as their contribution to FRC, using the Consumption Decision Model as the analytic tool for this investigation (Section 3).

1. HISTORY OF AUTOMOTIVE LAN PROTOCOL STANDARDIZATION

With the aim of realising technological innovation ('environment-friendliness', 'advanced safety', and 'riding comfort'), automobile manufacturers (hereafter OEMs) are confronted by the need to gather the increasing number of ECUs (electronic control units) into a single network with decentralised-coordination control (Reed Electronics Research, 2006; Riches, 2006). For instance, in Toyota's development of the 'environment-friendly' automobile PRIUS, coordination of the engine control unit with the braking control unit and the motor control unit was essential, while for the application known as the radar cruise system, which Honda fitted in the INSPIRE and ODYSSEY to realise an 'advanced safety' automobile, coordination was necessary between the vehicle speed control device, the adaptive cruise control device, the powertrain ECU, and the brake ECU.

For the development of such new applications, it has become necessary for OEMs to realise a decentralised-coordination control system by building the different ECUs into a network. We are moving from the phase of electronification of individual systems to the phase of network integration of a range of systems to create additional value (AUTOSAR, 2004; Beecham, 2006; Gerybadze, König, 2008). Since the new applications are realised by creating an ECU network, it is essential when building the systems to first standardize the communication protocol and then to ensure the interoperability of the networked ECUs. Especially in recent times, when automobile electronics has expanded rapidly, protocol standardization and interoperability of the networked systems have become indispensable for OEMs, especially when they have to source ECUs from a range of suppliers.

Today, there are a number of sets of specifications for automotive LAN protocols which serve as international *de facto* standards, differing according to the object of control (SAE, 2003). Here, we will trace the process leading to automotive LAN protocol standardization, which used to be centered on the individual specifications of each OEM.

1-1 From Individual Protocols to a Standard Protocol

Since the beginning of the 1980s, when automotive LAN protocol technology was introduced, many OEMs have developed their own individual bus systems. This development can be traced in Figure 1.

The introduction of automotive LAN protocols began with body control systems. However, since these control systems were based on optic fibers, there were issues in terms of cost and maintenance, and they failed to gain currency. The introduction of the LAN protocol began in earnest in the second half of the 1980s. The individual protocols for body control systems adopted by the respective manufacturers included the Chrysler C2D and the GM J1850VPW, followed in the 1990s by the Daimler CAN, the BMW I-BUS and K-BUS, the Chrysler J1850VPW, the Ford J1850PWM, the Toyota BEAN, the Honda MPCS, and the Nissan IVMS.

However, the main focus of protocol standardization was in the United States and Europe. In the 1990s, the US OEMs GM, Ford, and Chrysler adopted the J1850 standard set by the Society of Automotive Engineers (SAE). In Europe, after Daimler-Benz adopted CAN (Controller Area Network), BMW, Audi, and Volvo followed suit. From 2000, because CAN had the advantage of a faster communication speed than SAE J1850 and because the SAE had authorised CAN as its standard, CAN-based standardization was promoted in the United States too. Subsequently, CAN became the US standard with SAE J2411 (low speed) in 2000 and SAE J11898 (high speed) in 2002, and US OEMs also began to adopt CAN.

CAN is a protocol originally developed in the 1980s by the German system supplier Bosch. Bosch began the development of CAN in response to a request from Daimler-Benz in 1983, presented it in 1986 at the annual general meeting of SAE, and fitted it in 1992 on the Mercedes-Benz S-Class. In 1992, the standard consortium CiA (CAN in

Automation) was set up in Germany to promote standardization based on CAN, which became the international *de jure* standard through ISO 11898 (high speed) in 1993 and ISO 11519-2 (low speed) in 1994. This led to the widespread adoption and diffusion of CAN by European OEMs as a body control system and partly as a powertrain control system.

One of the reasons why the United States and Europe were ahead of Japan in moving forward with protocol standardization was that the major OEMs and suppliers in the United States and Europe (and in particular in Germany) determined the direction of travel for standardization at an early stage and undertook the required infrastructural preparation through industry-wide collaboration with the complementors responsible for the supply of the necessary electronic devices, tools, wire harnesses, software, diagnostic systems, and so on.

In Japan, by contrast, the development of a protocol was seen by the various OEMs as a domain for competition and the question of standardization was therefore not addressed by the automotive industry. CAN did however finally establish the position of international *de facto* standard in Japan, too, through the interaction of a range of factors. These included the following:

1. The expansion of electronic control systems and the resulting rapid increase in the required development resources strengthened moves among OEMs to declare protocol technology a non-competitive domain for joint development with other firms.

2. To allow OEMs to realise systemic innovation, the ECUs of different suppliers had to have interoperability, which led to CAN being declared the standard specification in the United States and Europe.

3. In its sales of systems such as the ESC anti-skid device, the ECU supplier Bosch adopted the marketing approach that 'as long as it is CAN-compatible, it does not

Figure 1. Transition from individual protocols to a standard protocol

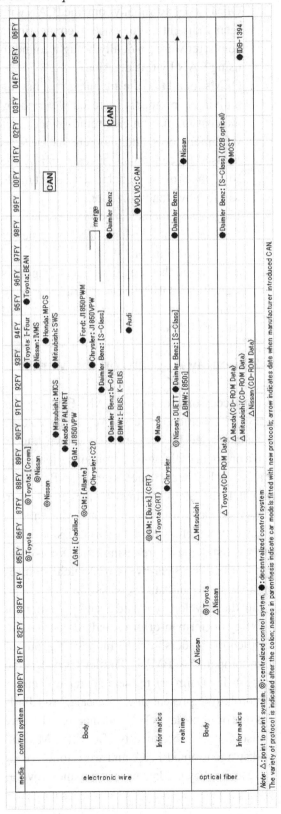

matter if the ECU with which the system is to be operated is not a Bosch product'. OEMs who had initially combined CAN with their individual protocols by connecting a converter were gradually brought round to using CAN by this decision.

4. OEMs found that the advantages of having individual protocols were outweighed by the cost savings on electronic devices, development tools, and maintenance systems realised by economies of scale and by the advantages of the global procurement made possible by standardization.

5. The software maintenance costs arising from changes in semiconductor processes began to weigh heavily on OEMs.

6. It was ruled that the US accident diagnosis regulations (OBD-II: On-Board Diagnostic System Stage II) were to be implemented through CAN.

1-2 FlexRay Appears on the Market

As a successor protocol to CAN, FlexRay has attracted attention. In recent years, the volume of data carried by networks has grown hugely and a protocol with higher communication speed than CAN has become necessary. FlexRay has a maximum bit rate of 10Mbps (10 times greater than CAN) and uses a time trigger method which allows precise timetabling of data transmission. This makes it suitable for realising such X-by-Wire[1] applications as Steer-by Wire, which requires high-reliability of data transmission.

In the development and standardization of FlexRay, a German-origin standard consortium fulfilled the leadership role. In 2000, a group of four companies – BMW, Daimler-Chrysler (the present-day Daimler), the semiconductor vendor Motorola (the present-day Freescale), and Phillips (the present-day NXP) – formed the FlexRay Consortium. Subsequently, Bosch, GM, and Volkswagen joined FRC, and were followed in 2002 to 2003 by the Japanese companies Toyota,

Nissan, Honda, and Denso (Murray, 2004). The aim of FRC was to establish an international *de facto* standard by jointly developing an automotive LAN protocol and corresponding systems. At the same time as promoting FlexRay with the SAE and marketing it to US manufacturers, FRC built up a collaborative framework with JasPar, thus promoting the diffusion of FlexRay as an international *de facto* standard.

The standardization activity of FRC was also aimed at responding to European competitor consortia. Responding to TTP/C, which was engaged in intense standardization competition with FlexRay, was a particularly important issue. TTP/C was a protocol which had originated at the Vienna University of Technology; it had been initially supported by EU projects such as BRITE-EURAM and had been developed mainly through the TTTech Computertechnik. Standardization under TTP/C was promoted by the TTA-Group consortium (originally TTA Forum) established in 2001 and whose original members had included Audi, Peugeot, Renault, Volkswagen, Honeywell, and Delphi. However, Volkswagen, which had been one of TTP/C's main promoters, was co-opted into FRC in 2003. Renault and then Peugeot also joined FlexRay in 2004[2]. By thus drawing OEMs from the competitor TTP/C camp over to FRC, FlexRay ultimately achieved the position of *de facto* standard for the next-generation automotive LAN protocol.

For suppliers, who face a heavy burden of investment for the development of parts compatible with a new protocol, a situation where they need to hedge their bets between two consortia while trying to guess which way the standardization will go is not ideal. For OEMs, meanwhile, given a market where it is very difficult to raise the final automobile price, a situation where they compete to develop a protocol technology that does not help to differentiate their product from that of competitors is similarly not ideal.

Among the factors which helped FlexRay become the *de facto* standard were that FRC succeeded in attracting the main OEMs into the consortium while at the same time encouraging the participation of semiconductor manufacturers, tool vendors, software houses, and other complementors by offering a competitive licensing policy[3]. In particular, in standardization competition at the pre-competitive stage, it seems to have been important that, having attracted many of the end users (OEMs) and complementors into the consortium, the expectation was created that this technology would become the *de facto* standard (Shapiro, Varian, 1998; Gawer, Cusumano, 2002).

1-3 Relations Between FRC and JasPar

JasPar is a consortium established in September 2004 chiefly through the efforts of the OEMs Toyota and Nissan (Nikkei Electronics, 2004; Tokuda, 2007). As of 2008, the membership consisted of five core members (Toyota, Nissan, Honda, Denso, and Toyota Tsusho Electronics), more than 100 regular and associate members, and academic members[4]. JasPar encompasses not only OEMs but also electronic system suppliers, software houses, tool vendors, semiconductor manufacturers, electronic parts manufacturers, trading companies, and other entities.

JasPar's main objective is to change the product architecture of automotive electronic control systems from a vertically integrated to a horizontally disintegrated structure by means of modularization of the system with standard interfaces. From the outset, the activity of JasPar has consisted of the standardization of the following three interfaces (*see* Figure 2):

1. Application programming interface[5] (API): activates the OS and device driver of each ECU (electronic control unit)
2. Automotive LAN interface (protocol): interoperates a number of ECUs (e.g. engine control unit, steering control unit, braking control, body control)
3. Hardware (e.g. microcontroller) and software (OS and device driver) interface

JasPar is said to have drawn many lessons from the activity of the German-origin standard consortia AUTOSAR (Automotive Open System Architecture)[6] and FRC. Within the automotive industry, Germany moved faster than Japan to create consortia to lead standardization activities. In Germany, there is less of a hierarchical relationship between OEMs and system suppliers (including independent manufacturers such as Bosch, Siemens VDO, and Continental) than in Japan in terms of that there are no interlocking shareholdings between them, thus the two sides are on a relatively equal footing. In Japan, on the other hand, there are strong vertical cooperative relationships known as *keiretsu*[7] between specific OEMs and specific suppliers (e.g. Toyota-Denso; Nissan-Hitachi Automotive; Honda-Keihin), and the competitiveness of each OEM is maintained

Figure 2. Interface standardization at JasPar (Source: JasPar Home Page)

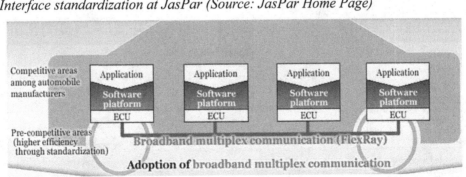

through a bottom-up coordinative relationship based on the expertise accumulated by the suppliers. However, due to the rapid advances in automotive electronics, it will in future be indispensable for OEMs to procure beyond the *keiretsu* and the importance of industry-wide standardization has therefore increased.

AUTOSAR and FRC are consortia of European origin, but are open to participation by Japanese firms. Nevertheless, because of the geographical disadvantage, Japanese firms were not able to become involved to the extent they wished in consortium activity. It is probably accurate to say that the establishment of JasPar was one approach to overcoming these disadvantages.

This does not however mean that the aim of JasPar is to join forces within the industry to establish a *de facto* standard of Japanese origin. Its policy is to seek strengthened collaboration with AUTOSAR and FRC while perfecting systems 'that work in practice' so that a Japanese contribution to Germany-centered standardization activity will be recognised by European firms (*see* Figure 3).[8]

2 THE THREE FEATURES OF THE COLLABORATIVE FRAMEWORK

The collaborative framework based on division of labour between FRC and JasPar has the following three distinctive features.

2-1 Differentiation from High-Speed FlexRay Version

Firstly, while the FRC standardization target envisages a FlexRay with maximum bit rate of 10Mbps, the JasPar target, although based on FlexRay specifications, separately promotes a FlexRay with a lower bit rate of 2.5Mbps or 5Mbps. One of the reasons why this distinction has arisen is that FRC is aiming to realise 'X-by-Wire' with a bit rate of 10Mbps, while JasPar also sees FlexRay as a replacement for CAN.

There is a trade-off relationship between the bit rate of the automotive LAN protocol on one hand and the degree of wiring freedom and the cost on the other hand: as speed increases, the degree of wiring freedom decreases and cost rises. JasPar's

Figure 3. Collaborative framework among consortia (Source: Renesas Technology Co.)

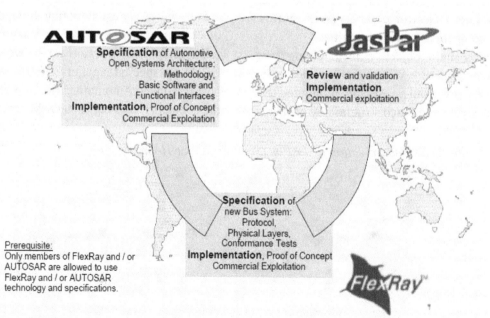

Source: Renesas Technology Co.

development strategy is to restrict cost increases by converting to high-speed while at the same time securing a degree of wiring freedom similar to that of CAN. On this point, the following comment was made by Mr. Noboru Osada, head of JasPar's FlexRay wiring working group:

'If the degree of wiring freedom is great, the task of wiring is easier, which means that the development cost drops. The smaller the degree of freedom, the more effort is needed to carry out the task and the higher the cost. The lower the speed, the greater the degree of wiring freedom; as the speed increases, the degree of wiring freedom decreases. When speed increases, noise becomes more of an issue, and so a whole range of limitations appear, for instance shield wires have to be used in the wiring, or only short distances can be wired, and so on. Even in the CAN currently in use with 500Kbps – 1Mbps, limitations in wiring are necessary, so at a rate several Mbps higher, wiring will take a lot of thinking about. If you ask me whether I would right now want to use a 10Mbps speed, where the limitations on wiring are very numerous, I would say that unless the system requires it specifically, I would prefer to use a more practical speed that is lower in cost and easier to handle. So I think that the idea at JasPar is not to move straight to 10Mbps but just to aim for applications faster than CAN.'[9]

The immediate task for JasPar is how to proceed with standardization of the low-speed FlexRay version (2.5Mbps, 5Mbps), which differentiates it from FRC, while at the same time maintaining collaboration with FRC, whose focus is on the 10Mbps that will realise 'X-by-Wire' applications, and obtaining FRC acknowledgement of the low-speed version.

2-2 Securing Interoperability

The second distinctive feature is that, while FRC drafts the specifications relating to FlexRay, JasPar contributes to FRC by validating these specifications to create finished systems 'that work in prac-

tice'. This means that JasPar carries out practical experiments to set concrete parameters and then proposes additions and adjustments to FRC.[10] To put it the other way round, FRC concentrates on drafting the specifications intellectual property (specification IP: proprietary information describing the details of the functions of the technology), while JasPar concentrates on drafting implementation intellectual property (implementation IP: proprietary information required for adaptation of the technology to actual products).[11]

Behind the emergence of this division of labour arrangement lay JasPar's intent with regard to the setting of its conformance test specifications. Namely, the specifications were to ensure seamless and reliable interoperability between ECUs and thus avoid repeating the mistakes of CAN. As we will explain below, this means that JasPar prefers to draft conformance test specifications with 'wider test coverage' than FRC. When CAN was introduced to the market, the description of its conformance test specifications was sometimes abstract, so that the different licensees (e.g. semiconductor manufacturers) were able to interpret them individually and discrepancies arose between individual sets of specifications. This affected bus traffic and caused ECU interoperability problems. As a result, although CAN was supposed to be the international *de facto* standard, when OEMs hooked up ECUs sourced from a number of different suppliers, they did not connect properly and ended up requiring repeated integration tasks.[12] The JasPar approach to the drafting of conformance test specifications is described as follows by Mr. Hiroshi Hashimoto, head of the JasPar conformance working group:

'With European conformance test specifications, validity is determined on the basis of a number of sampling points (representative values). The approach is to test a certain number of sampling points (values) and if they are OK to assume all values to be OK. But this approach means that you basically don't know whether all the values are right. In contrast, JasPar is willing to test all the values in the protocol specifications. If there is a fixed value in the specification, our approach is to give it 100% coverage in the conformance tests. Conformance basically means seeing whether the product matches the protocol specifications, so we should be laying down conformance test specifications that cover all the protocol specifications. The reason why we want to take this approach to conformance is of course that it was very loose in the initial stage of CAN. You were able to connect two ECUs from the same supplier but ECUs from different suppliers wouldn't connect, and even if they did connect, there was always still some hidden risk that might cause interoperability problems. So JasPar's approach is to make sure that we have reliable products where that kind of thing doesn't happen.'[13]

At JasPar, one method of eliminating this kind of interoperability problem is to increase the number of test items and use other ways of creating conformance test specifications with 'wider test coverage' than FRC. JasPar's next task will be to consider how to gain acknowledgement from FRC of its original conformance test specifications and how to incorporate them in the collaborative framework as a contributory activity of Japanese origin. Before undertaking this task, JasPar first needs to explain its ground clearly to FRC. We will refer to the point in the next section,

2-3 Differences in Handling of IPR

The third distinctive feature can be seen in the differences and similarities in IPR policy. Some researchers say that whereas royalty-free licensing of IPRs was a principle of conventional standardization, royalty-paying licensing of IPRs is becoming general in recent standardization (Kim, 2004). In other words, at present, even if a standard is set through the consensus-building process of a standard consortium, the standard cannot always be used freely. Where IPRs are embedded in a standard, their use is conditional on obtaining a license from the IPR holder.

The policy of JasPar on the handling of IPRs has been framed by the Intellectual Property Right Working Group, which, in contrast to the royalty-free IPR policy of FRC, laid down that IPRs should be available under royalty-free or RAND (reasonable and non-discriminatory) policy. JasPar's IPR policy is explained as follows by JasPar steering committee chairman Mr. Kazutaka Adachi:

'In JasPar, the technological side of the standardization activity is carried not by OEMs but by semiconductor manufacturers and Tier 1 suppliers. To motivate suppliers to take part in JasPar, an incentive mechanism is therefore needed. So we decided to make IPR available under RAND in addition to royalty-free conditions …. We adopted our IPR regulations after concluding that RAND was a good way of keeping suppliers' motivation going in the long term.'[14]

If everything became royalty-free, it might be hard to motivate suppliers competitively and to bring out their full capabilities. JasPar's IPR policy is to have suppliers make a patent statement of the IPRs embedded in the standard and to allow their use under RAND conditions. The RAND concept, however, is associated with a considerable degree of interpretative flexibility among the players involved. Because of this, the question of whether it provides a meeting ground where the motivation and capabilities of suppliers can flourish depends to a large extent on JasPar's normative judgments regarding its policy. And such judgments will to a certain extent be determined by JasPar's governance structure. As we mentioned above, the fact that JasPar's core membership does not include major semiconductor manufacturers of the kind found among FRC's core membership may have a substantial effect on its judgment. Moreover, in order for JasPar's IPR policy to work as a trigger to drive the motivation and capabilities of suppliers, a deepening of collaboration with FRC is essential for the reasons outlined below.

Some researchers note that the arrangement at FRC whereby IPRs embedded in a standard are basically available royalty-free seems to be sharply different from that at JasPar (Gerybadze, König, 2008), At FRC however, there is a separate set of regulations, the so-called 'application notes', on recommended procedures relating to the implementation of the FlexRay bus system and these require individual licensing negotiation with the IPR holders. Both consortia can thus be said to have made specifications relating to the implementation phase into a domain for competition.[15]

In connection, a point which IPR holders in JasPar need to be aware of is that, where RAND conditions are applied under JasPar, it is not clear whether the same IPRs will be treated by FRC as subject to RAND or to 'application notes'. According to JasPar's IPR regulations, where all or part of JasPar's specifications are adopted by FRC, FRC member firms that are also members of JasPar must follow FRC's IPR regulations. Accordingly, to derive the intended benefit from its IPR policy (RAND), it may become necessary for JasPar members not only to create precedents whereby latent IPR holders within FRC campaign to have the individual pieces of IPR recognised as 'application notes', but also to establish a system whereby JasPar members join forces to persuade FRC to apply the same conditions as JasPar.

3 COLLABORATIVE STRATEGY OF JASPAR

3-1 Trade-Off Between Interoperability and Universality

In this section, with the emphasis on ECU interoperability, we will analyze the strategic intent of JasPar as it works to develop its original conformance test specifications. The characteristics of JasPar's conformance test specifications are sharply different from those of FCS.

In connection, the term 'conformance test specifications' can be defined as the guideline information which describes the conformance test procedure used to verify whether a product is operating in conformity with the standardized protocol specifications; FRC and JasPar are nothing other than consortia for the drafting of these specifications. The conformance procedure can be described as follows:

1. The standard-setting organisations FRC and JasPar draft the conformance test specifications.
2. The third-party certification organisations carry out the tests.
3. Semiconductor vendors utilise third-party certification to obtain certification for communication-related drivers (e.g. transceivers) and controllers.
4. ECU suppliers source the certified drivers and manufacture ECUs incorporating devices that have passed the conformance test.
5. These ECUs are finally delivered to the OEMs.

One of the benefits we could expect to gain from this procedure is an enhancement of the reliability of the interoperability of different modules (devices, components, ECUs, etc.) implemented via FlexRay. The conformance test itself however is no more than a test to be performed as prescribed in the conformance test specifications. We therefore need to emphasise here that the 'quality' of interoperability of the system at the implementation stage depends to a certain extent on the 'characteristics' of the conformance test specifications. This means that even though a standard interface exists and we go through a series of test procedures, this does not necessarily ensure the degree of 'quality' which will satisfy ECU suppliers and OEMs. If securing the high-level interoperability of the system is a priority issue, this should be backed by conformance test specifications with 'reliable characteristics'.

Here, we attempt to understand the strategic significance of JasPar's contribution to FRC by applying the Consumption Decision Model.[16] With this model, we can analyze the amount of utility that standard consortia can derive from the characteristics of specifications and the circumstances of the consortium.

Dr. Hidemasa Kimura, an expert in aircraft aerodynamic structure who was involved in a trans-Pacific flight project after the First World War, maintained that as a basic principle of aircraft design, 'strength requirements' were decided by a 'compromise between safety and economy'. Meanwhile, to assess the maximum load and minimum required strength, he proposed that it would be necessary firstly to research theoretically and experimentally an incidental element consisting of the individual characteristics of the particular aircraft, the individual characteristics of its steering, and the individual characteristics of the weather; and then, avoiding simplification as far as possible, to factor these individual characteristics into the design (Kimura, 1932, 1933). The choice of whether to set complex and particular requirements in line with individual use cases and go for maximum aircraft performance improvement or to design with relatively simple and universal requirements with a view to the necessity of mass production for economies of scale needs to be made on the basis of careful judgment weighing the pros and cons of both sides and with due consideration of the political and economic situation (Hashimoto, 2000). Just as with aircraft 'strength requirements', the drafting of requirements for any transport vehicle is always subject to a trade-off between safety and economy.

In order to develop a safety-oriented LAN bus system, both FRC and JasPar will need conformance test specifications which include every tests for all potential individual use cases (we describe hereafter specifications of this kind as 'tight' and

the opposite as 'loose'). If they wish to develop a protocol with high universality for economies of scale, they will want conformance test specifications which include a relatively simple test available for all use cases (we describe this as 'wide' and the opposite as 'narrow'). 'Safety against economy' and 'interoperability depending on a range of test coverage from loose to tight against universality depending on a range of use cases from narrow to wide': each of these constitutes a trade-off relationship. The conformance test specifications decided under these circumstances will have the character of a combination of these goods. Then we refer to the amount of utility that the standard consortium derives from a character of conformance test specifications which is composed of a combination of goods they consume.

In connection, the goods to be combined are of course not limited to interoperability and universality. Other goods which may influence the amount of utility should also be envisaged. But here, when examining the relevant trade-offs, we assume that the other goods are fixed. In the presence of a given utility, all other things being equal, sets of characteristics for the conformance test specifications are represented by the various combinations of goods. These are present in an infinite series on the same indifference curve, stretching from those with reliable interoperability but poor universality (safety-oriented specifications: relatively tight and narrow specifications) to those with high universality but lacking in interoperability (economy-oriented specifications: relatively wide and loose specifications) (*see* Figure 4). Any one of the indifference curves shows various combinations of the goods that make the consortium equally happy[17].

Regarding the characteristics of these specifications, if there is no uncertainty present, relatively economy-oriented (wide and loose) conformance test specifications will likely be chosen by the consortium. However, at the implementation stage, incidental elements and situations not envisaged affect ECU interoperability. Accordingly, envis-

Figure 4. Indifference curves and characteristics of conformance test specifications

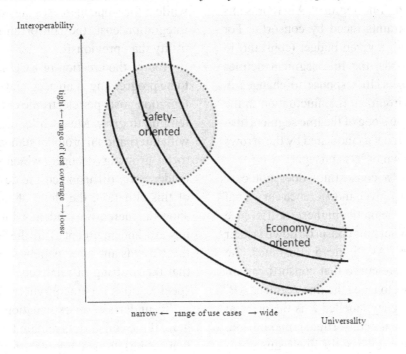

aging a range of circumstances to incorporate uncertainty and thereby develop specifications to a certain extent safety-oriented (tight and narrow) could be a realistic set of characteristics for the consortium. From this perspective, regardless of the initial position and the amount of utility, JasPar can be seen as moving its preference point to the top left of the indifference curves.

3-2 Constraints in Drafting Specifications

Even if specifications relating to protocol technology are standardized, the possibility that different suppliers (e.g. semiconductor manufacturers) may still have room to make individual interpretations is latent in the situation and cannot be ruled out. As mentioned above, with the former CAN, the description of the conformance test specifications was in parts abstract and lacking in detailed regulation. As a result, interoperability problems arose and OEMs were faced with massive integration tasks when it came to implementation. This kind

of inefficient system development needs to be remedied by reducing the burden of self-validation on suppliers and making the specifications tight. The opposite case could however be argued: that because the specifications are of a highly loose nature and everyone can make their own interpretation, they are readily accepted widely and are relatively easy to diffuse. But whichever the case, it should be emphasised that CAN and FlexRay are standards created at the cost of painstaking integration tasks at their implementation stage.

Approached in this way, the constraints when FRC and JasPar set conformance test specifications can be represented by the formula below.

diffusion cost × interoperability + integration cost × universality = constant

In this formula, diffusion cost is posited as the price of interoperability and integration cost as the price of universality. The constant on the right side of the equation should be thought of here as a numeric quantification of the constraints faced by consortia.

Figure 5 is a visual representation of this formula. Here, the line segment AB represents the budget constraints faced by consortia. For a consortium with a given budget (constant) to spend on the goods, the line segment defines its opportunity sets. In response to changes in the business environment (i.e. fluctuation in the price of goods), the slope of the line segment also changes (the intercept as indicated by the arrows moves up and down or left and right).

By definition, a consortium does not care where it sits on any given indifference curve, but it would prefer to be on the highest indifference curve possible. What pins consortia down is their budget constraint. As Figure 5 illustrates, the highest indifference curve that consortia attain is the one that just touches the line segment AB. The point of tangency labelled E is the point at which the utility for the consortium is maximised. Accordingly, if the slope of the line segment increases due a decrease in the diffusion cost, the

consortium will gain more utility than previously, while if the slope increases due to increase in the integration cost, the consortium will gain less utility than previously.

Today, the creation of ECU networks seems to be progressing at an accelerating pace and integration costs per electronic control system are tending to grow. Meanwhile, moves to progress with international protocol standardization seem to be growing stronger, which is producing a tendency for diffusion cost to decrease. Because of this situation, the slope of the line segment shows an increasing tendency (intercept A moves upward and intercept B to the left). Driven by these trends and anticipations, it can be deduced that the drafting of relatively tight and narrow specifications is being promoted by JasPar.

To undertake an explanation of the formula here, if the constraints remain the same, the first item on the left-hand side of the formula represents the circumstance that:

Figure 5. Indifference curve and budget constraints of consortium

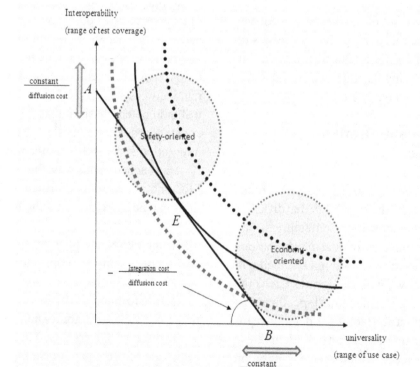

1. If the consortium tries to increase interoperability by designing tight conformance test specifications, because it becomes unavoidable to limit use cases to some extent, the diffusion cost of the specifications per unit expands. As a result, it attracts opposition from firms that want to see wide application of the protocol and from suppliers who want to deal in FlexRay-related devices and tools in large volumes.[18]

In contrast, the second item in the formula represents the circumstance that:

2. If the consortium tries to increase universality by designing wide conformance test specifications, by which an attempt is made to cut the cost of sourcing of related parts, integration costs for the sake of interoperability rise at the implementation stage, and concern will be registered in particular on this point by Japanese OEMs who do not want to repeat an old mistake experienced in the case of CAN.

3-3 Compromise Inside Consortia

The above gives a simple idea of the situation regarding the relationship of 'coopetition' (cooperation and competition) inside and outside consortia which arises when a large number of players with different interests, ranging from users to suppliers, join consortia. Taking into account this kind of relationship, it becomes clear that the players whose close cooperation JasPar OEMs should seek in their efforts to enforce tight and narrow specifications are the OEMs in FRC. The latter group, in particular OEMs such as Volkswagen and GM, whose high production volume means that sourcing ECUs from different suppliers is a pressing need, are very likely to show a generous understanding toward such specifications (or at least Toyota, whose high production volume means that sourcing from multiple suppliers is

absolutely essential, and Nissan, which is attempting to break out of the *keiretsu* system by sourcing from multiple suppliers).

Meanwhile in the abovementioned context, OEMs at JasPar need to provide to device suppliers with opposing interests a sufficiently persuasive argument that they will still have a surplus after covering their diffusion costs. To do this, OEMs should stimulate the expectation of the suppliers that, even if tight and narrow specifications are established, the use case in question will still provide a high product turnover. An important alternative strategy for doing this is to further deepen the collaboration between JasPar and FRC. In other words, to make a framework which allows even members of FRC to rapidly access the specifications drafted by JasPar and permits 'reasonable' utilisation thereof. Doing this would permit the stimulation of suppliers' expectations in such a way as to 'expand the range of users even if the range of use cases remains limited (thus producing high turnover per use case)'.[19] As a result, OEMs belonging to JasPar would be able to procure devices at low cost while maintaining their interoperability, while suppliers would be free of the risk that the specifications drawn up by JasPar and FRC could become a 'dual standard' or a 'double standard'. A win-win situation would result in this context.

3-4 Difficulties in Convergence

Finally, we will clarify the reason why JasPar decided to apply its tight and narrow specifications to a separate version (2.5Mbps, 5Mbps) by examining the difficulties of doing so for a uniform bit rate (10Mbps).

If we accept the argument so far, then, in the presence of constraint conditions accompanied by change (i.e. the change in integration cost and diffusion cost), both consortia will select conformance test specifications which maximise their utility. Let us assume that, under the constraint of the dotted line f*-f**, the optimal point for FRC

Figure 6. Strategy of JasPar toward FRC

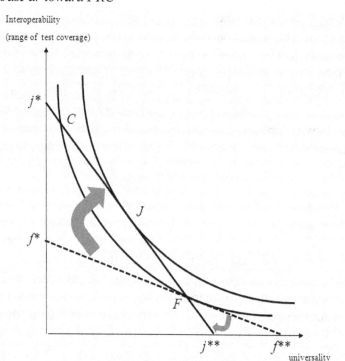

is point F (*see* Figure 6)[20]. Here, to reflect actual conditions, the characteristics are envisaged as relatively wide and loose in comparison with those of JasPar. In contrast, in preparation or anticipation of a change in the business environment in which budget constraint line j*j** inclines in the direction of the arrow, JasPar selects as optimal point J, which touches one of its indifference curves as drawn in the diagram. Thus it is situated on an indifference curve which offers JasPar a higher utility than point F.[21]

Here, if we allow for the situation where JasPar is obliged to follow the conformance test specifications decided by FRC (point F), although point F is acceptable to JasPar because it is also on JasPar's budget constraint line (segment j*j**), the utility which JasPar derives will be reduced. The reduction in utility is reminiscent of the bitter experience with CAN, which was convenient but a hindrance to ECU interoperability. In this situation, JasPar needs to work on FRC to get

it to move point F closer to point J. However, as we saw when we looked at the difference in the IPR policy of the two consortia, there is no incentive in place at FRC for suppliers to develop interoperability-reliable specifications for no reward. For this reason, as long as FRC continues with its present IPR policy, there is no logical reason for suppliers at FRC to cooperate in drafting and testing such specifications. The drafting of specifications with reliable interoperability is not the job of suppliers at FRC but of individual suppliers or OEMs. To put it another way, a certain level of quality premium relevant to ECU interoperability is achieved by the hand of the individual suppliers or engineering firms at FRC, whereas the quality premium is embedded in the specifications at JasPar.

In contrast, what about the option whereby the specifications characterised as point J can be used by FRC too? In this scenario, for OEMs who do not need to interconnect ECUs from multiple suppliers, ECUs conforming to JasPar's tight specifications may not quite be described as having 'excess quality', but in terms of cost performance it is hard to identify any superiority over their present specifications.[22] In addition, JasPar's narrow specifications may not be easy to handle for OEMs who wish to develop any applications they want without being bounded by any use cases.

Now let us focus on a point which is on JasPar's budget contraint line but at the opposite end to point F: point C. Although point C, like point F, represents a cut in utility for JasPar, it does fulfill JasPar's budget constraint and also constitutes a set of specifications that represent a risk hedge for point F in terms of securing interoperability. Although point C, along with point F, represents one of the maximum degrees of utility, in the case where JasPar has to compromise with FRC, it may be more difficult to let FRC make use of it for the same reason as in the case of point J, and it will attract opposition even from suppliers at JasPar, who will have to sustain higher diffusion costs than in the case of point J.

Because of the reasons outlined above, it would be no straightforward task to represent to FRC the value of tight and narrow specifications if they were being drafted for the same bit rate. We can therefore conclude that JasPar's strategic judgment was brilliant when it decided not to draft the specifications for the high-speed 10Mbps version but instead to separately sponsor 2.5Mbps and 5Mbps versions.

The result whether JasPar's original contribution in low-speed version will obtain an understanding at FRC seems to be announced by 2010.

CONCLUSION

As an approach to studying the interdisciplinary theme 'the world of international standardization', this chapter examined the example of actions and decision-making around the standardization of the automotive LAN protocol FlexRay. Focusing on the collaborative framework between FRC and JasPar, we traced the history of the standardization process for the LAN bus system and then examined three distinctive features of the collaborative framework with particular reference to the division of labour between the consortia; finally, by invoking the Consumption Decision Model, we investigated the reason why JasPar decided to draft tight and narrow specifications. Analysis of the collaborative framework led us to an understanding of the reason why JasPar decided to set specifications for a lower bit rate as their original contribution to FRC.

Now, when it comes to the formulation of specifications by JasPar for the 2.5Mbps and 5Mbps versions, there may be a limit to what individual suppliers can achieve alone. For example, a wire harness requires the electrical functions to ensure the reliability of the circuit of each harness, to reliably supply the required voltage and current values, and to prevent electromagnetic leaks to neighbouring circuits; since there are also great physical limitations, for instance the need for efficient wiring of the harness during assembly, ensuring interoperability calls for activities vertically coordinated with the concerned OEMs and suppliers.

It is no more than a hypothetical question, but compared to FRC, JasPar is possibly better equipped with the 'organizational capability' which facilitates ready vertical coordination among players for the drafting of tight and narrow specifications. Alternatively, it could be said that the two standard consortia deploy their respective strengths in the field of organizational capability and that these are arranged well in a complementary manner: FRC is relatively good at managing the horizontal coordination among players that could be advantageous in promoting the creation and diffusion of a standard interface while JasPar is relatively good at managing the vertical collaboration that could be advantageous in ensuring its interoperability.[23] For a concrete comparison of the organizational capabilities of the two consortia, further survey and analysis is now needed to identify what the respective characteristics are.

REFERENCES

Alder, K. (2002). *The measure of all things: The seven year odyssey and hidden error that transformed the world.* New York: Free Press.

AUTOSAR (2004). An industry-wide initiative to manage the complexity of emerging automotive E/E–architectures. *Proceedings of the 2004 international congress on transportation electronics, automobile electronics to digital mobility: the next generation of convergence,* (pp. 325-332).

Beecham, M. (2006). *Global market review of automobile electrical wiring systems – forecasts to 2012.* Aroq Limited.

Christensen, C. M., & Raynor, M. E. (2003). *The Innovator's Solution: Creating and Sustaining Successful Growth.* Boston: Harvard Business School Press.

Doz, Y. L., Olk, P. M., & Ring, P. S. (2000). Formation Processes of R&D Consortia. *Strategic Management Journal, 21*(3), 239-266.

Gawer, A., & Cusumano, M. A. (2002). *Platform Leadership: how Intel, Microsoft, and Cisco drive industry innovation.* Boston: Harvard Business School Press

Gerybadze, A., & König, R. (2008). Managing Global Innovation Networks: The Case of Automotive Electronics. *Presentation at Workshop on Managing Global Innovation Networks,* Duisburg University, 8 February.

Hashimoto, T. (2002). *Hyojun no tetsugaku : sutandado tekunoroji no sanbyakunen.* Tokyo:

Kodansha (*The Philosophy of Standards: 300 Years of Standard Technology; in Japanese*)

Hirschman, A. O. (1970). *Exit Voice and Loyalty: Responses to Decline in Firms, Organizations, and States.* Harvard University Press.

ISO&IEC (2004). *ISO/IEC guide 2: Standardization and related activities - General vocabulary (8th edition.)*

Kim, J. (2004). Technical Standard-Setting, Patent Pooling, and Competition Policy. *Report of the 2003 FY Industrial Property, Research Promotion Project.* Institute of Intellectual Property.

Kimura, M. (1932). Rationalization of load conditions. *Journal of the Aeronautical Research Institute, 99*(1), 815-820 (in Japanese). Tokyo Imperial University.

Kimura, M. (1933). Simplification of load conditions. *Journal of the Aeronautical Research Institute, 103*(1), 143-145 (in Japanese). Tokyo Imperial University.

Kurihara, S. (2006). The General Framework and Scope of Standards Studies. *Hitotsubashi Journal of Commerce and Management, 40*(1) (http://hdl.handle.net/10086/13784).

Murray, C. J. (2004). Four Asian automakers join FlexRay consortium. *Electronic Engineering Times,* March 1, 2004.

Nikkei Electronics (2004). Why Toyota and Nissan created JasPar. *Nikkei Electronics,* October 25, 2004, (pp. 61-62).

Reed Electronics Research (2006). *Automotive Electronics: A Profile of International Markets and Suppliers to 2010.* Reed Electronics Research.

Riches, I. (2006). *Automotive System Demand 2004 to 2013: Safety systems drive growth.* At:

http://www.strategyanalytics.net/default.aspx?mod=ReportAbstractViewer&a0=2868 (15th April 2008)

Ring, P. S., Doz, Y. L., & Olk, P. M. (2005). Managing Formation Processes in R&D Consortia. *California Management Review, 47*(4), 137-156.

SAE (2003). *Technical Paper Series,* SAE. 2003-01-0111

Shapiro, C., & Varian, H. R. (1998). *Information Rules: A strategic guide to the network economy.* Harvard Business School Press.

Tokuda, A. (2007). Standardization activity within JasPar: Initiatives of Renesas Technology Co., *Ritsumeikan International Affairs. 5*(1), 85-105.

WEB SITES

JasPar <https://www.jaspar.jp/guide/background.html>

FlexRay Consortium <http://www.flexray.com>

ISO <http://www.iso.org/>

ENDNOTES

[1] An X-by-wire system is a safety-related fault-tolerant automotive electronic system without mechanical backup. The "X" in "X-by-wire" represents the basis of any safety-related application, such as steering, braking, power train, suspension control, or multi-airbag systems. These applications will greatly increase overall automobile safety by liberating the driver from routine tasks and helping the driver to find solutions in critical situations.

[2] It is said that one of the reasons why these players had decided to change side was TTP/C had set a more strict licensing policy (e.g. to charge relatively higher licensing fee to the licensor) than that of FRC.

[3] Interview of 27th December 2006 with Mr. Hiroyuki Sugiyama, manager of the automotive technology lab at Freescale Semiconductor.

[4] The author has been an academic member of JasPar since April 2006.

[5] API is an interface for developing application software that can disregard the differences between OSs and device drivers.

[6] AUTOSAR came into being in Europe in July 2003. AUTOSAR is a consortium of German origin that aims to build a common platform for automotive software development and to standardize the interface between the software and hardware components of electronic control systems. The founder members were the OEMs BMW, Daimler-Chrysler, and Volkswagen and the system suppliers Bosch, Continental, and Siemens VDO.

[7] It is group of large Japanese financial and industrial corporations through historical associations and cross-shareholdings. In a keiretsu each firm maintains its operational independence while retaining very close commercial relationships with other firms in the group. Vertical keiretsu (such as Toyota Corp.) involve firms upstream and downstream of a manufacturing process.

[8] Only members of FlexRay are allowed to use FlexRay specifications at this moment. How to deal with non-members is one of the hot issues in the consortium.

[9] Interview of 23rd April 2007.

[10] For instance, there are a large number of parameters involved in the FlexRay specifications; determining the corresponding default values and other criteria for actual conditions of use through experimentation is the role of JasPar.

[11] FRC separately drafts 'application notes' in which recommended procedures relating to the implementation of the FlexRay EPL (electrical physical layer) specifications are prescribed.

[12] In addition, whenever the conformance test specifications for CAN were renewed,

semiconductor manufacturers and ECU suppliers had to shoulder significant additional investment to rewrite their conventional software assets.

[13] Interview of 13th July 2007.

[14] Interview of 5th May 2007.

[15] A set of 'application notes' is available at < http://www.flexray.com>.

[16] The model is normally employed in basic micro-economics as an analytical tool for consumption decision making under budget constraints.

[17] As a result of the principle of diminishing marginal rate of substitution, the slope of the difference curve becomes flatter from left to right along the curve.

[18] Of course, to draft a full set of specifications with limitless use cases and a complete range of test cases might be the best option for each consortium, but it would incur a huge development cost and would be redundant for most use cases.

[19] In addition, a crucial decision for JasPar would be deciding how to deal with specifications for other firms who do not participate in any consortia. The diffusion cost is greatly influenced by this judgment.

[20] In the diagram, we indicate one of the indifference curves of JasPar which touches point F.

[21] In order to locate point J on an indifference curve with higher utility than that containing point F, JasPar has to meet the condition whereby the degree of decrease of diffusion cost is greater than the degree of increase of integration cost. Therefore, it is an absolute requirement for JasPar to deepen the relationship so as to increase the utility which is derived from its specifications.

[22] The standard is the product of a compromise among the players in the consortium, and the normative judgment of FRC therefore reflects its governance structure, type of leadership, and so on. Conversely, this reminds us of the fact that there are some players who follow a judgment against their interest. If we compare the characteristics of their sets of specifications, we find that point F has a risky character for firms who source ECUs from multiple suppliers.

[23] In other words, JasPar is good at handling the verification of system integration in order to avoid the disadvantages of modular systems (i.e. interoperability problems).

Chapter XII
Between Supply and Demand:
Coping with the Impact of Standards Change

Tineke M. Egyedi
Delft University of Technology, The Netherlands

ABSTRACT

There is a continuous pressure for improvement in e-business. Increasing technical possibilities, new forms of outsourcing, the ongoing integration of business processes, the expansion of value chains, the emergence of new markets and new players; they affect the infrastructure and underlying ICT standards. Contrary to the inherent stability one might expect from standards, maintenance of and change in standards are rule rather than exception. The benefit of standards change is sometimes obvious. However, it can also pose severe problems (e.g. heavy switching costs and reduced market transparency). This chapter synthesizes research findings on standards change. A conceptual framework is developed to determine under which circumstances standards change is avoidable; if so, in what manner; and if not, which means exist to reduce the negative impact of change. While some change drivers are innovation-related, others stem from the standardization activity itself. They require distinct coping strategies: change control and quality control, respectively. Along these two lines, the chapter discusses strategies to cope with the impact of standards change.

1. INTRODUCTION

For different reasons, change is inherent to e-business and to the ICT sector in general. First, the high rate of technology change has led to a shortening of technology and product life-cycles. The shorter life-cycles are accompanied by a higher rate of standards change and an accelerated standards process. Second, the world-wide diffusion of ICT systems has facilitated the globalization of business and production. The distributed production of goods and services, including outsourcing of research and development (R&D) services, has created an additional demand for ICT standards.

This, in turn, challenges the standardization system. Next to the growing number of standards, the need to acquire consensus among a higher number of stakeholders with increasingly heterogeneous preferences is even more challenging. Even if consensus can be reached, the diversified context of those implementing ICT standards increases the likelihood of different implementations.

Third, related to the aforementioned two trends is the deregulation of many industries, and the telecommunication sector, in particular. Publicly owned companies have been privatized and legal framework conditions have been substituted by self-regulatory schemes, which include standardization. In sum, the need to develop standards has increased while the stability of the surrounding conditions has decreased. Therefore, the rate of standards change promises to be particularly high. (Egyedi & Blind, 2008)

Although standards change is systemic to the field of ICT (Blind, 2008; Egyedi & Heijnen, 2008) and is, as will be argued, not an unproblematic issue, until recently the topic has hardly been addressed. In order to draw attention to a number of studies that have recently been published, this chapter discusses and synthesizes their findings to determine the causes of standards change and how to deal with them. More specifically, the aim is to determine under which circumstances standards change is avoidable; if so, in what manner change can be avoided; and if not, which means exist to reduce the negative impact of change.

The chapter is structured as follows. In order to explain the problems attached to standards change (section 4), section 2 first argues that stability is crucial to standards. Nevertheless, different kinds of change exist (section 3). Their causes are manifold. However, they seem to fall into two main categories: standardization-internal and external causes (section 5). The causes can be conceptualized and modeled with help of two complementary, theoretical angles: innovation and management (section 6). The heuristic model provides a stepping stone for identifying

strategies to cope with standards change: avoiding unnecessary change, reducing its impact ex *post*, or dealing *ex ante* with future change in standards design (section 7). To conclude, the chapter's main findings are re-analyzed in terms of supply- and demand-side drivers of standards change (section 8).

2. THE VALUE OF STANDARDS

The term 'standard' is used in this chapter in two main senses, namely in the sense of *committee standards* and in the sense of *de facto* standards. A committee standard[1] is a very specific type of agreement. It is a specification developed by a committee for repeated use, or "a document established by consensus (…), that provides, for common and repeated use, rules, guidelines or characteristics for activities or their results, aimed at the achievement of the optimum degree of order in a given context" (adapted from ISO/IEC, 2004, p. 8).[2] This – adapted - definition covers the standards developed by formal standards bodies like the International Organization of Standardization (ISO) and from, for example, standards consortia (e.g. World Wide Web Consortium, W3C) and professional organizations (e.g. Institute of Electrical and Electronics Engineers, IEEE).

The second sense in which the term 'standard' is often used, refers to *de facto standards,* that is, to specifications that underlie products and services with a significant market share, and to widely adopted practices. An example is the PDF specification of Acrobat Reader[3]. Initially these specifications were not meant to become standards, that is, to be referred and built to by third parties, but their wide use turns them into such standards. De facto standards, too, undergo changes (e.g. software updates).

Standards make life easier because we can refer to them implicitly and explicitly, and thus reduce what economists term *informational transaction costs* (Kindleberger, 1983).[4] Moreover, they create compatibility (i.e. interoperability). They allow products to work together and equipment parts to be replaced. In anonymous markets complementary products can be used together based on standard interfaces. As points of reference, standards coordinate technology development (Schmidt & Werle, 1998). They structure and coordinate the way markets develop. Standards-based clusters of economic activity emerge. An example is the product cluster for paper processing equipment like printers, copiers, and fax machines which is based on the common A-series of paper formats (ISO 216).

There are many economic benefits to standards. As Table 1 indicates, standards facilitate trade and allow economies of scale. They increase economic efficiency.

3. CATEGORIES OF STANDARDS CHANGE

To be of value, however, standards need to be stable – at least for a certain period of time. The problem is that often they are *not*. Standards are revised, extended, replaced, succeeded, withdrawn, re-instated, etc.. In short, they are dynamic. *Standards dynamics* refers to the changes to and interaction between standards, that is, to what happens to standards *once they have been set* (Egyedi & Blind, 2008). Although its meaning includes competition between standards and the friction

Table 1. Main functions of compatibility standards (Source: Blind, 2004, adapted)

Function of standards	Effect on the market
Information	Reduce transaction costs Correct adverse selection[5] Facilitate trade
Compatibility	Create network externalities[6] Avoid lock-ins
Variety reduction	Allow economies of scale Build critical mass

between complementary standards, the emphasis in this chapter is on standards that change. There are four categories of *standards change*: implementation change, standard maintenance, standard succession, and formalization.

- Implementation change: a change introduced to the standard specification during its implementation in, for example, a product. When a standard is used, that is, implemented in a product, a service or a practice, it may undergo changes. The specification may only partly be implemented in order to suit the local situation (e.g. Timmermans & Berg, 1997); or it may be extended and implemented in a way that ties customers to a vendor. In such situations, where the implementation deviates from the standard, we speak of *implementation change*.

- Maintenance change or *horizontal dynamics* (Gauch, 2008): standards change that results from maintenance activities of standards bodies. It includes developing a new standard edition, a corrigendum, an amendment or a revision; merging standards, splitting them up, withdrawing a standard and re-instating it.

- Succession: the replacement of one standard by another one in an area of standardization. It includes what may retrospectively be seen to be a next generation standard. Where developed by the same committee, standard succession can be viewed as an extension to and special case of standard maintenance. However, different committees and even competing standards bodies may be involved in developing successors.

- Formalization or *vertical dynamics* (Gauch, 2008): the result of either ratifying a *de facto* standard in a standards consortium or a formal standards body (leading to a consortium standard or a formal standard, respectively), or by ratifying a consortium standard in a formal standards body. At stake is increased recognition and endorsement of the *de facto* or consortium standard.

Each category can be plotted onto the standard's life-cycle (see Figure 1). Figure 1 visualizes the relation between them. From the moment the standard specification has been defined, the cycle of standard maintenance starts. Feedback from implementers may be the reason to revise a standard (dotted arrow); while too many maintenance cycles may indicate that a more radical change is called for, i.e. a new standard. From the perspective of standards change, succession is an extension of the standard's life-cycle, as is formalization.

Although Figure 1 does not specify sources of change, the category 'implementation change' already fore-shadows the importance of the interplay between, on the one hand, standards use, a significant factor on the demand-side of standardization, and, on the other hand, the standard setting, that is, the supply-side. Vendor experience with implementing and localizing standards, and end-user experience with implementations are highly relevant triggers for standards maintenance.

4. PROBLEMS OF STANDARDS CHANGE

Change is a double-edged sword. On the one hand, standards change may well be valued positively when it accompanies innovation in science and technology. For example, in the field of medicine new research might result in a changed reference value for medical treatment. It may mean a lower dose of medication and less side-effect for patients. In this case, standards change is a regular occurrence and standards maintenance is part of what Kuhn (1970) calls 'normal problem solving'. Some regulatory and policy areas highly depend on standards, and therefore need to find ways to cope with this kind of standards change. The European Union has decided not to include standards in regulation precisely because standards change so often. Re-drafting regulation would require too much time and effort. Therefore, a *referential approach* has been developed, which allows standards to evolve without affecting the regulatory framework. This referential approach, which was confirmed in 1985 as the New Approach, is still in place.

Figure 1. Four categories of standards change: Implementation change, maintenance, succession and formalization in the extended life-cycle of a standard

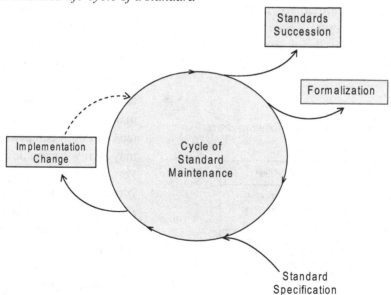

On the other hand, where the need for a standard is expressed, inherently, the need for a certain degree of stability is implied. From this angle standards change poses a problem. While stable standards create transparency and reduce informational transaction costs, changing them has the opposite effect; it decreases transparency and increases transaction costs. Standards change involves new costs (e.g. costs of updating the standard) and devaluates earlier investments (i.e. sunk cost). It diminishes self-evident interoperability because uncertainty may arise about the interoperability of products complying with different standard versions.

To follow, we highlight two difficulties that may arise: the economic costs of switching to the revised standard, and the issue of who actually benefits from and who carries the burden of change. We close this section with two well-recognized problems: the longevity of digital data and incompatibility between standard-compliant products.

4.1 Switching Costs

The work of economists on switching between competing de *facto* standards (e.g. Farrell & Saloner, 1985) provides a useful theoretical underpinning for understanding the difficulty of switching to a new standard version. The costs involved in switching from one standard to another are called *switching costs* (e.g. vonWeizsacker, 1982). Literature informs us that whether or not a party switches standards depends in particular on the size of the installed base, the improvements offered by the competing standard, and how quick network externalities are expected to be realized. In addition to a likely need to depreciate earlier investments in terms of time, effort and money, new investments have to be made. If the sum of switching costs, for example, investments in new equipment and the costs of learning how to use a new technology, is assessed as being too high *lock-in* occurs (Farrell, 1990).

Since similar switching costs are involved, thresholds for switching between competing standards also explain the hesitations which people have about switching to a new version of a standard or to a standard successor.

4.2 Who Bears the Costs

A core question is who benefits and who bears the costs of standards change. Some parties stand to gain more than others. The stakes are not only distributed asymmetrically between those who develop and change standards (the developers), but also between developers, standard implementers (i.e. those who adopt standards in products, services, regulation, etc.), and those who buy the standard-compliant products and services or are affected by them (end-users such as consumers).

Those who initiate the change are seldom the ones who bear its costs. In particular where lack of quality of an initial standard is the reason for a revision, the people responsible may not be the ones to pay (Sherif *et al.*, 2007). As Jakobs puts it

Users (...) are the ultimate sponsors of standardization (the costs of which are included in product prices). (...) Moreover, users will suffer most from inadequate standards that will leave them struggling with incompatibilities. (Jakobs, 2005, p. 5)

Staying close to home, these last years Microsoft products have become de facto standards in both the home and the work environment. They have undergone many updates in response to software bugs and virus attacks, updates which users initially had to act upon (i.e. downloads). In addition, new software releases have kept many large organizations in an almost constant flux of IT projects, which usually not only involved the roll-out of software and adapted configurations but included renewal of the stock of personal computers (Egyedi, 2002). In short: here, as in many cases, not the producer but the consumer bears the costs of change.

4.3 Salient Problem Areas

Next to the economic angle on the negative impact of change, there are a number of currently well-recognized problem areas in the field of ICT that illustrate the problematic side of standards change. Examples are, first, the increasingly urgent problem of sustainable digital data. Van der Meer (2008), for example, analyses the difficulty of maintaining access to archival digital data over time (i.e., *longevity*). The informational, legal, and cultural-historic value of archival data, "… are at risk as a result of standard dynamics". In most cases changes to standards make it very difficult to retain access.

A second example is that of standard-compliant, but incompatible IT products and services (Egyedi, 2008b). In particular implementation change leads to incompatibilities. Incompatible implementations may come about intentionally or unintentionally, for perfectly viable economic or functional reasons, or as part of an aggressive market strategy (embrace-and-extend). But whatever the reason, the consequences are the same. Implementation change undermines the open standards development setting and often results in needless market fragmentation.

5. CAUSES OF CHANGE

If change puts the value of standards at risk and can create serious problems, as the previous sections illustrate, then why *do* standards change? In order to know how to prevent, reduce and/or, retrospectively cope with the negative impact of standards change, insight is required in causes of standards change. The causes roughly fall into three complementary explanations, each with its own flow of reasoning:

- Standards change as part of innovation;
- Standards change as a market strategy; and
- Standards change as a learning phase in the standard's life-cycle.

5.1 Innovation

Standards change is endogenous to technology development (Egyedi, 1996). It is an intrinsic part of technology development and as such an unavoidable derivative of innovation. The pressure for change may stem from

- *Evolving user requirements*, that is, changes in the needs of consumers and organizations. Examples are the requirement for higher speed and more bandwidth in the case of wireless LAN (Jakobs, 2008); for more internet addresses in the case of IPv4 (Vrancken *et al.*, 2008); or for extended facilities (Meer, 2008). In addition, standards use - and localization (Timmermans & Berg, 1997) leads to new problems which then also need to be addressed (Vrancken *et al.*, 2008).

  The *expected* importance of a new functionality is often enough reason to initiate standards change - although in practice the functionality may never be used (e.g. added proprietary standard features such as encryption in the WLAN case; Jakobs, 2008).
- The emergence of *a new technical context*. An example is the new possibilities which the web-based environment offered for using standardized mark-up languages (Egyedi & Loeffen, 2008). A new context-of-use sets different requirements.
- The identification of *new application domains*. Examples are the intended use of a mark-up language for company-external document exchange (business-to-business), while the focus used to be on managing

complex, company-internal document flows (Egyedi & Loeffen, 2008); the expected use of IEEE 802.11 for imaging and voice transmission (IEEE 802.11a; Jakobs, 2008); and expansion of the Dublin Core to make it better suited for more types of digital objects, including software components and cultural heritage materials (Vander, Meer, 2008).

These developments lead to intensified standards maintenance as well as to more radical types of standards succession.

5.2 Market Strategy

ICT companies typically use standardization as a competitive tool. A company policy on standards, including standard's *change*, should therefore be part of their market strategy[7]. However, standards change can also be an outcome of market competition. Thus, in the case of wireless LAN competing technologies have led to different standard specifications (IEEE 802.11, 802.11a and 802.11b; Jakobs, 2008). Gauch's study of changes in the area of DVD recordables illustrates how competition can even spur a standard's race, and involve a high extent of change. He describes two largely stable, competing groups of companies tied together by patents and shared market interests. The two groups engage in R&D for increased speed and disc capacity to prolong revenue streams from their respective patents. This, in turn, leads to a string of competing standards versions and initiatives to formalize them (*horizontal* and *vertical dynamics*; Gauch, 2008). Standards change is here an outcome of market competition as well as part of a market strategy.

In the same vein implementation change can be a company strategy (e.g. embrace-and-extend strategy). A standard may be implemented with proprietary extensions or be otherwise 'improved' (as in the case of IEEE 802.11b+ implementations and Access Point that supports 128 bit link layer encryption; Jakobs, 2008); or, alternately, organi-

zations may implement a standard prematurely and comply to a draft standard which is subsequently changed (Jakobs, 2008).

5.3 Standardization Factors

Overall standards research ignores life-cycle issues of standardization and the relevance of maintenance therein. In addition to innovation- and market-related factors that give rise to standard updates and revisions, factors intrinsic to the activity of standardization occasion maintenance change. Factors are at work that are standardization-specific and stem from the context in which standards are developed, that is, the supply-side, and implemented, that is, the demand-side. There are four main sources of tension and change (Egyedi, 2008b). The source of change may lie in

- A flaw or a weakness in the idea that underlies the standard (e.g. aim at a standard which is too comprehensive to be workable),
- How the standard process takes place (e.g. not involving an important category of standard users in its development),
- The standard specification itself (e.g. ambiguous terminology), and
- The way the standard is implemented (e.g. partial implementation due to cost-constraints).

For example, a standard which is perceived as too complex for implementers may signal that the standard's scope has been too wide (Thomas *et al.*, 2008), but also that possibly too many compromises have clouded the standards process. Complex standards may only be partially implemented - as in the case of OSI standards (Egyedi, 2008b). Sometimes revisions are desired because experience with implementing a standard has uncovered ambiguities and omissions. Ambiguities may lead to different implementations and irreproducible outcomes as in the case of Z39.50

Table 2. Causes of incompatibility and their origin (source: Egyedi, 2008b)

CAUSES OF INCOMPATIBILITY	PHASE C= conceptual idea SP= standard process S= standard spec IP=implem. process
Errors, ambiguities, inconsistencies	SP/S
Ambiguity of natural language	SP/S
Missing details, monopoly on tacit knowledge	S/IP
Ill-structured standards	S
Unclear how to handle options	S
Uncertain compatibility of non-binding recommendations	S
Complexity of comprehensive, ambitious standards	C
Too many options and parameters	SP/S/IP
'Bugward compatibility'	C
Unclear official status of standard's companion book	S
Single company pushing for standard; weak specs	SP
Overload of standards	C/IP
Deviation from and partial implementation of a standard	IP
Interference between standards	C/IP

(Van der Meer, 2008). Table 2 summarizes a number of salient, standardization-related causes of incompatibility and assigns them to phases in the standards life-cycle.

A number of factors influence the level of maintenance change. To note the most salient ones, the timing of standardization with respect to the technology life-cycle is influential (Egyedi & Sherif, 2008). It matters whether the technology to be standardized is mature (responsive standardization) or immature (anticipatory standardization). In the latter case experience with the technology comes after the standard and will sooner lead to revisions (Egyedi & Heijnen, 2008).

Technical immaturity not only increases the likelihood of change. It also increases the scope of change. More radical changes to standards may be expected. Incidentally, the same applies to standards that switch development environment and are elaborated in a different standards setting – that is, a different committee or standard body. Such a switch also facilitates the adoption of more radical – and incompatible - changes to the original standard (e.g. XML; Egyedi & Loeffen, 2008).

Lastly, although one might assume a direct relation between a low quality standards process, a dire need for maintenance and a high level of maintenance activity, this line of reasoning needs to be put into perspective: some standards bodies adopt a more elaborate and intensive maintenance policy, and are therefore more likely to show a higher number of revisions.

6. HEURISTIC MODEL

The aforementioned findings point to two clusters of causes of standards change: the *external causes* of change typically also identified as causes of technology change in innovation literature (i.e. the innovation and market strategy angle), and the *internal causes* of change that are specific to the activity of standardization development and use. See Figure 2. With regard to the external causes, ICT standards are intrinsic to ICT. Where there is pressure to innovate in ICT, ICT standards will be subject to the same pressure for change. That is, the forces that lead to technology dynamics, such as regulatory change, market dynamics, and innovations in related technologies, also lead to changes in standards. In Figure 1 these forces are portrayed by the arrow 'external causes of change'.

The internal causes of standards change, which are standardization-specific and stem from the context in which standards are developed and implemented, are evident across all standards areas and directly affect standards. Institutional factors such as weaknesses in committee procedures fall within this explanatory category.

Figure 2. External factors lead to technology change and therefore also to standards change. Internal factors in the settings of standard development and implementation may directly cause standards change.

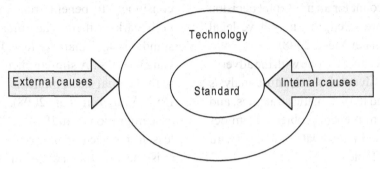

The two sets of causes are analytically distinct but, as the figure indicates, not mutually independent: external factors such as a fiercely competitive market may well underlie internal causes of change such as ambiguity in the standard. That is, external causes may intensify internal causes of change.

External pressures for technology change - and hence standards change – are difficult to withstand. Standards must follow technology innovation and remain up-to-date. Standards change is therefore unavoidable, and should therefore preferably be well-orchestrated (i.e. change control). Where internal causes of change are concerned (Table 2), many of them are a consequence of the way the standards process has been managed and can be addressed (i.e. quality control). See Table 3.

The distinction between avoidable internal causes and unavoidable external causes points to two different directions for systematically

dealing with standards change: measures that focus on the quality of the standards process, and measures that mediate the impact of standards change. These two directions are explored in the following section.

7. COPING WITH THE IMPACT OF CHANGE

Sometimes standards change has little impact. For example, the users of the Aachen Wireless LAN had few problems with the transition from IEEE 802.11b to IEEE 802.11g (Jakobs, 2008). However, in many cases revisions and extensions do create difficulties. For example, different standard versions may become competitors as in the case of the compatible short-term solution to IPv4 addressing problems (i.e. NAT) and the incompatible long-term solution (i.e. IPv6). Or, in the case of

Table 3. Drivers for standards change and their implications (source: Egyedi & Sherif, 2008)

Drivers for Change	External Causes	Internal Causes
Source of change	Co-evolution with technology	Standardization process
Characteristics of change	Inevitable	Consequence of a standardization management process (intentional or accidental)
Framework	Innovation	Management and business
Overall aim	Create up-to-date standard	Create a stable standard
Management objectives	Change control	Quality control

Z39.50, different standard implementations may lead to different query results. If a query result is later needed to account for an important decision and cannot be reproduced, this may have legal repercussions (Van der Meer, 2008).

What means are there to cope with the adverse impact of standards dynamics? Literature analysis points to ad hoc and to systematic strategies, and strategies that try to prevent problems from occurring (*ex ante*) and those that try to deal with them *ex post*. See Table 4.

7.1 Ex Post Measures

Standards change cannot be always be prevented. In such a situation, the main problem which implementers and end-users must deal with is market fragmentation and lack of interoperability between different standards versions, generations and implementations. The solution depends on the type of incompatibility concerned. In data communication, for example, bridges, multi-protocol stacks and routers are used to re-create interoperability between competing standards (Egyedi & Loeffen, 2008). More in general, in the field of ICT and consumer electronics *multiprotocol implementations* are made, that is, single devices in which competing standards are implemented (Gauch, 2008). In all these solutions producers and users of one standard still have access to the market segment of the competing standard and its externalities. They reduce the consumer's fear that the market will tip towards the competing standard leaving them with an obsolete technology. However, apart from the extra costs involved,

Gauch argues that these solutions sustain market competition and fragmentation. Since they allow consumers to benefit from the externalities of both markets, there is no urgent need to integrate standards and markets (e.g. DVD recordables; Gauch, 2008). A similar phenomenon is at stake with the dual stack implementation of IPv4 and IPv6 (Vrancken *et al.*, 2008). Although aimed to ease migration from IPv4 to IPv6, the dual stack lessens the need to migrate because it allows co-existence. Inefficiencies remain.

Where the sustainability of digital data is concerned, there are a number of partial and temporary solutions (Van der Meer, 2008): data refreshment, migration and conversion, and the emulation of earlier data handling devices. The emulation option is required if there is no strategy to archive and update the data handling devices, as was the case with tools that could handle ODA/ODIF (Van der Meer, 2008).

Although crosswalks between a standard and its successor sometimes seem possible (e.g. from DC to DCQ; Van der Meer, 2008), the results of such efforts are likely to be ambiguous - as were the results of multiple efforts to re-establish compatibility between SGML and its successor XML (Egyedi & Loeffen, 2008).

In principle these ex post measures temporarily resolve the adverse effects of standards dynamics. Moreover, in rapidly evolving fields of technology 'temporariness' need not always pose a problem. But they are usually costly and laborious, and are often unsatisfactory because they only solve part of the problem and do so inadequately.

Table 4. Strategies for coping with standards change

Type of Solutions	Ad hoc	Systematic
Ex ante	-	Quality standards process Flexible, future-proof standard design
Ex post	Patchwork: converters, bridges, multi-protocol stacks, etc.	Downward compatibility

7.2 Quality of the Standards Process

Standardization-specific, internal causes of standards change can to large degree be avoided by improving the quality of the standards process (Sherif *et al.*, 2007). Quality standards may sometimes take longer to develop but are more stable and therefore less disruptive for the market.

Improving the quality of the process means intervening in the causes of dynamics. As indicated in Table 2, there are numerous examples of internal causes of standards change, causes that can be traced back to the scope of the standards project, the standards process, the standards specification, and the implementation process. There are several options open to standards management for addressing these internal causes and intensifying quality control measures. A number of suggestions are made in Egyedi (2008b). See Table 5.

Paying attention to the quality of the standards process will not always be able to prevent change. First of all, standards development is not a one-size-fits-all occurrence. Besides, there are design and participation dilemmas which by definition cannot be fully resolved. Learning and feedback is part of the process and will often lead to changes. Moreover, standards work is difficult to manage because there is no real hierarchy between the voluntary committee participants. It is difficult for the committee chair to manage – much more so than projects usually are (Sherif *et al.*, 2007).

Sometimes standards change is a by-product of the chosen standards strategy. Quick and dirty standardization allows standardizers to make an early claim to market, but it also increases the likely need for improvements at a later stage.

Table 5. Recommendations

Institutional measures towards reducing standard-based interoperability problems
Drafting of standards • provide institutional support for editors and rapporteurs on standards engineering • involve technical editors • use pseudo-code or formal languages in a focused way • adopt a unified naming convention • clarify the type of options involved • specify how to deal with options (e.g. profiles) • specify the consequences of (not) implementing options • make explicit the rationale that underlies choices in the specification • issue a reference guide with the standard • organize wider scrutiny of the standard • translate the standard to uncover ambiguities • coordinate the interrelated processes of different standards bodies
Pre-implementation • validate standards before implementation in products ("walk throughs") • develop a reference implementation / pre-implementation • develop a reference environment • include standard conformance and interoperability testing • organize interoperability events with different vendors (e.g. plug tests) • organize dialogues between standard developers and implementers
Post-implementation • supply test suites • improve consistent use and integrity of standards with e.g. compliance and interoperability conformance statements, compatibility logos, certification programs
Standards policy • prioritize implementability as a standard's requirement • reconsider the desired level of consensus across all areas

7.3 Standards Design: Downward Compatible & Future-Proof

Whereas high quality standards lessen the need for change, standards change is to a large degree unavoidable and even desirable where standards need to co-evolve with technology innovation. In many cases standards change actively contributes to the development of technologies and markets. In such situations, the only option is to intervene on the negative impact of standards change and design standards in way that causes the least upheaval. Two design strategies, each departing from a different point in time, would seem to be most promising: designing in downward compatibility and developing 'future-proof' standards (i.e., robust and flexible).

Standards change can lead to technology disruption and fragmentation between the markets of the successor standard and its predecessor. Whether or not this will happen depends to a large degree on whether standard versions and successors are downward compatible and grafted. The incremental nature of most changes makes grafting[8] a viable option and reduces the negative impact of change. In particular where the longevity of digital archival data is concerned, grafting would seem the most viable *ex ante* strategy (Van der Meer, 2008).

Grafting also partly alleviates the problem that most standards are not stand-alone artifacts but part of a web of interrelated standards. To keep abreast with changes in the 'core' standard, related standards must be updated. Grafting lessens the pressure for change on related standards. However, it comes at a cost. Sometimes a less burdensome clean start is preferred, as the SGML- XML succession showed (Egyedi & Loeffen, 2008). 'Downward compatibility or a clean start' is one of the fundamental dilemmas in standards design.

Backward compatibility is easier said than done (Thomas *et al*, 2008). The backward compatibility effort itself can become a source of

problems. For example, when the STEP standard was introduced in the UK defense environment, end-users saw too few differences between the implemented versions. Moreover, compatibility between the versions was not fully achieved, which led to extra work and delays in the project (i.e. 1999, 2001, 2006 editions of AP224; Thomas *et al*).

Furthermore, there is the problem of seeking backward compatibility with legacy systems that contain bugs - as in the case of AP224 with UNIX (Thomas *et al.*, 2008) and CSS1 in Internet Explorer (Egyedi, 2008b). 'Bugward compatibility', as this is referred to, lays a burden on current and future interoperability with other systems.

The second design angle relevant for coping with standards change is the development of 'future-proof' or robust *ex ante* standards. The need for robustness applies to sets of interrelated standards as well as individual standards. Where information architectures or otherwise composed systems are concerned, a modular and layered design approach to standardization is a well-tested and proven concept. In essence, the idea is here that modularity and layering allow one standard to evolve without affecting related standards. The archetypical example for layering is the Open Systems Interconnection reference framework for data communication (Tanenbaum, 1989).

In respect to separate standards, standards must be flexible to be able to cater to uncertain future needs. What makes a standard flexible? Although there have been incidental studies exploring the characteristics of flexible system and product standards (Egyedi & Verwater-Lukszo, 2005), it is an area of research that deserves more systematic attention in the context of standards dynamics.

8. CONCLUSION

The occurrence of change in ICT standards is caused by an interplay of supply- and demand-side factors. In this respect, e-business standards are no exception. On the demand-side, evolving user requirements, new technological possibilities, and new application domains create a pull for innovation-driven standards change; while experience gained with implementing standards in products and services and localizing standard-compliant systems make manifest the need to improve them.

On the supply-side of setting standards, sources of change may play at any stage of the standards life-cycle (i.e., problems with the scope of the standard, the standards process, the specification, and the implementation process). In this chapter, these standardization-related factors, together with implementation feedback (a demand-side factor), have been categorized as internal causes of change. The resulting changes can partly be avoided by improving the standards process, that is, by improved quality control. However, standards change that is caused by external, demand-side factors, such as the emergence of new technological opportunities, is in the long run inevitable – and desirable where it supports innovation. To cope with the negative side of change such as switching costs and reduced transparency, change control is required. There are *ad hoc* as well as more systematic approaches to support change management. Some of them cope with change ex post and focus on repairing compatibility; while others try to prevent incompatibility by including change requirements in standards design. In particular in the latter area, that is, the area of developing 'future-proof', robust and flexible *ex ante* standards, much work still needs to be done to minimize the negative effects of standards change.

ACKNOWLEDGMENT

I sincerely thank the contributors to the NO-REST workpackage on standards dynamics (EU project), the Europeon Commission and Sun Microsystems for their valuable contributions and financial support and the two anonymous reviewers of this chapter for their constructive comments. This chapter is a strongly revised version of and extension to Egyedi (2008a).

ABBREVIATIONS

CSS: Cascading Style Sheets

DC: Dublin Core

DCQ: Dublin Core Qualifi ers

DVD: Digital Versatile Disc

ICT: Information and Communication Technology

IEC: International Electrotechnical Commission

IEEE: Institute of Electrical and Electronics Engineers

IPv4: Internet Protocol version 4

IPv6: Internet Protocol version 6

ISO: International Standardization Organization

IT: Information Technology

LAN: Local Area Network

NAT: Network Address Translation

ODA: Open Document Architecture

ODIF: Open Document Interchange Format

OSI: Open Systems Interconnection

R&D: Research and Development

SGML: Standard Generalized Markup Language

STEP: STandard for the Exchange of Product model data

W3C: World Wide Web Consortium

WLAN: Wireless Local Area Network

XML: EXtensible Markup Language

REFERENCES

Blind, K. (2008). Factors influencing the lifetime of telecommunication and information technology standards In T. M. Egyedi & K. Blind (Eds.), *The dynamics of standards* (pp. 155-177). Cheltenham, UK: Edward Elgar.

Egyedi, T. M. (1996). *Shaping Standardisation: A Study of Standards Processes and Standards Policies in the Field of Telematic Services.* Delft, the Netherlands: Delft University Press.

Egyedi, T. M. (2002). *Trendrapport Standaardisatie. Oplossingsrichtingen voor problemen van IT-interoperabiliteit.* Delft: Ministerie van Verkeer en Waterstaat, Rijkswaterstaat/ Meetkundige Dienst.

Egyedi, T. M. (2008a). Conclusion. In T. M. Egyedi & K. Blind (Eds.), *The dynamics of standards* (pp. 181-189). Cheltenham, UK: Edward Elgar.

Egyedi, T. M. (2008b). An implementation perspective on sources of incompatibility and standards' dynamics. In T. M. Egyedi & K. Blind (Eds.), *The dynamics of standards* (pp. 181-189). Cheltenham, UK: Edward Elgar.

Egyedi, T. M., & Blind, K. (2008). *Introduction.* In T. M. Egyedi & K. Blind (Eds.), *The dynamics of standards* (pp. 1-12). Cheltenham, UK: Edward Elgar.

Egyedi, T. M., & Heijnen, P. (2008). How stable are IT standards? In T. M. Egyedi & K. Blind (Eds.), *The dynamics of standards* (pp. 137-154). Cheltenham, UK: Edward Elgar.

Egyedi, T. M., & Loeffen, A. (2008). Incompatible successors: The failure to graft XML onto SGML. In T. M. Egyedi & K. Blind (Eds.), *The dynamics of standards* (pp. 82-97). Cheltenham, UK: Edward Elgar.

Egyedi, T. M., & Sherif, M. H. (2008). *Standards' Dynamics through an Innovation Lens: Next Generation Ethernet Networks.* Paper presented at the Conference Name|. Retrieved Access Date|. from URL|.

Egyedi, T. M., & Verwater-Lukszo, Z. (2005). Which standards' characteristics increase system flexibility? Comparing ICT and Batch Processing Infrastructures. *Technology in Society, 27*(3), 347-362.

Farrell, J. (1990). Economics of Standardization. In J. L. B. H. Schumny (Ed.), *An Analysis of the Information Technology Standardization Process.*

Farrell, J., & Saloner, G. (1985). Standardization, Compatibility and Innovation. *RAND Journal of Economics, 16*, 70-83.

Gauch, S. (2008). + vs. − , Dynamics and effects of competing standards of recordable DVD media In T. M. Egyedi & K. Blind (Eds.), *The dynamics of standards* (pp. 47-67). Cheltenham, UK: Edward Elgar.

ISO/IEC. (2004). *ISO/IEC Directives, Part 2: Rules for the structure and drafting of International Standards.* Geneva: ISO/IEC.

Jakobs, K. (2005). The Role of the 'Third Estate' in ICT Standardisation. In S. Bolin (Ed.), *The Standards Edge: Future Generation*: The Bolin Group.

Jakobs, K. (2008). The IEEE 802.11 WLAN installation at RWTH Aachen University: A case of voluntary vendor lock-in. In T. M. Egyedi & K. Blind (Eds.), *The dynamics of standards* (pp. 99-116). Cheltenham, UK: Edward Elgar.

Jones, P., & Hudson, J. (1996). Standardization and the Cost of Assessing Quality. *European Journal of Political Economy, 12*, 355-361.

Kindleberger, C. P. (1983). Standards as Public, Collective and Private Goods. *Kyklos, 36*, 377-396.

Kuhn, T. S. (1970). *The structure of scientific revolutions* (2 ed.). Chicago: University of Chicago Press.

Meer, K. v. d. (2008). The sustainability of digital data: Tension between the dynamics and longevity of standards. In T. M. Egyedi & K. Blind (Eds.), *The dynamics of standards* (pp. 15-27). Cheltenham, UK: Edward Elgar.

Reddy, N. M. (1990). Product of Self-Regulation. A Paradox of Technology Policy. *Technological Forecasting and Social Change, 38*, 43-63.

Schmidt, S. K., & Werle, R. (1998). *Co-ordinating Technology. Studies in the International Standardization of Telecommunications.* . Cambridge, Mass: MIT Press.

Sherif, M. H., Jakobs, K., & Egyedi, T. M. (2007). Standards of quality and quality of standards for Telecommunications and Information Technologies. In M. Hörlesberger, M. El_Nawawi & T. Khalil (Eds.), *Challenges in the Management of New Technologies* (pp. 427-447). Singapore: World Scientific Publishing Company. .

Tanenbaum, A. S. (1989). *Computer Networks* (2 ed.): Prentice-Hall .

Thomas, J. W., Probets, S., Dawson, R., & King, T. (2008). A case study of the adoption and implementation of STEP. In T. M. Egyedi & K. Blind (Eds.), *The dynamics of standards* (pp. 117-134). Cheltenham, UK: Edward Elgar.

Timmermans, S., & Berg, M. (1997). Standardization in Action: Achieving Local Universality through Medical Protocols. *Social Studies of Science, 27*(2), 273-305.

Vrancken, J., Kaart, M., & Soares, M. (2008). Internet addressing standards: A case study in standards dynamics driven by bottom-up adoption. In T. M. Egyedi & K. Blind (Eds.), *The dynamics of standards* (pp. 68-81). Cheltenham, UK: Edward Elgar.

Weizsacker, C. C. v. (1982). Staatliche Regulierung - positive und normative Theorie. *Schweizerische Zeitschrift fur Volkswirtschaft und Statistik, 2*, 325-243.

ENDNOTES

[1] The term 'open standards' is avoided because it raises more questions than that it provides answers, and the term committee standard suffices for our purposes. For the interested reader we point to Krechmer (2006), who distinguishes different aspects of openness and angles (openness from the perspective of standard creators, implementers, and users).

[2] The phrase "and approved by a recognized body" was omitted from the definition in order to widen its applicability to other committee standards as well.

[3] In 2005 a PDF version became an ISO committee standard.

[4] *Transaction costs* are costs like the time and resources required to establish a common understanding. Standards reduce transaction costs of negotiation because "both parties to a deal mutually recognize what is being dealt in..." (Kindleberger, 1983, p. 395) Standards reduce transaction costs between producers and costumers by improving recognition of technical characteristics and avoidance of buyer dissatisfaction (Reddy, 1990). They reduce e.g. *search costs* since there is less need for customers to spend time and money evaluating products (Jones & Hudson, 1996).

5   *Adverse selection* takes place if a supplier of inferior products gains market share through price competition because the supplier of high quality products has no means to signal the superior quality of its products to consumers. Quality standards support the latter in signaling activities, foster the co-existence of low and high quality market segments, and therefore minimize the likelihood that consumer selection is based on wrong assumptions.

6   The term network externalities refers to the situation that every new user in the network increases the value of being connected to the network (Farrell & Saloner, 1985).

7   Because company strategies on standardization are usually not made public, it is un-certain whether company policies include a standards change paragraph. Since standards change has not yet been widely addressed, its business relevance may not have drawn their attention.

8   The term *grafting* refers to the process of developing a standard (successor) based on another standard (predecessor) with the intention to improve the latter's functionality and/or usefulness in other respects (e.g. ease or cost of implementation) while preserving compatibility and interoperability with its predecessor's context of use (Egyedi & Loeffen, 2008, p.84)

Section V
Policy Issues

Chapter XIII
Open Standards and Government Policy

Mogens Kühn Pedersen
Copenhagen Business School, Denmark

Vladislav V. Fomin
Vytautas Magnus University, Lithuania

Henk J. de Vries
Erasmus University, The Netherlands

ABSTRACT

The fast growth in globalization stimulates the trend of open standards and challenges governments in devising policies for the national information infrastructures to foster equal access to and even distribution of knowledge among citizens and business. In response, governments may seek a more active role in standardization as they face challenges from being stakeholders in use of standards; a need for new standards may drive governments to become participants in the standardization process, and to require conformance assurance by the market, and search for a policy on migration from an installed base of proprietary solutions. In this chapter the authors identify some critical issues, which can help government decision makers opt for select positions and interventions in standardization.

INTRODUCTION

The role of national governments in the context of global informatization is fostering information infrastructures that create equal access to and an even distribution of knowledge among citizens and businesses (Castells, 1996). Efficient func-

tioning of the information infrastructure requires standards for effectively implementing interoperability and interchange of information-based processes and products in the society, which, in turn, requires competent government policy for choosing and adopting broadly recognized standards that do not bias solutions towards specific implementations (Fomin, Pedersen, & de Vries, 2008). Adoption of relevant standards is also required for protection of the critical infrastructure (GAO, 2004).

An increasing interest in standards across governments may be traced to the understanding of the huge economic impact a *lack* of standards policy can have upon national economies (Garcia, 1992), and government budgets in particular. It is through sharing a common standard that anonymous partners in a market can communicate, can have common expectations on the performance of each other's product, and can trust the compatibility of their joint production. Thus, standards are necessary for the smooth functioning of anonymous exchanges – and therefore, for the efficient functioning of the market (WTO, 2005). The sheer size of the information technology markets, representing a growing share (more than 10 percent) of the global economy, attests to the economic magnitude of standards' influence on products. Practically all ICT products implement one or more standards – de facto or de jure. This is due to the component nature of all ICT hardware and the many software and hardware interfaces that need being specified.

Compatibility and information and services exchange come with a cost in the age of rapidly developing technology. With major shifts of technology paradigm taking place every decade, governments and businesses alike are facing the huge migration costs of ICT structures built in previous eras of computerization to make them meet the requirements of the present day operations (Hertz, Lucas, & Scott, 2006).

Given the technical criticality and economic importance of standards in the functioning of modern information society, there has been an increasing interest in *open* standards across governments (IBM, 2005). *Open standards* are understood as "technologies whose specifications are public and without any restriction in their access and implementation" (Reding, 2008). In the context of this work, we refer to open standards along

the lines defined by European standardization organizations: open standards are (1) developed and/or affirmed in a transparent process open to all relevant players, including industry, consumers and regulatory authorities; (2) either free of Intellectual Property Rights (IPR) concerns, or licensable on a fair/reasonable and non-discriminatory (F/RAND) basis; (3) driven by stakeholders, whereas user requirements must be fully reflected; (4) publicly available; and (5) maintained (ICT Standards Board, 2005, p.10). Following these process requirements, the standard should not favour a single company or group of companies against others in implementing the specifications. While this technological condition echoes the pluralist rhetoric of democratic society (Oksala, Rutkowski, Spring, & O'Donnell, 1996, p.11), it often presents a challenge for policy-makers, as almost all technologies have vested commercial interests driving their development into standards though specific proprietary technologies.

The novelty of the open standards trend (IBM, 2005) and challenges it brings to government decision-making implies the lack of government expertise in policy formulation. In the tradition of providing academic intellectual vision for building government decision-supporting expertise (Helmer & Rescher, 1959), in this paper we review some of the standards and standardization issues and challenges that governments, ICT industries, and non-ICT industries face in the coming years. We do not aim to provide a comprehensive policy guideline, as such task would be near to impossible given the diversity of national interests and ICT infrastructures from country to country. However, by engaging in the debate, we can sketch out general directions for future developments, and identify some critical issues, which can help government decision makers harness the complexity of the issue (Axelrod & Cohen, 1999).

This paper is structured as follows. First we explore the contemporary challenges ICT infrastructure build-out imposes on the government policy. Then we discuss the role of open standards in coping with these challenges. We conclude the paper with a summary and managerial implications.

STANDARDS, STANDARDIZATION AND MARKETS

The industrial revolution created the conditions for booming economies in many countries of the world. The national economies grew as local markets became regional and eventually national. This was caused by new means of transport (roads, steam trains, harbours, and steam boats), new means of energy (steam, later electrification, diesel engines, turbines, etc.), and new means of communication (telegraph and telephony). Industrialization, therefore, developed a range of interdependencies due in part to an increased division of labour. It was particularly due to the network effects of power supply from utilities, telecommunication networks, and governments active in promoting their industries internationally. Technological progress meant agreements between industrialists—at some point in the technological development—to accept certain standards needed to connect machines, to apply utensils, to rig boats and vessels, and to connect private, local operating telephony networks into national networks. In brief, the industrial revolution would not have succeeded without a concomitant standardization. Many of the standardization bodies around today trace their origin to the early days of industrialization. The history of active government involvement in standardization also traces back to at least the beginning of the 20th century (Garcia, 1992), although since then standards development responsibility has gradually shifted to the private standards development organizations (SDOs).

While the Age of Industrial Revolution is long past, standardization shows no tendency to slow down. On the contrary, standards seem to have become a driving force for furthering economic development. To ascertain this proposition, German and English economists have undertaken a major study (Blind, 2004; DTI, 2005). It shows that standards may be held accountable for as much as 13 percent of the rate of growth of productivity in the economy in the latter third of the last century in Britain and in Germany—the rate ridiculed by some as far too small, since no growth without standards in the industrialized world would be possible at all.

Already a decade ago, new standards development for the ICT domain surpassed that of other industrial areas (Oksala, et al., 1996). Are there particularities of standardization of ICT compared to the standardization of industrial age products? For ICT, the numerous layers and their interfaces account for a high level of complexity. To manage the complexity, testing "machines" are built to facilitate compatibility to product specifications and compliance to standard specifications. Yet, it is still not possible to build a complete testing machine because standards documents cannot (and should not) be a complete specification of all future product implementations. Compatibility and interoperability requirements imposed upon end users (consumers) have been used as a strong reason for government to assure and support international standards organizations and/or formal standards. The government involvement here is prompted by public-good considerations in government efforts to assure the public access, public safety, and public welfare (Oksala, et al., 1996, p.11).

The role of standards as a mechanism to achieve economic goals represents another important reason for government's active involvement in standardization. Steinmueller (2005) points to two mechanisms for using standards as a market regulation tool. First, licensable standards may allow the owner of standard's specifications "to capture the definition of the technological trajectory, the direction and, to some degree, the rate at which future technological progress is made" (Steinmueller, 2005, p.26). As an example, Microsoft can force the market to adopt new versions of its software due to compatibility issues between different components of Microsoft OS and applications. Second, the owner of an industry standard's IPR may be able to extend market power by licensing its standard vertically: that is to the market for components (Steinmueller, 2005). As an example, the "compatibility" of Microsoft Windows and Internet Explorer versus "non-compatibility" of the former with Firefox or Opera browsers.

The basic point of these market strategies is to give the standard's owner an advantage over rivals in defining and implementing the next incremental step in technological advance (e.g., when to introduce the new version of MS Office) (Steinmueller, 2005).

Open standards carry a potential to reconcile the economic and public-good rationales of standardization: in markets where open standards operate to reduce entry barriers for competitors, the network effects of complementary product and service suppliers may buttress the position of the dominant firm (Steinmueller, 2005, p.28). While the increased competition in the short run can not be guaranteed, adoption of open standards provides assurance that long run market development will not falter as a consequence of technological mistakes made by the dominant firm. This is a desirable outcome from a social welfare point of view (Steinmueller, 2005).

ICT Challenges Beyond the Industrial Age Standards

The ICT domain represents complexity that goes beyond the imagination of the industrial world. The myriad of disparate information systems on firm, local, government, and global levels can be made somewhat interoperable through the use of (open) standards. The EC recently issued a report on the challenges of eEurope which emphasizes the challenge of achieving interoperability between the information systems that differ due to the diversity of administrative law and practices between countries, identity management, reliability, security and other issues (Commission of the European Communities, 2003). As an example, seven out of ten local governments in Denmark – a country touted by many as the global leader in the informatization of the state (Fomin, 2008; ITU, 2003) – reported to lack common public sector solutions and infrastructure, while roughly the same number were lacking common standards for data exchange (Ministry of Science Technology and Innovation, 2003).

The lack of interoperability is difficult to quantify for economic assessment, but one aspect of non-open standards is directly related to economic impact: the vendor lock-in or "the ability of proprietary software vendors to use their de facto standards for protocols and data formats to perpetuate their own software products in volume and over time" (SSRC, 2005). The use of proprietary standards (for example, for word-processing and spreadsheets, currently dominated by Microsoft's proprietary Office standards) forces not only consumers (citizens), but also administrations (government(s)), to lock-in to the software vendor (Microsoft). Then they are forced or enticed to undergo software and hardware upgrades at a pace more frequent than economically viable and/or justifiable, much less needed. This may affect other stakeholders as well: for example, a software and/or hardware upgrade by a local municipality may force its residents and businesses to undergo the same upgrade in order to maintain access to the (online) services provided by the municipality.

Another difference between the industrial products and software is that of a material nature and the rights of use. Software is different from that of industrial products (DTI, 2002):

- It is intangible and can easily be reproduced;
- Its lifetime is dependant on infrastructure evolution;

- It doesn't have a value as a physical product, but as a right to be used;
- It is well suited for opportunistic pricing, due to the cost of copying-distribution being zero, while the value of right of use varies depending on the needs/capabilities of its owners;
- There are no "production" capacity limits once the software has been developed—it is only limited to the size of the market;
- Due to high profit margins and "unlimited" market, there is a trend towards monopolistic behaviour by producers.

The economics of maintenance is much more complicated than the economics of rights of use though the latter has imposed non-negligible administrative costs and complexity in some cases. Comparing standard compliant to non-standard software in network communication has proven the former to be dominant. The Internet has wiped out most non-standard computing networks, except for a few global, industry networks such as e.g., the inter-bank financial SWIFT network. Yet, when considering database software, the proprietary standards remain in power, only yielding to the SQL standard of inquiry. Thus, standardization drivers are not working equally across the field of ICT but are subject to competitive strategies of large companies each guarding their market.

Costs of software use depend upon which contractual terms apply to the customer. A conclusive and pre-emptive copyright is imposed on every purchase of licensed software with strict, limited rights of use of proprietary software. Pricing of rights of use may be anything but transparent. An example is the famous "battle" in 2002-3 that led Microsoft to withdraw a pricing scheme after strong protests from corporate buyers. Because it left most customers uncertain as to the price they should pay, it resulted in customers abandoning contracts with Microsoft. Less than a year later Microsoft released a new scheme.

When devising a policy for adoption of ICT standards, one must consider the life-span of those standards. That consideration would include the evolution of ICT infrastructure, as well as the emergence of new(er) standards with a greater value (offering higher productivity for the user). In addition, consideration must be given to such socio-economic issues as (re-)training.

Finally, compatibility and interoperability requirements imposed upon end users (citizen) have been evoked as justification for government to assure that international standards organization procedures take precedence over consortia, and in particular, vendor organizations' standards. This is in line with a call for open standards that harness the powers of dominant vendors in the middle to the long run.

POLICY OF STANDARDIZATION

Given the role of standards in the functioning of markets, as explored before, issues in standardization that government would be inclined to address must include competition policy and consumer protection measures to achieve workable competitive markets, secure and reliable products, and incentives for innovation activities in the marketplace. Besides general competition and consumer protection policies, there is a range of standardization issues where ICT standards have become essential to the long-term interests of government in securing and accessing electronic documents.

This leaves the core of standards issues as:

1. Considerations of whether to take an active part in bringing about open standards (policies) where they are lacking but needed for governments' ICT operations.
2. Timing for an open standards' adoption (early vs. late).
3. Conformance clause in ICT public procurement (enforcing vs. avoiding/ignoring).

4.   Discrimination against non-compliant ICT products.

The first issue to arise is a response to the digitalization of government documents and of government-to-business and government-to-citizen communication. In realizing the importance of standards to the ICT markets, governments find themselves as stakeholders with a long-term interest that may seem inconclusively addressed or subject to a biased impact from other stakeholders that may jeopardize competition objectives of governments.

The second issue arises as governments acknowledge their responsibility for their own long-term interests. How can or how should governments position themselves in the standardization process? Participation as an end user selecting among market products with a set of selection criteria has been the prevalent procedure. Yet, this strategy may not succeed if there is no opportunity for standards creators to develop standards that meet the long-term requirements of governments who have not helped formulate them. It is only if governments have a stated policy that standard creators can take stock of them and respond. Governments therefore cannot rely only on their role as end users. They need to look at the early phase of standardization to make their requirements known.

Therefore governments also need to address the third issue of a conformance clause in ICT public procurement. They must look for ways to guide and evaluate implementations to ensure that their requirements are met in the products. The latter may not be necessary before a government decides to procure a product, though the means for assessing standard conformance should be in place long before the procurement of products.

The fourth issue emerges as standard compliant products become available while proprietary products form the major part of the installed base of government ICT. The very co-existence of proprietary and standard-compliant products may conflict with the objective of interoperability. Therefore, learning how to deal with an installed base of non-compliant technologies cannot be dismissed as irrelevant. Governments need to determine a period of transition. It is rarely possible to determine such a transition period for a single product at a time because of needs of interchange of files and data and the process dependencies embedded in applications. In addition, it is not economically sound to adopt a mechanistic approach to transition.

Each of the aforementioned issues of standards policy deserves government's attention. In the following, we explore these issues in more detail.

Government Participation in Standardization

The distinction between propriety standards and open standards in ICT has arisen partly because of the increasing impact of consortia standardization on general communication and interoperability requirements in society and in governments.

Studies show there is a relative reduction in activity in formal standardization bodies and a relative increase in consortia for overall activity in the field of ICT (Blind & Gauch, 2005). If formal standardization bodies are open, consortia are not always so (Egyedi, 2003). One explanation of this shift may be the relatively decreasing share of telecommunication standards with a traditional involvement of public owned service providers in telecommunications since 1998. Another explanation is the speed of technological development; formal standardization is perceived to be slower (which is not always true). A third explanation is that due to the highly-specialized technical knowledge needed to make the standards, only a few companies are able to contribute and it thus does not make sense to have a "democratic" process with involvement of many countries (Garcia, 1992, p.535). A fourth reason is that these standards are related to product development and that for confidentiality reasons the companies prefer to have a non-disclose agreement. A fifth reason may be related to IPRs: formal standardization organizations allow inclusion of IPR in standards only in case licenses are available 'on reasonable and non-discriminatory' (RAND) terms, whereas consortia have more flexibility in this sense. Irrespective of the reasons causing the shift, the increasing share of consortia leaves governments and consumers with a lesser representation in total ICT standardization activities.

The legitimate objectives of these stakeholders may be achieved by engaging in international standards organizations where governments and consumers organization may have a say. CEN/ISSS has estimated that there are 250 consortia, according to their June 2007 list (which is 19 less than in 2000). This can be compared to the ETSI, CEN and CENELEC and the technical committees (TCs) of international standardization bodies (i.e., ISO and IEC) with 55 TCs in the ICT area (Blind & Gauch, 2005). Yet, we see international standardization organizations adopt a filtering role leaving the technical specification process to consortia. This may become a productive coexistence of standardization bodies, although it challenges the ideal of an open standardization process: a case for concern is the possibility of accepting "biased" standards as international standards by the public bodies. In this way, standardization processes may come to halt innovation, jeopardizing the overall economic growth effects of standards.

The other side of consortia standardization concerns interoperability, which is a prime end user standards objective. It is next to impossible to assure complete (i.e., conformance test) interoperability of a software product with a proprietary source code. However that does not equally strongly exclude establishing interoperability between open source products, even though there is no perfect "testing machine" available to guarantee complete interoperability. Unfortunately, the issue in the case of open source is often interoperability with a proprietary product where the inaccessibility of the source code constrains the testing.

Controlling which specifications find their way into a standard requires participation in the standardization process. If all relevant technical minded representatives are to be assured access to participate, this requires only one known model: open standards. It is the only model where there is no right to veto access of a participant and there is not an economic entry barrier. While government participation per se does not fulfil this objective, it is still a way better to monitor and intervene in the process. A subsidy instead of participation buys the government legitimacy but provides no assurance of a useful specification of a standard enhancing interoperability. A truly free and open access would shift the governments' burden of ensuring interoperability to a wide range of interests. There is little we know in terms of predicting the outcome of such a policy.

Early Adoption of Open ICT Standards

The economics of standards leaves little doubt that economic growth is well served by (some) standardization. The questions today are: when, which, and how much standardization best serves economic growth and which standardization process best supports the development of the innovation capacity of the economy? Should standardization in ICT become an issue of high concern (again) to governments, and can it avoid the "nationalistic" bent that it has had previously? These questions should be raised regarding adoption of a standard whether published by a consortium or later by an open standards organization.

Adoption of standards by businesses, governments, and organizations cannot be taken for granted. The reason is simply because producers of standards-compliant products need to adopt the standard for their product *before* it reaches the end users so that it is an alternative to non-standard compliant products. Therefore, early adoption of standards means it is necessary to select standards before they may have been able to prove they can gather a broad acceptance in the industry. This is generally obtained if a standard is found in several competing vendor products.

A model of early adoption should balance the trade-off of getting a good deal on a (proprietary) standard compliant product today versus the long term effects of a high degree of certainty through the broad adoption of an (open) standard by an industry and its customers. The danger in buying a proprietary standard compliant product today is that it could lead to becoming either locked-in or abandoned, i.e., becoming a so-called "angry orphan" (King & West, 2002). This is kind of a-procurement-today versus an-information-infrastructure-policy-of-tomorrow argument. It is unbalanced and needs to be separated into its component parts.

Meeting proprietary or industry standard compliant products in the market exposes the dilemma of coming late to standardization. Several types of standards may no longer be available if the installed base in society has been dominated by a single (proprietary) standard for a while. If government needs to adopt a competition policy view of this type of a market then there are reasons for concern. Therefore one option would be policy intervention requiring the incumbent to open up the specific standard for an inspection and change by a SDO technical committee that submits the (adapted) standard to an open standardization body in conformance to the (fast track) PAS procedure of ISO. Another way for government to deal with late coming to the market would be to embark upon the development of an open standard following the rules of an open SDO, itself.

Coordination of government standards policies would bring them a long way toward ensuring critical mass for a standard and therefore becoming a kind of self-fulfilling prophecy of a technological trajectory based on an open standard.

Presently, this is hard to achieve because many governments still seem to see themselves as protagonists of their own companies in a world market perspective rather than as their citizens'

guardians of interoperability and competitive ICT markets. Pressures from government representatives in international standard bodies may turn the tide.

Conformance to Standards in Public Procurement

Governments' specific interests in standardization of ICT have arrived late on the standards scene. Therefore, many proprietary products are installed in governments today. Coping with the coexistence of proprietary and open standard ICT requires certified third parties to apply conformance testing according to firmly established criteria based upon the open standard. Public procurement will be able to manage in the heterogeneous market of competing products only in so far as such third parties are present in the marketplace.

The ISO Strategic Plan 2005-10 stresses the aim of "one standard, one test and one conformity assessment procedure accepted everywhere" (ISO, 2004) that seems to fulfil the very objective of managing the coexistence of competing standards reliant products. Yet, one more condition applies to the issue of creating open standard compliant ICT products: timing of the adoption of an open standard.

In the case of coming late to a market, governments therefore face problems of creating proper incentives to industry and smoothing the process of adoption of new, standard compliant ICT products in government agencies, amongst citizens and in business.

Discrimination Against Non-Compliant ICT Products

When non-standard products proliferate in government, there is a definite case for considering a migration policy. Migration from proprietary to an industry/open standard compliant product depends upon the degree of urgency to embark upon a new technological track and upon a cost-benefits calculus of the migration of all partners to the transaction. These conditions will vary across technologies. This is due to their degree of penetration into government, the rate of penetration in dependent industries and among citizens, and the profitability (or advantages) of the corresponding, non-standard products.

On the part of government and other users, objective measures of usage, scope of usage, and prospects of usage can all be obtained for specific instances. However, they will often make sense only if obtained for a domain rather than within a single office or department of an organisation or of government. Since objective conditions do not pre-empt the factors determining ICT procurement decisions, it may be necessary to adopt economic measures that will reveal the relative strength of hard-to-quantify objective factors' impact on the cost-benefits of adoption of a standard compliant product. Economic measures would then enter into the calculus representing the degree to which non-standard compliant products could be discriminated against in a tender. The degree of discrimination would mean that the non-compliance could be tolerated at a price for a limited time period after which the vendor would have to offer a smooth transition according to contract. This would require having conversion tables or other technical equipment ready-made for the purpose of a smooth migration.

These and other measures would combine incentives to both vendors and buyers in terms of their respective transitions to a standard compliant ICT product. Because of this, they would lower barriers-to-change more than if solutions to manage the migration phase for ICT vendors and the users were left out of the process. To industry, this would mean a phasing out of (profitable) products that were bound to lose in the market anyway given sufficient time. In particular, government bodies would have the powers required to conduct a coordinated and flexible transition to open standards not only in government but where relevant also in society.

SUMMARY AND CONCLUSIONS

The Trend of the Open Standards

The trend of open standards for government policy (Fomin, et al., 2008; IBM, 2005) is being enforced by the growing globalization. The need for such standards increases along with the fast growth in global trade, manufacturing, services, capital and labour.

Governments and citizens need standards. If "remnants" of proprietary standards are found, they need to be filtered out to ensure the nations' global connectivity by enforcing open standards. Here it makes little sense to apply a "comply or explain" principle, since it is only to the disadvantage of the national interest to opt out of interoperability.

In the latter case, two types of issues need to be addressed. If we do not have a completely mature technology but a variety of technologies defying interoperability, then we are still chasing the spirit of innovation but at higher costs to industry than necessary. If innovation is a vendor strategy for market share protection, then innovations may come about reluctantly and not necessarily in the interest of end-users. If innovation is an "open market operation", then there will be no dominant players in that market to bias future innovations. If this is a clause that cannot be validated, then incentives to innovation will be biased against governments' interests – at least if government policy is that of a globalization policy.

Transitioning from Proprietary to Open Standards

Researching the transition from a proprietary standard to an open one shows that the change process encounters network effects and path dependency impacts. A study of 1394 firms in the US on the migration from an EDI to an open standard IOS came to the conclusion that prior use of EDI reduced adoption costs for open standard IOS adoption, but that it tended to increase switching costs (Zhu, Kraemer, Gurbaxani, & Xu, 2006). This finding validates the path dependency effects in standards migration. The network effects of a standard were translated into significant economies if associated with a trading community. Managerial complexity, as opposed to financial costs, was a more significant determinant of adoption costs (Zhu, et al., 2006, p.534). The findings of studies on the economics of standards so far have not provided useful insights how government could facilitate transition from industry standards to open standards.

If government itself adopts an open standard and industry and citizens have to comply, then government inflicts on the industry and citizens the migration costs. Those migration costs will depend on previous standards' use in industry. The adoption costs would then need to be balanced by benefits spillover from government adoption and from concomitant reduced coordination costs in industry.

Managerial Implications

Government can have a unique role in standards policy for the national information infrastructure, because it can prescribe certain standards, stimulate its use by its procurement policy, and/or decide about the public good status of a particular technology. The latter may lead to a preference for 'open standards'. However, experts disagree on the willingness as well as the ability of governments to deal with such issues.

Governments' requirement of conformance to open standards in public procurement can counter the proprietary developments by large corporations, thus helping avoid vendor lock-in by promoting or even enforcing conformity to general standards. However, demanding or recommending compliance is not easy, it is necessary to specify precisely how suppliers should comply.

For governments to take a more active role in standardization processes, government representatives could monitor relevant industry consortia developments and define grey areas and common interests where market fails to get agreement. However, the governments lack competence and resources needed for effective participation.

Concluding Remarks

To conclude, we believe that while governments are disadvantaged participants in standardization due to a range of factors explored here, the powers of globalization should motivate governments to opt for select positions and interventions in standardization.

This article does not provide final answers to any of the issues raised. In a global economy, the obstacles to true interoperability are formidable, yet in practice the ICT industry has proven itself capable of delivering products meeting the criteria. Governments should not perceive the issues presented here as far away opportunities but surely within the orbit of today's policy, industry will be able to meet governmental requirements.

ACKNOWLEDGMENT

This work was supported by research grant from the Danish Ministry of Science, Technology, and Innovation, Grant #5798000416642.

LIST OF ABBREVIATIONS

CEN: European Committee for Standardization

CENLEC: European Committee for Electrotechnical Standardization

EC: The European Council

EDI: Electronic Data Interchange

ETSI: European Telecommunications Standardisation Institute

F/RAND: Free/Reasonable and Non-Discriminatory

ICT: Information and Communication Technology

IEC: The International Electrotechnical Commision

IOS: Interorganizational System

IPR: Intellectual Property Right

ISO: International Organization for Standardization

ISSS: Information Society Standardization System

SDO: Standards Development Organization

SQL: Structured Query Language

SWIFT: Society for Worldwide Interbank Financial Telecommunication

TC: Technical committee

REFERENCES

Axelrod, R. M., & Cohen, M. D. (1999). *Harnessing complexity : organizational implications of a scientific frontier.* New York: Free Press.

Blind, K. (2004). *The Economics of Standards. Theory, Evidence, Policy.* Cheltenham, UK: Edward Elgar.

Blind, K., & Gauch, S. (2005, September 21-23). *Trends in ICT Standards in European Standardisation Bodies and Standards Consortia.* In the Proceedings of the 4th International Conference on Standardization and Innovation in Information Technology (SIIT), Geneva.

Castells, M. (1996). *The Rise of the Network Society* (2nd ed. Vol. I). Oxford: Blackwell Publishers, Ltd.

Commission of the European Communities (2003). *Commission staff working document "Linking up the Europe: the importance of interoperability for e-government services"* (Commission staff working document No. SEC(2003)801). Brussels: Commission of the European Communities.

DTI (2002). *Open source software in e-government* (report). Copenhagen: Danish Board of Technology (DTI).

DTI (2005). *The Empirical Economics of Standards* (DTI Economics Paper No. 12). London: Department of Trade and Industry (DTI). Available at http://www.berr.gov.uk/files/file9655.pdf

Egyedi, T. M. (2003). Consortium Problem Redefined: Negotiating 'Democracy' in the Actor Network on Standardization. *International Journal of IT Standards & Standardization Research, 1*(2), 22-38.

Fomin, V. V. (2008). Snow, Buses, and Mobile Data Services in the Information Age. *Journal of Strategic Information Systems, 17*(3), 234-246.

Fomin, V. V., Pedersen, M. K., & de Vries, H. J. (2008). Open Standards And Government Policy: Results Of A Delphi Survey. *Communications of the Association for Information Systems, 22*(April), 459-484.

GAO (2004). *Technology Assessment. Cybersecurity for Critical Infrastructure Protection:* United States General Accounting Office (GAO). Available at http://www.gao.gov/new.items/d04321.pdf

Garcia, D. L. (1992). Standards Setting in the United States: Public and Private Sector Roles. *Journal of the American Society for Information Science, 43*(8), 531-537.

Helmer, O., & Rescher, N. (1959). On the Epistemology of the Inexact Sciences. *Management Science, 6*(1), 25-52.

Hertz, J. C., Lucas, M., & Scott, J. (2006). *Open Technology Development. Roadmap Plan*: Prepared for: Ms. Sue Payton, Deputy Under Secretary of Defense.

IBM (2005, May 10). Governments and public policy. Corporate responsibility report Retrieved Nov 29, 2005. Available at http://www.ibm.com/ibm/responsibility/world/government/

ICT Standards Board (2005, April 27). *Critical Issues in ICT Standardization* (report). ICT Standards Board. Available at http://www.ictsb.org/ictsfg/ictsfg_report_2005-04-27.pdf

ISO (2004). *ISO Strategic Plan 2005-2010 : Standards for a sustainable world*. Geneve: ISO Central Secretariat.

ITU (2003, 19 Nov). *ITU Digital Access Index: World's First Global ICT Ranking. International Telecommunications Union (ITU)*. Available at http://www.itu.int/newsarchive/press_releases/2003/30.html

King, J. L., & West, J. (2002). Ma Bell's orphan: US cellular telephony, 1974-1996. *Telecommunications Policy, 26*(3-4), 189-204.

Ministry of Science Technology and Innovation (2003). *The Danish Software Strategy* (report). Copenhagen: Ministry of Science Technology and Innovation.

Oksala, S., Rutkowski, A., Spring, M., & O'Donnell, J. (1996). The Structure of IT Standardisation. *StandardView, 4*(1), 9-22.

Reding, V. (2008). *Digital TV, Mobile TV: let's push for open technologies in Europe and worldwide* (Speech No. SPEECH/08/144). Budapest.

SSRC (2005). *The Politics of Open Source Adoption*: Social Science Research Council (SSRC).

Steinmueller, E. W. (2005, 10-11 January). *Technical Compatibility Standards and the Co-Ordination of the Industrial and International Division of Labour*. Paper presented at the Advancing Knowledge and the Knowledge Economy, Washington, DC.

WTO (2005). *World Trade Report 2005: Exploring the Links between Trade, Standards and the WTO*. Geneva, Switzerland: World Trade Organization (WTO).

Zhu, K., Kraemer, K. L., Gurbaxani, V., & Xu, S. X. (2006). Migration to Open-Standard Interorganizational Systems: Network Effects, Switching Costs, and Path Dependency. *MIS Quarterly, 30* (Special Issue. Standard Making: A Critical Research Frontier for Information Systems Research), 515-540.

Section VI
Additional Readings

Chapter XIV
Developing Measures and Standards for the European Electronic Signatures Market

Ioannis P. Chochliouros
Hellenic Telecommunications Organization S.A. (OTE), Greece

Anastasia S. Spiliopoulou
Hellenic Telecommunications Organization S.A. (OTE), Greece

Tilemachos D. Doukoglou
Hellenic Telecommunications Organization S.A. (OTE), Greece

Elpida Chochliourou
General Prefectorial Hospital "Georgios Gennimatas," Greece

ABSTRACT

The European Authorities have promoted a specific and innovative framework for the use of electronic signatures, allowing the free flow of electronic signature-related products and services cross borders, and ensuring a basic legal recognition of such facilities. The core aim was to promote the emergence of the internal market for certification products, mainly intending to satisfy various requirements for the proper use and immediate "adoption" of electronic signature applications related to e-government and personal e-banking services. Thus, a number of technical, procedural, and quality standards for electronic signature products and solutions have been developed, all conforming to the requirements imposed by the EU regulation and the relevant market needs. In the present work, we examine the role of standardization activities for the promotion of several needs of an "open" European market based on the effective usage of e-signatures, and being able to affect a great variety of technological, business-commercial, regulatory, and other issues. In any case, the transposition of legal requirements into technical specifications (or business practices) needs to be harmonized at a European member-states' level in order to enable adequate interoperability of the final solutions proposed. Appropriate technical standards for the sector can help to establish a presumption of conformity that the electronic signature products following or implementing them comply with all the legal requirements imposed, in the background of the actual European policies. Thus we discuss recent European and/or national initiatives to fulfil such a fundamental option. The European Electronic Signature Standardization Initiative (EESSI) has been set up under the auspices of the European Commission for the carrying out of a work program aiming at the development of standards (be it technical specifications or policy practices) that would facilitate the implementation of the basic legal instrument (the "Electronic Signatures Directive"). Two major streams of possible standards-setting work have been determined, covering: (i) Qualitative and procedural standards for the provision of certification services and (ii) technical standards for product interoperability. We identify (and evaluate at a primary level) the basic components/modules of EESSI's specific results, already developed and offered in the market either as technical regulations and/or as recognized standards, with respect to essential requirements imposed by the European regulation. We also discuss relevant "feedback" already gained from various market areas and we focus on challenges for further implementation, progress, adoption, and development, especially in the framework for the promotion of converged broadband (Internet-based) communications facilities. It is important for the market that expected standardization work takes into account new technological developments as, in the future, users will move their e-signature key from device-to-device in a connected world. The added value of standards in the e-signatures sector, for both end users and assessing parties (judge, arbitrator, conformity assessment body, etc.) is of extreme importance for the future of the European electronic communications market.

INTRODUCTION

The digital technological landscape has changed significantly during the past decade. New communication technologies, new media, the Internet, and devices carrying new functionalities are expected to meet consumers' demand for seamless, simple, and user-friendly digital tools providing access to an extended range of services and content (i2010 High Level Group, 2006). In fact, electronic communication via open networks such as the Internet has been remarkably increased and expanded, on a scale unimaginable some years ago. As a consequence, electronic communication networks and information systems have been developed exponentially in recent years and are now an essential part of the daily lives of almost all European citizens (European Commission, 2002); in addition, they both constitute fundamental "tools" to the success of the broader European economy in the international scenery (Chochliouros & Spiliopoulou, 2005).

In particular, networks and information systems are converging and becoming increasingly interconnected, thus creating a variety of potential opportunities for all categories of "players" involved. This rapid expansion concerns all sectors of human activity, whether business, public services, or the private sphere. Actually, global networks have truly become the "lifeblood" of our societies and economies: An overwhelming number of employees use a mobile phone, a laptop, or a similar device to send or retrieve information for their work. Furthermore, in multiple cases, such information can represent a considerable value, for instance, describe a business transaction or contain technical knowledge (Lalopoulos, Chochliouros, & Spiliopoulou, 2004).

Despite the many and obvious benefits of the modern electronic communications development, this evolutionary process has also brought with it the worrying threat of intentional attacks against information systems and network infrastructures (European Commission, 2000). As cyberspace gets more and more complex and its components more and more sophisticated, *especially due to the fast development and evolution of (broadband) Internet-based platforms*, new and unforeseen vulnerabilities may emerge.

Moreover, as Internet becomes ubiquitous for all business and personal communications, the sensitivity and economic value of the content of information transmitted is highly increasing (Shoniregun, Chochliouros, Laperche, Logvynovskiy, & Spiliopoulou, 2004). The economic damage caused by network and/or service disruptions is becoming larger. Unfortunately, due to the transnational and borderless character of modern information systems, it is possible to launch an attack from anywhere in the world, to any place, at any time. This constitutes a severe threat (PriceWaterhouseCoopers, 2001) to the achievement of a safer information society and to an area of freedom and security, and therefore requires a "proper" and immediate response at the level of the European Union (EU). In particular, the economic burden imposed by various illegal actions on public bodies, companies, and individuals is considerable and threatens to make information systems more costly and less affordable to all potential users. Therefore, as so much depends on networks and information systems, their secure functioning has nowadays become a key concern, especially for the smooth operation of both internal EU market and society (European Commission, 2001).

BACKGROUND: THE NECESSITY FOR ENHANCED SECURITY

Development of a Proper Strategic Framework

As already pointed out, communication infrastructures have now become a "critical" part of the backbone of modern economies. Users should be able to rely on the availability of information services and have the confidence that their communications (and data) are safe from unauthorized access and/or modification. Thus, security is a major global challenge that has recently come to the fore due to world events and societal changes and it has therefore become an "enabler" for e-businesses and a prerequisite for privacy (Chochliouros & Spiliopoulou, 2006). Innovative solutions relying on emerging technologies are replacing previous "traditional" security approaches: the former may involve the extensive use of encryption and "digital signatures," new access control and authentication tools, and software filters of all kinds.

Ensuring secure and reliable information infrastructures and corresponding (offered) facilities not only require a range of technologies but also their correct deployment and effective use to respond to practical needs. At the European level, a variety of legislative action (Chochliouros & Spiliopoulou, 2003b; Weber, 2002) has mainly taken the form of measures especially in the fields of the protection of the fundamental right to privacy and data protection, together with electronic commerce (and other relevant electronic services) and electronic signatures (Kamal, 2005). (In the context of the present work, e-services can be considered as those providing the specific needs of businesses conducting commerce on the Internet by using Web technology to help businesses streamline processes, improve productivity, and increase efficiencies.) To adopt European legislation is sometimes a challenging task; but to put it into real life and in real business conditions is an even bigger challenge.

The practical application of e-communications in various spheres of activity, and specifically in that of electronic commerce, depends on the efficient removal of any "obstacles" to the expected harmonized development (Chochliouros & Spiliopoulou, 2004). These "obstacles" can be described as probable insecurities typical to "open" networks; that is, messages can be intercepted and manipulated, the validity of documents can be contested, and personal data can be illicitly collected and several forms of communication can be used for illegal purposes. Electronic commerce and many other applications of the information society will only develop if confidentiality can be guaranteed in a user-friendly and cost-efficient way. Therefore, it is necessary to create a secure environment that will enable the establishment of an information society that will safeguard the public against misuse, and the development of e-commerce on bases at least as assured as those which currently govern paper currency transactions in the business world.

To this aim, the international practice/experience has suggested two fundamental goals: digital signatures and encryption (European Commission, 1997; Richards, 2000). The first guarantees the identity of the user and the origin of the message (authentication), while the second protects against illegal interference (integrity) and ensures the confidentiality of communications. The regulation of this area had to be approached with a clear overall vision: on the one hand, there is a need to proceed with flexibility so as not to hamper technological advances and their applications while, *on the other hand*, the fundamental principles of the EU should be preserved including, *among others*, consumer protection, a level playing-field in terms of competition, free movement of services, and mutual recognition. General rules have to be established, leading to greater confidence in electronic commerce but providing guarantee that it remains flexible and open enough to allow for new technological developments.

Consequently, both electronic communication and commerce (European Parliament & Council of the European Union, 2000b; Ford & Baum, 2001) necessitate proper solutions and related services allowing data authentication. However, divergent rules with respect to legal recognition of electronic signatures and the accreditation of certification-service providers in the EU may create a significant barrier to the use (and growth) of e-communications and e-commerce.

The development and use of authentication products and services is still in progress, even at the global level. Up to now, several systems existed, which all made use of authentication for commerce, administration, and public services; however, it was necessary to create and to endorse a complete "set" of internationally agreed industry standards (or technical specifications) for their use. Without such standards, it is impossible to provide a common level of security, recognized as "valid for use" at national/regional level, even less at international level (Dempsey, 2003).

Open networks such as the Internet are of increasing importance for worldwide communication. They offer new ways of doing business, such as teleworking and virtual shared environments, and they offer opportunities for communication between parties which may not have pre-established relationships. Electronic signatures open up opportunities to exploit the (broadband) Internet for secure document exchange, for purchase requisitions, contracts, and invoice applications. To date, the most common form of electronic signature is the "digital signature." For the problem of authentication and integrity of data, digital signatures can provide a solution creating a proper framework at the European level to ensure mutual compatibility and to encourage the development of a range of certification arrangements that will suit different applications between public bodies and citizens (Kaufman, 2002).

It is quite important for the EU not only to guarantee practices and/or measures for the effective adoption of such digital signatures, but to establish appropriate procedures in the field of standardization and product which are interoperable with other international ones, or (at least) have a common interface with them. The aim for such an initiative is to encourage all sectors of society, and particularly the European industry, to design, develop, and endorse commonly accepted standards not only at national level but also at international level (bearing in mind the importance of ensuring that such standards comply with best practice and the state-of-the-art) (Dumortier, Kelm, Nillson, Skouma, & Van Eecke, 2003).

The Basic European Regulatory Initiatives

The "digital signature" is a digital code that can be attached to an electronically transmitted message that uniquely identifies the sender (Aalberts & Van der Hof, 1999). Like a written signature, its purpose is to guarantee that the individual sending the message really is who he or she claims to be. Digital signatures are based on public key technology (Chochliouros, Chochliouros, Spiliopoulou, & Lambadari, 2007), a special form of encryption invented in the 1970s which uses two different keys. Due to this specific usage, this form of encryption is also known as asymmetric cryptography. One key is kept secret (the so-called "private key") whereas the other key is made publicly available (the so-called "public key"). Both keys are generated simultaneously and they are collectively known as a "key pair." Once a message has been encrypted using one of them, it can only be decrypted by the other key. To be effective, digital signatures must be unforgeable. There are a number of different encryption techniques to guarantee this level of security. A signature is not part of the substance of a transaction, but rather of its representation or form. Digital signatures identify and authenticate the originator of the information. They allow the receiver to ascertain the identity of the sender and to determine (and verify) whether the message has changed during transit.

The Internet has created a borderless space for information exchange, and the keyword for the deployment of corresponding applications in all sectors of the worldwide economy is trust. Rapid technological development and the global character of all underlying platforms (and infrastructures) impose the requirement/necessity for an effective approach, adequately "open" to various technologies and services, and capable of authenticating data electronically (Kamal, 2005; Shoniregun et al., 2004).

Consequently, a very important and identifiable challenge (ISO, 2005; OECD, 2004) is to exploit Internet for secure document exchange, originating from various thematic areas. Recognizing that Internet's expansion and progress in e-commerce offer an unrivaled occasion for economic integration, after appropriate consultation procedures the EU has very early endorsed the *"Electronic Signature Directive"* (hereinafter as the "Directive") aimed at ensuring the proper functioning of the internal European market in the field of electronic signatures by creating a harmonized and appropriate legal framework for their use (European Parliament & Council of the European Union, 2000a). A clear European Community framework regarding the conditions applying to e-signatures can strengthen confidence in, and general acceptance of, the new corresponding technologies.

The Directive establishes a set of detailed criteria, which form the basis for en effective legal recognition of electronic signatures and create an open environment and infrastructure for secure transactions, while it promotes interoperability of related products and/or similar facilities. More specifically, it intended to create a suitable framework for electronic signatures and certain certification services, in order to ensure the proper functioning of the European marketplace (thus avoiding several divergent national laws in the area). Without any doubt, as a result of international experience, global electronic communication and commerce are dependent upon the progressive adaptation of international and domestic laws to the rapidly evolving technological infrastructure (Commission of the European Communities, 2005) ensuring conditions for a proper functioning of the market and supporting interests of all actors involved.

The Directive also identifies requirements that have to be met by service providers supporting e-signatures and prerequisites both for signers and verifiers. These obligations need to be supported by detailed technical standards and open specifications which also meet the requirements of European business, so that products and services supporting electronic signatures can be known to provide legally valid signatures, thus furthering the competitiveness of European business in the international market arena.

Transpositions of legal requirements into technical specifications (or business practices) need to be harmonized at a European member states' level in order to enable interoperability of electronic signature-creation products and cross-border availability of all related services, to the extent possible. Simultaneously, the Directive's wording is wide enough to prescribe security requirements that should be met by electronic signature-creation systems and products, but without mandating the use of a specific technology, thus preserving the sense of technical neutrality, which composes a core axis of the present European regulation. For an extensive range of issues enounced in the approach performed, that is, from the "electronic signing" process to business applications and policies supporting the e-signature creation (e.g., supply of certification services), the corresponding regulatory requirements need to find a more concrete "echo" in several business practices. A means to achieve this coherence between law and practices is by the efficient adoption and usage of standardization processes.

STANDARDIZATION ACTIVITIES FOR ELECTRONIC SIGNATURES

Reliable electronic signatures are essential in the creation of open markets, enabling the development of cross-border trust services and increasing competitiveness, with consequent benefit to service providers, manufacturers, and, *ultimately*, the whole user community (Treasury Board of Canada Secretariat, 1999).

The European Authorities have taken various initiatives to stimulate further standardization and interoperability in the area, while efforts have also been performed at the level of the member states. The Directive lays down a number of functional requirements that cannot be addressed through law only. More specifically, the Directive identifies several requirements for qualified certificates, qualified Certification Service Providers (CSPs), and security-creation devices. In addition, it allows the European Commission to establish and publish references of generally "recognized standards" for e-signatures products, under the scope of these conditions. Therefore, national legislation needs to presume compliance with the relevant prerequisites/requirements, when one of these products meets the reference standards. Such "recognition" could for instance be achieved if the standards in question become finally widely accepted in the market practices, because of their undisputable added value, their wide availability, cross-border acceptability, and so forth (Boyd & Mathuria, 2003; Feghhi, Williams, & Feghhi, 1998).

In order to guarantee wider acceptance of any proposed standards, a broad range of participants has been involved in the relevant activities, including: different departments and agencies of national governments, individual corporations, industry associations, civil society organizations, intergovernmental organizations at the regional and global levels, and other international groups and organizations, some of which are multipartite while others may represent a single stakeholder group.

The work of the European Committee for Standardization/Information Society Standardization System (CEN/ISSS) and the European Telecommunications Standards Institute (ETSI) in providing technical specifications and guidance material for their implementation and market adoption was hence "decisive" to the future of e-commerce, to provide timely standards permitting full and efficient implementation of a commonly adopted framework. These two authorized standardization bodies work in close cooperation with each other and with other standardization organizations around the world as appropriate. Their work follows a number of core principles, mainly including openness, transparency, consensus, effectiveness, and relevance.

In fact, industry and the European standardization bodies together with service providers, vendors, users and consumers, national authorities, and/or other interested organizations have all joined under the auspices of the Information and Communication Technologies Standards Board (ICTSB) to identify and to analyze, *in a coherent manner*, the exact Europe's standardization needs in the sector (Sherif, 2006).

Several standardization initiatives had already been launched at the national, regional, and international levels by organizations and industry fora. Worthy of mention were the activities of the International Chamber of Commerce, the ILPF (Internet Law Policy Forum), the IETF (Internet Engineering Task Force), the W3C (World Wide Web Consortium), and the ABA (American Bar Association) standardization activities. In January 1999, therefore, to initiate and coordinate the necessary standardization effort, a new initiative was launched (i.e., the European Electronic Signature Standardization Initiative, or EESSI), bringing together industry, market players, public authorities, and legal and technical experts (http://www.ict.etsi.org/EESSI_home.htm). Its basic task was to develop the standardization activities required to enable electronic signatures in a coherent manner (particularly in the business environment) and to monitor the implementation of a proper work program to meet this need and to harmonize specifications at the international level to maximize market take-up (Nilsson, Van Eecke, Medina, Pinkas, & Pope, 1999). Three key areas were identified:

- Quality and functional standards for CSPs;
- Quality and functional standards for signature creation and verification products; and
- Interoperable standardization requirements.

The initiative had no desire to "reinvent the wheel," and, *wherever possible*, new standards were built on existing specifications from the International Telecommunication Union (ITU), the International Organization for Standardization (ISO) and the IETF.

In the fast moving domain of information and communications technologies, CEN/ISSS was responsible for the part of the work program dealing with quality and functional standards for signature creation and verification products, as well as quality and functional standards for CSPs (http://www.cenorm.be/isss/Workshop/e-sign/Default.htm).

Several related responsibilities have been focused on the following distinct issues:

- Security requirements for trustworthy systems and products;
- Security requirements for secure signature creation devices;
- Signature creation environment;
- Signature verification process and environment; *and*
- Conformity assessment of products and services for electronic signatures.

Various EESSI deliverables have been published as CEN Workshop Agreements (CWA) and ETSI Technical Specifications (TS). Since a number of valuable documents have been published in this area, national supervisory authorities can now make use of these specifications, to facilitate the proper functioning of their markets. Many countries are now promoting, using, or planning to use several of these specifications. More specifically, the interoperability standards developed by ETSI have also been accepted as "de-facto standards" by multiple market players, although further work is still needed to enhance interoperability at different approaches.

Within ETSI, the Electronic Signature Infrastructure (ESI) Working Group has promoted a variety of corresponding activities (http://portal.

etsi.org/esi/el-sign.asp). Its core responsibilities under EESSI have been focused on the subsequent areas:

- The use of X.509 public key certificates as qualified certificates (ITU, 2001);
- Security management and certificate policy for CSPs issuing qualified certificates;
- Security requirements for trustworthy systems used by CSPs issuing Qualified Certificates;
- Security requirements for signature creation devices;
- Signature creation and verification;
- Electronic signature syntax and encoding formats (occasionally in XML);
- Technical aspects of signature policies; *and*
- Protocol to interoperate with a Time Stamping Authority.
- In certain cases, apart from the above context, there is the additional possibility to examine signature policies for extended business models, together with harmonized provision of CSP status information.

Each of these thematic categories of standards addresses a range of requirements including those of Qualified Electronic Signatures as specified in relevant EU Directive (*article 5.1 of the Directive*). However, they also address general prerequisites related to the proper and the effective use of e-signatures for business activities and for realizing various forms of e-commerce (which all fall into the category of *article 5.2 of the Directive*). Such a variation in requirements may be identified in the standards either as different levels or different options (European Parliament & Council of the European Union, 2000a).

The standardization work is still ongoing in a number of areas, with emphasis given in the fundamental thematic domains covering:

- The development of certification services (*according to the provisions of Annexes I & II of the Directive*); and

- Work on signing process and signature creation products (*according to the provisions of Annexes III & IV of the Directive*).

More specifically, the former category includes standards describing, *among others*:

- Policy requirements for certification authorities issuing qualified certificates (ETSI, 2006d)
- Profile for qualified certificates (ETSI, 2006a)
- Electronic Signature Formats (ETSI, 2007a)
- Time Stamping Profile (ETSI, 2006b)
- Security requirements for trustworthy systems managing certificates for electronic signatures (CEN Workshop Agreement, 2003a; 2003b)
- XML advanced electronic signatures (ETSI, 2006c)
- International harmonization of policy requirements for CAs issuing certificates (ETSI, 2005)
- Signature policies report (ETSI, 2002a)
- Policy requirements for time stamping authorities (ETSI, 2003)
- Provision of harmonized Trust Service Provider status information (ETSI, 2002b)
- XML Format for signature policies (ETSI, 2002c)
- Policy requirements for certification authorities issuing Public Key Certificates (ETSI, 2007b)

In the context of effort performed on signing process and signature creation products are included the following works:

- Guidelines for the implementation of secure signature-creation devices (CEN Workshop Agreement, 2004a)
- Secure signature-creation devices (CEN Workshop Agreement, 2001; 2004b)

- Security requirements for signature creation applications (signature creation process and environment) (CEN Workshop Agreement, 2004c)
- Procedures for electronic signature verification (CEN Workshop Agreement, 2004d)
- Conformity assessment guidance (CEN Workshop Agreement, 2004e), where work that has been realized includes general approach, provision of certification services, security of certificate management systems, procedures for signature creation (and verification), and provisions for secure signature creation devices

EESSI's deliverables have been developed on Public Key Infrastructure (PKI) and related certificate techniques. PKI technology is known by the industry as a reference tool for digital signature (Chochliouros et al., 2007). It is however clear that other technologies are relevant and consideration is already being given to these. EESSI has put all its effort towards the definition of operating procedures and security environment assisting users and trust service providers in the implementation of electronic signature applications. The produced deliverables contribute to fundamental objectives of the EU strategic framework as: *on the one hand*, they propose to providers of trust products and service solutions for compliance with the critical requirements of the basic European Directive in the area, thus contributing to a harmonized implementation of electronic signatures in the EU (in respect of the free movement of goods and services in the internal market); *on the other hand*, they contribute to the creation of an open, market-led environment for the availability of interoperable products and services, thus enabling the development of cross-border trust services with a view to increasing competitiveness and favoring exploitation of services in the internal market for the benefits of the whole user community.

EESSI's activities have been well publicized outside Europe, links have been established with various fora and consortia worldwide, and representatives of international organizations participated in several among its working groups. With the detailed publication of a full set of standards, EESSI has fulfilled its mandate and consequently ICTSB decided to close EESSI WG in October 2004. However, standardization work in the area is still ongoing and carried out by various European bodies, mainly on the basis of the results performed by the previous corresponding effort. A great part of the relevant work has been considered as the basis for solutions already applied in several national legislative regimes (i.e., in Italy and in Germany).

The Impact of Standardization Activities in the Sector

With convergence effects in the electronic communications sector, the marketplace has fundamentally changed: the monolithic world of the past has been replaced by a heterogeneous technology development and standards environment and new complex relationships have arisen between networks and business models as well as contractual and strategic business relationships, often at a global level, between all "key players." Standardization consortia (and/or fora) become a common practice in the sector and some of the suggested standards have reached large market acceptance, challenging the role of the formal European Standardization Organizations. In order to respond to new market requirements, the standardization structures were flexible and able to evolve quickly (De Vries, 2006).

It is widely recognized that one of the impediments to electronic commerce is the lack of standards to support the use of electronic signatures and certificates. The EU standardization initiatives for supporting e-signatures addressed two major aspects of openness: one was to support fast and easy establishment of trust between parties who desired to do business online; the other option was to take care of the technical compatibility of services and components. Such a context can support new business relationships, while it "minimizes" risks involved with investments by corporations and/or by private users. An open environment is favorable for public services to the citizen and for all kinds of business activity.

Thus, partnership/collaboration of all relevant stakeholders is always regarded as "essential" to the successful standardization of electronic signatures. By involving all interested parties, a common and harmonized framework can be agreed and interoperability, at least within Europe, can be ensured (European Commission, 2003). As already mentioned, the e-signatures Directive allows the European Commission to establish and publish reference numbers of "generally recognized standards" for several corresponding products. Consequently, compliance with the requirements laid down in the Directive when an e-signature product meets those standards is presumed.

In the context of a Decision published by the European Commission in July 2003 (European Commission, 2003), there were particular references to CEN standards for the requirements related to the creation of qualified electronic signatures. The validity of these CWAs was initially expected to expire after three years of their publication, with the possibility for further temporal extension, *if needed*. In the meantime, other standards could also be developed and accepted, as long as they could be considered as being "generally recognized standards." In this framework, it is important for the market that future standardization work takes into account new technological developments as users will move their e-signature key from device to device in a digitally connected world.

The purpose of the original EESSI initiative was to ensure that the legal requirements imposed by the (commonly accepted) European legal framework should be implemented by work-

able, interoperable solutions, to develop effective market solutions and underpin the development of e-business in Europe, on the basis of a proper consensus among all actors involved, representing public authorities, industry, and the private sector.

The initiative was an open and neutral platform, bringing together expertise from different fields and regions and supporting "co-regulation" initiatives. "Co-regulation" represents a sharing of responsibilities between public authorities and private market players: This is particularly important for the e-economy, as the new information society services require a high level of trust and security, and this in a business environment where technologies are rapidly changing. In this circumstance, the suggested standards can all be taken into account as a practical effort for developing detailed technical rules on how qualified e-signatures have to be made and become applicable. These rules need to become essential part of the national legal framework, if progress and efficiency is expected.

In order to support a "wider" acceptance, international standards adopted and/or developed by industry had to avoid the need for detailed regulations, *to the extent possible*. As necessity of standards was (and still is) urgent, reference to existing recognized international standards has to be preferred to the development of new standards, wherever possible. The complete effort in the area has represented the first coordinated initiative on a large scale in Europe, being led by formal standardization bodies that attempted to provide an agreed framework for an open, "market-oriented" implementation of the corresponding legal requirements, through a consensus-based approach.

Without any doubt, under the current circumstances practical guidance and technical specifications are necessary to help the private sector and the public authorities to put into practice the legal EU framework in a clear, well-organized, efficient, and cost effective manner (European Parliament

& Council of the European Union, 2000a). The e-signatures Directive is, *by definition*, "technology neutral." Standards, however, are not. Thus, they have to be structured upon specific business models that are considered to be as relevant. At the same time, security aspects must be fully respected to give legal recognition to any suggested electronic signatures and, *simultaneously*, to be conformant to specific national conditions. Taking these requirements together, the suggested standards must be adequately open and internationally agreed. They have to be satisfactorily flexible to cover different business models and to provide quite secure solutions. These basic criteria are fully met by the recent European standardization works, including EESSI's works.

The added value of the European standardization system is to ensure the transparency, openness, inclusiveness, and accountability of the consensus-building process for creating standards for adoption and use (Chochliouros & Spiliopoulou, 2003a). As a consequence, all efforts performed for the development of a series of proper "guidelines" for an efficient e-signatures standardization are more than "simply important" for the internal European market and have a growing contribution to different policies and thematic areas such as: sustainable development; global trade; avoidance of market fragmentation, European governance, *and*; support of several strategic initiatives. In any case, it is essential to develop, as widely as possible, measures based on existing technical solutions, representing the "state-of-the-art" and, *most importantly*, a wide consensus among market players (European Commission, 2005, 2006).

Building strong user commitment is one of the key requirements for successful standardization in the e-signatures sector. For this reason, it would be essential that EESSI deliverables are as widely disseminated and promoted as possible (for example, making these deliverables available for downloads from the Internet can also be an important matter). In addition, guidelines for practical implementa-

tion can further help in testing and certifying secure software European-wide in a consistent manner. This cannot only support the creation of an internal market for the corresponding facilities, but it can provide immediate response to current challenges, due to the fast development of various (global) e-commerce activities. The entire initiative has been well performed, in order to be more open to direct industry participation and more internationally oriented for secure business solutions, supporting the European approach for security in the international literature.

Many countries are now promoting, using, or planning to use several of the EESSI deliverables. Recent works (such as Commission of the European Communities, 2006; Dumortier et al., 2003; Hayat, Leitold, Rechberger, & Rössler, 2004) provide a detailed overview of the state in the European environment, demonstrating that significant progress has been realized on the basis of EESSI's works. (In these references, exact informative data is listed, correlated to the specific national legislation. Further information about the current status of the implementation of the e-signatures Directive at national level, the existing regulatory framework, and exact depiction of all appropriate progress for each separate member state can be found at http://ec.europa. eu/information_society/eeurope/2005/all_about/ security/esignatures/index_en.htm.)

There is a strong requirement for technical interoperability standards for electronic signature functions in an open and competitive marketplace, to achieve interoperability between products and services. In fact, users want standardized and interoperable products to enable them to buy different components from different vendors, while vendors prefer standards to enable them to sell products on an international market.

Interoperability depends on standardization, but standardization cannot be the only and unique answer. The lack of common standards in a converged area (like the sector of e-signatures) is an inhibitor to its development. However, variable and competing standards can also raise serious concerns. The interoperability standards developed by ETSI have been accepted as "*de-facto*" standards by many European actors, although further work may still be necessary to promote their actual use, as it may be probably "unwise" to integrate such standards into the legal framework at a very early stage. When different national authorities set different standards as to what attributes are required for an electronic signature before it will be considered enforceable, businesses face daunting practical difficulties in using e-signatures for transactions nationwide and internationally. Any lack of technical interoperability at national and at cross-border level causes a severe obstacle for the market acceptance of e-signatures. This has resulted in many "isolated" islands of e-signature applications, where certificates can only be used for one single application. EESSI has worked on the promotion of interoperability and has supported the definition of specifications that will encourage the emergence of interoperable competitive solutions; but most of the EU member states have specified national standards in order to promote the option for enhanced interoperability; for example, the ISIS-MTT specifications in Germany (Giessler & Lindemann, 2003) aimed at creating technical interoperability between the related e-signatures products.

Anyway, according to the actual European legislation, the responsibility for the recognition of electronic signatures remains with the national authorities, whether common standards exist or not. This may occasionally led to conflicts (and case law) about various kinds of e-signatures, while national laws can be enacted, *in several instances,* with various security requirements with regards to authentication issues, and so forth. Thus, legislation ranges from a "minimalist" approach that simply authorizes the use of electronic signatures in very limited circumstances, to legislation that establishes some evidentiary presumptions and default provisions that parties can contract out of, to a very formal and highly regulatory

approach governing the manner in which digital signatures may be used and certification authorities may operate (Hayat et al., 2004; Van Eecke, Pinto, & Egyedi, 2007).

From an EU perspective, national legislation with differing requirements risks holding back the effective establishment of the internal market especially in areas which depended on e-signature related products and services. Avoiding disruption of the internal market in an area considered as "critical" to the future of electronic transactions in the European economy is at the basis of the proposed harmonization measures at all levels. The European Commission sees a clear need to further encourage the development of these services/applications and therefore to monitor market and technological developments. Thus, particular emphasis is given on the interoperability and cross-border use of e-signatures. The European Commission has recently announced that will encourage further standardization work in order to promote the interoperability of all corresponding systems within and across borders and the use of all kinds of technologies for qualified e-signature in the single market (Commission of the European Communities, 2006).

With the globalization of trade and the (expected) growth of e-commerce, the flexibility and the ability of national law to deal with contracts concluded in cyberspace are severely tested. There is a widely held belief that the law is slow moving and not able to properly cope with the demands of modern technology. But standards such as the EESSI deliverables have proved that they can help EU member states to work towards interoperable and mutually recognized solutions, able to support market expansion, conformingly to the national legislation systems. EESSI standards may spur the use of e-signatures and will help European countries to "transpose" effectively, from a legal point of view, the basic EU common regulatory provisions of the (e-signature) Directive. International experience has demonstrated that only standards that are widely used can have an essential impact on the market. Thus, the aim of standardization in the domain is to "push the market forward," while standards have to remain voluntary and flexible (European Commission, 2004; Van Eecke et al., 2007).

CONCLUSION

To make fullest use of the opportunities offered by the Internet, secure electronic signatures are essential to verify the authenticity and integrity of a communication activity. In fact, security is a key priority for e-business, e-procurement, and e-government in the global digital environment. Electronic signatures can now be used in a large diversity of circumstances and applications, resulting in a wide range of new services and products. It is so expected that online purchasing, e-marketplaces, and e-procurement will further promote the use of e-signatures, in parallel with the immense Internet penetration affecting international businesses between various players, mainly from the private sector. Electronic signatures can be also used in the public sector within national and European Community administrations and in communications between such administrations and with citizens and economic operators (for example, in the public procurement, taxation, social security, health, and justice systems).

The definition of e-signatures products and services will not be limited to the issuance and management of certificates, but will also encompass any other service and product using, or ancillary to, electronic signatures, such as registration services, time-stamping services, directory services, computing services, or consultancy services. In fact, e-signatures increase the (state's and/or private and/or public) businesses' efficiency by ensuring trusted and secure end-to-end electronic processes. A reliable system of electronic signatures that work across intra-EU borders is vital to safe electronic commerce and the efficient electronic delivery of public services

to businesses and citizens, in the context of a remarkably converged world.

The European Union has promoted effective several regulatory measures, mainly on the basis of the "e-Signatures Directive." These initiatives have even influenced international standardization initiatives as well as other legal and technical activities, *to a great extent*. All EU member states have now implemented the general principles of this fundamental legislative tool, and the EU rules that all member states have transposed into their national laws make e-signatures legally recognized on their territory. For e-commerce to develop and flourish, both consumers and businesses must be confident that their transaction will not be intercepted or modified, that the seller and the buyer are "who they declare," and that transaction mechanisms are available, legal, and secure. However, for promoting practical solutions to current market needs, it is necessary to support specific technical solutions of the wider possible acceptance. The solution may be through the adoption and the endorsement of appropriate standards, created on the basis of the common EU practice, as those created in the context of the EESSI initiative. For Europe to benefit fully from the information society, standardization is an important prerequisite. The traditional standards environment, in the face of the sheer pace of technological innovation and changes in market demands, is responding to the challenge. The EESSI deliverables came in the form of an implementation model (technical specifications or guidelines) with the double objective to satisfy the requirements of the e-signatures Directive and to propose effective answers to market needs in the current timeframe.

The full work performed in the scope of the European standardization entities to fulfill the requirements imposed by the European regulation has achieved remarkable effects to facilitate a consistent and coherent implementation for validity and cross-recognition of e-signatures. Current open issues in the area of electronic signatures are

European interoperability, European coordination of supervision, European accreditation schemes, European Root Authority, and sustainable business models; but EESSI standards have been a first important step towards the solution of these open issues. Several solutions for specific corresponding requirements have been already adopted in the market and have been implemented to a wide area of activities at national level, thus supporting the development towards an *"information society for all citizens.*

REFERENCES

Aalberts, B., & Van der Hof, S. (1999). *Digital signature blindness: Analysis of legislative approaches toward electronic authentication.* Tilburg, The Netherlands: Tilburg University. Retrieved June 1, 2008, from http://www.buscalegis.ufsc.br/busca.php?acao=abrir&id=15433

Boyd, C., & Mathuria, A. (2003). *Protocols for key establishment and authentication.* Berlin/Heidelberg, Germany: Springer-Verlag GmbH & Co.

CEN Workshop Agreement (2001). *CWA 14168: Secure signature-creation devices.* Brussels, Belgium: CEN (European Committee for Standardization).

CEN Workshop Agreement (2003a). *CWA 14167-1: Security requirements for trustworthy systems managing certificates for electronic signatures* (Part 1: System security requirements). Brussels, Belgium: CEN.

CEN Workshop Agreement (2003b). *CWA 14167-2: Cryptographic module for CSP signing Operations with backup: Protection profile (CMCSOB-PP).* Brussels, Belgium: CEN.

CEN Workshop Agreement (2004a). *CWA 14355: Guidelines for the implementation of secure signature-creation devices.* Brussels, Belgium: CEN.

CEN Workshop Agreement (2004b). *CWA 14169: Secure signature-creation devices "EAL 4+."* Brussels, Belgium: CEN.

CEN Workshop Agreement (2004c). *CWA 14170: Security requirements for signature creation applications.* Brussels, Belgium: CEN.

CEN Workshop Agreement (2004d). *CWA 14171: General guidelines for electronic signature verification.* Brussels, Belgium: CEN.

CEN Workshop Agreement (2004e). *CWA 14172: EESSI conformity assessment guidance. General introduction.* Brussels, Belgium: CEN.

Chochliouros, I.P., Chochliouros, S.P., Spiliopoulou, A.S., & Lambadari, E. (2007). Public key infrastructures (PKI): A means for increasing network security. In L.J. Janczewski & A.M. Colarik (Eds.), *Cyber warfare and cyber terrorism* (pp. 281–290). Hershey, PA: Information Science Reference.

Chochliouros, I.P., & Spiliopoulou, A.S. (2003a). European standardization activities: An enabling factor for the competitive development of the information society technologies market. *The Journal of The Communications Network (TCN), 2*(1), 62–68.

Chochliouros, I. P., & Spiliopoulou, A.S. (2003b). Innovative horizons for Europe: The new European telecom framework for the development of modern electronic networks and services. *The Journal of the Communications Network (TCN), 2*(4), 53–62.

Chochliouros, I.P., & Spiliopoulou, A.S. (2004). Potential and basic perspectives of the European Electronic Commerce (e-Commerce) Directive for the Effective Promotion of Modern Business Applications in the Internet (article in Greek). *Telecommunications Audit and Law of New Technologies Magazine, 1*(4), 502–535.

Chochliouros, I.P., & Spiliopoulou, A.S. (2005). Broadband access in the European Union: An enabler for technical progress, business renewal and social development. *The International Journal of Infonomics (IJI), 1,* 5–1.

Chochliouros, I.P., & Spiliopoulou, A.S. (2006, August 30–September 02). Privacy protection vs. privacy offences in the European regulatory context: The cases for interception of communications and the retention of traffic data. In Federation of telecommunications Engineers of the European Union (Ed.), *Proceedings of the 45th International Congress: "Telecom Wars—The Return of the Profit,"* Athens, Greece (pp. 197–203). Athens, Greece: FITCE.

Commission of the European Communities (2005). *Communication on i2010: A European Information Society for growth and employment* [COM(2005) 229 final, 01.06.2005]. Brussels, Belgium: Commission of the European Communities.

Commission of the European Communities (2006). *Report on the operation of Directive 1999/93/EC on a community framework for electronic signatures* [COM(2006) 120 final, 15.03.2006]. Brussels, Belgium: Commission of the European Communities.

Dempsey, J.X. (2003). Creating the legal framework for ICT development: The example of e-signature legislation in emerging market economies. Washington, DC: Center for Democracy and Technology. *Information Technologies and International Development (ITID), 1*(2), 39-52. Washington, DC: Center for Democracy and Technology. Retrieved June 1, 2008, from http://www.internetpolicy.net/e-commerce/20030900esignature.pdf

De Vries, H.J. (2006). IT standards typology. In K. Jakobs (Ed.), *Advanced topics in information technology standards and standardization research, 1,* 1–26.

Dumortier, J., Kelm, S., Nillson, H., Skouma, G., & Van Eecke, P. (2003). *The legal and market aspects of electronic signatures: Study for the European Commission* (DG Information Society, Service Contract No. C28.400). Brussels, Belgium: The Interdisciplinary Centre for Law & Information Technology & Katholieke Universiteit Leuven. Retrieved June 1, 2008, from europa.eu.int/information_society/eeurope/2005/all_about/security/electronic_sig_report.pdf

European Commission (1997). *Communication on ensuring security and trust in electronic communication: Towards a European framework for digital signatures and encryption* [COM(97) 503 final, 01.10.1997]. Brussels, Belgium: European Commission.

European Commission (2000). *Communication on creating a safer information society by improving the security of information infrastructures and combating computer-related crime—eEurope 2002* [COM(2000) 890 final, 26.01.2001]. Brussels, Belgium: European Commission.

European Commission (2001). *Communication on network and information security: Proposal for a European policy approach* [COM(2001) 298 final, 06.06.2001]. Brussels, Belgium: European Commission.

European Commission (2002). *Communication on eEurope 2005: An information society for all* [COM(2002) 263 final, 28.05.2002]. Brussels, Belgium: European Commission.

European Commission (2003). *Communication decision 2003/511/ERC of 14 July 2003 on the publication of reference numbers of generally recognized standards for electronic signature products in accordance with Directive 1999/93/EC of the European Parliament and of the Council* [Official Journal (OJ) L175, 15.07.2003, pp. 45–46]. Brussels, Belgium: European Commission.

European Commission (2004). *Communication on the role of European standardisation in the framework of European policies and legislation* [COM(2004) 674 final, 18.10.2004]. Brussels, Belgium: European Commission.

European Commission (2005). *Communication on more research and innovation: Investing for growth and employment: A common approach* [COM(2005) 488 final, 12.10.2005]. Brussels, Belgium: European Commission.

European Commission (2006). *Communication to the Council, the European Parliament, the European Economic and Social Committee and the Committee of the Regions, on Bridging the Broadband Gap* [COM(2006) 129 final, 20.03.2006]. Brussels, Belgium: European Commission.

European Parliament & Council of the European Union (2000a). *Directive 1999/93/EC of the European Parliament and of the Council of 13 December 1999 on a community framework for electronic signatures* [Official Journal (OJ) L13, 19.01.2000, pp. 12–20]. Brussels, Belgium: European Parliament & Council of the European Union.

European Parliament & Council of the European Union (2000b). *Directive 2000/31/EC of the European Parliament and of the Council of 8 June 2000 on certain legal aspects of information society services, in particular electronic commerce, in the internal market (Directive on Electronic Commerce)* [Official Journal (OJ) L178, 17.07.2000, pp. 1–16]. Brussels, Belgium: European Parliament & Council of the European Union.

European Telecommunications Standards Institute (2002a). *ETSI TR 102 041 V1.1.1 (2002-02): Signature Policies Report.* Sophia-Antipolis, France: ETSI.

European Telecommunications Standards Institute (2002b). *ETSI TR 102 030 V1.1.1 (2002-03): Provision of harmonized trust service provider status information.* Sophia-Antipolis, France: ETSI.

European Telecommunications Standards Institute (2002c). *ETSI TR 102 038 V1.1.1 (2002-04): TC Security - Electronic Signatures and Infrastructures (ESI); XML format for signature policies.* Sophia-Antipolis, France: ETSI.

European Telecommunications Standards Institute (2003). *ETSI TR 102 023 V1.2.1 (2003-01): Electronic signatures and infrastructures (ESI); Policy requirements for time-stamping authorities.* Sophia-Antipolis, France: ETSI.

European Telecommunications Standards Institute (2005). *ETSI TR 102 040 V1.3.1 (2005-03): Electronic signatures and infrastructures (ESI); International harmonization of policy requirements for CAs issuing certificates.* Sophia-Antipolis, France: ETSI.

European Telecommunications Standards Institute (2006a). *ETSI TS 101 862 V1.3.3 (2006-01): Qualified certificate profile.* Sophia-Antipolis, France: ETSI.

European Telecommunications Standards Institute (2006b). *ETSI TS 101 861 V1.3.1 (2006-01): Time stamping profile.* Sophia-Antipolis, France: ETSI.

European Telecommunications Standards Institute (2006c). *ETSI TS 101 903 V1.3.2 (2006-03): XML advanced electronic signatures (XAdES).* Sophia-Antipolis, France: ETSI.

European Telecommunications Standards Institute (2006d). *ETSI TS 101 456 V1.4.2 (2006-12): Electronic signatures and infrastructures (ESI); Policy requirements for certification authorities issuing qualified certificates.* Sophia-Antipolis, France: ETSI.

European Telecommunications Standards Institute (2007a). *ETSI TS 101 733 V1.7.3 (2007-01): Electronic signatures and infrastructures (ESI); CMS Advanced Electronic Signatures (CAdES).* Sophia-Antipolis, France: ETSI.

European Telecommunications Standards Institute (2007b). *ETSI TS 102 042 V1.2.4 (2007-03): Electronic Signatures and Infrastructures (ESI); Policy requirements for certification authorities issuing public key certificates.* Sophia-Antipolis, France: ETSI.

Feghhi, J., Williams, P., & Feghhi, J. (1998). *Digital certificates: Applied Internet security.* Addison-Wesley.

Ford, W., & Baum, M. (2001). *Secure electronic commerce* (2nd ed.). Upper River Saddle, NJ: Prentice Hall.

Giessler, A., & Lindemann, R. (2003, July 29). *ISIS-MTT compliance criteria* (Version 1.1). Berlin, Germany: T7 & TeleTrusT. Retrieved June 1, 2008, from teletrust.de/fileadmin/files/ag8_isis-mtt-compliancecrit-v1.1.pdf

Hayat, A., Leitold, H., Rechberger, C., & Rössler, T. (2004, August 10). *Survey on EU's electronic-ID solutions* (Version 1.0). Vienna, Austria: Secure Information Technology Center (A-SIT). Retrieved June 1, 2008, from www.a-sit.at/pdfs/A-SIT_EID_SURVEY.pdf

i2010 High Level Group (2006, December). *The challenges of convergence* (Discussion paper). Brussels, Belgium: European Commission. Retrieved June 1, 2008, from http://ec.europa.eu/information_society/eeurope/i2010/docs/i2010_high_level_group/i2010_hlg_convergence_paper_final.pdf

International Organization for Standardization (2005). *ISO/IEC 17799: Information technology: Security techniques: Code of practice for information security management.* Geneva, Switzerland: ISO.

International Telecommunication Union (2001). *ITU-T recommendation X.509 (2000)/ISO/IEC 9594-8: Information technology: Open Systems Interconnection: The Directory: Public-key and attribute certificate frameworks.* Geneva, Switzerland: ITU.

Kamal, A. (2005). *The law of cyber-space.* Geneva, Switzerland: United Nations Institute of Training and Research (UNITAR).

Kaufman, C. (2002). *Network security: Private communication in a public world* (2nd ed.). Prentice Hall.

Lalopoulos, G.K., Chochliouros, I.P., & Spiliopoulou, A.S. (2004). Challenges and perspectives for Web-based applications in organizations. In M. Pagani (Ed.), *The encyclopedia of multimedia technology and networking* (pp. 82–88). Hershey, PA: IRM Press.

Nilsson, H., Van Eecke, P., Medina, M., Pinkas, D., & Pope, N. (1999, July 20). *Final report of the EESSI Expert Team.* European Electronic Signature Standardization Initiative (EESSI). Retrieved June 1, 2008, from http://www.ictsb.org/EESSI_home.htm

Organization for Economic Coordination and Development (2004). *Digital delivery of business services (JT00162724).* Paris, France: OECD.

PriceWaterhouseCoopers (2001). European Economic Crime Survey 2001. *European Report.* Retrieved June 1, 2008, from http://www.pwcglobal.com

Richards, J. (2000). The Utah Digital Signature Act as a "model" legislation: A critical analysis. *The John Marshal Journal of Computer & Information Law, XVII*(3).

Sherif, M.H. (2006). Standards for telecommunication services. In K. Jakobs (Ed.), *Information technology standards and standardization research.* Hershey, PA: Idea Group Publishing.

Shoniregun, C.A., Chochliouros, I.P., Laperche, B., Logvynovskiy, O., & Spiliopoulou, A.S. (2004). *Questioning the boundary issues of Internet security.* London: e-Centre for Infonomics.

Treasury Board of Canada Secretariat (1999). *Digital signature and confidentiality: Certificate policies for the Government of Canada public key infrastructure* (Government of Canada (GOC), PKI Certificate Policies version 3.02).

Van Eecke, P., Pinto, P., & Egyedi, T. (2007, July). *EU study on the specific policy needs for ICT standardisation* (Final Report, Ref. ENTR/05/059). Brussels, Belgium: DG Enterprise, European

Commission. Retrieved June 1, 2008, from http://www.ictstandardisation.eu/

Weber, R. (2002). *Regulatory models for the online world.* Zurich, Switzerland: Schulthess Juristische Medien.

Chapter XV
Quality Standardization Patterns in ICT Offshore

Esther Ruiz Ben
Technische Universität Berlin, Germany

ABSTRACT

In recent years, the ICT branch has experienced new internationalization impulses through the improvement of offshore practices. Particularly the development of modularization and standardization of some production processes have crucially contributed to enabling offshoring in globalized areas of ICT. Competencies as well as innovation sources have increasingly fragmented; resting upon cooperation and trust principles. Quality standards play a crucial role to satisfy and optimize these coordination and regulation needs so to warrant quality outcomes. In this chapter, I will give an overview of the development of quality standards related to offshore projects, focusing particularly on recent practices in Europe. To illustrate the importance of quality standards and quality management for ICT off- and nearshore projects, and moreover for the internationalization of the ICT branch, I present some preliminary results of my work in progress. From the perspective of project managers in large ICT firms, quality standards play a very important role as the internal controlling instrument of working and communication processes; as well as an external mechanism beyond the ICT network in order to get market advantages.

INTRODUCTION

During the late 1990s and particularly in 2000, the ICT sector has shown an enormous expansion, especially influenced by the development of the Internet, extended application areas and the former favorable economic situation. The commercialization and expansion of the Internet as a working basis, particularly in the 1990s, played in this phase a crucial role to begin enabling compatibilities in cross-national working practices; as well as creating a basis to build common knowledge exchange arenas that are fundamental for the further internationalization of the ICT branch. Thus, the use of the internet as an exchange working platform represented one of the first enabling steps toward the organization of work in global contexts in the sector, overcoming time and space barriers in working processes (Castells, 2001) (Editor note: Castells is not listed in the references section.) Whereas organization control during the early 1990s concentrated on core firms that operated with local outsourcing companies to compete in an increasingly dynamic environment, involving new actors and customers around the world. In the late 1990s, the new diffusion and communication basis, supported by the Internet, contributed to the development of a new organizational paradigm known as network organization. Competencies, as well as innovation sources, have increasingly fragmented; resting upon cooperation and trust principles. Nonetheless, networks need to coordinate their operation activities and their innovation expectancies to guarantee the quality of their working processes, their staff and their customer-focused outcomes. And moreover, they are often bound to national and international regulations of working and production practices.

Network organizations must find a consensus regarding customer groups, innovation, quality and performance goals. Once these goals, as well as coordinative and regulative standards, are integrated within quality management systems, they serve as a legitimate basis for network performance.

Particularly in recent years, the ICT branch has experienced new internationalization impulses through the improvement of task delegation to foreign organizations, or in other words, offshore practices. The development of modularization and standardization of these production processes have crucially contributed to enabling offshoring in globalized areas of ICT.

Offshore tasks and production segments in the ICT sector are part of the internationalization of the sector and must be understood in the context of the globalization of the whole economy (Ruiz Ben & Wieandt, 2006). In the last few years, offshoring has expanded in the ICT sector due to

the maturity of the branch in terms of standardization and consolidation of certain segments of the sector, mostly within the production part and related to the development of standard products. Some authors argue that offshoring constitutes a "prelude to software automation and mechanization," taking for example the automation of labor-intensive tasks in data centers, software customization, translation, website hosting and reuse of code that is currently taking place in software service companies (Carmel & Tjia, 2005, p. 7). Although, this argument is still far away from the present situation. Particularly important in the adoption of international quality standards by the current impulse towards internationalization and the increasing global competition in the ICT sector. Thus, even if resistance towards the adoption of international quality standards exists in ICT organizations, due to the additional work it represents for the employees by way of documentation pressure, particularly large ICT organizations adopt them in order to accomplish the perceived expectations in the sector (Boiral, 2006). Another way to accomplish such market expectations is for the organization to develop particular quality management systems on the basis of internationally recognized quality standards (Ruiz Ben, 2007). However, the speed of innovation in the ICT sector is often too fast and the documentation of software development process needed in quality management systems is often neglected due to time pressure or lack of habitualization among employees (Ruiz Ben, 2005). In the context of the internationalization of the ICT sector, the adoption and adaptation of quality standards and documentation practices are not yet very well researched. Questions such as the existence of quality management systems in organizations or of the dynamics brought about in organizations when new quality standards are implemented to address qualification development, task definition and performance in international settings are still unexplored. In this chapter, I will give an overview of the development of quality standards and management mechanisms related to offshore projects, focusing particularly on recent practices in Europe and especially in the German ICT branch. I will present definitions of offshoring in ICT, explanations about quality standards in this field and discuss the institutions involved in the development of international standards. Moreover, I will present some of the results of my research regarding the transformation of tasks and qualifications in the internationalization process of the ICT branch, focusing on the importance of quality standards and management systems.

BACKGROUND

Quality Management and the Current Internationalization Process of the ICT Sector

The increasing development and introduction of quality standards in management systems experienced an important impulse during past years due to the expansion of ICT offshore practices. Quality standards support the foundation of tasks and work processes and represent a common communication base for international teamwork. Quality initiatives such as Six Sigma serve as a tool to implement existing quality standards, defined by organizations such as ISO, using data and statistical analysis to measure business processes, recruiting and outcomes. Principally, Six Sigma represents the practical realization of the total quality management (TQM) approach. The main philosophy of this tool is to define and identify defects as failures in relation to the customers' demands. Moreover, from the perspective of the market, quality standards are important for competing in a very dynamic environment. Particularly, quality standards are becoming a crucial role for the orientation of customers, but also for ICT enterprises, in order to better choose their partners in the framework of a globalized economy and international ICT industry.

In India for instance, managers in major ICT firms have developed their own teams to identify customers' needs and have designed various pathways towards TQM. Nevertheless, the transfer of knowledge and technology also becomes necessary for emerging smaller ICT firms that play a very important role in consolidating the market (Dutka & Sekhar, 2004). Thus, the establishment of interaction and learning platforms among ICT firms are very important for industry improvement (Crevoisier, 1999). Moreover, the national environment in which the firm is embedded plays an important role to establish a competitive ICT industry in the country and also the regional conditions of the country, which we can especially observe in the case of the EU. The political environment from a national, regional and international perspective influences offshoring and also standardization processes regarding quality management in aspects related to working practice regulations.

At the same time, as (author's first name needed) Jakobs (2005) remarks, standardization politics change and national interests can become more important. Thus, Jacobs (2005, p. 25) comments, "…governments now have a vested interest in pushing such standards to support domestic firms. These firms, in turn, will look to standards setting for several reasons which are typically, though not necessarily, related to their own economic well-being." Therefore, standardization can be considered, according to this author, as an arena in which technical and non-technical (e.g., economic, organizational, or social) issues concur due to the importance of social interactions between diverse stakeholders (e.g., vendors, service providers, users, consumers, administrations, etc.) and technical experts who develop the standards. The gap between the needs and perspectives of the standard developers in the organization and the users who abide by the standards often leads to ad hoc solutions that do not always bring an effective and timely output. Especially for examining quality standardization patterns in relation to ICT offshore projects, it is important to take into account the actors interacting in the standardization process of quality systems and how they legitimate the establishment of standard settings in organizations. Intercultural aspects, as well as national regulations and rules, must also be considered in the analysis of this process; not to mention the financial aspects and embedded risks in offshoring practices that ICT organizations have to confront and that standardization may sometimes even veil.

Quality Standards in the Context of the ICT Branch in Europe

According to the British Standard Institution, a quality standard in accordance with ISO (2001, p.2000) provides an organization "with a set of processes that ensure a common sense approach to the management." Moreover, "the system should ensure consistency and improvement of working practices, which in turn should provide products and services that meet customer's requirements. ISO 9000 is the most commonly used international standard that provides a framework for an effective quality management system."[1] ISO Standards are widely used in the ICT branch and represent a very important basis for the development of management systems in organizations.

The ISO 9000 series of quality system standards have been applied to industrial practices for a long time (Van der Wiel, van Iwaarden, Williams, & Dale, 2004). By origin, they were developed on the basis of military standards (e.g., AQAP) and the British Standards (BS 5750) and were first published in 1987. Since then, two upgrades have followed in 1994 and 2000.

Following these authors, the initial aim of the ISO 9000 series was to build a trust basis for suppliers and manufacturers practicing business-to-business transactions. Tummala and Tang (1996) explain that the basic concept behind ISO 9000 is the notion that a set of characteristics of quality systems can be standardized and yield benefits

both for organizations, as well as for their suppliers, due to the common certainty that they both should meet certain requirements.

ISO 9000 standards help ensure that organizations follow well-documented procedures in the production process, as well as in the delivery of their products or services. These procedures aim to guarantee that the products or services of an organization comply with customer specifications, but are still basic recommendations that must be further adapted to the special situation of the organization, its environment and its production scope.

Thus, the tension between the quests for universality embedded in ISO standards and the need to take into account the various stages of technological and commercial development are reflected in the adaptation of new quality management systems; especially in its implementation.

Nonetheless, ISO is not the only existing standard used to develop quality management systems in the ICT branch. Standards in this branch are very heterogeneous. Several classifications have been suggested. For instance, the one suggested by Blind (2004) distinguishes among product standards, control standards and process standards. Regarding the way standards are produced, Blind talks about three additional categories: standards that are set through the market (such as IBM's systems network architecture [SNA] and Microsoft Windows); standards that are set by government, through a regulatory process (mandatory standards); and standards that are negotiated through a voluntary consensus process (formal public standards developed by a publicly recognized standardization organization such as ISO, IEC and ITU) (2004).

Moreover, standards can also be defined in relation to their use: mandatory by law for every product concerned (for example when safety considerations have prompted regulations); those requested by a vendor or system integrator; or those including numerous instances where the application of a standard is mandatory for public procurement (as in the case of the European Handbook for Open

Systems according to a decision of the European Council).

Therefore, considering this complexity regarding standard types, the definition of a typology of standards is still not totally satisfactory (OECD, 2001).

Regarding the motivation to implement formal standardization in organizations, some authors point out that the focus tends either to be on the reduction of transaction costs, especially related to information, or it is associated with network externalities (Schmidt & Werle, 1998). Standards can also be associated with reducing uncertainty or with enhancing competition by clearly defining the information required to serve a market. Mansell (1995) refers to the use of standardization for the facilitation of scale economies, either for suppliers or for influencing the distribution of cost and benefits related to the building and operating of large, complex technical systems.

Moreover, in order to develop themselves in new markets while protecting established ones, companies utilize standardization so to prevent compatibility and avoid the participation of competitors in the market. Thus, as some authors remark, companies use standards as strategic tools to consolidate a market position and gain advantage over competitors (Cargill, 1989; Bonino & Spring, 1991).

Particularly regarding quality standards, Van der Wiele, van Iwaarden, Williams, and Dale (2004) remark on the basis of a literature review that there is evidence of a positive impact created by ISO standards in some business countries and sectors. Heras (2002) points out that most of the studies conducted on the benefits of ISO standards are mainly anecdotal, case study based, and report descriptive statistics (Van der Wiele, van Iwaarden, Williams, & Dale, 2004).

Van der Wiele, van Iwaarden, Williams, and Dale (2004) report a positive impact of ISO 9000 on companies in The Netherlands and in the UK. Nevertheless, it is important to consider that the implementation of ISO needed changes in the organizations, especially when the last version of ISO 9000 was used. The participation of auditors in the process was also very important in the implementation of the quality recommendations.

Especially the participation of external and internal consulting in ICT offshoring plays a crucial role to legitimate the consequent organizational change (Ruiz Ben & Claus, 2005; Ruiz Ben & Wieandt, 2006; Wieandt, 2006; Ruiz Ben, 2006). Thus, as we mention elsewhere (Ruiz Ben, Wieandt, & Maletzky, 2008) in offshore processes, the selection of the providers in host offshore countries involves legal and consulting costs, and contracting issues (Morales, 2005). When organizations do not have experience with ICT offshoring, they usually work with benchmarking companies, utilizing consultants that provide an overview and evaluation of the specific chances and risks of ICT offshoring for the company (Amberg & Wiener, 2004).

Thus, from my point of view, to analyze quality standardization patterns in ICT offshore processes, it is important to consider the actors involved in the development of quality standards and the embedded environments of ICT organizations and networks, especially regarding legal, social and financial issues. Moreover, at the organizational level, we must take into account in which way the workers adopt or resist the introduction of quality standards in their working routines, particularly when they work on international projects.

In the next section, I will focus on the actors involved in the development of quality standards, considering the particular situation in Europe and especially the framework of the European Union after previously explaining the role of standards in ICT offshoring.

QUALITY STANDARDIZATION PATTERNS IN ICT OFFSHORE

Standards play a particularly important role as a 'selection mechanism', especially in the case of

ICT networks in which alliances are often based upon trust and efficiency and in which narrowing diversity can benefit internal cohesiveness and support stability against external threats. Particularly in ICT offshoring processes, the standardization of working processes through methodologies such as CMM has played a crucial role in some offshore countries. These formal processes explain, in part, the tremendous success of the offshore industry in India (Carmel & Tjia, 2005). Nonetheless, particularly regarding quality standards, the Indian ICT Branch has played a very important role in developing new settings. A significant number of major Indian ICT companies have adopted a central measure for achieving quality, particularly Six Sigma methodology and/or its multivariate branches like TQM, supply chain management (SCM), and customer relationship management (CRM). Also, ITIL recommendations aligns with the international standards of ISO 20000 and represents a customizable framework that defines how service management is applied within an organization and how it plays an important role in the development of off- and nearshore projects.

Regarding production standards, already in the previous phases of the Internet expansion, the Directive on ICT Standardization of 1996 formulated by the Expert Group of the OECD represents an important milestone in the establishment of ICT standards. In order to assess the implications of emerging globalization and the consequent need for standardization in the ICT, the OECD sought the advice of a group of experts, who were responsible for the standardization of ICT in their respective companies. This group formulated several recommendations regarding the development of ICT standards, their coordination, management, tasks distribution, participation of the users, standardization ethics, etc. Particularly relevant in the recommendations is the role assigned to official standardization agencies, which shall be referred to below as "Standards Development Organizations," or "SDOs." The question is, how

do these organizations define standards and how do they support their stability and diffusion? Werle and Iversen (2006) examined in a recent article the legitimacy of committee standardization in comparison to market processes of the technical standardization of ICT. Responsible for the development of a significant number of standards in the ICT branch are SDOs, in which agents of firms represent the majority of participants, due to the fact that enrollment in standardization development constitutes a time-consuming and resource-intensive activity requiring technical expertise (Werle & Iversen, 2006). Thus, these authors remark on the bias existing in SDOs towards industry interest representation. Blind (2005) also refers to the requirement of qualified personnel for the participation in standard development in SDOs (2005). Therefore, the chances for the enrollment of persons from developing countries or even from small- and medium-sized enterprises (SMEs) are rather limited (Jackobs, 2005). Taking into account the composition of the ICT branch in Europe that in its majority is represented by SMEs, also in Europe such bias is something important to consider. Nevertheless, in the framework of the EU, where the exchange of services and goods is free, due to recent regulations (OECD, 2004), European ICT companies can develop a self-reinforcing dynamic, gaining cost or quality advantages through offshoring (OECD, 2005; see also Aspray, Mayadas, & Vardi, 2006). At this point, it is very important to consider labor and employment rights, as well as issues related to privacy and data transfer, that are related to ICT offshoring processes in Europe.

Regarding data privacy laws, the European Union Data Privacy Directive adopted in 1995, applies to companies collecting or processing data within the EU or reciving data from the EU and is implemented by the respective EU countries through their national legislation (Eisner, 2005). Eisner (2005) points out that EU-approved transfer contract clauses are the most efficient way to handle data transfer in ICT offshoring processes in the EU. These clauses consist of an agreement between the transferring parties about a set of contracted provisions consistent with data privacy laws, allowing enforcement by EU authorities.

Another important issue related to EU regulations in the context of ICT offshoring is the EU Acquired Rights Directive, approved in 1977, that gives employees protection in the event of a business transfer[2]. This means that transferred employees must maintain the same working conditions that they had before the transfer took place. In the case of replacement, employees must be informed and consulted about related measures and sometimes be awarded a particular payment (Eisner, 2005).

These regulations are very important in the development of ICT offshoring in the EU context. Nevertheless, at the level of the implementation of working policies in organizations, and particularly regarding the employer's representation in the decision processes of the companies, there are many differences among the European Member States. Especially the differences between the former EU15 and new European Member States are very significant.

Because of the political divide in Europe before 1989, we can show specific conditions in regards to off- and onshoring. The former division led to the establishment of a highly developed and well performing western part (the Europe-15 Member States, Norway, and Switzerland) and a transforming, but well qualified and low regulated eastern part (the new member states Bulgaria and Romania). Thus, in Europe, even both home and host countries using offshoring practices occur in one market area regulated by the European Union. According to specific historical, political and socio-cultural conditions, and also in regard to the particular economic and industrial situation, as well as to the special position in the global ICT branch, each country has developed specific strategies to confront innovation demands and to cope with high qualified labor shortages and skill mismatches.

ICT companies, each depending on their size and market scope, had to react very fast to innovation pressures developing special internal training measures as well as hiring foreign workforces.

Particularly important for the adoption of quality standards in an organization is the speed of change. At the international, as well as the European level, some measures have been developed to confront this problem. Egeydi (2001, p. 39) comments the following:

According to the ISO/IEC Directives, 7 years were needed to take a standard from start to Draft International Standard in 1989, while in the Directives of 1992 this period had been reduced to 3 years.

... the approval time of recommendations in the ITU-T has been reduced from 4 years in 1988 to a maximum of 9 months in 2000 (ITU-T, 2000).

This represents an improvement in standardization processes; however, ICT networks often adopt their own quality standards embedded in more general management systems, such as Six Sigma. At the regulative level, Egeydi (2001, p. 44) remarks that formal standards constitute an important point of reference for European regulation: "The European Commission requires a degree of democratic accountability if it is to refer to such standards in a regulatory context. However, in the field of ICT standards have emerged with a high market relevance, standards that stem from standards consortia."

Egydi (2001) points out, however, that in the field of ICT, standards will seldom be part of regulation. Thus, this author pleads for more clarity from European regulators about what type of democracy is needed and for what purpose. Additionally, Egydi remarks that a systematical monitoring of democratic requirements by 'democratic' standards by developing organizations should be considered.

In sum, especially for ICT offshoring practices, this kind of monitoring would be positive and would establish clear cooperation environments among the EU15 countries and the new European Member States. However, the rapid dynamics in the ICT sector and the need to develop quality standards in line with the velocity of change lead to an internal adaptation of quality standards in organizations on the basis of internationally recognized standards. Adding to the problem of high dynamic changes in the ICT sector, increasing internationalization of the sector means that intercultural problems can emerge among project networks that use quality management systems established in home enterprises (Ruiz Ben, 2006). Thus, it is crucial to consider emerging expertise in international teamwork and prevent the overemphasizing of focusing on narrowed, organizational quality management standards and systems. The awareness of network interactions in projects and beyond them of emerging expertise and knowledge creation is crucial to developing effective quality management systems in internationalized ICT organizations. In the next section I will focus on this issue, presenting some results of our work in progress regarding the transformation of tasks and qualifications related to ICT off- and nearshoring.

Preliminary Empirical Results: Quality Standards and Quality Management Systems in the Internationalization of the German ICT Branch

In our current research about the transformation of tasks and qualifications in the framework of the internationalization of the German IT sector (INITAK), we have conducted interviews with personnel and quality managers in several IT enterprises (see description above and in appendix) that expand their activities in foreign countries and especially in Eastern Europe. The preliminary analysis regarding qualification and expertise requirements are related to one of our case studies in a large software development enterprise (F3). This enterprise is an affiliated company of a large, multinational enterprise with many establishments all around the world. Academically acknowledged persons founded the German establishment in the early 1980s. During the 1980s and 1990s, the enterprise expanded and founded six further locations in Germany, Switzerland and recently in Eastern Europe. The enterprise has an academic origin which still remains, as it is reflected for instance in the links to academicallybased professional federations (GI – Gesellschaft für Informatik). The motivation for off- and nearshore is basically to reduce costs, but also to expand the firm market scope and moreover to remain innovative in the rapidly internationalizing environment of the ICT sector.

Particularly the German establishment of F3, where we conducted our interviews in 2006 has itself experience with nearshore since 2004 in Eastern Europe. In the first phases of this nearshore project, the enterprise used the platforms of the multinational enterprise they belong to, which brings advantages regarding the availability of adequate personnel and infrastructure and the knowledge management of the enterprise. Nearly 50 employees are working in the nearshore establishment of F3. The standard integration procedure for these individuals is a visit in Germany for a training period of one year, in which they learn the project and quality standards of the enterprise.

Regarding the tasks that the F3 firm keeps in Germany during its current internationalization, the first specification phases of software development projects, during which the contact with customers is very intensive, remain in the German headquarters. However, some nearshore workers participate sometimes in the discussions with the customers, as a part of their integration training. The architecture phase also remains in Germany, whereas the developers in the nearshore center conduct the detailed design of the architecture. Therefore, the recruitment strategy of the firm F3 in its nearshore center is oriented towards hiring both very young university graduates and also experienced personnel that can rapidly adapt to the growing present project demands, as well as train and help to integrate young newcomers. The long-term internationalization perspective of F3 in the nearshore location is to expand their market opportunities in the country, building an increasingly autonomous center with high-qualified personnel. Apart from the high qualification requirements in computer science, one of the pre-requisites for recruitment is high communication skills and an ability to speak in German.

For coordinating international teamwork between German and the software developers in the nearshore center due to the differences in work habits in Germany and in the nearshore country perceived by personnel managers, firm F3 uses as a common background the German institutionalized sense of professionalism and an especially strong hierarchical quality management system that goes beyond the firm through to the core, multinational owner enterprise. This system has been developed and institutionalized in the enterprise through the years, taking internationally recognized quality standards as a basis and functions as the internal control system for the whole, teamwork-oriented organization. Although the software developers who took part in our interviews were satisfied with the quality systems in the organization, a quality manager in firm F3 argues that this kind of system sometimes makes the organization "self-blind" if it does not permit acting in a reflexive way from the ground floor to reflect the typical, workday problems within projects. Thus, according to the quality manager, communication and social skills are especially important for two main reasons: first, to understand the problems of the software developers, as well as the technical and management problems within a project and second, to solve these problems according to three basic quality principles, or in the words of a quality manager, "the magical triangle for decision making: budget, timing and quality."

The quality manager in firm F3 emphasizes the importance of the "social component" in teamwork to reach high quality in production. Thus, in contrast to offshore projects in India, nearshore projects in Eastern Europe, as the quality manager points out, are easier to coordinate because the team members and the quality and project managers know each other and can more easily establish a communication basis:

We need the social component. We have observed this precisely in our nearshore center; the nearshore center people were first here and thus we could build a social relationship. You know each other, you get out together for a drink and then, when we telephone it is like as if he were in the neighbor room.

However, the firm plans to expand in the nearshore center country market, so that the autonomy requirements for software developers in the nearshore country will grow and they will have to act as mediators between different cultural backgrounds. Taking into account that the nearshore experience of the firm F3 beginning 2004 is still very short, I cannot yet give a clear picture about the teamwork culture in this international software development environment. However, it is important to note that although the German based corporate professionalism dominate the expectations of the personnel managers, due to some reported misunderstandings in teamwork practices between nearshore center and German software developers, the firm F3 has reacted initiating the design of common "corporate rules" for the nearshore projects that sometimes are developed "ad hoc" within the project, but takes also international quality standards as a basis. In which way the German based corporate professionalism will prevail or coexist with local habits in the international software development environment of the firm F3 or in other words, how expertise in both locations will be institutionalized is yet an open question that we will seek to answer in the next phases of our research.

The second firm about which I report in this paper, F1a, is an operation segment of a multinational company operating in the telecommunication and software areas of the ICT branch. F1a was recently established as operation segment and has since its origins experience with off- and nearshoring in India and Eastern Europe. As a part of a multinational company, F1a is tied to the cultural identity of its owner and particularly rooted in the tradition of the German industrial culture with a strong "Beamtentum" influence.

The experiences with off- and nearshore of F1a remain linked to the long internationalization tradition of the core owner company. This means a good starting basis for projects, since F1a can use the existing recruitment pool with experience in the company in base countries. Moreover, some team workers and specially the team coordinators often travel to the home or host locations of the nearshore projects to maintain face to face contacts, which is high valued to improve the communication and interaction of the team members. Particularly F1a has currently nearshore projects in Poland, Romania, and Slovakia. The programming phases of ICT projects have been delivered to these countries. The consequences for the organization of work processes are that tasks, work modules and deliveries must be clearly defined as well as the interfaces between work modules. This strong definition requirement in off- and nearshore projects is the main difference to local focused projects in the opinion of a project manager. This means a stronger standardization of processes and documentation practice as it was the case in the past and a rapid adaptation to current needs selecting just some aspects of past documented processes. Documentation represents at this point a double-edged sword, since at the one hand it is needed to identify possible process failures and to find solutions as well as to check

the processes with quality standards, but on the other hand it retards the working process and moreover, it is sometimes not clear what is relevant to be documented. As a project manager in the enterprise F1a remarks, definition of modules and tasks, documentation and process adaptation run parallel in successive constant iteration moments. In the words of the project manager:

The whole experience stored since an eternity resides somehow inside documentation and we cannot adopt just as it is. We look at what makes more sense and what makes less, in order to bring it to an extension that we can use in the project. Otherwise we lose too much time. We make everything parallel, we begin to define everything, to document and then the processes are adapted. And it is a kind of iterative process in which everything size by size puzzles together.

Quality management systems live and develop together within this process and they are extremely important for the improvement of the working process in internationalized software development environments. However, such systems did not exist in the past years or they were only available on the call, and were moreover not documented. Currently, in the enterprise F1a, documentation plays a crucial role in relation to quality systems and particularly in relation to offshore, since the teams work within an integrated global environment and structure in which the communication of work steps and developments, but specially the secure run of the process must be guaranteed and arbitrated. As the project manager puts it:

(...) looking back to the past, regarding the configuration system, there were no quality criteria or only few ones just on the call and not documented. And here due to this ongoing structure that we have set up, and taking into account the conjunction and succession of work process parts, we must of course lay down on something and we must document. Specially because with such an ongoing system, in which we say to sales and marketing department: work with it, they can in

fact work with it in the whole world just with the push of a button and in a critical moment they can also risk lots of money.

Particularly risks in the interfaces among several modules in home and host locations in off- and nearshore projects represent a difficult problem, which has sometimes lead to relocating offshore projects to nearer host destinations. As a controlling instance, consulting firms play a crucial role.

In the case of F1a, the supervision of the projects is conducted by an external consulting enterprise, which in the particular case of the project to which the interviewed project manager belongs, is extremely important due to its huge volume and complexity. As the consultant working in this project comments, quality standards are crucial in off- and nearshore projects, both for coordination and also as a basis to find solutions in case of work process problems. Quality standards are important for the external consultant also as a legitimating basis for possible changes in work processes that the consultant has to achieve and implement in the "client" enterprise, to which somehow he plays a twofold role as a external worker and also interacting in the day to day practice of the project with the employees "clients" as a colleague and supporter within the project. Thus, quality standards are the instrument to legitimate decisions in the work processes. The knowledge of such standards and also of the quality management systems of the company is also important for the team workers, since they have to implement them in the day to day project life. Thus, quality standards, as well as quality management, becomes more and more institutionalized in the company, which is reflected in the increasing number of courses that the company offers to the employees. Moreover, employees can only learn about quality standards and their implementation as well as about quality management within the company, since, first, it is not usual to get training in these issues at the universities and second, even if the employees have some knowledge having studied informatics or mathematics, they do not have the particular knowledge of their implementation in such a complex environment of a multinational company. As the project manager puts it:

What we make here you cannot learn at the university. Either I know it from my studies, if I learn informatics or mathematics and there also especially software development and I know what a docmentation and a test as a whole means or I do not know. And even if I know it, I have never known it in such an environment like this.

Thus, internal continuous training in quality standards and in quality management is crucial for the employees working in off- and nearshore projects. And this means both in home and host countries. Nevertheless, quality standards must be also developed in line with the different internal improvement of quality management systems in different companies, which means that training about quality issues remains within the organization. This training should attend to the needs of the organization including its foreign locations, in which differing qualification and working habits exist and also different interpretations of the recommendations included in quality management systems. Thus, as quality managers in our two case studies remark, quality standards and management systems represent a double-edged sword making the organization blind about day-to-day problems among project workers in international teams. A balance between the recommendations included in quality management systems and the day-to-day expertise emerging in different projects and locations is needed in order to integrate working experiences into future projects and to establish an organizational knowledge basis. In other words, quality standardization as coordination tool for off- and nearshore projects should both establish a common working basis for different organizational settings and represent a dynamic process of self-reflection on working experiences.

In off- and nearshore projects distance play a crucial role that is very often underestimated. At the organizational level the participation of project workers from different locations in the development of quality standards could represent a chance to establish more realistic working and communication patterns in international ICT organizations. Moreover, the cooperation of ICT organizations with educational institutions for the integration of quality standard and management issues in educational curricula in computer science or other related studies could support a common basis for the implementation of ICT qualifications in different national settings. In the next section I comment some future trends regarding quality standardization patterns in offshore in Europe.

FUTURE TRENDS

Taking into account the development in the European ICT Branch regarding offshoring (Ruiz Ben & Wieandt 2006; Ruiz Ben, Wieandt, & Maletzky, 2006), quality standardization will gain importance, first as coordination instruments in the development of the ICT branch in new geographical areas of the European Union. Due to this increasing significance of quality standards in the region, there will be a growing need for professionals with skills needed to engage in both standard setting activities in ICT companies and in Standard Setting Organizations. This represents an additional challenge for the educational institutions in the respective countries of the European Union that sum to the long-discussed problem of qualification mismatch in the ICT branch (Ruiz Ben & Claus, 2005; Ruiz Ben, 2003; Dostal, 2004). Educational institutions should more intensively cooperate with companies to prevent qualification mismatch in quality management, but also in project management issues. Internships about quality management should be established as a part of the curricula.

Intercultural aspects will gain also importance in the development of quality standards. The need to address these issues is crucial, in order to ensure equal access and opportunity for all European countries. From a global perspective, the World Summit on the Information Society represents an example for creating a discussion forum for these kinds of issues. Global SDOs like the ITU are also assigning growing focusing to equity aspects.

Considering the future trend towards increasing standardization, German companies seem to play in an advantage position, since as Tate (2001, p. 472) remarks:

In Germany, firms have been world leaders at creating a transnational infrastructure for standards, transferring their routine national standards work to the European and international levels which in turn remain closely integrated with more specialized national standards capable of supporting diversified quality strategies.

Nevertheless, as Tate further remarks, national varieties in standard settings in Europe are being compressed, but not eliminated. In the case of Germany, firms need "a comprehensive standards infrastructure capable of supporting high level product engineering" (2001, p. 472). Particularly at the process level, it is very important that standards develop in the line of process innovation rhythms. Therefore, firms will probably increasingly use international standard setting organizations for establishing their own standards in trans-national arenas. Particularly in Europe, this trend will be enhanced with the participation of the EU as harmonization, for instance. This could be a chance to better involve small and medium enterprises and also the new European Member States in the development of quality standards in the ICT branch.

CONCLUSION

In this chapter, I have shown which role quality standards play in the current internationalization process of the ICT branch focusing in the situation in Europe and particularly in Germany presenting some preliminary results of my work in progress.

First, I have given an overview of the importance of quality standards for the development of ICT off- and nearshore processes, as well as the role of the main actors in standards setting processes. Firms very often adopt ad hoc solutions in order to try to timely bring production outputs in line with the innovation rhythm of the market, due to the gap between the needs and perspectives of the standard developer, the organizations and the users of the standards. However, such solutions are very often ineffective. ICT companies practicing off- and nearshore mostly use quality standards as an instrument to reduce transaction costs, especially related to information and communication efforts among home and host centers, or as a basis to confront network externalities related to market competition. Thus, we can distinguish two main aspects of the adoption of quality standards in relation to off- and nearshore processes: an internal controlling aspect of working and communication processes and an external one beyond the network in order to get market advantages. Such advantages are mostly dominated by large enterprises playing the mayor role in the process of standards setting in SDOs and moreover due to their time and personnel resources to implement and adapt quality management systems in their network environments and to continually train their employees in order to implement quality standards in their day to day working practices.

In order to improve more democratic processes for the development of quality standards, the EU could adopt a harmonization entity role in the European context of the ICT branch. At the national level, a more intensive cooperation among small, medium and large enterprises with educational institutions and especially with universities could serve as a basis to reduce the particular disadvantages mentioned above and reduce possible qualification mismatches.

FUTURE RESEARCH DIRECTIONS

The research on quality standardization patterns in ICT off- and nearshore projects has been mainly focused on the level of the institutional support and composition development of quality standards. Also, management issues have been an important focus of research (Boiral, 2006; Tate, 2001; Carmel & Tjia 2005; Tummala & Tang, 1996). From the point of view of the day-to-day working practices, the question about how quality standardization patterns influence the working habitus of ICT professionals at different levels of the organizations is still open. Also, the transformation of tasks profiles in off- and nearshore projects and the related importance of quality managers for the implementation of international ICT projects are not yet fully researched. Aspects such as the balance between standardization of working processes and the emerging expertise of off- and nearshore projects in quality management systems are in some cases internally considered in organizations and represent an important problem in off- and nearshore projects. Here it is important to investigate which interaction and communication models between home and host organizations are best suited and how different actors in participating organizations can integrate their working experiences in the development of quality management systems. Moreover, the relation between innovation and implementation of quality standards in ICT organizations from an international perspective is another important issue for research. The question at this point is how quality standards contribute to the development of product and working process or on the contrary, they hindering dynamics of innovation. Particularly the adaptation of host organizations in off- and nearshore locations to quality standards implemented in home organization countries represents interpretation risks that can constitute a communication and creativity obstacle. Furthermore, the acceptance of imported quality management systems in host organizations should be better investigated in order to confront conflicts among workers in international ICT projects.

From an institutional perspective, the integration of quality standardization and quality management issues in university curricula is an important theme for research in order to confront the persisting mismatch between ICT educational and industrial development. At this point, it is important to investigate which models of institutional knowledge transferred in different regional settings have more successfully contributed to establishing learning patterns between educational institutions and ICT organizations. The chances and challenges for transferring such models to other contexts should be furthermore researched.

REFERENCES

Boiral, O. (2006). La certification ISO 14001: une perspective néoinstitutionnelle. *Management International, 10*(3), 67-79.

Carmel, E., & Tjia, P. (2005). *Offshoring information technology.* Sourcing and outsourcing to a global workforce. Cambridge: Cambridge University Press.

Crevoisier, O. (1999). Innovation and the city. In E. J. Malecki & P. Oinas (Eds.), *Making connections: Technological learning and regional economic change.* UK: Ashgate Publishing Company.

Dutka, D., & Sekhar, A. (2004, April 27-28). *Major Indian ICT firms and their approaches towards achieving quality.* Paper presented at an International Conference to Mark 20 Years of ASARC, University House, Australian National University.

Eisner, R. (2005). Offshore legal issues. In E. Carmel & P. Tjia (2005). *Offshoring information technology. Sourcing and outsourcing to a global workforce* (pp. 112-129). Cambridge: Cambridge University Press.

OECD. (2002a). *Technology outlook: ICTs and the information economy.* OECD & Dev.

OECD. (2002b). *Reviewing the ICT sector definition: Issues for discussion.* Paper DSTI/ICCP/IIS(2002)2. Retrieved August 25, 2006, from http://www.oecd.org/dataoecd/3/8/20627293.pdf

OECD (2002c). *Measuring the information economy.* Retrieved August 25, 2006, from http://www.oecd.org/dataoecd/16/14/1835738.pdf

Ruiz Ben, E., & Claus, R. (2004). Offshoring in der deutschen IT Branche. Eine neue Herausforderung für die Informatik. *Informatik Spektrum,* (4), 1-6.

Ruiz Ben, E., & Wieandt, M. (2006). *Growing East:* Nearshoring und die neuen ICT Arbeitsmärkte in Europa. FifF-Ko, (3). (forthcoming)

Tate, J. (2001). National varieties of standardization. In P. A. Hall & D. Soskice (Ed.), *Varieties of capitalism* (pp. 442-474). Oxford: Oxford University Press.

Tummala, V.M.R., & Tang, C.L. (1996). Strategic quality management. Malcolm Baldrige and European Quality Awards and ISO 9000 certification: Core concepts and comparative analysis. *International Journal of Quality and Reliability Management, 13*(4), 8-38.

van der Wiele, T., van Iwaarden, J., Williams, R., & Dale, B. (2004). *Perceptions about the ISO 9000 (2000) quality system standard revision and its value: The Dutch experience. ERIM Report Series ERS-2004-081-ORG (Organizational be-*

havior and HRM). Rotterdam: Erasmus Research Institute of Management.

ADDITIONAL READINGS

Adam, E.E. Jr., Corbett, L.M., Flores, B.E., Harrison, N.J., Lee, T.S., Rho, B., Ribera, J., Samson, D., & Westbrook, R. (1997). An international study of quality improvement approach and firm performance. *International Journal of Operations and Production Management, 17*(9), 842-73.

Askey, J.M., & Dale, B.G. (1994). From ISO 9000 series registration to total quality management, an examination, *Quality Management Journal,* July, 67-76.

Binney, G. (1992). *Making quality work: Lessons from Europe's leading companies.* The Economist Intelligence Unit, London. Special Report No. P655.

Blind, K. (2001). *Standardisation, R&D and export activities: Empirical evidence at firm level.* Proceedings of the Third Interdisciplinary Workshop on Standardization Research at the University of the German Federal Armed Forces (pp. 165-186). Hamburg, Germany: Univ. der Bundeswehr.

Bradley, M. (1994). Starting total quality management from ISO 9000. *The TQM Magazine, 6*(1), 50-4. Brecka, J. (1994). Survey of registrars for ISO 9000: Prices down, success rate up. Quality Progress, February, 20-1.

Brown, A., & Wiele, A. van der (1996). A typology of approaches to ISO certification and TQM. *Australian Journal of Management, 21*(1), 57-72.

Brown, A., Loughton, K., & Wiele, A. van der (1998). Smaller enterprises' experiences with ISO 9000. *International Journal of Quality and Reliability Management, 15*(3), 273-85.

Buttle, F. (1997). ISO 9000: Marketing motivations and benefits. *International Journal of Quality and Reliability Management, 14*(9), 939-47.

Corrigan, J. (1994). *Is ISO 9000 the path to TQM?* Quality Progress, May, 33-6.

Ebrahimpour, M., Withers, B.E., & Hikmet, N. (1997). Experiences of US- and foreign-owned firms: A new perspective on ISO 9000 implementation. *International Journal of Production Research, 35*(2), 569-76.

Flynn, B.B., Schroeder, R.G., & Sakakibara, S. (1995). The impact of quality management practices on performance and competitive advantage. *Decision Sciences, 26*(5), 659-92.

Forker, L.B., Vickery, S.K., & Droge, C.L. (1996). The contribution of quality to business performance. *International Journal of Operations and Production Management, 16*(8), 44-62.

Gotzamani, K.D., & Tsiotras, G.D. (2001). An empirical study of the ISO 9000 Standards' contribution towards total quality management. *International Journal of Operations & Production Management, 21*(10), 1326-42.

Heras, I., Casadesus, M., & Dick, G.P.M. (2002). ISO 9000 certification and the bottom line: A comparative study of the profitability of Basque companies. *Managerial Auditing Journal, 17*(1/2), 72-8.

Institute of Quality Assurance. (1993). *Survey on the use and implementation of BS5750.* London: Institute of Quality Assurance.

Hawkins, R. (2000). *Study of the standards-related information requirements of users in the information society.* Final report to CEN/ISSS. Retrieved February 14, 2000, from www.cenorm.be/isss

International Organisation for Standardization (ISO) (2004). T*he ISO survey of ISO 9000 and ISO 14000 Certificates (Twelfth Cycle).* International Organisation for Standardisation, Geneva.

Jacobson, R., & Aaker, D. (1987). The strategic role of product quality. *Journal of Marketing, 51*(4), 31-44.

Johannsen, C.G. (1995). Application of the ISO 9000 standards of quality management in professional services: An information sector case. *Total Quality Management, 6*(3), 231-42.

Jones, R., Arndt, G., & Kustin, R. (1997). ISO 9000 among Australian companies: Impact of time and reasons for seeking certification on perceptions of benefits received. *International Journal of Quality and Reliability Management, 14* (7), 650-60.

Kanji, G.K. (1998). An innovative approach to make ISO 9000 standards more effective. *Total Quality Management, 9*(1), 67-78.

Kochan, A. (1993). ISO 9000: Creating a global standardisation process. Quality, October, 26-34.

Lee, T. (1995). The experience of implementing ISO 9000 in Hong Kong. *Asia Pacific Journal of Quality Management, 4*(4), 6-16.

Llopis, J., & Tarí, J.J. (2003). The importance of internal aspects in quality improvement. *International Journal of Quality and Reliability Management, 20*(3), 304-24

McAdam, R., & McKeown, M. (1999). Life after ISO 9000: An analysis of the impact of ISO 9000 and total quality management on small businesses in Northern Ireland. *Total Quality Management, 10*(2), 229-41.

Meegan, S.T., & Taylor, W.A. (1997). Factors influencing a successful transition from ISO 9000 to TQM: The influence of understanding and motivation. *International Journal of Quality & Reliability Management, 14*(2), 100-17.

Meeus, M.T.H., Faber, J., & Oerlemans, L.A.G. (2002). *Why do firms participate in standardization?* An empirical exploration of the relation between isomorphism and institutional dynamics in standardization. Working Paper Department of Innovation Studies, Utrecht: University of Utrecht.

Phillips, L.W., Chang, D.R., & Buzzel, R.D. (1983). Product quality, cost position, and business performance: A test of key hypotheses. *Journal of Marketing, 37*(1), 26-43.

Quazi, H.A., & Padibjo, S.R. (1998). A journey towards total quality management through ISO 9000 certification. A study of small and medium sized enterprises in Singapore. *International Journal of Quality & Reliability Management, 15*(5), 364-71.

Rada, R. (1998). Corporate shortcut to standardisation. *Communications of the ACM, 41*(1), 11-15.

Rada, R. (2000). Consensus versus speed. In K. Jakobs (Ed.), *IT standards and standardisation: A global perspective* (pp. 19-34). Hershey, PA: Idea Group Publishing.

Rust, R.T., Zahorik, A.J., & Keiningham, T.I. (1994). Return on quality (ROQ): Making service quality financially accountable. *Journal of Marketing, 59*(2), 58-70.

Seddon, J. (1997). Ten arguments against ISO 9000. *Managing Service Quality, 7*(4), 162-8.

Singles, J., Ruel, G., & Van de Water, H. (2001). ISO 9000 series—Certification and performance. *International Journal of Quality and Reliability Management, 18*(1), 62-75.

Stephens, K.S. (1994). ISO 9000 and total quality. *Quality Management Journal, 2*(1), 57-71.

Taylor, W.A. (1995). Senior executives and ISO 9000. *The International Journal of Quality and Reliability Management, 12*(4), 40-57.

Terziovski, M., Samson, D., & Dow, D. (1997). The business value of quality management systems certification: Evidence from Australia and New

Zealand. *Journal of Operations Management, 15*(1), 1-18.

Terziovski, M., Power, D., & Sohal, A.S. (2003). The longitudinal effects of the ISO 9000 certification process on business performance. *European Journal of Operational Research, 146*(3), 580-95.

Tsiotras, G., & Gotzamani, K. (1996). ISO 9000 as an entry key to TQM: The case of the Greek industry. *International Journal of Quality and Reliability Management, 13*(4), 64-76.

Tummala, V.M.R., & Tang, C.L. (1996). Strategic quality management, Malcolm Baldrige and European Quality Awards and ISO 9000 certification: Core concepts and comparative analysis. *International Journal of Quality and Reliability Management, 13*(4), 8-38.

Weiss, M., & Cargill, C. (1992). Consortia in the standards development process. *Journal of the American Society for Information Science, 43*(8), 559-565.

Weiss, M.B.H., & Sirbu, M. (1990). Technological choice in voluntary standards committees: An empirical analysis. *Economics of Innovation and New Technology, 1*, 111-133.

Wiele, A. van der, Dale, B.G. & Williams, A.R.T. (1997). ISO 9000 series registration to total quality management: The transformation journey. *International Journal of Quality Science, 2*(4), 236-52.

Williams, N. (1997). ISO 9000 as a route to TQM in small to medium sized enterprises: Snake or ladder? *The TQM Magazine, 9*(1), 8-13.

Yahya, S., & Goh, W.K. (2001). The implementation of an ISO 9000 quality System. *International Journal of Quality and Reliability Management, 18*(9), 941-66.

ENDNOTES

[1] http://www.bsi-emea.com/Quality/Overview/WhatisaQMS.xalter (Retrieved August 20, 2006)

[2] The following example illustrates the use of the EU Acquired Rights Directive for ICT offshoring: *"When multinational companies are applying 'global sourcing' strategies, suppliers can be played off against one another and as a result, they can either win or lose a contract. In the case of long-term contracts for service delivery, staff can be transferred together with their jobs to do the same work for their new boss. This is necessary to ensure the continuity and quality of the service delivery. Such transfer of employees from one service provider to another requires special attention to maintaining the acquired working conditions. Recently, Siemens Business Services (SBS) took over a contract of Electronic Data Systems (EDS) to supply business services to the Coca-Cola Company. SBS agreed with the EDS on the transfer of a number of dedicated employees from the latter to the former in certain countries. These transfers were carried out within the EU Acquired Rights Directive that regulates the transfer of working conditions."* Accessed August 29, 2006, from http://www.union-network.org/Uniindep.nsf/f73728e0eb1f5ca5c125700e003ccdbb/$FILE/MOOSNewsletter3.pdf#search=%22acquired%20rights%20directive%20eu%20offshoring%22

This work was previously published in Handbook of Research on Global Information Technology Management in the Digital Economy, edited by M. Raisinghani, pp. 312-327, copyright 2008 by Information Science Reference (an imprint of IGI Global).

Chapter XVI
An Overview of Models and Standards of Processes in the SE, SwE, and IS Disciplines

Manuel Mora
Autonomous University of Aguascalientes, Mexico

Ovsei Gelman
Universidad Nacional Autónoma de México, Mexico

Rory O'Connor
Dublin City University, Ireland

Francisco Alvarez
Autonomous University of Aguascalientes, Mexico

Jorge Macías-Luévano
Autonomous University of Aguascalientes, Mexico

ABSTRACT

This chapter develops a descriptive-conceptual overview of the main models and standards of processes formulated in the systems engineering (SE), software engineering (SwE) and information systems (IS) disciplines. Given the myriad of models and standards reported, the convergence suggested for the SE and SwE models and standards and the increasing complexity of the modern information systems, we argue that these ones become relevant in the information systems discipline. Firstly, we report the rationale for having models and standards of processes in SE, SwE and IS. Secondly, we review their main characteristics. Thirdly, based on the identified aims and principles, we report and posit the concepts of process, system and service as conceptual building blocks for describing such models and standards. Finally, initial theoretical and practical implications for the information systems discipline of such models and standards are discussed, as well as recommendations for further research are suggested.

... in the current marketplace, there are maturity models, standards, methodologies, and guidelines that can help an organization improve the way it does business. However, most available improvement approaches focus on a specific part of the business and do not take a systemic approach to the problems that most organizations are facing. (SEI, 2006, p. 3)

INTRODUCTION

The manufacturing of products and the provision of services in the modern world has increased process engineering (including manufacturing or provision) and process managerial complexity (Boehm & Lane, 2006). The engineering complexity has been raised because of the variety of design, manufacturing or provision process, machines and tools, materials and system-component designs, as well as for the high-quality, cost-efficiency relationships, and value expectations demanded from the competitive worldwide markets. The process managerial complexity has increased because of disparate business internal and external process must be coordinated. To meet the time to market, competitive prices, market sharing, distribution scope and environmental and ethical organizational objectives, among others financial and strategic organizational objectives contribute to increased organizational pressures and organizational complexity (Farr & Buede, 2003).

Such process engineering and/or managerial complexity is manifested in: (1) the critical failures of enterprises information systems implementations (CIO UK, 2007; Ewusi, 1997; Standish Group, 2003), (2) the unexpected appearance of large batches of defective products that have had a proved high-quality image for decades, and (3) the increasing of system downtimes and/or low efficiency and effectiveness in critical services such: electricity, nuclear plants, health services and governmental services (Bar-Yam, 2003).

Organizations with global and large-scale operations have fostered the exchange of the best organizational practices (Arnold & Lawson, 2004). The purpose is to improve business processes and avoid critical failures in the manufacturing of products and provision of services. Best practices have been documented (via a deep redesign, analysis, discussion, evaluation, authorization, and updating of organizational activities) through models and/or standards of process by international organizations for the disciplines of systems engineering (SE), software engineering (SwE) and information systems (IS). Some models and standards come from organizations with a global scope, like the International Organization for Standardization (ISO) but others limit their influences in some countries or regions, like the US-based Software Engineering Institute (SEI). Whilst both types of organizations can differ in their geographic scopes, both keep a similar efficacy purpose: to make available a set of generic process (technical, managerial, support and enterprise) that come from the best international practices to correct and improve their organizational process, with the expected outcome being improved quality, value and cost-efficiency issues with respect to the software products and services generated.

However, because of the myriad of models and standards reported in the three disciplines, the convergence suggested for SE and SwE engineering process, models and/or standards (Boehm 2000; Hecht, 1999; ISO, 2006c; ISO, in press; Sommerville, 1998; Thayer, 1997) and the increasing complexity of the modern information systems (Mora et al, 2008), we argue that these models and standards of processes become relevant in the Information Systems discipline. Then, in this chapter we develop a conceptual description (Glass, Armes & Vessey, 2004; Mora, 2004) of the main models and standards of processes formulated in the SE, SwE and IS disciplines with the general purpose to identify aims, purposes, characteristics, and core building-block concepts. Firstly, we report the rationale for having models and standards of processes in such disciplines. Secondly, we review their main characteristics. Thirdly, based in the identified aims and principles, we report and posit the concepts of *process*, *system* and *service* as the conceptual building-blocks for describing such models and standards. Finally, initial theoretical and practical implications for the Information Systems discipline of such models and standards are discussed, as well as recommendations for further research are suggested.

REVIEW ON MODELS AND STANDARDS OF PROCESSES

The Rationale of Models and Standards of Processes

Currently the global and large-scale organizations are faced with the challenge to meet the highest customer's expectations for their products and services, as well as to satisfy their own organizational financial and strategic objectives. To cope with such external and internal complexities, organizations have fostered the utilization (deployment and exchange) of best organizational practices. These global best practices have been documented via models and standards of processes. According to Succi, Valerio, Vernazza, and Succi (1998, p. 140) *"standardization means that there is an explicit or implicit agreement to do certain things in a defined and uniform way"*.

Whilst the models are considered as *de facto* standards (not a legal mandatory use) and the standards as *de jure* (legal mandatory use when a country or business sector agrees use it), both help the organizations to improve the quality of their internal processes and to align them with international practices. In this way, the organizations foster an efficient and effective international exchange of goods and services. We consider that an insightful understanding of the models and standards concepts is required for their further analysis. The Table 1 (from several sources: Mora, Gelman, O'Connor, Alvarez & Macías, 2007a;

Table 1. Models and standards of processes in SE and SwE

FEATURE	MODELS OF PROCESSES	STANDARDS[1] OF PROCESSES
General aim	To provide a set of best and generic management, engineering and organizational practices for performing high-quality processes (e.g., efficiency and effectiveness) related with SE, SwE and IT practices.	
Main purpose	- To improve processes -To measure the capability maturity level of organizational processes	- To define the processes - To measure compliance or not compliance of processes with the normative processes
	- To provide a generic map of processes	
Definition	*"A process model is a structured collection of practices that describe the characteristics of effective processes."* (SEI, 2006)	A set of the state-of-the-art practices and their related vocabulary that provides a model to be strictly followed and fulfilled by organizations in order to be certified in its utilization.
Origin	Any organization with resources (knowledge, time, money)	An industry-approval and/or nation-endorsed is required.
Mandatory utilization	No, but some of them are become in *de facto* standards	No, but these are merged with national or industry-based regulations or are directly adopted for being mandatory (*de jure*)
Life-cycle uniqueness	No, these are open to any life cycle (but usually suggest a generic one)	No, but lifecycle reported as example are taken as the best recommended
What vs How recommendations	Both have been designed to provide only what-alike recommendations on what must be done and produced (activities, tasks and deliverables) rather than on the detailed specifications on how doing these (specific procedures, techniques and profiles of deliverables). However, some could provide how-alike guidelines.	

Sheard & Lake, 1998; Tantara, 2001; Wright, 1998) shows the main conceptual attributes of the models and standards of process.

The main similarities between models and standards are the following: (1) both provide a map of generic processes from the best international practices; (2) both establish what-alike and must-be instructions rather than how-alike specific procedures, and (3) both do not impose a mandatory life-cycle but suggest a demonstrative one that is usually taken as a starting point. The implementers must complement such recommendations with detailed procedures and profiles of the deliverables. Regarding to the differences: (1) the models (at least the early reported[2]) have been focused on process improvement efforts (and consequently include a capability maturity level assessment such CMMI) while that the standards, on an overall complaint and not complaint general assessment (e.g., ISO, 1995), (2) models are used under an agreement between companies to legitimate their industrial acceptance (e.g., CMMI in the Americas) while that standards are used under a usually obligatory country-based agreement (e.g., ISO, 2003 in Europe and Australia), and (3) the models can be originated from any organization while that the standards are strongly endorsed by nations.

It is worth noting that the first standards were product-oriented (Tripp, 1996) (design and final product attributes, tolerances, specifications) and could be objectively assessed through testing and evaluation of the devices using physical instruments. However, the standards for process convey additional difficulties for automatic assessment. Observations, records, interviews, analysis and questionnaires applied to core people in site are required. Furthermore, for the case of the software as a product/artifact, additional complications emerge. While that the standard ISO 9126:1991 offers an initial solution, their set of attributes still requires a final interpretation on how to measure them. Other sources of complexity are the time and the human resource performance variability

in the certification of standards of processes.

It has been reported also the critical roles that are played by the information and communications technologies (ICT) and the systems of information systems (SoIS) for supporting practically all business process in worldwide organizations (Mora, Gelman, Frank, Paradice, Cervantes & Forgionne, 2008). This assertion implies that for such organizations, the ICT infrastructure and the SoIS (and IS function), have become an essential resource and macroprocess (e.g., a system of systems of processes) for that the organization operates efficient and effectively. Relevant economic losses from ICT infrastructure downtimes or SoIS failures are present evidences of the high-dependability that worldwide organizations have on the correct availability, capacity, and reliability of such ICT resources and process.

Models and/or standards of processes for engineering and management of ICT and SoIS resources have been also developed. However, such development and deployment have increased the engineering and management complexity per se. To cope holistically with the technical and socio-organizational problems for their efficient and effective engineering and management, this chapter supports the premise[3] that an integrative and holistic approach based in an extended Systems Engineering philosophy and methods (Forsberg & Mooz, 1997; INCOSE, 2004; Sage, 1992, 2000; Sage & Amstrong, 2000) can provide the suitable conceptual lenses and methodological tools to study and cope with the increasing managerial, technical and organizational complexity of the engineering and management (E&M) of ICT and SoIS resources and processes. Overall expected contribution is to increase our understanding and control of such E&M processes.

This chapter then, is motivated by the reasons identified previously by authors (Mora et al., 2007a):

(i) the SE models and standards of processes have been ignored in IT&S or scarcely analyzed in

SwE; (ii) the SwE literature has wrongly equaled the concept of software system with the concept of information systems when both constructs are ontologically different (Mora et al., 2003) *and consequently relevant organizational issues have been ignored in SwE models and standards of processes; and (iii) the Systems Engineering field and the Systems Approach philosophy has proved to be very successful in large scale projects when it is correctly applied* (Barker & Verma, 2003; Honour, 2002).

Furthermore, we have identified also (idem) core facts that become relevant the interaction of SE, SwE, and IT standards and models of processes for the IS discipline:

(i) the recognition that the scope and effects of software systems do not end with its completion but with its successful deployment of the whole (information) system (Boehm, 2000; Sommerville, 1998)*; (ii) the acceptance of the software engineering process involves also managerial, organizational, economic, sociopolitical, legal and behavioral issues* (Fuggetta[4], 2000; Kellner, Curtis, deMarco, Kishida, Schulemberg & Tully, 1991)*; (iii) the proposal of the integration of Systems Engineering (SE)[5] with Software Engineering[6] to enhance mutually their engineering and managerial process* (Andriole & Freeman, 1993; Bate, 1998; Boehm, 2000, 2006; Deno & Feeney, 2002; Hecht, 1997; Hole, Verma, Jain, Vitale & Popick, 2005; Johnson, 1996; Johnson & Dindo, 1998; Nichols & Connaughton, 2005; Sommerville, 1998; Thayer, 1997, 2002)*; (iv) the identification that the Information Technology and Systems (IT&S) field, which traditionally has its focus in the management and evaluation of IT-intensive systems, is highly dependent of the engineering activities* (Hevner, March, Park & Ram, 2004; Nunamaker, Chen & Purdin, 1991) *conducted in SwE and SE, and despite this has generated its own set of models and standards of processes, their conceptual relation with SwE and*

SE models and standards has been few explored, and (v) the proposal to widen the scope of SE standards of processes to define business process architectures in organizations (Arnold & Lawson, 2004; Farr & Buede, 2003).

History and Aims of the Main SE, SwE and IS Models of Standards of Processes

A generic aim of the SE, IS and SwE is the definition, development and deployment of large-scale cost-effective and trustworthy integrated systems, system of information systems or software-intensive systems respectively (Sage, 1992, 2000; Sage & Amstrong, 2000; Thayer, 1997). In pursuit of this aim, these disciplines have generated models and standards of processes to guide and control the engineering and managerial activities involved in the creation of such systems. The models and standards provide a set of processes for good (or best) SE, SwE and IS practices, but differs in some items exhibited in Table 1. The Table 2 (derived from Collin, 2004; Garcia, 1998; ISO, 2005; ITGI, 2000; Sheard & Lake, 1998; SEI, 2006; Tantara, 2001; Wright, 1998) shows the history of the main models and standards in SE, SwE, and IS.

The main finding from Table 2 is the lack of models and standards of processes for IS area. Except for the ISO 20000 standard (published in 2006 but based in ITIL v.2.0 model from 1995) and the model CobIT, no significant model or standard of process has been posed[10]. SE and SwE disciplines have developed more standards in the last two decades but both face the challenge of integration toward single standards (e.g., ISO 15289, CMMI for SE and SwE). From the descriptions of the aims of the standards and models of processes in Table 3, we identify two core purposes: (1) the improvement/assessment of processes and (2) the definition/provision of processes.

Mora et al (2007a) report that such standards and models also exhibit a(n):

Table 2. History of models and standards of processes in SE, SwE, and IT

YEAR	STD/ MOD	ORIGIN	SE	SwE	IS
1987, 2000	Std	TC 176/SC 2/WG 18		ISO 9001:2000 (Standard Base)	
1995, 2002, 2004	Std	JTC 1/ SC7		ISO/IEC 12207	
1999, 2002	Std	EIA	SECM (EIA-731)		
1996, 2002	Std	JTC 1/ SC7	ISO/IEC 15288		
2003, 2004, 2006	Std	JTC 1/ SC7	ISO/IEC 15504		
2004	Std			ISO/IEC 90003:2004	
1995, 2001, 2006	Mod	SEI	CMMI-DEV+IPPD 1.2 (SE,SW,HW)		CMMI-SVC[7] 1.2
1996, 2000, 2006	Std	ISACA			CobIT[8]
2005	Std	JTC 1/ SC7			ISO/IEC 20000[9]
2006	Std	JTC 1/ SC7	ISO/IEC 15289		

1. *... rationality to organize the managerial and engineering functions to define, develop and deploy products and services in a generic organization through a process approach;*

2. *... acknowledgement of the increasing interrelationship between software, hardware and general IT-based products, services and/or systems, [that] has fostered the integration of SwE and SE standards and models to address the needs a whole product, service or system to be engineered;*

3. *... emergence of the service-oriented approach in the future (as the forthcoming CMMI-SVC, and the current ISO20000 standard)*

4. *... implicit need for an interdisciplinary body of knowledge and research related to the management and engineering of process from SE, SwE and IT&S disciplines including BPM;*

5. *... implicit utilization of the Systems Approach to establish the initial foundations such as concepts, principles and philosophy, for the design of standards.*

The aforementioned characteristics are based on the fact of the ISO 9000 family of standards (which deal with a generic industry-independent quality management system and an organizational encouragement toward a continuous process improvement) is identified as the main source for the SE, SwE, and IT standards and models of process. Table 3 shows the official self-description and status of these models and standards.

The Core Building-Block Concepts for Understanding Models and Standards of Processes: Process, Service and System

The ISO 9000 standard in its 2000-year version has established eight management principles where two of them (Principle 4 and 5) endorse the **process approach** and the **systems approach** as critical management paradigms respectively. Principle 4 establishes that an organization will be more likely to achieve the results expected efficiently, if the resources and activities are managed as **processes**. In turn, the Principle 5 sets forth that an

Table 3. Official description and status of models and standards of processes in SE, SwE and IT

STD/MOD	OFFICIAL DESCRIPTION OF THE STANDARD OR MODEL'S AIM	STATUS
ISO 9001:2000	*"Quality management systems – Requirements: ISO 9001:2000 specifies requirements for a quality management system where an organization needs to demonstrate its ability to consistently provide product that meets customer and applicable regulatory requirements, and aims to enhance customer satisfaction through the effective application of the system, including processes for continual improvement of the system and the assurance of conformity to customer and applicable regulatory requirements. All requirements of this International Standard are generic and are intended to be applicable to all organizations, regardless of type, size and product provided" (ISO, 2006a).*	Code ISO 90.92 (International Standard to be revised)
ISO/IEC 12207	*"Information technology – Software life cycle processes: Establishes a system for software life cycle processes with well-defined terminology. Contains processes, activities and tasks that are to be applied during the acquisition of a system that contains software, a stand-alone software product and software services" (ISO, 1995).*	Code ISO 90.92 (International Standard to be revised)
ISO/IEC 15504-1 to 5	*"Information technology – Process assessment: ... ISO/IEC 15504 (all parts) provides a framework for the assessment of processes. This framework can be used by organizations involved in planning, managing, monitoring, controlling and improving the acquisition, supply, development, operation, evolution and support of products and services" (ISO, 2003).*	Code ISO 60.60 (International Standard published)
ISO/IEC 90003	*"Software engineering -- Guidelines for the application of ISO 9001:2000 to computer software: ... ISO/IEC 90003:2004 provides guidance for organizations in the application of ISO 9001:2000 to the acquisition, supply, development, operation and maintenance of computer software and related support services ... identifies the issues which should be addressed and is independent of the technology, life cycle models, development processes, sequence of activities and organizational structure used by an organization" (ISO, 2004a).*	Code ISO 60.60 (International Standard published)
SECM (EIA/IS 731)	*System Engineering Capability Model: "... describes the essential systems engineering and management tasks that an organization must perform to ensure a successful systems engineering effort" (Minnich, 2002); "...(is) a method for assessing and improving the efficiency and effectiveness of systems engineering" (same core idea shared with SECAM former standard, INCOSE, 1996).*	(International Standard published)
ISO/IEC 15288	*"Systems engineering System life cycle processes: ... this standard encompasses the life cycle of man-made systems, spanning the conception of the ideas through to the retirement of the system. It provides the processes for acquiring and supplying system products and services that are configured from one or more of the following types of system components: hardware, software, and human interfaces. This framework also provides for the assessment and improvement of the project life cycle" (ISO, 2002; Magee, 2006).*	Code ISO 90.92 (International Standard to be revised)
ISO/IEC 15289	*"Systems and software engineering -- Content of systems and software life cycle process information products (Documentation): ... ISO/IEC 15289:2006 was developed to assist users of systems and software life cycle processes to manage information items (documents) ... may be applied to any of the activities and tasks of a project, system or software product, or service life cycle. It is not limited by the size, complexity or criticality of the project" (ISO, 2006c).*	Code ISO 60.60 (International Standard published)
CobIT	*"COBIT provides good practices for the management of IT processes in a manageable and logical structure, meeting the multiple needs of enterprise management by bridging the gaps between business risks, technical issues, control needs and performance measurement requirements" (ITGI, 2000).*	(International Model published)

continued on following page

Table 3. continued

ISO/IEC 20000	*"Information technology -- Service management: defines the requirements for a service provider to deliver managed services ... promotes the adoption of an integrated process approach to effectively deliver managed services to meet business and customer requirements. For an organization to function effectively it has to identify and manage numerous linked activities. Coordinated integration and implementation of the service management processes provides the ongoing control, greater efficiency and opportunities for continual improvement"* (ISO, 2005).	Code ISO 60.60 (International Standard published)
CMMI-DEV	*"CMMI® (Capability Maturity Model® Integration) is a process improvement maturity model for the development of products and services. It consists of best practices that address development and maintenance activities that cover the product lifecycle from conception through delivery and maintenance. This latest iteration of the model as represented herein integrates bodies of knowledge that are essential for development and maintenance, but that have been addressed separately in the past, such as software engineering, systems engineering, hardware and design engineering, the engineering "-ilities," and acquisition. The prior designations of CMMI for systems engineering and software engineering (CMMI-SE/SW) are superseded by the title "CMMI for Development" to truly reflect the comprehensive integration of these bodies of knowledge and the application of the model within the organization. CMMI for Development (CMMI-DEV) provides a comprehensive integrated solution for development and maintenance activities applied to products and services"* (SEI, 2006).	(International Model published)

organization can identify, understand and manage more efficiently and effectively the ***processes*** if they conceptualized them as a ***system***. Furthermore, the ISO 9001:2000 standard remarks that *"... concerns the way an organization goes about its work ... concern processes not products—at least not directly"* (ISO, 2006b). However, this standard admits also that, *" ... the way in which the organization manage its processes is obviously to affect its final (quality of) product"* (ibid).

This ***process management premise*** (e.g., *"the quality of a system is largely governed by the quality of the process used to develop and maintain it"*) has been largely used in quality management

Table 4. Definitions of the concept of process

AREA	DEFINITION OF THE CONCEPT: PROCESS	SOURCE
Quality Management Systems	*"Set of interrelated or interacting activities, which transforms inputs into outputs. These activities require allocation of resources such as people and materials."*	ISO 9001:2000
SwE	*"The means by which people, procedures, methods, equipment, and tools are integrated to produce a desired end result." A process can be also considered the "glue that ties them"* in order to get a work done. (Based in CMMI-DEV (SEI, 2006)	CMM-SW, CMMI-DEV 1.2
SwE	*"... a (software development) process is a collaboration between abstract active entities called roles that perform operations called activities on concrete, tangible entities called artifacts."*	UPM (OMG, 2005)
BPM	*"A Process is an activity performed within a company or organization. In BPMN a Process is depicted as a graph of Flow Objects, which are a set of other activities and the controls that sequence them. The concept of process is intrinsically hierarchical. Processes may be defined at any level from enterprise-wide processes to processes performed by a single person. Low-level processes may be grouped together to achieve a common business goal."*	BPMN (OMG, 2006)
SE	*"A set of inter-related functions and their corresponding inputs and outputs, which are activated and deactivated by their control inputs."*	SysUML (2005)
IS	*"A connected series of actions, activities, changes, etc., performed by agents with the intent of satisfying a purpose or achieving a goal."*	ITIL (2004)

Table 5. Definitions of the concept of service

AREA	DEFINITION OF THE CONCEPT: SERVICE	SOURCE
Quality Management Systems	An explicit definition is not reported.	ISO 9001:2000
SwE	*"a service is a product that is intangible and non-storable."*	CMMI-DEV 1.2
SwE	*An explicit definition is not reported.*	UPM (OMG, 2005)
BPM	*An explicit definition is not reported.*	BPMN (OMG, 2006)
SE	*Missing concept. Instead of it, the concepts of: operation, function, activity and action are reported. In particular, the concept of operation is defined as "A feature which declares a service that can be performed by instances of the classifier of which they are instances."*	SysUML (2005)
IS	*"One or more IT systems which enable a business process."*	ITIL (2004)
SSME	*"Service can be defined as the application of competences for the benefit of another, meaning that service is a kind of action, performance, or promise that's exchanged for value between provider and client. Service is performed in close contact with a client; the more knowledge-intensive and customized the service, the more the service process depends critically on client participation and input, whether by providing labor, property, or information."*	Spohrer et al. (2007)

systems (Paulk, Chrissis, Weber & Perdue, 1987). With these insights, we posit that the concepts of **process**, **system** and **service** and their conceptual systemic interrelationships become critical to understanding the different standards and models under study. The relevance of the notion of **process** is self-evident. The notion of **service**, for SwE is becoming of critical relevance for the shifting from the object and component-based paradigm toward the Web service-computing paradigm. In SE and IS, the broad initiative on Service Science, Management and Engineering (SSME) (Chesbrough & Spohrer, 2006; Demirkan & Goul, 2006) justifies its relevance. The notion of **system** is justified by the ISO 9000:2000 principles.

In order to describe the relationships between **process, service** and **system** in the context of standards and models of process, we develop the Tables 4, 5 and 6 (updated from Mora et al., 2007a) to report the main definitions from such concepts.

Definitions in the Table 4 show that the concept of **process** is not unique. However several attributes are shared in the definitions: (1) an overall purpose (transform inputs in outputs), (2)

activities interrelated, and (3) utilization of human and material resources, procedures and methods. Then, a **process** –based in all definitions-, can be defined as "an ordered set of processes (called sub-process) and/or activities that are performed by agents (either people and/or mechanisms) exercising roles and using procedures, tools and machines for its realization, to transform a set of inputs in a set of expected outputs" (extended from Mora et al., 2007a).

In the Table 5, the concept of **service** is implicitly used for most standards except by those focused on such an issue. Because the most important standards and models of processes for IS (ITIL, CobIT, ISO 20000) and for SwE/SE (CMMI-SVC) are now oriented toward services, a plausible generic definition of what is a **service** is fundamental. Similar to the notion of **process**, there is not unique definition but several attributes are also shared by the definitions: (1) intangible, (2) non-storable, (3) ongoing realization, and (4) people involved for the value appreciation attribute. Whilst the human beings can assess the value scale of nonliving artifacts, the automated processes (by using tools) can assess quality attributes (e.g., agreed physical specifications). Therefore, a *service* can be defined as "the intangible, non-storable and user value-appreciated ongoing outcome (but with a start and end time point) from a system of processes" and consequently a **product** can be defined as "the tangible, storable and quality-measured for instruments or users from a system of processes" (extensions from Mora et al., 2007a).

Hence, the main visible distinctions between **product** and **service** are: (1) its tangibility property that leads to the quality (e.g., the attributes expected in the product) vs. the value (e.g., the benefits to quality-prices rate perceived from a customers' perspective (e.g., human beings), and (2) the ongoing service experience (Teboul, 2007) vs. the time-discrete (includes also periods) utilization of products. An additional difficult to define the building blocks is the omission of the responsible entity that generates a *service*. The definitions proposed (because these appear in the standards) are the notions of *system* and *process*. Still, the difference between both concepts has not been still well reported.

For the aforementioned arguments and definitions showed in the Table 6, the construct *system* becomes a critical concept to link logically the *process* and *service/product* constructs. Hence, the utilization of a Systems Approach (Ackoff, 1971, 1973; Bertalanffy, 1972; Checkland, 2000) as well as the relevance of the correct conceptualization of what is a *system* can be considered fundamental notions to be untapped. Despite, it could be considered that the concept system is a well defined and understood construct, Gelman and Garcia (1989), Gelman et al. (2005), Mora, Gelman, Cervantes, Mejia, and Weitzenfeld (2003) and Mora, Gelman, Cano, Cervantes, and Forgionne (2006) studies on the formalization of the construct *system*, have proved the ambiguity, incompleteness and informality of main definitions reported in the context of SE and IS. Then, the concept of *system* used in these standards, despite can be considered practically illustrative and useful is theoretically incomplete from a systems science discipline. In Mora et al. (2007a) it is argued that "it has diminished the clarity on the critical role of the Systems Approach as the

Table 6. Definitions of the concept of system

AREA	DEFINITION OF THE CONCEPT: SYSTEM	SOURCE
Quality Management Systems	From the Principle 5 and other arguments reported in available documents, a system can be considered *as a network of interdependent processes connected for achieving expected products and services.*	ISO 9001:2000 (2000)
SwE	An explicit definition is not reported.	CMMI-DEV 1.2
SwE	An explicit definition is not reported.	UPM (2000)
BPM	An explicit definition is not reported.	BPMN (2006)
SE	*"An item, with structure, that exhibits observable properties and behaviors."*	SysUML (2005)
SE	*"An integrated set of elements that accomplish a defined objective. These elements include products (hardware, software, firmware), processes, people, information, techniques, facilities, services, and other support elements."*	INCOSE (2004)
IS	*"An integrated composite that consists of one or more of the processes, hardware, software, facilities and people, that provides a capability to satisfy a stated need or objective."*	ITIL (2004)
SSME	*"... a service system [is] a value-coproduction configuration of people, technology, other internal and external service systems, and shared information (such as language, processes, metrics, prices, policies, and laws). This recursive service system definition highlights the fact that service systems have internal structure (intraentity services) and external structure (interentity services) in which participants coproduce value directly or indirectly with other service systems."*	Spohrer et al. (2007)

philosophical and practical source to establish the principles and methods of such standards and has increased consequently the complexity for a mutual understanding and integration. Whilst Process Approaches have been the corner stone for the development and utilization of standards and models of processes, we claim that the Systems Approach is in turn the corner stone that holds to the Process Approach."

However, from a practical worldview and with the purpose to propose a plausible relationship between the three concepts, a *system* as an abstract entity, can be defined as "*a whole into a wider system, with unique attributes co-generated by their parts, where the main attribute is its purpose, function or mission*". Given that such a definition is open, a specific definition of a *system* abstraction in the context of organizations is required. In particular, the notion of *organizational system* is relevant for the context of standards and models of processes. In concordance with system foundations (Gelman & Garcia, 1989; Mora et al., 2006), this concept can be defined as: "a whole (the real physical system) into a wider system (the wider real physical system), with unique attributes co-generated by their parts (subsystems and process (that include the parts of every process has)), which the main attribute is its purpose, function or mission (to manufacturing a product or provision a service)". Such a notion is also congruent with the SSME's notion of **service system** (Spohrer et al., 2007).

As illustration, from a high practical worldview perspective, the following eleven conceptual relationships between the core building-block concepts can be posed[11].

- **R1:** a <S: system> is whole into a wider <SS: system>, with unique <A: attributes: a1,a2,...> co-produced by their (at least two) parts called <sB: subsystems>, where the main attribute is its purpose, function or mission <attribute: a*>.

- **R2:** a <sB: subsystem> is just a <S: system> that is part of a wider <SS: system>.

- R3: a <C: component> is a constituent of a <sB: subsystem> that is not decomposable in parts (from a modeling viewpoint) but with attributes.

- **R4:** an <O: organization> is a <S: system> composed of <OsS: organizational sub-systems>.

- **R5:** an <OsB: organizational sub-system> is a <S: system> composed of <OsB: organizational sub-systems> and/or <BP: business processes>.

- **R6:** a <BP: business process> is a <S: system> composed of <BsP: business sub-process> and/or <BA: business activities>.

- **R7:** a <BA: business activity> is a <C: component> with the <A: attributes: a-tasks, a-personnel, a-tools-infrastructure, a-methods-procedures and a-socio-political-mechanisms-structures>

- **R8:** a <Sv: service> is an intangible ongoing <BO: business outcome> of a <BP: business process> into an <OsB: organizational sub-system>

- **R9:** a <Pr: product> is a tangible and discrete <BO: business outcome> of a <BP: business process> into an <OsB: organizational sub-system>

- **R10:** a <BsP: business sub-process> is just a <BP: business process> that is into a <process>.

- **R11:** a <BO: business outcome> is a perceived output of a <BP: business process> with either <VoP: value-oriented people attributes: v1,v2, ...> or <QoM: quality-oriented machines attributes: q1,q2, ...>.

Hence, the manufacturing of *products* and the provision of *services* needs a *business process approach* where the *business process* can be conceptualized as a *system* (composed of *business subprocesses* and/or *business activities*) contained in an *organizational system* that affects to and it is affected by a wider system called the *suprasystem*. Initial but substantial theoretical and practical implications of such relationships are discussed in the final section.

INITIAL THEORETICAL AND PRACTICAL IMPLICATIONS FOR THE IS DISCIPLINE

This chapter is part of a research in progress and an extensive discussion of their contributions is out of the planned scope. However, initial results on the how to apply such a set of conceptual relationships have been reported in Mora et al. (2007a, 2007b). From a theoretical viewpoint, however, we can argue that these conceptual findings contribute: (1) to identify the building-block concepts of the highest abstraction level to define and understand the rationale of standards and models of processes; (2) to establish a conceptual hierarchical set of initial relationships between such conceptual building-blocks that permits the development of a further formalization via an ontology; (3) to keep a theoretical congruence with the formal notions of what is a *system*, *subsystem* and *suprasystem*; and (4) to provide a parsimonious theoretical model of what is a *business organization*, *business process*, *business activity*, *service* and *product*.

From a practical viewpoint, this study contributes: (1) to help to practitioners to understand the conceptual relationships between *process*, *system* and the final outcomes of *services* and *products* using a domain vocabulary linked to formal systemic foundations; (2) to provide the foundation for the development of a computerized ontology for standards and models of processes that would permit automated knowledge-based inquires; and (3) to provide the foundations for the development of a framework/model to describe and compare the standards and models of processes from a top-bottom perspective according to the level of detail required by the modeler (Mora et al., 2007b).

CONCLUSION

In this chapter, we have developed a conceptual description of the main models and standards of processes formulated in the disciplines of SE, SwE and IS. Based in such descriptions, we have developed a conceptual analysis of the concepts of *process*, *system* and *service*. Such concepts have been identified as the core building blocks for describing models and standards of processes. Eleven semi-formal conceptual relationships between the building-blocks concepts have been also posed. The main theoretical contribution is the generation of a parsimonious model theoretically congruent with the Theory of Systems. The main practical contribution is the provision of a conceptual tool to describe and compare standards and models of processes. Two recommendations that emerge for further research are: (1) the refinement of the relationships to describe and compare standards and models of processes and (2) the development of a computerized ontology based in this theoretical model for permitting knowledge-based inquires on the digital description of standards and models of processes in SE, SwE and IT. These two research recommendations are part of the research goals of this study under progress.

ACKNOWLEDGMENT

This research is being developed with the financial support of the Autonomous University of Aguascalientes (www.uaa.mx) (Project PIINF-06-8) as well as from the Mexican National Council of Science and Technology (CONACYT, www.conacyt.mx) (Project P49135-Y).

REFERENCES

Ackoff, R. (1971). Towards a system of systems concepts. *Management Science, 17*(11), 661-671.

Ackoff, R. (1973). Science in the systems age: Beyond IE, OR and MS. *Operations Research, 21*(3), 661-671.

Andriole, S., & Freeman, P. (1993). Software the case systems engineering: For a new discipline. *Software Engineering Journal*, May, 165-179.

Arnold, S., & Lawson, H. W. (2004). Viewing systems from a business management perspective: the ISO/IEC 15288 standard. *Systems Engineering, 7*(3), 229-242.

Barker, B., & Verma, D. (2003). System engineering effectiveness: A complexity point paradigm for software intensive systems in the information technology sector. *Engineering Management Journal, 15*(3), 29-35.

Bar-Yam, Y. (2003). When systems engineering fails—Toward complex systems engineering. In *Proceedings of the 2003 International Conference on Systems, Man & Cybernetics* (pp. 2021- 2028), Piscataway, NJ: IEEE Press.

Bate, R. (1998). Do systems engineering? Who, Me? *IEEE Software*, Jul-Aug, 65-66.

Bertalanffy, L. von (1972). The history and status of general systems theory. *Academy of Management Journal*, December, 407-426.

Boehm, B. (2000). Unifying software engineering and systems engineering. *Computer*, 114-116.

Boehm, B., & Lane, J. (2006). 21st century processes for acquiring 21st century software-intensive systems of systems. *Crosstalk: The Journal of Defense Software Engineering*, May, 1-9.

Checkland, P. (2000). Soft systems methodology: a 30-year retrospective. In P. Checkland (Ed.), *Systems thinking, systems practice*. Chichester: Wiley.

Chesbrough, C., & Spohrer, J. (2006). A research manifesto for services science. *Communications of the ACM, 49*(7), 35-40.

CIO UK Website. (2007). *Late IT projects equals lower profits*. Retrieved May 15, 2008, from http://www.cio.co.uk/concern/resources/news/index.cfm?articleid=1563

Collin, R. (2004). *An introductory overview of ITIL*. London: ITSMF.

Deno, P., & Feeney, A. B. (2002). Systems engineering foundations of software systems integration. In *Proceedings of the OOIS Workshops*.

Demirkan, H., & Goul, M. (2006). AMCIS 2006 panel: Towards the service oriented enterprise vision: Bridging industry and academics. *CAIS, 18*, 546-556.

Ewusi, K. (1997). Critical issues in abandoned information systems development projects. *Communication of the ACM, 40*(9), 74-80.

Farr, J., & Buede, D. (2003). Systems engineering and engineering management: Keys to the efficient development of products and services. *Engineering Management Journal, 15*(3), 3-9.

Forsberg, K., & Mooz, H. (1997). System engineering overview. In R. Thayer & M. Dorfman (Eds.), *Software requirements engineering* (pp. 44-72). Los Alamitos: IEEE Computer Society Press.

Fuggetta, A. (2000). Software process: A roadmap. In *Proceedings of the International Conference on Software Engineering*, Limerick, Ireland.

Garcia, S. (1998). Evolving improvement paradigms: Capability maturity models & ISO/IEC 15504 (PDTR). *Software Process Improvement and Practice, 3*(1), 1-11.

Gelman, O., & Garcia, J. (1989). Formulation and axiomatization of the concept of general system. *Outlet IMPOS (Mexican Institute of Planning and Systems Operation), 19*(92), 1-81.

Gelman, O., Mora, M., Forgionne, G., & F. Cervantes (2005). Information systems and systems theory. In M. Khosrow-Pour (Ed.), *Encyclopedia* of information science and technology, (Vol. 3, pp. 1491-1496). Hershey, PA: Idea Group.

Glass, R., Armes, V., & Vessey, I. (2004). An analysis of research in computing disciplines. *Communications of the ACM, 47*(6), 89-94.

Hecht, H. (1999). Systems engineering for software-intensive projects. In *Proceedings of the ASSET Conference*, Dallas, TX.

Hevner, A. R., March, S. T., Park, J., & Ram, S. (2004). Design science in information systems research. *MIS Quarterly, 28*(1), 75-105.

Hole, E., Verma, D., Jain, R., Vitale, V., & Popick, P. (2005). Development of the ibm.com interactive solution marketplace (ISM): A systems engineering case Study. *Systems Engineering, 8*(1), 78-92.

Honour, E. (2004). Understanding the value of systems engineering. In *Proceedings of the 2004 INCOSE Conference*, 1-16.

INCOSE (1996). *SECAM: Systems engineering capability assessment model* (version 1.5). INCOSE.

INCOSE (2004). *Systems engineering handbook*. INCOSE-TP-2003-016-02. INCOSE.

ISO (in press). *ISO/IEC NP 24748 Systems and software engineering—Life cycle management*. Geneva, Switzerland: ISO/IEC.

ISO (1995). *ISO/IEC 12207: Information technology—Software life cycle processes*. Geneva, Switzerland: ISO/IEC.

ISO (2002). *ISO/IEC 15288: Systems engineering—Systems life cycle processes*. Geneva, Switzerland: ISO/IEC.

ISO (2003). *ISO/IEC 15504-2: Information technology—Process assessment*. Geneva, Switzerland: ISO/IEC.

ISO (2004a). *ISO/IEC 90003:2004 software engineering—Guidelines for the application of*

ISO 9001:2000 to computer software. Geneva, Switzerland: ISO/IEC.

ISO (2004b). *ISO/TMB Policy and principles statement global relevance of ISO technical work and publications*. TMB/SC/GR 2004-06-30. Geneva, Switzerland: ISO/IEC.

ISO (2005). *ISO/IEC 20000:2005 Information technology—Service management -- Part 1: Specification*. Geneva, Switzerland: ISO/IEC.

ISO (2006a). *Where ISO 9000 came from and who is behind it*. Retrieved May 15, 2008, from www.iso.org

ISO (2006b). *ISO 9000 and ISO 14000 in plain language*. Retrieved May 15, 2008, from www.iso.org

ISO (2006c). *ISO/IEC 15289: Systems and software engineering—Content of systems and software life cycle process information products (Documentation)*. Geneva, Switzerland: ISO/IEC.

ITGI (2000). *COBIT 3rd edition framework*. Illinois: IT Governance Institute..

Johnson, D. M. (1996). The systems engineer and the software crisis. *ACM SIGSOFT Software Engineering Notes, 1*(2), 64-73.

Johnson, K., & Dindo, J. (1998). Expanding the fcus of software process improvement to include systems engineering. *Crosstalk: The journal of defense software engineering*, 1-13.

Kellner, M., Curtis, B., deMarco, T., Kishida, K., Schulemberg, M., & Tully, C. (1991). Non-technological issues in software engineering. In *Proceedings of the 13th International Conference on Software Engineering*. Retrieved digital library at www.acm.org

Magee, S. (2006). *A successful software quality strategy using ISO/IEC 12207 &15288*. Retrieved May 15, 2008, www.15288.com

Minnich, H. (2002). EIA IS 731 Compared to CMMI-SE/SW. *Systems engineering journal, 5*(1), 62-72.

Mora, M. (2004). *Manual of Conceptual Research* (Internal Tech. Rep. IS-2004-01). Autonomous University of Aguascalientes, Mexico.

Mora, M., Gelman, O., Cervantes, F., Mejia, M., & Weitzenfeld, A. (2003). A systemic approach for the formalization of the information system concept: Why information systems are systems? In Cano, J. (Ed.), *Critical reflections of information systems: Systemic approach* (pp. 1-29). Hershey, PA: Idea Group.

Mora, M., Gelman, O., Cano, J., Cervantes, F., & Forgionne, G. (2006). Theory of systems and information systems research frameworks. In *Proceedings of the 50th Annual Meeting of the International Society for the Systems Sciences*, Somona State Universiy, CA.

Mora, M., Gelman, O., O'Connor, R., Alvarez, F., & Macías, J. (2007a). On models and standards of processes in SE, SwE and IT&S disciplines: Toward a comparative framework using the systems approach. In K. Dhanda & R. Hackney (Eds), In *Proceedings of the ISOneWorld 2007 Conference Track in System Thinking/Systems Practice*, Las Vegas, Nevada.

Mora, M., Gelman, O., & Alvarez, F. (2007b). A systemic model for the description and comparison of models and standards of processes in the SE, SwE and IT disciplines. In *e-Proceedings, International Conference on Complex Systems 2007, NECSI*, Boston, MA.

Mora, M., Gelman, O., Frank, M., Paradice, D., Cervantes, F., & Forgionne, G. (2008). Toward an interdisciplinary engineering and management of complex IT-intensive organizational systems: A systems view. *The International Journal of Information Technologies and the Systems Approach, 1*(1), 1-24.

Nichols, R., & Connaughton, C. (2005). *Software process improvement journey: IBM Australia application management services* (A Report from the Winner of the 2004 Software Process Achievement Award). Technical Report CMU/SEI-2005-TR-002, ESC-TR-2005-002.

Nunamaker, J. F., Chen, M., & Purdin, T. D. (1991). System development in information system research. *Journal of Management Information Systems, 7*, 89-106.

OMG (2005). *Software process engineering management: The unified process model (UPM)*. Document ad/2000-05-05. Object Management Group

OMG (2006). *Business process modeling notation (BPMN) specification*. Document dtc/06-02-01. Object Management Group.

Paulk, M., Chrissis, M., Weber, C. & Perdue, J. (1987). *The capability maturity model for software, Version 2B*. SEI/CMU Presentation. Retrieved May 15, 2008, from a www.sei.cmu.edu

Sage, A. P. (1992). *Systems engineering*. New York: Wiley.

Sage, A. P. (2000). Systems engineering education. *IEEE TSMC-Part C, 30*(2), 164-174.

Sage, A. P., & Amstrong, J. (2000). *Introduction to systems engineering*. New York: Wiley.

Sheard, S., & Lake, J. (1998). *Systems engineering and models compared*. retrieved May 15, 2008, from www.software.org

SEI (2006). *CMMI for development, version 1.2: CMMI-DEV, V1.2. Software engineering institute. CMU/SEI-2006-TR-008, ESC-TR-2006-008*. retrieved May 15, 2008, from www.sei.edu

Sommerville, I. (1998). Systems engineering for software engineers. *Annals of Software Engineering, 6*, 111-129.

Spohrer, J., Maglio, P., Bailey, J., & Gruhl., D. (2007). Steps toward a science of service systems. *IEEE Computer*, January issue, 70-71.

Standish Group International (2003). *The extreme CHAOS report*. Retrieved May 15, 2008, from www.standish-group.com

Succi, G., Valerio, A., Vernazza, T., & Succi, G. (1998). Compatibility, standards and software production. *Standarview, 6*(4), 140-146.

Tantara (2001). *History and relationship of process standards/models*. Retrieved May 15, 2008, from www. tantara.ab.ca

Teboul, J. (2007). *Service is front stage: Positioning services for value advantage*. Paris: INSEAD.

Thayer, R. H. (1997). Software systems engineering: An engineering process. In R. Thayer & M. Dorfman (Eds.), *Software requirements engineering* (pp. 84-106). Los Alamitos: IEEE Computer Society Press.

Thayer, R. H. (2002). Software systems engineering: A tutorial. *IEEE Computer*, April, 68-73.

Tripp, L. (1996). International standards in system and software integrity. *Standardwiew, 4*(3), 146-150.

Wright, R. (1998). Process standards and capability models for engineering software-intensive systems. *Crosstalk*, October, 1-10.

ENDNOTES

1. A standard is a " *... document, established by consensus and approved by a recognized body, that provides, for common and repeated use, rules, guidelines or characteristics for activities or their results, aimed at the achievement of the optimum degree of order in a given context.*" (ISO, 2004b)

2. Most recent standards have incorporated such improvement purpose (e.g., ISO 15504).

3. The initial results from such a premise have been reported in Mora et al (2007a) and final findings will be reported in a further study.

4. In particular, Fuggetta (2000, p. 28) points out that ".. rather, we (e.g., the software process community) must pay attention to the complex interrelation of a number of organizational, cultural, technological and economic factors."

5. SE is an older discipline than SwE that copes with the definition, development/acquisition and deployment of large scale systems comprised of multiples components of people, facilities, hardware, software, mechanical, and so forth.

6. SwE is defined as the discipline to generate software components or systems on time, on budget and with the expected technical requirements achieved.

7. CMMI-SVC will be the constellation focused on the management and engineering of process for delivering services. It is planned be released in 2007. Other CMMI-ACQ constellation for acquisition process is also being developed for 2007.

8. In this chapter is analyzed the version 3.0 released in 2000. The new version 4.0 has been recently released ending 2006.

9. This standard is derived from the BS15000 standard. In turn, the later evolved from the ITIL V.2.0 (1995) Model. Because the ITIL V.3.0 was liberated during the ending of this study, this is not considered. Major change realized is a lifecycle approach to arrange the previous main six categories of processes.

10. Other IS standards (e.g., Computer standards) are oriented to computer sciences and

these are not considered in this chapter. ICT security standards can be considered hybrid but are out of the scope of this research.

[11] These definitions are based in Gelman & Garcia (1989), Mora et al. (2003), Gelman et al. (2005) and Mora et al. (2006, 2007b)

Chapter XVII
E–Business Standardization in the Automotive Sector:
Role and Situation of SMEs

Martina Gerst
The University of Edinburgh, UK

Kai Jakobs
RWTH Aachen University, Germany

ABSTRACT

Successful cooperation between large manufacturers and their suppliers is a crucial aspect, especially in the automotive industry. Such mutually beneficial cooperation requires at least a certain level of integration and interoperation of the partners' IT and e-business systems. This chapter looks at two approaches in order to achieve this goal: sector-specific harmonization (in the form of electronic marketplaces) and international, committee-based standardization. This chapter shows that SMEs are facing a severe disadvantage in both cases. This is, however, less pronounced in a formal standards setting, in which capabilities of the individual representatives are more important, at least at the working level.

INTRODUCTION

The automotive industry is facing a number of challenges to the established relations among its players. Issues to be addressed include, for instance, shorter product life cycles, increasing cost pressure in stagnant markets, and higher complexity of the embedded electronic systems. In order to meet the associated production require-ments, standardization of processes, systems, and data is inevitable. This industry is characterized by vertical integration in terms of the business relationship structures between OEMs[1] and suppliers (Adolphs, 1996; Lamming, 1993). A current trend in manufacturing is that OEMs attempt to cooperate with fewer suppliers but on a worldwide scale. As a result, small and medium-sized suppliers become suppliers to tier 1 or tier 2 suppliers rather than directly to the OEMs.

The use of ICT-related technologies, particularly e-business systems, facilitates the creation of a network of relationships within a supply chain. Yet such interorganizational integration requires interoperability that cannot be achieved without widely agreed upon standards. But who has a say in the standardization process? This already has led to a range of transformations in the structure of the automotive supply chain. Large OEMs have been forced to create networks to replace the existing one-to-one relations with their suppliers, which are typically SMEs[2]. According to a study of Nexolab in 2001, standards were a major headache for SMEs, and 75% of the suppliers saw the lack of standardization as a major obstacle for closer collaboration. Therefore, it might be useful for companies to rethink their standardization strategies.

In many cases, an SME supplier does business with more than one OEM. In this situation, bilateral standardization to improve cooperation between OEMs and suppliers and between different suppliers, respectively, is inefficient. Still, this has been the approach of choice in many cases. However, possible alternatives are available, including sector-specific harmonization (e.g., in the form of an electronic marketplace) and, particularly, international committee-based standardization.

However, the challenges and the pressure for collaboration have led organizations in the automotive sector to become involved in a range of projects by means of interorganizational systems (IOS). Examples include electronic collaboration projects, the integration of engineering processes, and electronic catalogue projects to present product and service data. Such IOSs are adopted not only to achieve operational effectiveness by reducing coordination costs and transaction risks (Kumar & van Dissel, 1996) but also to improve communication and information presentation. Collaboration and integration shift the emphasis from stand-alone initiatives to the development of standardized and integrated solutions (Koch

& Gerst, 2003). In this context, one form of IOS that fulfills the criteria of collaboration and integration is business-to-business/supplier portals that incorporate standardized business processes. Covisint, an e-marketplace founded in 2000 by large OEMs, is a very good example to analyze the standardization process in an industry, which is characterized by a large number of SMEs.

The remainder of the chapter is structured as follows: using the automotive industry as an example, this chapter looks at two approaches toward standardization, both of which involve large companies and SMEs. One approach is based on the use of international standards, and proactive participation in the open standards-setting process by all relevant stakeholders. The alternative comprises a standardized, albeit sector-specific, electronic marketplace. The design and development was pushed by a group of large car manufacturers. It turned out that the situation of SMEs was not very favorable in either case—both processes were largely dominated by the big guys. Nonetheless, the chapter makes some recommendations how this situation may be changed for open standards setting.

SOME BACKGROUND

The Automotive Industry

According to a study by McKinsey (2003), the automotive industry in the next 10 years will be shattered by a third revolution that follows the invention of assembly-line production by Henry Ford and the lean production of Toyota. Customers are expecting better value for the same money, resulting in continuous cost pressure and innovation marathons for OEMs.

This has led to a range of transformations in the automotive supply chain. For example, in order to improve customer satisfaction and to increase revenue growth and shareholder value, large OEMs and their suppliers started establishing large automotive networks. Yet, the added value of these collaborative networks is beginning to shift from the OEMs to suppliers and to other business partners such as system integrators (see Figure 1).

In the 1980s, the relations between an OEM and its suppliers were similar. In the 1990s, this changed to a tier-x structure in which the main collaboration partners of an OEM were the tier-1 suppliers that, in turn, collaborated through tier-2 suppliers, and so forth. Today, OEMs are collaborating not only with their supply base but also with other business partners; for example, system integrators. In the future, the relations between OEMs and their suppliers are expected to change dramatically (Gerst & Bunduchi, 2004).

Apart from shifts in the value chain, the industry is confronted with a number of transformations that challenge the established relations among industry players. The automotive industry is characterized by extremely complex processes, and the standardization of processes and data is inevitable in order to meet production requirements. Driven by challenges such as shorter product life cycles, increasing cost pressure in stagnant markets, and higher complexity of the electronics embedded in modules and systems, OEMs gradually increase the outsourcing of manufacturing, which is expected to rise from 25% to 35% within the next 10 years (McKinsey, 2003).

The supplier community also is undergoing major changes as the result of this pressure. Increasingly, platforms and model varieties require advanced deals and project management capabilities, which means that in terms of innovation management, suppliers have to be able to provide leading-edge technology and efficient simultaneous engineering processes. This change primarily affects the tier-1 suppliers, which are taking over systems integration responsibility and management of the supply chain from the OEMs. At the same time, they also take an increasing share of risk, which used to be incurred by the OEMs. As a result, the industry is forced to collaborate more closely (e.g., by adopting portal) technology.

Standardization

Standards Setting in General

Over the last three decades, the world of IT standardization has become extremely complex. Figure 2 gives an impression of the situation in the 1970s (not complete, though). Back then, standards-setting bodies were few, national bodies contributed to the work of CEN/CENELC[3] at the European level and to ISO/IEC[4] at the international level. These bodies were responsible for all areas of standards setting, with the exception of the then highly regulated telecommunication sector, which was the realm of the CCITT[5]. The only other international organization of some importance was ECMA.[6]

Since then, the situation has changed dramatically, especially for the IT and e-business sectors. Figure 3 depicts an excerpt of the situation that today may be found in these sectors. In addition to the newly established regional Standards Developing Organizations (SDOs; e.g. ETSI[7] in Europe, TIA[8] in the U.S., etc.), a considerable number of standards-setting industry for a and consortia have been founded as well (W3C[9], OASIS[10], etc.); a recent survey found around 190 such entities (ISSS, 2004). In a way, these organizations have successfully created a parallel universe of standards setting that is partly in competition with the older, formal bodies, partly in cooperation and partly without any relations to them at all.

The complexity of this environment represents a major obstacle for those who are considering active participation in standardization and, most notably, for SMEs. In most cases, they have neither the resources nor the knowledge necessary for a meaningful participation in this highly complex process. Questions they need to address include why, how, where, and when to participate.

At first glance, "Why participate at all?" seems to be a very valid question. After all, standardization is a costly business and is time-consuming, and the return on investment is uncertain in many cases. This normally is not a major problem for large vendors and manufacturers, who may want to push their own ideas, prevent success of competing specifications, or are just driven by the desire to gather intelligence in the work groups.

Things look very different for user companies and SMEs. They cannot easily commit considerable resources to activities with very intangible direct benefits. Yet, all users need to recognize that they will suffer most from inadequate standards. Such standards will leave them struggling with incompatibilities, which, at the end of the day, may well drive them out of business. On the other hand, they will reap major benefits from well-designed standards that address real needs. In addition, at least large and/or well-off users may find a standards committee to be a very suitable platform for cooperation with vendors and manufacturers. Here, technical requirements can be mapped onto system capabilities at a very early design stage (in fact, this is rather more a pre-design stage), thus making the process far more efficient.

Accordingly, (SME) users who participate in standards setting will be driven by the desire to (Jakobs, 2003).

Avoid Technological Dead-Ends

Users want to avoid purchasing products that eventually leave them stranded with an incompatible technology. A number of issues need to be considered in this context. For instance, it has to be decided if and when a new technology should be purchased and which one should be selected. Too early adoptions not only bear the risk of adopting a technology that eventually fails in being successful in the market but also ignore the considerable time and money that have gone into the old technology. It has to be decided if and when to switch from a well-established technology to a new one. Investments in the old technology need to be balanced with the prospective benefits potentially to be gained from this

move. On the other hand, late adopters may lose competitive advantage while being stuck with outdated technology.

Reduce Dependency on Vendors

Being locked in into a vendor-specific environment increasingly is becoming a major risk for a user, despite the advantages that can be associated with integrated proprietary solutions. In particular, problems occur if a vendor misses an emerging development and its users are forced to switch to completely new (and different) systems, which is a very costly exercise. Accordingly, standard compliant products from a choice of vendors appeal to the users, who can pursue a pick-and-mix purchasing strategy and also stand to benefit from price cuts as a result of increased competition.

Promote Universality

Ultimately, users would like to see seamless interoperability among all hardware and software, both internally (between different departments and sites) and externally (with customers and business partners). With the ongoing globalization of markets, this only can be achieved through international standards. Clearly, this holds especially for communications products. Ideally, it should not matter at all which vendor or service provider has been selected; interoperability always should be guaranteed, which implies that user needs and requirements are met by the standards (and the implementations). In addition to seamless communication and the business value that lies herein alone, there is another major economic benefit to be gained: the cost of incompatibility may be tremendous.

The next issue to be considered is "how to participate." In general, there seems to be consensus that large users, especially those with an urgent need for standardized systems or services, should participate directly in the technical work. In fact, some do. However, especially for smaller companies, there are obvious barriers to this form of participation, which are largely rooted in the lack of sufficient financial resources and knowledgeable personnel. Here, participation via umbrella organizations would be an option, as would be participation at the national level with a mandate for national representatives to act as the voice of these SMEs in the international arena.

Considering the complexity of the IT standardization universe, "where to participate" is another relevant issue. Equivalent systems may well be standardized in parallel by different SDOs and consortia, and participation in all these work groups is well beyond the means of all but the biggest players. The correct decision here is crucial, as backing the wrong horse may leave a company stranded with systems based on the wrong (i.e., non-standard) technology. This holds for both users and manufacturers.

Especially SMEs and users should also ask themselves, "When should we participate?" In most cases, the standardization process is viewed as an atomic entity that cannot be subdivided any further. Yet, the standards life cycle depicted in Figure 4 suggests otherwise. Participation in profile development, for example, would be the option of choice, if interoperability of implementations were to be assured. On the other hand, there is little point in specifying a profile for a base standard that does not meet the requirements in the first place.

Standards in the Automotive Industry

Standardization in the automotive industry has a long tradition. According to Thompson (1954), engineers and industrialists in the American automobile industry initiated in 1910 for the first time an extensive program of intercompany technical standards. Technical standards made parts interchangeable so that mass production was facilitated, which led to production economies. In relating the growth of intercompany technical standards in the automotive industry up to about 1930, the study of Thompson (1954) attempts to show the influence of changing business conditions on standardization and, hence, on the mechanical technology of a car.

Some decades later, in the rising technology age, the launch of Electronic Data Interchange (EDI), was the next step of the automotive industry in order to collaborate more closely with suppliers by means of Interorganizational Systems (IOS) (Graham, Spinardi, Williams & Webster, 1995). IOS refers to the computer and telecommunications infrastructure developed, operated, and/or used by two or more companies for the purpose of exchanging information that supports a business application or process (Cunningham & Tynan, 1993). These companies can be suppliers and customers in the same value chain, strategic partners, or even competitors in the same or a related market. The integrative potential of networked computer systems that enabled information sharing and facilitated collaboration of hitherto competing organizations was well recognized (Monse & Reimers, 1995; Webster, 1995; Williams, Graham, & Spinardi, 1995).

Contemporary IOSs are complex Information and Communication Technology (ICT) systems that incorporate a multitude of standards. Consequently, for a company, the decision to integrate business partners with IOS requires an initial strategic decision whether to implement standardized technology that supports standardized business processes or to implement and customize off-the-shelf proprietary systems. The latter, of course, means to stick to the homemade processes and systems. This decision is influenced by various factors (e.g., economical, organizational, technical, social) and actors (e.g., players of internal business units, software suppliers, consultants) situated in a highly dynamic environment.

Today, SMEs in this sector are under enormous pressure from their frequently large customers to deploy e-business systems (and the necessary underlying ICT infrastructure) that are compatible with the customers' respective systems. Yet, as these systems typically differ, SMEs accordingly would have to set up and maintain a number of different systems. This is hardly a realistic option, and the use of standards-based systems is an SME's only chance to keep both its ICT environment manageable and all its customers happy.

Unfortunately, few standards take into account SMEs' unique requirements. Major standards setting initiatives already have failed because of this[11]. Thus, it seems to be about time to have a closer look at the current standardization practice with respect to SMEs' needs.

SMES BETWEEN A ROCK AND A HARD PLACE

SMEs in Standards-Setting Bodies

For SMEs, a potential route toward standards that also cover their specific needs and requirements would be through participation standards setting bodies (SSBs) that produce open specifications. In the following, we will have a closer look at the prospects of SMEs in this environment. This section, therefore, will analyze what would have to be done in order to make standards setting in the ICT domain more accessible and useful for small and medium enterprises.

The study on the role of SMEs in committee-based standardization is based on desk research and several (small) studies. Here, data were collected through different questionnaires, each comprising a number of open-ended questions. Qualitative methods have been deployed to analyze the data.

Motivation

Today, the standards-setting processes in the Information and Communication Technologies (ICT) and e-business sectors are dominated very much by the large companies and other financially potent stakeholders. As a consequence, there is a real danger that standards, and thus, ultimately, policies, are based on the needs and requirements of a comparably small, albeit powerful, group of stakeholders. The action plan for innovation, Innovate for a Competitive Europe, rightly says, "Voluntary standards, properly used, can help establish the compatibility of innovative concepts and products with related products and so can be a key enabler for innovation. ... SMEs should be more involved in standardization in order to exploit their potential for innovation and to enhance the accountability, openness, and consensus-based character of the European standardization system" (European Commission, 2004).

Yet, the working groups (WGs) of almost all standards-setting bodies are populated by representatives of large, multinational companies. The comparably few representatives of SMEs typically come from highly specialized vendors or manufacturers. SME users (i.e., those who merely deploy ICT systems) are hardly represented at all, and neither are their umbrella organizations.

Today, SMEs are under enormous pressure from their frequently large customers to deploy e-business systems (including the necessary underlying ICT infrastructure) that are compatible with the customer's respective systems. Yet, as these systems typically differ, SMEs accordingly have to set up and maintain a number of different systems. This is hardly a sustainable option, and the use of standards-based systems is an SME's only chance to keep both its ICT environment manageable and all its customers happy.

Some Background

There seems to be general agreement that participation of all stakeholders, particularly users, is a *sine qua non* in order for an ICT standardization activity to be successful. In fact, increased user participation often is considered the panacea for all problems.

Typically, SMEs opt for readily available off-the shelf systems and services that need to be inexpensive and easy to install, maintain, and use. Proprietary systems also are used frequently, and SMEs are compelled to do so by, for example, a major business partner (with all associated problems). The non-use of many standards-based services by SMEs is due largely to the fact that insufficient knowledge and resources are available to employ these systems, which are perceived as being extremely complicated to deal with. In fact, this perception may be considered a major impediment to a more successful uptake of standards-based systems by SMEs. This exemplifies an urgent need for simpler standards.

The procedures adopted by the individual standards-setting bodies suggest that the degree of control over and influence on the standards-setting process is about equally distributed among the different stakeholders (see Figure 5).

Unfortunately, this does not quite capture reality. Especially, the assumption of an equal influence of all stakeholders appears to be flawed (Swann, 2000). In fact, it appears that, so far, development of IT standards almost exclusively has been technology-driven. This can be attributed largely to the fact that relevant standardization committees typically have been dominated by vendors and service providers. Accordingly, a more realistic model is called for and will be presented in section 5.

SMEs in Standards Setting: A Small Study

As part of a project co-funded by the European Commission, one of the authors did a small study of selected ITU and ISO working groups in order to learn about some issues relating to SME users in standards setting[12]. In summary, it became clear that both ITU and ISO are indeed dominated by large companies. SME representation (if any, that is) occurs primarily through small consultancy firms, as opposed to actual users. Also, the influ-

ence that real SMEs (i.e., excluding consultants) have on the process is said to be very limited.

Respondents' opinions were split about SMEs' influence at the technical level. A sizable minority basically stated that in many cases, influence is related to market power. This holds particularly for the voting level, in which appropriate (and perhaps national) strategies are playing an important role. Obviously, SMEs, if represented at all, stand little chance of competing with the big multinationals.

Things look slightly different at the working level, though (i.e., in working groups in which the actual technical standardization work is being done). The majority of respondents noted that the individual capabilities of the representatives (i.e., technical skills, language proficiency, willingness to take on responsibility, etc.) are the deciding factors.

SME participation would broaden technical expertise of a WG, as they are frequently closer to state-of-the-art technical development than big companies and less bound by internal rules and administrative procedures. Also, they would be welcome as a counterweight to the interests of the big companies. This holds particularly if they represent fora or some other form of umbrella organizations. However, it was also noted that the typical sporadic or infrequent participation of SME representatives might lead to inadequate familiarity with both technical aspects discussed and procedures, thus causing unnecessary delays to the process.

Cost of participation is considered the major obstacle that SMEs will face if they want to become active in standards setting. Suggestions how this could be overcome include increased deployment of electronic media to replace meetings, lower or waived fees for SMEs, and provision of dedicated travel money. In addition, it was suggested that SMEs join forces and co-sponsor representatives.

Electronic Marketplaces: Two Examples

So far, we have looked at the role that SMEs may play in the context of largely proprietary, sector-specific standardization processes that are driven and dominated by large companies. An additional case study about the development of standardized business processes of two electronic marketplaces in the automotive industry will describe if and how SMEs, which are supposed to be the main target audience for the use of such marketplaces, were involved in the development of standardized business processes of those marketplaces.

Each OEM has an extensive network of suppliers. They, in turn, frequently supply more than one OEM. In this situation, bilateral standardization of the complex processes and technology that enable the cooperation both between OEMs and suppliers and between different suppliers is less than effective, as it would leave suppliers with the need to maintain one system per OEM. Still, this is the approach of choice in many cases. This is the reason that sector-specific electronic marketplaces absolutely would make sense.

Introduction

In order to enable increased collaboration and outsourcing, all large OEMs since the 1980s have launched a number of strategic programs to ensure networking across their entire value chain, including electronic collaboration in the form of EDI systems and electronic catalogue projects. The implementations of IOS such as EDI have been linked strongly with the need to move away from competitive supply chain relationships and toward closer collaborative relationships. EDI implementations thus were seen to support the changes toward higher outsourcing and collaboration in the industry (Webster, 1995). Despite its advantages, EDI systems adoption was limited to large companies (OEMs and tier-1 suppliers), with small suppliers lagging behind. One of the

reasons was the significant investment associated with EDI deployment, which impeded the ability of smaller suppliers to participate in the EDI game and reap the benefits.

The expectations of the OEMs were built around a vision to standardize intra- and inter-organizational processes in an effort not only to reduce costs but also to increase the efficiency of information exchange on a global basis by taking advantage of leading-edge technologies. To support this vision toward global collaboration, OEMs in the late 1990s began to deploy Internet-based portals in order to integrate applications and give real-time data access to their suppliers.

Example One: Covisint

In 1999, the Internet hub Covisint[13] (**Co**nnectivity, **Vi**sibility, **Int**egration) was founded by a number of large OEMs such as DaimlerChrysler, Ford, and General Motors, and software companies such as Oracle and Commerce One. The aim of Covisint was to connect the automotive industry to a global exchange marketplace with the offer of one single point of entry to all connected applications and functionalities. It thus aimed to represent a de-facto industry standard for the entire automotive industry. First of all, Covisint offered different e-services; for example e-auction or e-collaboration tools. Second, the e-service offer aimed to improve the interconnection between and integration of OEMs and suppliers through standardized portal technology. This technology provided uniform personalized access from any location and any device between networked organizations. The functionality and infrastructure that characterizes such open architecture allowed the integration of diverse interaction channels. To a large extent, the supplier community is the same for all OEMs. Concretely, the same suppliers were using the same OEM-own applications that always needed different log-ins and passwords. Therefore, the big picture behind Covisint was the idea of one single point of entry for suppliers of every company size in order to facilitate and enable integration and collaboration. The vision behind Covisint was to enable the connection of the entire automotive industry to a single, global exchange marketplace with one single point of entry, standardized business processes, and standard applications. Covisint thus aimed to represent a de-facto industry standard and open integration framework for business process integration.

The development process was characterized by an iterative approach. Before Covisint started to develop and implement the standardized portal technology, one of the OEM founders already had started to develop a portal registration process, one of the core processes in a supplier portal (based on the best practice in the industry: the development of standards has benefited from the development of portals by other organizations before). Since all the founders were very interested in taking the most benefit out of Covisint on a short-term basis, they were highly motivated to develop standard processes that later could be implemented in their own organizations.

In a first instance, standards development was related to best practices in the industry and had been worked out by a limited number of specialists from the OEMs that were involved in Covisint. In a later stage, this small-group approach to standard development has been replaced by a consortium of the Covisint stakeholders and the software companies that delivered pieces of software to complete the offer of the Internet hub. The consortium approach was more similar with the typical approach to standard development following specific procedures and having different working groups that met regularly. Additionally, industry experts of associations were invited to presentations and workshops to contribute to the standards development. In a second phase, in order to increase legitimacy among suppliers, they were included in the process. However, participation in the consortium was closely controlled, and the working procedures were less rather than more transparent and open. Only well-known, mostly tier-1 suppliers, who already had participated in other pilot projects, were asked about their input in the form of commentary feedback to already developed processes. The restrictions in participation and the lack of transparency and openness regarding the work within the consortium could be explained by the desire of the OEMs to achieve the initial goal of a standardized industry solution.

Due to the fast-to-market strategy of Covisint, the standards were developed in parallel with systems development and implementation. The emphasis of the standardization itself was on speed and on finding compromise solutions that fitted all parties rather than on long-term quality solutions. The development phase of the standardized portal was very complex with regard to the existing complexity of already existing IT infrastructure and the difficulty to integrate all different systems and applications in an overall company architecture. The overall inconsistent strategy of the OEMs with respect to the implementation of the e-collaboration tools, particularly online bidding, significantly affected the suppliers' negative perceptions of portals in general. Whereas some of the OEMs preferred the standardized industry solution managed by an electronic marketplace, others, such as the VWGroup, voted for the in-house option, which meant not to draw on a third party service.

According to a representative of a tier-1 supplier, the supplier community was "deeply concerned and felt threatened" by the sheer market power concentration. One result of these concerns was SupplyOn, founded by a number of large tier-1 suppliers. It became one of the major competitors of Covisint in the field.

Example Two: SupplyOn

Whereas Covisint was envisaged by its founders to streamline the business processes of all participants and to enable them to collaborate seamlessly across organizations' borders, this was not necessarily the perception of the suppliers. There were two reasons for this.

First, the suppliers were excluded from the early development process, with only a few of the largest and most powerful tier-1 suppliers being asked to become involved during a later stage of the development phase. However, even at this stage, the suppliers' involvement was limited mainly to providing feedback over the OEMs' decisions rather than actively participating in negotiations. The decisional power remained almost entirely with the OEMs. As a result, by and large, suppliers' requirements were neither part of the Covisint vision nor included in the development of the standardized technology. Therefore, despite the acclaimed aim of Covisint to address the costs and risks reduction pressures across the entire industry, the development stage included the requirements and visions of only a limited number of OEMs.

Second, suppliers already struggled with the administration of a number of such standardized portals, and the suppliers who were approached at an early stage showed mixed feelings regarding the OEMs' approach to volume bundling and pricing.

The development of Covisint was the trigger for the tier-1 supplier community to set up SupplyOn to counterbalance the OEMs' obvious power consolidation and the Goliath gigantic-like marketplace. In April 2000, the tier-1 suppliers Robert Bosch GmbH, Continental AG, INA Werk Schaeffler oHG, SAP AG, and ZF Friedrichshafen AG signed a letter of intent and kicked off a new e-marketplace business—SupplyOn.

The basic vision behind SupplyOn was the same as for Covisint; namely, to join forces, to bundle know-how, and in a collaborative effort to set up industrywide standards (e.g., for logistic processes). However, whereas the initial objective of SupplyOn was the same as the Covisint approach to the development of standardized business processes, in the end, it diverged from the original vision. In contrast with Covisint, which followed the U.S. management model, the founders of SupplyOn made explicitly clear

from the beginning that they denied the American way of doing business, opting in contrast for an approach based on smaller but concrete step-by-step efforts and results rather than big visions that, they argued, were often impossible to implement. SupplyOn thus was positioning itself in direct competition with Covisint, representing the suppliers' approach to the development of a standardized industrywide portal.

However, even though SupplyOn was the brainchild of suppliers, one should take into consideration that large tier-1 suppliers initiated a competing standard, pretending that they would better understand the business requirements of the supplier world. But, as in the case of Covisint, SMEs were not very involved in the SupplyOn development process, either. SME participation was reduced to feedback, as well.

Summary

Today, most would agree that both electronic markets, Covisint and SupplyOn, by and large failed or, at least, struggled to set up a de-facto industry standard for business processes for a number of major reasons with an organizational, economical, and technical nature[14]. Certainly, SMEs played a weighty role in the whole e-game; they simply did not participate and even tried to escape the new electronic (and supposedly better) world offered by the OEMs.

Organizationally, SMEs did not have a great say in the development processes of the e-marketplaces. This holds despite the fact that the original idea of electronic marketplaces in general, and sector-specific marketplaces such as Covisint and SupplyOn, in particular, was to integrate all suppliers, particularly SMEs. Covisint did not fulfill the expectations of the industry; most members of the supplier community were disappointed with the way Covisint was set up. In particular, tier-1 suppliers feared the dominance of Covisint (and the resulting power of the participating OEMs) and, consequently, formed their own marketplace—SupplyOn. In the case of Covisint, the relation between the founding OEMs and Covisint was difficult to handle for the OEMs (in terms of roles and responsibilities) and difficult to understand for SME suppliers. An SME supplier had a business relationship with its OEM, which was manifested in a written contract. With Covisint, this relation was getting more complex in two ways: first, the use of Covisint required the supplier to become a member of Covisint. Although initially the participating OEMs paid the membership fee for their suppliers, a lack of enthusiasm clearly was shown by the supplier community, because it (rightly) feared additional cost of participation in a later phase. Second, some of the OEMs forced their suppliers to sign an additional document called an e-marketplace contract in order to avoid warranty claims of suppliers in the case of the nonavailability of Covisint.

Another important organizational issue was to harmonize the business processes of the different consortium partners. The requirements of the participating companies were very difficult to understand for third parties. This led, for example, to difficulties in the development of the portal registration processes. For SME suppliers that were working on an international basis, it turned out to be difficult to register with Covisint due to an inadequate registration processes (despite the promise that Internet technologies would help to simplify business and make it faster).

As a result, this quick-to-market approach led to incomplete solutions (at a technical level) that were difficult to integrate into already existing IT infrastructures and were expensive to realize. Here, as well, SME suppliers mistrusted the OEMs, fearing larger investments for their back-end integration.

Economically, the inability of Covisint to manage the business and the technology development and standardization as well as the inability of its founders to attract the potential users to buy into the Covisint vision led to the formation of two competitive standardized solutions in the industry, with the majority of SME suppliers favoring SupplyOn. Neither the founding OEMs nor Covisint was able to explain clearly the distribution of benefits of working with Covisint. Suppliers did not see a win-win situation. Thus, when severe technical problems and intractable project management issues arose later during the implementation of Covisint, suppliers withdrew their support for Covisint altogether.

Another reason for the lack of participation could be the fact that both e-marketplaces were sector-specific, and, from a certain tier level, most SMEs did business not only with the automotive sector but also with other industries.

In conclusion, the development of standardized electronic marketplaces was much more complex in organizational, technical, and economic terms than was expected by the founders of both Covisint and SupplyOn. In the case of Covisint, OEMs had significant difficulties adapting their internal processes to the marketplace. Moreover, the integration of the portal's different components into an overall standardized architecture was extremely difficult. Additionally, because of the organizational and technological difficulties integrating the often divergent OEMs' business requirements within a standardized approach, the benefits of adhering to the standardized processes associated with using the portal were not directly evident to potential users and led to the formation of SupplyOn.

Discussion

Today, according to the study, active participation in ICT and e-business standards-setting is limited largely to large, multinational companies. In particular, SMEs hardly stand a chance to make their voice adequately heard. Since standardization and policymaking are mutually dependent, this is an extremely unsatisfactory situation. Ultimately, it means that the influence of globally acting multinationals on European policy is out of proportion with, for example, the number of jobs they provide in Europe. In a way, SMEs are part of a modern-day Third Estate with respect to their capability to influence standardization and, thus, ultimately, policymaking. This holds despite the fact that there are more than 20 million SMEs in the EU.

Standardization processes should provide a platform in which opportunities for technologies, requirements of various types of companies from all sectors, consumer preferences, and other societal needs (e.g., protection of the environment) are mediated efficiently. Standards that are useful for all relevant stakeholders should be the outcome of these processes.

Unfortunately, it appears so far that development of IT standards almost exclusively has been technology-driven with standards produced that solely reflect providers' and implementers' priorities such as manageability rather than usability. Most other stakeholders, including the general public, consumer organizations, and, most notably here, SME users, constitute what one might call the Third Estate of IT standards setting (see Figure 6).

The figure shows that the members of the Third Estate (specifically, SMEs) are separated largely from the key players, with SME umbrella organizations perhaps located somewhere in between. Although they represent the vast majority of standard users, these groups have extremely little say in the standards-setting process. This holds, despite the fact that organizations such as ANEC, the European Association for the Co-ordination of Consumer Representation in Standardization, and NORMAPME, the European Office of Crafts, Trades and SMEs for Standardization, are participating actively in selected standard working groups on behalf of their constituencies.

Four reasons for the current, less-than-adequate representation of (individual) SMEs in ICT standards setting may be identified: inadequate technical expertise[15], very limited interest, lack of funding, and dependency from vendors. The former two are interrelated. A minimum of tech-

nical expertise and sophistication is required in order to make meaningful contributions to standards setting. Thus, limited expertise contributes significantly to the considerable lack of SMEs' interests in active participation in standards setting that may be observed today. Moreover, it is very unlikely that such active participation will to offer any short-term return on investment. Thus, getting involved in standardization is simply not economically feasible for many SMEs.

Inadequate technical expertise, lack of funding, and, particularly, dependency from vendors could be overcome if SMEs with similar interests and/or in similar situations joined forces. For example, it is easily conceivable that a group of tier-1 or tier-2 suppliers in the automotive industry would join forces in order to fund a standards specialist to represent them in the relevant working groups. In addition to a better representation at the technical level, the combined economical power also should lead to a more adequate representation at the strategic decision level.

Moreover, user and SME representatives may have to prove their credibility (i.e., demonstrate that they are actually representing a constituency broader than just one single company) (e.g., the SME community as such, as opposed to just their respective employers). This was never demanded from technical people representing large vendors, manufacturers, or service providers; it may be expected that the representative of an SME umbrella organization would not face this problem, either.

It frequently has been observed that individuals may drive and direct the activities of an entire standards working group, at least at the technical level (Egyedi, Jakobs & Monteiro, 2003; Jakobs, Procter, & Williams, 2000). Being represented by such an individual would not only solve (or at least reduce) the credibility problem but also would allow a group of SMES (or an umbrella organization) to punch well above its weight.

The Covisint study shows that standardization efforts are triggered by a complex array of non-technical and technical considerations. The case illustrates that ICT standardization is not only about bridging the gap between the technologies and business processes of different companies but also about bridging complex social processes.

As suggested by the SST perspective, this vision of industrywide collaboration has been used actively by OEMs in order to mobilize resources internally and to attract suppliers into buying into Covisint. However, a number of factors has shaped the OEMs' and suppliers' choices during the development and implementation of the standardized technology, which eventually has led to a very different outcome than what initially was envisaged by the founding OEMs.

Each of the founding OEMs has an extensive network of suppliers. They, in turn, frequently supply more than one OEM. In this situation, bilateral standardization of the complex processes and technology that enable collaboration both between OEMs and their suppliers and between the different suppliers, is less than effective, as it would leave suppliers with the need to maintain one system for each OEM. Moreover, market pressures were forcing OEMs to reduce costs, increase the efficiencies in the industry, and enhance collaboration with their suppliers. Therefore, the idea to join forces in order to provide a single point of entry and set an industry standard seemed advantageous for both groups. Furthermore, when the Covisint idea emerged in late 1999, the use of leading-edge Internet technology to reorganize internal and external business processes to support collaboration across the entire supply chain was on every company's agenda. Consequently, the foundation of Covisint was a natural step in order to increase the effectiveness of the industry through a collaborative effort of the largest industry players. Indeed, such collaboration was required in order to share the risks and costs among a number of players.

The three founders showed their commitment to the Covisint vision through an initial investment of about $500 million. However, due to the distribution of power that historically characterized the relations between OEMs and suppliers, the latter were apprehensive of Covisint. They saw it as just than another exercise to intensify OEMs' power pressure. Some suppliers also feared that Covisint would require significant additional resources and investments from their side, whereas the benefits would materialize mostly at the OEMs' side.

However, on the OEM side, significant resources involving not only additional budget but also extra human resources were required in order to address the pending integration issues. The need for these additional resources led to negotiations concerning their allocation across different Bus (Business Units) within the OEMs. As a result of these negotiations, some application owners (the BUs within the participating OEMs) abandoned the idea of adopting standardized business processes and started blaming Covisint for not providing mature, workable solutions. It even was claimed that suppliers already working with the applications did not see any of the benefits. Consequently, far from reaching stabilization and closure, the choices made by the OEMs further deepened the disagreement regarding the approach to an industrywide standardized portal, which was deserted not only by suppliers but also by some of the BUs within the founding OEMs.

The previous discussion seems to indicate that SME suppliers were not particularly satisfied with the standardized solution developed by their large customers. Yet, it would appear that SMEs do not necessarily fare any better in today's open standards-setting processes.

CONCLUSION

Regarding the role of SMEs in open standards setting, "standardization is a prerequisite for a broad deployment and use of ICT, and will trigger and enable new business" (PWC, 2004, p. 7) (see also Blind et al. [1999] and Swann [2000] for similar accounts). With the creation of new businesses high on the agenda in Europe, it would be extremely unhelpful if SMEs, which, after all, form the employment and growth engine of the EU, were excluded from shaping this infrastructure upon which they rely very much.

However, there is no one-size-fits-all solution in order to give SMEs a greater say in actively participating in standardization development. One possible approach would be to provide funding for suitable SME umbrella organizations (we are not even starting to think about the potentially resulting or, at least, claimed distortion of competition). It then would be their task to identify those standards committees whose work is of particular relevance to SMEs and to represent their constituency's interests there. Yet, in this case, two problem areas need to be addressed.

First, SME users are not a homogeneous group. Accordingly, something needs to be done about the problem of diverse and context-specific user requirements (Jakobs, Procter & Williams, 1998). In particular, there is a need for a mechanism to align these requirements. This ideally should happen prior to the actual standardization process. Dedicated SME user groups might be an option worth considering, despite the problems that have to be associated with this approach (Jakobs, 2000).

Along similar lines, sector-specific standards may be a way to raise the interest of SMEs to actively participate in standards setting, as such standards might be closer to their specific business interests. This approach, however, carries the risk of introducing incompatibilities among different sectors.

Here, the sectoral organizations, such as the Verband deutscher Automobilindustrie (VDA) at the German level or the Organization for Data Exchange by Tele Transmission (ODETTE) at the European level, actively could take part in informing and influencing their members (mainly SMEs). In the past, they struggled to reach a common position regarding the development and implementation of Internet-based technologies and their standards

and the related consequences for suppliers. Such organizations reach a large number of suppliers of all sizes and, therefore, have the chance not only to inform but also to educate SME suppliers. Moreover, provision of additional information (through Web sites or brochures) could help to keep suppliers informed about developments of standards in their areas. Regional associations also might consider redefining their roles and trying to actively represent the interests of their members in European organizations.

This, of course, would imply the need for a mechanism to guarantee intersector interoperability. Another related option would be to deploy the national standards bodies to a greater extent as SME representatives in the far more important international arena. Lower travel budgets and the prospect of communicating in their native languages might be an incentive for more SMEs to participate in standards setting and to let the national bodies represent them in the international/global arena. This might also resolve at least partly the problem of requirements alignment.

The task of developing and implementing standardized business processes in order to collaborate more effectively across the full supply chain is more challenging than ever. Supplier portals are one of the options to collaborate more closely and to harmonize cross-company business processes. Apart from the technical issues surrounding the development of standardized business processes across the entire industry (i.e., the complexity of technology, integration issues, and security concerns), a range of organizational, social, and economic factors has influenced the OEMs' and the suppliers' choices and actions, which eventually have led to the undesired outcome of failing to accomplish the initial vision of industrywide collaboration supported by common industrywide standards.

However, given the failure of the large portals, the industry at least should consider turning to committee-based standards in the future instead. Such standards could be developed under the responsibility of a standards-setting body based on consensus and due process and with all stakeholders having the chance to participate and to contribute their ideas and needs.

REFERENCES

Adolphs, B. (1996). *Stabile und effiziente geschäftsbeziehungen—Eine betrachtung von vertikalen koordinationsstrukturen in der deutschen automobilindustrie* [unpublished doctoral dissertation]. University of Cologne, Germany.

Blind, K., et al. (1999). *Economic benefits of standardization* (in German). Berlin: Beuth Publishers.

Cargill, C. F. (1995). A five segment model for standardization. In B. Kahil & J. Abbate (Eds.), *Standards policy for information infrastructure* (pp. 79-99). Cambridge: MIT Press.

Cunningham, C., & Tynan, C. (1993). Electronic trading, inter-organizational systems and the nature of buyer and seller relations: The need for a network perspective. *International Journal of Information Management, 13,* 3–28.

Dankbaar, B., & van Tulder, R. (1992). The influence of users in standardization: The case of MAP. In M. Dierkes, & U. Hoffmann (Eds.), *New technologies at the outset—Social forces in the shaping of technological innovations* (pp. 327-349). Frankfurt; New York: Campus/Westview.

Egyedi, T., Jakobs, K., & Monteiro, E. (2003). *Helping SDOs to reach users* (Report for EC DG ENT, Contract No. 20010674). Retrieved January 16, 2006, from http://www-i4.informatik.rwth-aachen.de/~jakobs/grant/Final_Report.pdf

European Commission. (2004). *Innovate for a competitive Europe: A new action plan for innovation*. Retrieved January 16, 2006, from http://europa.eu.int/comm/enterprise/innovation/consultation/docs/innovate.pdf

Gerst, M., & Bunduchi, R. (2004). The adoption of standardised technology in the automotive industry. In P. Cunningham, & M. Cunningham (Eds.), *E-adoption and the knowledge economy: Issues, applications, case studies* (pp. 287–294). Amsterdam, The Netherlands: IOS Press.

Graham, I., Spinardi, G., Williams, R., & Webster, J. (1995). The dynamics of EDI standard development. *Technology Analysis & Strategic Management, 7*(1), 3–20.

ISSS. (Eds.). (2004). *ICT standards consortia survey* (9th ed.). Retrieved January 16, 2006, from http://www.cenorm.be/cenorm/businessdomains/businessdomains/isss/consortia/survey+table+of+content.asp

Jakobs, K. (2000). *User participation in standardisation processes—impact, problems and benefits*. Braunschweig, Wiesbaden, Germany: Vieweg Publishers.

Jakobs, K. (2003). Information technology standards, standards setting and standards research: Mapping the universe. In *Proceedings of the Stanhope Center's Roundtable on Systematic Barriers to the Inclusion of a Public Interest Voice in the Design of Information and Communications Technologies,* Cotswolds, UK (pp. 118-123).

Jakobs, K. (2004). *E-business & ICT) standardisation and SME users—Mutually exclusive?* In *Proceedings of the Multi-Conference on Business Information Systems, Track 'E-Business—Standardisierung und Integration,* Göttingen, Germany.

Jakobs, K., Procter, R., & Williams, R. (1998). Infrastructural technologies to enable electronic commerce. In *Proceedings of the 3rd International Conference on the Management of Networked Enterprises,* Montreal.

Jakobs, K., Procter, R., & Williams, R. (2000). The making of standards. *IEEE Communications Magazine, 39*(4).

Koch, O., & Gerst, M. (2003). E-collaboration-initiative bei DaimlerChrysler. In R. Bogaschewsky (Ed.), *Integrated supply management—Einkauf und beschaffung: Effizienz steigern, kosten senken* (pp. 207–234). Cologne: Deutscher Wirtschaftsdienst.

Kumar, K., & van Dissel, H.G. (1996). Sustainable collaboration: Managing conflict and cooperation in interorganisational systems. *MIS Quarterly, 20*(3), 279–300.

Lamming, R. (1993). *Beyond partnership, strategies for innovation and lean supply.* Upper Saddle River, NJ: Prentice Hall, International.

McKinsey. (2003). Studie HAWK 2015—Wissensbasierte veränderung der automobilen wertschöpfungskette. *VDA 30 Materialien zur Automobilindustrie, 30.* Franfurt: Verband der Authomobilindustrie.

Monse, K., & Reimers, K. (1995). The development of electronic data interchange networks from an institutional perspective. In R. Williams (Ed.), *The social shaping of interorganizational IT systems and electronic data interchange* (pp. 109–127). Luxembourg: European Commission.

PWC. (2004). *Rethinking the European ICT agenda: Ten ICT-breakthroughs for reaching Lisbon goals.* Retrieved January 16, 2006, from http://www.eskills2004.org/files/Rethinking%20the%20European%20ICT%20agenda_def.pdf.

Swann, P.G.M. (2000). *The economics of standardization* (Final Report for DTI). Retrieved January 16, 2006, from http://www.dti.gov.uk/strd/economic%20benefits%20of%20standardisation%20-%20EN.pdf

Thompson, G. (1954). Intercompany technical standardization in the early American automobile industry. *Journal of Economic History, 14*(1), 1–20.

Webster, J. (1995). Networks of collaboration or conflict? The development of EDI. In R. Williams (Ed.), *The social shaping of interorganizational IT systems and electronic data interchange* (pp. 17–41). Luxembourg: European Commission.

Williams, R., Graham, I., & Spinardi, G. (1995). The social shaping of EDI. In R. Williams (Ed.), *The social shaping of interorganizational IT systems and electronic data interchange* (pp. 1-16). Luxembourg: European Commission.

ENDNOTES

[1] Original Equipment Manufacturers

[2] Small and medium-sized enterprises

[3] The European Committee for Standardization/The European Committee for Electrotechnical Standardization

[4] The International Organization for Standardization/The International Electrotechnical Commission

[5] The International Telegraph and Telephone Consultative Committee, later ITU-T (see the following)

[6] The European Computer Manufacturers Association

[7] The European Telecommunications Standards Institute

[8] The Telecommunications Industry Association

[9] The World Wide Web Consortium

[10] The Organization for the Advancement of Structured Information Standards

[11] General Motors' Manufacturing Automation Protocol (MAP) and Boeing's Transport and Office Protocol (TOP) are particularly instructive cases in point. At that time, specifically GM had to spend millions of dollars annually to interconnect incompatible IT systems at their plant floors. Thus, the idea behind MAP and TOP was to define precisely the individual protocols and optional protocol features of the then popular OSI protocol stack (Open Systems

Interconnection) to be implemented in plant floors and office environments, respectively. This was at least due to the fact that only very large companies (like the two initiators) participated in the initiative. In particular, no SMEs were involved, despite the fact that they represented the majority of suppliers. As a consequence, their needs and requirements largely were ignored. Yet, SMEs were not able to implement this highly complex technology, and the initiative eventually failed dramatically (Dankbaar & van Tulder, 1992).

[12] The full report may be found at http://www-i4.informatik.rwth-aachen.de/~jakobs/grant/Final_Report.pdf

[13] In 2004, Covisint was bought by Compuware, which still offers some e-marketplace functionalities, including the portal functionality.

[14] In general, most of the electronic marketplaces, whether or not they were sector-specific, were not successful in the sense of making money out of the e-marketplace business model; for example, Connextrade (Swiss e-marketplace for commodities) and Answork (French e-marketplace for commodity buying of banks) did not fare very well, either.

[15] With the possible exception of specialist vendor (Jakobs, 2004).

This work was previously published in Small Business Clustering Technologies: Applications in Marketing, Management, Economics, Finance, and IT, edited by R. MacGregor, pp. 281-314, copyright 2007 by Information Science Publishing (an imprint of IGI Global).

Compilation of References

Abbate, J. (1999). *Inventing the internet.* Cambridge, Mass.: MIT Press.

Abernathy, W. J., & Utterback, J. M. (1978). Patterns of industrial innovation. *Technology Review, 80*(7), 40-47.

Afuah, A., & Tucci, C. (2001). *Internet Business Models and Strategies.* Boston: McGraw-Hill Irwin.

AIM, Radio Frequency Identification – RFID. A basic primer, AIM White Paper, 1.11, September 28th, (1999), http://www.aimglobal.org, Access Date: January, 2005

Alder, K. (2002). *The measure of all things: The seven year odyssey and hidden error that transformed the world.* New York: Free Press.

Amor, D. (2000). The E-business (R)Evolution. Living and Working in an Interconnected World. USA: Prentice Hall.

AMR Research (2005). *The Auto Industry and RFID.*

Andel, T. (1998). Managing supply chain relationships. *Transportation & Distribution, 39*(10), SCF10-SCF14.

Anonymous (2008). The Way Forward. *Discussion document for the Open Meeting of the Conference. European ICT Standardization Policy at a Crossroads: A New Direction for Global Success.* organized by the European Commission - Directorate-General for Enterprise and Industry, Brussels, 12 February 2008.

Arthur, B. (1989). Competing Technologies, Increasing Returns, and Lock-In by Historical Events. *Economic Journal, 99*, 116-131.

AUTOSAR (2004). An industry-wide initiative to manage the complexity of emerging automotive E/E – architectures. *Proceedings of the 2004 international congress on transportation electronics, automobile electronics to digital mobility: the next generation of convergence,* (pp. 325-332).

Axelrod, R. M., & Cohen, M. D. (1999). *Harnessing complexity : organizational implications of a scientific frontier.* New York: Free Press.

Ballon, P., & Hawkins, R. (2008). Standardization and business models for platform competition: the case of mobile television. *International Journal of Information Technology Standards Research* (forthcoming).

Ballon. P. (2007). Changing business models for Europe's mobile telecommunications industry: The impact of alternative wireless technologies. *Telematics and Informatics, 24*(3), 192-205.

Barrat, M. (2004). Understanding the meaning of collaboration in the supply chain. *Supply Chain Management: An International Journal, 9*(1), 30-42.

Bearing Point, Beyond compliance: the Future promise of RFID. White Paper: communications, consumer, industrial & technology.

Beecham, M. (2006). *Global market review of automobile electrical wiring systems – forecasts to 2012.* Aroq Limited.

Bekkers, R. (2001). *Mobile Telecommunication Standards: GSM, UMTS, TETRA and ERMES.* Boston: Artech House.

Bellissard, L., et al (1999). An Agent Platform for Reliable Asynchronous Distributed Programming. *Proc. 18th IEEE Symposium on Reliable Distributed Systems table of contents*. IEEE Computer Society.

Besen, F. M. (1995). The standards process in telecommunication and information technology. In R. W. Hawkins, et al. (Eds.), *Standards, Innovation and Competitiveness*. Edward Elgar Publishers.

Besen, S. M. (1990). The European Telecommunications Standards Institute: A Preliminary Analysis. *Telecommunications Policy, 14*(6), 521-530.

Besen, S. M., & Farrell, J. (1991). The Role of the ITU in Standardization: Pre-eminence, Impotence or Rubber Stamp? *Telecommunications Policy, 15*(4), 311-321.

Besen, S., & Saloner, G. (1988). Compatibility Standards and the Market for Telecommunication Services. In R. W. Crandall & K. Flemm, (Eds.), *Changing Rules: Technological Change, International Competition and Regulation in Telecommunications*. Brookings Institution, Washington, DC.

Blind, K. (2004). *The Economics Of Standards - Theory, Evidence, Policy*. Edward Elgar, ISBN 1 84376 793 7.

Beyer, S. (1982). *Regulation and its Reform*. Cambridge Mass: Harvard Univ. Press.

Blind, K. (2006). A Taxonomy of Standards in the Service Sector: Theoretical Discussion and Empirical Test. *The Service Industries Journal, 26*(4), 397-420.

Blind, K. (2008). Factors influencing the lifetime of telecommunication and information technology standards In T. M. Egyedi & K. Blind (Eds.), *The dynamics of standards* (pp. 155-177). Cheltenham, UK: Edward Elgar.

Blind, K., & Gauch, S. (2005). Trends in ICT Standards in European Standardisation Bodies and Standards Consortia. *Proceedings of the 4th IEEE Conference on Standardisation and Innovation in Information Technology,* (pp. 29-39).

Blind, K., & Gauch, S. (2005, September 21-23). *Trends in ICT Standards in European Standardisation Bodies and Standards Consortia*. Paper presented at the Proceedings of the 4th International Conference on Standardization and Innovation in Information Technology (SIIT), Geneva.

Blind, K., & Thumm, N. (2004). Interrelation between patenting and standardisation strategies: empirical evidence and policy implications. *Research Policy, 33*(10), 1583-1598.

Blind, K., Gauch, S., & Hawkins, R. (2007). How Stakeholders View the Impacts of International ICT Standards. *In the Proceedings of the 12th EURAS Workshop*, **16-17 May,** Thessaloniki, Greece.

Blind, K., Thumm, N., Bierhals, R., Hossein, K., Iversen, E., van Reekum, R., & Rixius, B. (2002). *Study on the Interaction between Standardisation and Intellectual Property Rights*. Final Report to the DG Research of the European Commission (EC Contract No G6MA-CT-2000-02001), Karlsruhe.

Borders, A. L., Johnston, W. J., & Rigdon, E. E. (2001). Beyond the Dyad: Electronic Commerce and Network Perspectives in Industrial Marketing Management. *Industrial Marketing Management, 30*(4), 343-358.

Borisov, N., Goldberg, I., & Wagner, D. (1999). *802.11 Security*. Retrieved 2007-01-30, from http://www.isaac.cs.berkeley.edu/isaac/wep-faq.html

Borras, J. (2003). *E-Government Challenges and Perspectives-the UK Perspective*. Office of the E-Envoy.

Bresnahan, T., Greenstein, S., Brownstone, D., & Flamm, K. (1996). Technical progress and co-invention in computing and in the uses of computers. *Brookings Papers on Economic Activity – Microeconomics,* (pp. 1-13).

Britt, F. F. (2002). *Multiplying business value: The fusion of business and technology*. IBM Institute for Business Value, http://managementconsult.profpages.nl/man_bib/rap/ibm06.pdf

Broadbent, M., Weill, P., & St. Clair, D. (1999). The implications of information technology infrastructure for business process redesign. *MIS Quarterly. 23*(2).

Bukowski, R. W. (2003). The Role of Standards in a Performance-based Building Regulatory System. http://fire.nist.gov/bfrlpubs/fire02/PDF/f02032.pdf.

Cargill, C. (1989). *Information Technology Standardization: Theory, Process, and Organizations.* Digital Press.

Cargill, C. (2002). Uncommon Commonality – A Qust for Unitiy in Standardization. In S. Bolin, (Ed.), The Standards Edge.

Cargill, C. (2005). Open Source, Open Standards, Open Issues: Structuring a Busienss perspective. In S. Bolin, (Ed.), *Standards Edge – Open Season.*

Cargill, C. F. (1995). A Five-Segment Model for Standardization. In B. Kahin & J. Abbate (Eds.), *Standards Policy for Information Infrastructure.* MIT Press.

Cargill, C. F. (1995). *Open Systems Standardization – A Busienss Approach.* Prentice Hall.

Cargill, C., & Bohlin, S. (2007). Standardization: A falling paradigm. In S. Greenstein & V. Stango (Eds.), *Standards and Public Policy.* Cambridge: Cambridge University Press, (pp. 296-328).

Cargill, C., & Bolin, S. (2007). Standardization: A Failing Paradigm, Standards and Public Policy. In S. Greenstein & V. Stango (Eds.), *Standards and Public Policy.* Cambridge University Press. (pp. 296-328).

Cash, D., Clark, W., Alcock, F., Dickson, N., Eckley, N., & Jäger, J. (2002). *Salience, Credibility, Legitimacy and Boundaries: Linking Research, Assessment and Decision Making.* John F. Kennedy School of Government Faculty Research Working Paper RWP02-046. John F. Kennedy School of Government, Harvard University.

Castells, M. (1996). *The Rise of the Network Society* (2nd ed. Vol. I). Oxford: Blackwell Publishers, Ltd.

CEN (2005). *Analysis of standardization requirements and standardization gaps for eProcurement in Europe, CEN Workshop Agreement*, Brussels.

CEN/ISSS (2008). *ICT Standards Consortia survey*, 14th edition. http://www.cenorm.be/cenorm/businessdomains/businessdomains/isss/consortia/index.asp.

CEPT. (1991). *Recommendation T/R 10-01 (Oslo 1991, revised in Madrid 1992), Wide band data transmission systems using spread-spectrum technology in the 2.5 GHz band. Superseded by T/R 70-03.*

CEPT. (1992). *Recommendation T/R 22-06 (Madrid 1992, revised at Nicosia 1994), Harmonised radio frequency bands for high performance radio local area networks (HIPERLANs) in the 5 GHz and 17 GHz frequency range. Superseded by T/R 70-03.*

Chandler, A. (1962). *Strategy and Structure: Chapters in the History of American Industrial Enterprise.* Cambridge MA: MIT Press.

Chesbrough, H. (2003). *Open innovation: The new imperative for creating and profiting from technology.* Cambridge: Harvard University Press.

Chesbrough, H., & Rosenbloom, R. S. (2002). The role of the business model in capturing value from innovation: Evidence From Xerox corporation's technology spin off companies. *Industrial and Corporate Change, 11*(3), 529-555.

ChinaLabs (2004, July). *New Globalism: A Research Report on China's High Technology Standards Strategy.* Beijing.

Christensen, C. M., & Raynor, M. E. (2003). *The Innovator's Solution: Creating and Sustaining Successful Growth.* Boston: Harvard Business School Press.

Cohen, W., & Levinthal, D. (1990). Absorptive Capacity: A New Perspective On Learning And Innovation. *Administrative Science Quarterly;* March, *35*(1), 128-152.

Collaborative Planning Forecasting and Replenishment (CPFR), operated by VICS USA www.vics.org

Commission of the European Communities (2003). *Commission staff working document "Linking up the Europe: the importance of interoperability for e-government services"* (Commission staff working document No. SEC(2003)801). Brussels: Commission of the European Communities.

Cooke, P., & Morgan, K. (1998). *The Associational Economy.* Oxford: Oxford University Press.

Core Components – developed by UN/CEFACT with ISO, ITU and IETC. To be used, hopefully, by EDIFACT, ebXML, OASIS, and 'all' of e.business. – 2001-08. See also UNe.docs. www.unece.org/cefact

Cowan, R., Cowan, W., & Swann, P. (1997). A model of demand with interactions among consumers. *International Journal of Industrial Organization, 15*(6), 711-33.

Crane, M. (2007). *Stealing Starbuck's Wi-Fi customers*. Retrieved 2007-08-28, from http://www.forbes.com/2007/02/23/fonbucks-wifi-starbucks-ent_cx_mc_0226fonbucks_print.html

Crane, R. J. (1978). Communication Standards and the Politics of Protectionism. *Telecommunications Policy, 2*(4), 267-281.

D.I.A.M.O.N.D.– a General Theory of Value Chain Management Data – adding strength and sparkle to your value chain ' Tom McGuffog. UK Partners for electronic business. London, 2004.

Dankbaar, B., & van Tulder, R. (1992). The Influence of Users in Standardization: the Case of MAP. In M. Dierkes & U. Hoffmann (Eds.), *New Technology at the Outset: Social Forces in the Shaping of Technological Innovations*. Frankfurt and New York: Campus Verlag, (pp. 327-349).

David, P. A. (1985). Clio and the Economics of QWERTY. *American Economic Review, 75*(2), 332-337.

David, P. A., & Greenstein, S. (1990). The Economics of Compatibility Standards: An Introduction to Recent Research. *Economics of Innovation and New Technology, 1*(1) 3-41.

David. P. A., & Steinmueller, E. (1990). The ISDN Bandwagon is Coming, But Who Will Be There To Climb Aboard?: Quandaries in the Economics of Data Communication Networks. *Economics of Innovation and New Technology, 1*(1), 43-62.

Davis, L. E., & North, D. C. (1971). *Institutional Change and American Economic Growth*. Cambridge: Cambridge University Press.

Davydov, M. M. (2000). e-Commerce Solutions for Business and IT Managers. *Corporate Portals and e-business Integration*. New York, USA: McGrow Hill.

De Leeuw, G. J. (2006). *Wi-Fi in the Netherlands*. Paper presented at the 9th Annual International Conference Economics of Infrastructure, Delft, the Netherlands.

De Leeuw, G. J. (2007). *A snapshot of the Wi-Fi world in 2007*. Delft, the Netherlands: TUDelft.

De Vries, H. (1999). *Standardization: A Business Approach to the Role of National Standardization Organizations*. Springer.

De Vries, H. J. (1999). *Standardization*. A Business Approach to the Role of National Standardization Organizations. Kluwer Academic Publishers, Boston/Dordrecht/London.

De Vries, H. J. (2001). *Systematic services standardization from consumer's point of view*. Contribution to the ISO Workshop in Oslo.

De Wit, B., & Meyer, R. (2004). *Strategy: process, content, context - An international perspective*. London: Thomson.

Dixit, A. (1996). *The Making of Economic Policy: A Transaction-Cost Politics Perspective*. The MIT Press.

Dosi, G. (1982). Technological paradigms and technological trajectories - A suggested interpretation of the determinants and directions of technical change. *Research Policy, 11*, p147-162.

Doz, Y. L., Olk, P. M., & Ring, P. S. (2000). Formation Processes of R&D Consortia. *Strategic Management Journal, 21*(3), 239-266.

DTI (2002). *Open source software in e-government* (report). Copenhagen: Danish Board of Technology (DTI).

DTI (2005). *The Empirical Economics of Standards*: Danish Board of Technology (DTI).

EANCOM Standards supported by GS1 - www.gs1.org

EC (2003). The Role of eGovernment for Europe's Future, COM(2003) 567, European Communities. European Communities, Brussels

EC (2006). Directive 2006/123/EC of the European Parliament and of the Council of 12 December 2006 on services in the internal market, Brussels.

EC (2006). i2010 eGovernment Action Plan: Accelerating eGovernment in Europe for the Benefit of All, COM(2006) 173, European Communities Brussels.

EC (2006). Interoperability for Pan-European eGovernment Services, COM(2006) 45, European Communities Brussels.

Economides, N., & Flyer, F. (1998). Technical Standards Coalitions for Network Goods. *Annales d'Economie et de Statistique, 49/50*, 361-380.

EDIFACT EDI Standards – United Nations Economic Commission for Europe, Standards for Administration, Commerce and Transport – version D.08A. Geneva, 2008

Eertink, H., & Demchenko, Y. (Eds.) (2000). Notes from the European Middleware Workshop (EMW2000). http://www.terena.nl/tech/projects/middleware/emw2000notes01.html

Egyedi, T. (2001). Why Java™ was not standardized twice. *Computer Standards & Interfaces, 23*(4), 253-265.

Egyedi, T. (2006). Beyond Consortia, Beyond Standardization? In K. Jakobs (Eds.), *Advanced Topics in Information Technology Standards and Standardization Research, 1.* Idea Group Publishing.

Egyedi, T. M. (1996). *Shaping Standardisation: A Study of Standards Processes and Standards Policies in the Field of Telematic Services.* Delft, the Netherlands: Delft University Press.

Egyedi, T. M. (2002). *Trendrapport Standaardisatie. Oplossingsrichtingen voor problemen van IT-interoperabiliteit.* Delft: Ministerie van Verkeer en Waterstaat, Rijkswaterstaat/ Meetkundige Dienst.

Egyedi, T. M. (2003). Consortium Problem Redefined: Negotiating 'Democracy' in the Actor Network on

Standardization. *International Journal of IT Standards & Standardization Research, 1*(2), 22-38.

Egyedi, T. M. (2008). Conclusion. In T. M. Egyedi & K. Blind (Eds.), *The dynamics of standards* (pp. 181-189). Cheltenham, UK: Edward Elgar.

Egyedi, T. M. (2008). An implementation perspective on sources of incompatibility and standards' dynamics. In T. M. Egyedi & K. Blind (Eds.), *The dynamics of standards* (pp. 181-189). Cheltenham, UK: Edward Elgar.

Egyedi, T. M., & Blind, K. (2008). *Introduction.* In T. M. Egyedi & K. Blind (Eds.), *The dynamics of standards* (pp. 1-12). Cheltenham, UK: Edward Elgar.

Egyedi, T. M., & Heijnen, P. (2008). How stable are IT standards? In T. M. Egyedi & K. Blind (Eds.), *The dynamics of standards* (pp. 137-154). Cheltenham, UK: Edward Elgar.

Egyedi, T. M., & Loeffen, A. (2008). Incompatible successors: The failure to graft XML onto SGML. In T. M. Egyedi & K. Blind (Eds.), *The dynamics of standards* (pp. 82-97). Cheltenham, UK: Edward Elgar.

Egyedi, T. M., & Sherif, M. H. (2008). *Standards' Dynamics through an Innovation Lens: Next Generation Ethernet Networks.* Paper presented at the Conference Name|. Retrieved Access Date|. from URL|.

Egyedi, T. M., & Verwater-Lukszo, Z. (2005). Which standards' characteristics increase system flexibility? Comparing ICT and Batch Processing Infrastructures. *Technology in Society, 27*(3), 347-362.

EQOS Ltd. For details see www.equos.com

ETSI. (1993). *ETS 300 328 Radio Equipment and Systems (RES); Wideband transmission systems; Technical characteristics and test conditions for data transmission equipment operating in the 2,4 GHz ISM band and using spread spectrum modulation techniques.*

European Commission (2001). On Actions Taken Following the Resolutions on European Standardisation Adopted by the Council and the European Parliament in 1999. *COM*(2001) 527 final.

European Commission (2004). The role of European standardisation in the framework of European policies and legislation. Communication from the Commission to the European Parliament and the Council. *COM*(2004) 674. http://europa.eu.int/comm/enterprise/standards_policy/role_of_standardisation/doc/communication_en.pdf.

Evans, C. D., Meek, B. L., & Walker, R. S. (Eds.) (1993). *User Needs in Information Technology Standards*. Oxford: Butterworth-Heinemann

Farrell, J. (1990). Economics of Standardization. In J. L. B. H. Schumny (Ed.), *An Analysis of the Information Technology Standardization Process.*

Farrell, J., & Saloner, G. (1985). Standardisation, Compatibility and Innovation. *Rand Journal of Economics, 16*(1), 70-83.

Farrell, J., & Saloner, G. (1985). Standardization, Compatibility and Innovation. *RAND Journal of Economics, 16*, 70-83.

Farrell, J., & Saloner, G. (1988). Coordination through Committees and Markets. *Rand Journal of Economics, 19*(2), 235-251.

FCC. (1981). *GEN Docket 81-413, Authorization of spread spectrum and other wideband emissions not presently provided for in the FCC rules and regulations. Notice of Inquiry, June 30, 1981.* Retrieved 2008-01-30, from http://www.marcus-spectrum.com/documents/SpreadSpectrumNOI.pdf

FCC. (1985). *GEN Docket 81-413 Report and Order in the matter of: Authorization of spread spectrum.* Washington, D.C.: Federal Communications Commission.

FCC. (1999). *ET Docket 99-231, Amendment of Part 15 of the Commission's rules regarding spread spectrum devices. Notice of Proposed Rulemaking, released June 24, 1999.* Retrieved 2008-02-08, from http://www.fcc.gov/searchtools.html

FCC. (2007). *About the FCC.* Retrieved 2007-01-05, from http://www.fcc.gov/aboutus.html

Fleisch, E. et al. (2004b). *From operations to strategy: The potential of RFID for the automotive industry.*

Study of the M-Lab St. Gallen/Zurich with Booz Allen Hamilton, April 2004.

Florida, R. (2002). *The Rise of the Creative Class.* New York: Basic Books.

Fomin, V. V. (2008). Snow, Buses, and Mobile Data Services in the Information Age. *Journal of Strategic Information Systems, 17*(3), 234-246.

Fomin, V. V., Pedersen, M. K., & de Vries, H. J. (2008). Open Standards And Government Policy: Results Of A Delphi Survey. *Communications of the Association for Information Systems, 22*(April), 459-484.

FON. (2007). *What's Fon?* Retrieved 2007-08-30, from http://www.fon.com/en/info/whatsFon

For details about OASIS see - www.oasis-open.org

For STEP standards, see - www.steptools.com . See also – www.ukceb.org.uk

Foray D. (1995). Coalitions and committees: How users get involved in information technology standards. In R. W. Hawkins, R. Mansell, & J. Skea (Eds.), *Standards, Innovation and Competitiveness: The Politics and Economics of Standards in Natural and Technical Environments.* Cheltenham: Edward Elgar.

Fox, M. (2004). E-commerce Business Models for the Music Industry. *Popular Music and Society, 27*(2), 201-220.

Freeman, C. (1994) Critical survey: The economics of Technical change. *Cambridge Journal of Economics, 18*, 463-514.

Freeman, R. (1996). *Developing Standards: A Market-Driven Approach.* http://www.peostri.army.mil/E-DIR/ED/SEI/documents/013.pdf.

Funk, J., & Methe, D. (n.d.). Market- and Committee-Based Mechanism in the Creation and Diffusion of Global Industry Standards: the Case of Mobile Communication. *Research Policy 30*, 589-610.

GAO (2004). *Technology Assessment. Cybersecurity for Critical Infrastructure Protection.* Available at http://www.gao.gov/new.items/d04321.pdf.

Gao, P. (2007). Counter-Networks in Standardization: a Perspective of Developing Countries. *Information Systems Journal, 17*, 391-420.

Garcia, D. L. (1992). Standards Setting in the United States: Public and Private Sector Roles. *Journal of the American Society for Information Science, 43*(8), 531-537.

Garud, R., Jain, S., & Kumarasawamy, A. (2002). Institutional entrepreneurship in the sponsorship of common technological standards: The case of Sun Microsystems and Java. *Academy of Management Journal, 45*(1).

Gauch, S. (2008). + vs. – , Dynamics and effects of competing standards of recordable DVD media In T. M. Egyedi & K. Blind (Eds.), *The dynamics of standards* (pp. 47-67). Cheltenham, UK: Edward Elgar.

Gawer, A., & Cusumano, M. A. (2002). *Platform leadership: How Intel, Microsoft and Cisco drive industry innovation*. Boston: Harvard Business School Press.

Gerst, M., & Bunduchi, R. (2005). *Challenges in the adoption of RFID standards, published by the European Commission, Strengthening Competitiveness through Production Networks – A perspective from European ICT research project in the field of 'Enterprise Networking'.* pp. (pp. 81-90).

Gerybadze, A., & König, R. (2008). Managing Global Innovation Networks: The Case of Automotive Electronics. *Presentation at Workshop on Managing Global Innovation Networks*, Duisburg University, 8 February.

Graham, I., Spinardi, G., Williams, R., & Webster, J. (1995). *Technology Analysis & Strategic Management, 7*(1), 3–20.

Graham, I., Spinardi, G., Williams, R., & Webster, J. (1995). The Dynamics of EDI Standards Development. *Technology Analysis & Strategic Management, 7*(1), 3-21.

Grebe, A. (1997). *Standards: Today's Trade Barriers Are Tomorrow's Global Markets.* http://www.ses-standards.org/displaycommon.cfm?an=1&subarticlenbr=56.

Gulati, R., Nohria, N., & Zaheer, A. (2000). Strategic Networks. *Strategic Management Journal, Special Issue: Strategic Networks, 21*(3), 203-215.

Harrington, L. H. (1998). Software tools to revamp your supply chain. *Transportation & Distribution, 39*(11), 59-70.

Hashimoto, T. (2002). *Hyojun no tetsugaku : sutandado tekunoroji no sanbyakunen.* Tokyo: Kodansha (*The Philosophy of Standards: 300 Years of Standard Technology; in Japanese*)

Hawkins, R. & P. Ballon (2007). When standards become business models: reinterpreting 'failure' in the standardization paradigm, *Info – the Journal of Policy, Regulation and Strategy for Telecommunications, Information and Media, 9*(5), 20-30.

Hawkins, R. (1992). The Doctrine of Regionalism: A New Dimension for International Standardization in Telecommunication. *Telecommunications Policy, 16*(4), May/June, 339-353.

Hawkins, R. (1995). Enhancing the User Role in the Development of Technical Standards for Telecommunication. *Technology Analysis & Strategic Management, 7*(1), 21-40.

Hawkins, R. (1995). Standards-Making as Technological Diplomacy: Assessing Objectives and Methodologies in Standards Institutions. In R. Hawkins, R. Mansell, & J. Skea (Eds.), *Standards, Innovation and Competitiveness: the Politics and Economics of Standards in Natural and Technical Environments*. Cheltenham: Edward Elgar, (pp. 147-158).

Hawkins, R. (1999). The Rise of Consortia in the Information and Communication Technology Industries: Emerging Implications for Policy. *Telecommunications Policy, 23*(2), 159-173.

Hawkins, R. (2003). Looking beyond the .com bubble: exploring the form and function of business models in the electronic marketplace. In H. Bouwman, B. Preissl, & C. Steinfield, (Eds.), *E-Life after the dot-com Bust*. Hamburg: Springer/Physica, (pp. 65-81).

Hawkins, R., & Puissochet, A. (2005) Estimating Software activity in European Industry, paper prepared for the FISTERA consortium in the European Union Sixth Framework (IST-2001-37627).

Helmer, O., & Rescher, N. (1959). On the Epistemology of the Inexact Sciences. *Management science, 6*(1), 25-52.

Hemenway, D. (1975). *Industrywide Voluntary Product Standards.* Cambridge: Ballinger.

Hertz, J. C., Lucas, M., & Scott, J. (2006). *Open Technology Development. Roadmap Plan*: Prepared for: Ms. Sue Payton, Deputy Under Secretary of Defense.

Heywood, P., Jander, M., Roberts, E., & Saunders, S. (1997). Standards, The Inside Story: Do Vendors have too much Influence on the Way Industry Specs are Written and Ratified? *Data Communications,* March, (pp. 59-72).

Hill, S. Jr, (2002). True supply chain management. *Manufacturing Systems, 20*(2), 48-49.

Hills, A. (1999). Wireless Andrew. *IEEE Spectrum, 36*(6), p49-53.

Hills, A., & Johnson, D. B. (1996). A wireless data network infrastructure at Carnegie Mellon University. *IEEE Personal Communications, 3*(1), 56-63.

Hirschman, A. O. (1970). *Exit Voice and Loyalty: Responses to Decline in Firms, Organizations, and States.* Harvard University Press.

Hogart-Scott, S. (1999). Retailer-supplier partnerships: hostages to fortune or the way forward for the millennium? *British Food Journal, 101*(9), 668-682.

Hong, J. I., & Landay, J. A. (2001). An Infrastructure Approach to Context-Aware Computing. *Human-Computer Interaction, 16*(2, 3 & 4), 287-303.

Howgego, C. (2002). Maximising competitiveness through the supply chain. *International Journal of Retail & Distribution, 30*(12), 603-605.

Hudson, H. E. (2006). *Municipal wireless broadband: Lessons from San Francisco.* San Francisco: University of San Francisco.

IBM (2005, May 10). Governments and public policy. Corporate responsibility report Retrieved Nov 29, 2005. Available at http://www.ibm.com/ibm/responsibility/world/government/

IBM (2008). *IBM Announces New I.T. Standards Policy.* http://www-03.ibm.com/press/us/en/pressrelease/25186.wss.

ICT Standards Board (2005, April 27). Critical Issues in ICT Standardization Retrieved March 30, 2006. Available at http://www.ictsb.org/ictsfg/ictsfg_report_2005-04-27.pdf

IDABC (2004). European Interoperability Framework for Pan-European eGovernment Services - Version 1.0: Office for Official Publications of the European Communities.

IDABC (2007) eID Interoperability for PEGS Analysis and Assessment of similarities and differences - Impact on eID interoperability, European Communities Brussels.

IDABC eGovernment Observatory (2005). eGovernment in the Member States of the European Union, European Communities Brussels.

Instat. (2007). Personal communication.

ISO (2004). *ISO Strategic Plan 2005-2010 : Standards for a sustainable world.* Geneve: ISO Central Secretariat.

ISO&IEC (2004). *ISO/IEC guide 2: Standardization and related activities - General vocabulary (8th edition.)*

ISO/IEC. (2004). *ISO/IEC Directives, Part 2: Rules for the structure and drafting of International Standards.* Geneva: ISO/IEC.

ITU (2003, 19 Nov). ITU Digital Access Index: World's First Global ICT Ranking Retrieved March 8, 2005. Available at http://www.itu.int/newsarchive/press_releases/2003/30.html

ITU. (1965). *From semaphore to satellite.* Geneva: International Telecommunication Union.

Jakobs K., Procter, R., & Williams, R. (1996). Users and standardization: Worlds apart? The example of electronic mail. *StandardView, 4*(4), 183-191.

Jakobs, K. (2000). *User Participation in Standardisation Processes - Impact, Problems and Benefits.* Vieweg Publishers.

Jakobs, K. (2003). *Information Technology Standards, Standards Setting and Standards Research: Mapping the Universe.* Presented at: Stanhope Center's Roundtable on systematic barriers to the inclusion of a public interest voice in the design of Information and Communications Technologies. http://www.stanhopecentre.org/cotswolds/papers.htm.

Jakobs, K. (2004). (E-Business & ICT) Standardisation and SME Users – Mutually Exclusive? *Proc. Multi-Conference on Business Information Systems, Track 'E-Business – Standardisierung und Integration,* Cuviller Verlag, Göttingen.

Jakobs, K. (2005). The Role of the 'Third Estate' in ICT Standardisation. In S. Bolin (Ed.), *The Standards Edge: Future Generation:* The Bolin Group.

Jakobs, K. (2008). The IEEE 802.11 WLAN installation at RWTH Aachen University: A case of voluntary vendor lock-in. In T. M. Egyedi & K. Blind (Eds.), *The dynamics of standards* (pp. 99-116). Cheltenham, UK: Edward Elgar.

Jakobs, K., & Mora, M. (2008). Co-ordinating Rule Setters – Co-operation in ICT Standards Setting. *Proc. 2008 International Conference on Information Resources Management (Conf-IRM).*

Jakobs, K., Egyedi, T., & Monteito, E. (2003). *Helping SDOs to Reach Users. – Final Report.* http://www-i4.informatik.rwth-aachen.de/~jakobs/grant/FinalReport.pdf.

Jakobs, K., Hayes, V., Tuch, B., Links, C., & Lemstra, W. (Forthcoming). Towards a wireless LAN standard. In W. Lemstra & J. P. M. Groenewegen (Eds.), *The genesis of Wi-Fi and the road toward global success.*

Jakobs, K., Procter, R., & Williams, R. (2001). The Making of Standards. *IEEE Communications Magazine, 39*(4).

Jakovljevic, P. J. (2004). RFID – A new technology set to explode? *TechnologyEvaluation.Com,* (12th of April 2004), http://www.technology-evaluation,com/Research/ResearchHighlights/Scm/2004/04/research_notes/TU_SC_PJ_04_22_04_1.asp, Access Date: February.

Johnson, D. B. (2007). Personal communication.

Jones, P., & Hudson, J. (1996). Standardization and the Cost of Assessing Quality. *European Journal of Political Economy, 12*, 355-361.

Kamlani, D. (2005). ICT Standards and the New Arms Race – The Rule of 3 (+N). In S. Bolin, (Ed.), *Standards Edge, Future Generation.*

Kamp, D. (2005). *Analysis of the emergence of Wi-Fi.* Delft: TUDelft.

Katz, M. L., & Shapiro, C. (1985). Network Externalities, Competition, and Compatibility. *American Economic Review, 75*, 424-440.

Katz, M. L., & Shapiro, C. (1986). Technology Adoption in the Presence of Network Externalities. *Journal of Political Economy, 94*, 882-841.

Kauffman, S., Lobo, J., & Macready, W. G. (2000). Optimal search on a technology landscape. *Journal of Economic Behavior & Organization, 43*, 141–166.

Kim, J. (2004). Technical Standard-Setting, Patent Pooling, and Competition Policy. *Report of the 2003FY Industrial Property, Research Promotion Project.* Institute of Intellectual Property.

Kimura, M. (1932). Rationalization of load conditions. *Journal of the Aeronautical Research Institute, 99*(1), 815-820 (in Japanese). Tokyo Imperial University.

Kimura, M. (1933). Simplification of load conditions. *Journal of the Aeronautical Research Institute, 103*(1), 143-145 (in Japanese). Tokyo Imperial University.

Kindleberger, C. P. (1983). Standards as Public, Collective and Private Goods. *Kyklos, 36*, 377-396.

Kindleberger, C. P. (1983). Standards as Public, Collective, and Private Goods. *Kyklos, 36*(3), 377-396.

King, J. L., & West, J. (2002). Ma Bell's orphan: US cellular telephony, 1974-1996. *Telecommunications Policy, 26*(3-4), 189-204.

Klingenstein, K. J. (1999). Middleware: The Second Level of IT Infrastructure. *Cause And Effect Journal, 22*(4), EduCause.

Knospe, H., & Pohl, H. (2004). RFID Security. Information Security *Technical Report, 9*(4), 39-50.

KPMG (2004). KPMG's Auto Executive Survey 2004 – Client Preview.

Kraemer, K. L., Dedrick, J., & Yamashiro, S. (2000). Redefining and extending the Business Model with Information Technology: Dell Computer Corporation. *The Information Society, 16*(1), 5-21.

Kraemer, K., & Dedrick, J. (2002). Strategic use of the Internet and e-commerce: Cisco Systems. *Journal of Strategic Information Systems, 11*(1), 5-29.

Krechmer, K. (2000). Market Driven Standardization: Everyone Can win. *Standards Engineering, 52(4)*, 15–19.

Krechmer, K. (2003). Face the FACS. *Proc. 3rd. Int. Conf. On Standardization and Innovation in IT.* IEEE Press.

Kuhn, T. S. (1970). *The structure of scientific revolutions* (2 ed.). Chicago: University of Chicago Press.

Kurihara, S. (2006). The General Framework and Scope of Standards Studies. *Hitotsubashi Journal of Commerce and Management, 40*(1) (http://hdl.handle.net/10086/13784).

Lane, R. E. (1991). *The Market Experience*. Cambridge: Cambridge University Press.

Lansford, J. (1999). HomeRF: Bringing wireless connectivity home: Intel.

Lansford, J. (2007). Personal communication.

Leaver, S. (2004, August). Evaluating RFID Middleware. *Forrester,* (pp. 1-21).

Lemstra, W. (2006). *The Internet bubble and the impact on the development path of the telecommunication sector.* TUDelft, Delft, The Netherlands.

Lemstra, W., & Hayes, V. (Forthcoming). License exempt: Wi-Fi complement to 3G. *Telematics & Informatics.*

Lemstra, W., Hayes, V., & Van der Steen, M. (2009). Network modernization in the telecom sector - The case of Wi-Fi. In R. W. Künneke (Ed.), *The governance of network industries: Redefining rules and responsibilities.* Cheltenham, UK: Edward Elgar.

Levinthal, D. (1997). Adaptation on rugged landscapes. *Management Science, 43*(7), 934-950.

Liebowitz, S. J. & Margolis, S. E. (1995). Path Dependence, Lock-In and History. *Journal of Law, Economics and Organization, 11*(1), 205-226.

Links, C. (2007). Personal communication.

Lipsey, R., Carlaw, K., & Bekar, C. (2005). *Economic Transformations: General Purpose Technologies and Long Term Economic Growth*. Oxford: Oxford University Press.

Macdonald, S. (2004). When means become ends: considering the impact of patent strategy on innovation. *Information Economics and Policy, 16*, 135-158.

Mahadevan, B. (2000). Business Models for Internet-Based E-Commerce: An Anatomy. *California Management Review, 42*(4), 55-69.

Majone, G. (1984). Science and Trans-Science in Standard Setting. *Science, Technology and Human Values, 9*(1), 15-22.

Marcus, M. (2000). *Commercial spread spectrum*. Retrieved 2007-06-28, from http://www.marcus-spectrum.com/documents/Orlando_000.ppt

Marcus, M. (2007). Personal communication.

Marincu, C., & McMullin, B. (2004). A comparative assessment of Web accessibility and technical standards conformance in four EU states. *First Monday, 9*(7).

Mazzoleni, R., & Nelson, R. (1998). Economic theories about the benefits and costs of patents. *Journal of Economic Issues, 32*(4), 1031-1052.

McGinity, M. (2004). Staying Connected. *Communications of the ACM, 47*(1), 15-18.

McKinney, J., & Barraclough, G. (2003). Radio Frequency Identification Technology Overview. *Pharmatech*, (pp. 110-112).

McMeekin, A., Green, K., Tomlinson, M., & Walsh, V. (2002). *Innovation by Demand: An Interdisciplinary Approach to the Study of Demand and its Role in Innovation*. Cheltenham: Edward Elgar.

Meer, K. v. d. (2008). The sustainability of digital data: Tension between the dynamics and longevity of standards. In T. M. Egyedi & K. Blind (Eds.), *The dynamics of standards* (pp. 15-27). Cheltenham, UK: Edward Elgar.

Middleton, R. W. (1973). Standardization and International Economic Co-operation. *Journal of World Trade Law, 7*(5), 500-510.

Ministry of Science Technology and Innovation (2003). *The Danish Software Strategy* (PDF). Copenhagen: Ministry of Science Technology and Innovation.

Mock, D. (2005). *The Qualcomm equation*. New York: AMACOM.

Montalvo, C. (2002). *Environmental policy and technological innovation: Why do firms adopt or reject new technologies?* Cheltenham: Edward Elgar.

Moore, G. A. (1995). *Inside the tornado*. New York: Harper Business.

Morath, P. (2000). *Success@E-Business. Profitable Internet Business & Commerce*. London: McGraw Hill.

Morgan, R. M., & Hunt, S. D. (1994). The Commitment-Trust Theory of Relationships Marketing. *Journal of Marketing, 58*(3), 20-38.

Mörschel, I., & Schwengels, C. (2002). Standardisierungspotenziale für Dienstleistungen—Ergebnisse einer allgemeinen Bedarfserhebung. In DIN (Ed.), *Standardisierung in der deutschen Dienstleistungswirtschaft – Potenziale und Handlungsbedarf*, DIN-Fachbericht 116, Berlin et al.: Beuth Verlag GmbH, (pp. 51-65).

Mowery, D. C., & Rosenberg, N. (1979). The influence of market demand upon innovation: a critical review of some recent empirical studies. *Research Policy, 8*, 102-53.

Murmann, J. P., & Frenken, K. (2006). Toward a systematic framework for research on dominant designs, technological innovations, and industrial change. *Research Policy, 35*, 925-952.

Murray, C. J. (2004). Four Asian automakers join FlexRay consortium. *Electronic Engineering Times*, March 1, 2004.

Negus, K. J., Stephens, A. P., & Lansford, J. (2000). HomeRF: Wireless networking for the connected home. *IEEE Personal Communications, Feb.*

Nelson, R. R., & Winter, S. G. (1977). In search of a useful theory of innovation. *Research Policy, 6*, 36-76.

Nelson, R. R., & Winter, S. G. (1982). *An evolutionary theory of economic change*. Cambridge, MA: The Belknap Press of Harvard University Press.

Nikkei Electronics (2004). Why Toyota and Nissan created JasPar. *Nikkei Electronics*, October 25, 2004, (pp. 61-62).

North, D. (1990). A Transaction Cost Theory of Politics. *Journal of Theoretical Politics, 2*(4), 355-367.

North, D. C. (1981). *Structure and Change in Economic History*. New York: Norton.

North, D. C. (1990). *Institutions, Institutional Change, and Economic Performance*. Cambridge: Cambridge University Press.

North, D. C. (1993). Institutions and Credible Commitment. *Journal of Institutional and Theoretical Economics, 149*(1), 11-23.

Ohrtman, F., & Roeder, K. (2003). *Wi-Fi Handbook - Building 802.11b wireless networks*. New York: McGraw-Hill.

Oksala, S., Rutkowski, A., Spring, M., & O'Donnell, J. (1996). The Structure of IT Standardisation. *StandardView, 4*(1), 9-22.

Orlikowski, W. J., & Robey, D. (n.d.). Information technology and the structuring of organizations. *Information Systems Research, 2*(2).

Oudshoorn, M. (2003). Scheduling and Latency—Addressing the Bottleneck. In N. S. Shi & V. K. Murthy (Eds), *Architectural Issues of Web-Enabled Electronic Business*. Idea Group Publishing.

Palo Wireless. (2003). *HomeRF overview and market positioning*. Retrieved 2007-08-07, from http://www.palowireless.com/homerf/homerf8.asp

Paolucci, M., & Sycara, K. (2003). Autonomous Semantic Web Services. *IEEE Internet Computing, 7*(5).

Papazoglou, M. P. (2003). Web Services and Business Transactions. *World Wide Web: Internet and Web Information Systems, 6*, 49–91. Kluwer Academic Publishers.

Penrose, E. (1959). *The Theory of the Growth of the Firm*. London: Blackwell.

Peteraf, M. A. (1993). The cornerstone of competitive advantage: A resource-based view. *Strategic Management Journal*, (pp. 179-191).

Pharmanet served the pharmaceutical industry; Istel and Motornet served the vehicle industry, which tended to use the Odette standards; Limnet served the London insurance market .

Raza, N., Bradshaw, V., & Hague, M. (1999, October). Applications of RFID technology. *IEEE Colloquium on RFID Technology*. London.

Reale, K. (2006). *RFID continues to take Back Seat in Automotive*. AMR Research Report.

Reck, D. (Ed.) (1956). *National Standards in a Modern Economy*. New York: Harper & Brothers.

Reddy, N. M. (1990). Product of Self-Regulation. A Paradox of Technology Policy. *Technological Forecasting and Social Change, 38*, 43-63.

Reding, V. (2008). *Digital TV, Mobile TV: let's push for open technologies in Europe and worldwide* (Speech No. SPEECH/08/144). Budapest.

Reed Electronics Research (2006). *Automotive Electronics: A Profile of International Markets and Suppliers to 2010*. Reed Electronics Research.

Reimers, K., & Mingzhi, L. (2005). Antecedents of a Transaction Cost Theory of Vertical IS Standardisation Processes. *Electronic Markets, 15*(4), 301-312. (Special Issue on Vertical Industry Information Technology Standards and Standardization).

Reimers, K., & Mingzhi, L. (2005). Should Buyers Try to Shape IT Markets Through Non-Market (Collective) Action? Antecedents of a Transaction Cost Theory of Network Effects. *International Journal of IT Standards & Standardization Research, 3*(1) (January-March 2005), 44-67.

Reimers, K., & Mingzhi, L. (2007). Effectiveness of the International 3G standardization Process and Implications for China's 3G Policy. *International Journal of Public Policy, 2*(1/2), 124-139.

Riches, I. (2006). *Automotive System Demand 2004 to 2013: Safety systems drive growth*. At:

Ricketts, M. (2002). *The economics of business enterprise - An introduction to economic organisation and the theory of the firm*. Cheltenham, UK: Edward Elgar Publishing.

Riggins, F. J., & Rhee, H. (1998): Toward a Unified View of Electronic Commerce. *Communications of the ACM, 41*(10), 88-95.

Ring, P. S., Doz, Y. L., & Olk, P. M. (2005). Managing Formation Processes in R&D Consortia. *California Management Review, 47*(4), 137-156.

Roberts, H. M. (2000). *Robert's rules of order - Newly revised*. Cambridge MA: DaCapo Press.

Ruppel, C. (2004). An information systems perspective of supply chain tool compatibility: The roles of technology fit and relationships. *Business Process Management Journal, 10*(3), 311-324.

SAE (2003). *Technical Paper Series*, SAE. 2003-01-0111

Sahal, D. (1981). *Patterns of technological innovation*. Reading, MA: Addison-Wesley.

Sahal, D. (1985). Technology guideposts and innovation avenues. *Research Policy, 14*, 61-82.

Salter, L. (1988). *Mandated Science: Science and Scientists in the Making of Standards.* Dordrecht: Kluwer.

Sarma, S. E., Weis, S. A., & Engels, D. W. (2005). RFID Systems and Security and Privacy Implications. *Workshop on Cryptographic Hardware and Embedded Systems,* (pp. 454-470), http://citeseer.ist.psu.edu/sarma02rfid.html, Access Date March, 2005.

Schindler, E. (2003). Location, Location, Location. *netWorker, 7*(2), 11-14.

Schmidt, S. K., & Werle, R. (1998). *Co-ordinating Technology. Studies in the International Standardization of Telecommunications.* . Cambridge, Mass: MIT Press.

Schmitt, P., Michahelles, F., & Fleisch, E. (2006). *An Adoption Strategy for an Open RFID Standard - Potentials for RFID in the Automotive Aftermarket.* Auto-ID Labs White Paper WP-BIZAPP-024.

Schmookler, J. (1966). *Invention and Economic Growth.* Cambridge, Harvard University Press.

Schumpeter, J. A. (1912). *Die Theorie der Wirtschaftlichen Entwicklung.* Duncker & Humblot: Leipzig

Schumpeter, J. A. (1939). Business Cycles: A Theoretical, Historical and Statistical Analysis of the Capitalist Process (Volume 1 and 2). McGraw Hill: New York.

Schumpeter, J. A. (1942). *Capitalism, Socialism and Democracy.* George Allen and Unwin: New York.

Schwartz, M. (1987). *Telecommunication networks: Protocols, modelling and analysis.* Reading, MA: Addison-Wesley.

Seddon, P. (1997). *Defining Electronic Commerce.* Department of Information Systems, University of Melborne, http://www.dis.unimelb.edu.au/staff/peter/research/InternetEra.htmlTapscott.

Semantic Web. L. Feigenbaum, I. Herman, T. Hongsermeir, E. Neumann, S. Stephens. Scientific American Vol 297 No 6, December 2007

Setterfield, M. (2002). *The Economics of Demand-Led Growth: Challenging the Supply-Side Vision of the Long Run.* Cheltenham: Edward Elgar.

Shapiro, C., & Varian, H. (2002). The art of standards wars. In R. Garud, A., Kumaraswamy, & R. Langlois (Eds.), *Managing in the Modular Age: Architectures, Networks, and Organizations.* Oxford: Blackwell, (pp. 247-315).

Shapiro, C., & Varian, H. R. (1998). *Information Rules: A strategic guide to the network economy.* Harvard Business School Press.

Sherif, M. H. (2003). When is standardization slow? *Int. J. on IT Standards & Standardisation Research, 1*(1).

Sherif, M. H., Jakobs, K., & Egyedi, T. M. (2007). Standards of quality and quality of standards for Telecommunications and Information Technologies. In M. Hörlesberger, M. El_Nawawi & T. Khalil (Eds.), *Challenges in the Management of New Technologies* (pp. 427-447). Singapore: World Scientific Publishing Company. .

Silva, F., & Senger, H. (2004). Digital Communities in a Networked Society: e-Commerce, e-Business and e-Government. *Proc. Third IFIP Conference on e-Commerce, e-Business and e-Government.* Kluwer.

Simpl.e.business – paper by Tom McGuffog, Nigel Fenton and Nick Wadsley - e.centre.uk : b. 'B.e.e. Business enabled electronically, the future for e.business' – Tom McGuffog. UK Partners for electronic business. London, 2002.

Simpl.e.business – proposals from UK Delegation to plenary of UN/ECE.CEFACT. Papers in 1997/CRP10; 1998/4; 2000/24; 2002/32

Spring, M. B., Grisham, C., O'Donnell, J., Skogseid, I., Snow, A., Tarr, G., & Wang, P. (1995). Improving the Standardization Process: Working with Bulldogs an Turtles. In B. Kahin & J. Abbate, (Eds.), *Standards Policy for Information Infrastructure.* MIT Press.

SSRC (2005). *The Politics of Open Source Adoption*: Social Science Research Council.

Steinbock, D., & Noam, E. (2003). *Competition for the Mobile Internet.* Kluwer Academic Publishers.

Steinmueller, E. W. (2005, 10-11 January). *Technical Compatibility Standards and the Co-Ordination of the*

Industrial and International Division of Labour. Paper presented at the Advancing Knowledge and the Knowledge Economy, Washington, DC.

Straube, F., Bensel, P., & Vogeler, S. (2007). RFID Standardisierungslandkarte. *PPS Management, 12*(4), 20–23.

Su, S. Y. W., Lam, H., Lee, M., Bai, S., & Shen, Z. J. (2001). An Information Infrastructure and E-Services for Supporting Internet-Based Scalable E-Business Enterprises. *In Proceedings of the Fifth IEEE International Enterprise Distributed Object Computing Conference,* http://csdl.computer.org/comp/proceedings/edoc/2001/1345/00/13450002abs.htm

Sullivan, C. D. (1983). *Standards and Standardization: Basic Principles and Applications.* New York: Marcel Dekker Inc.

Suttmeier, R., & Yao, X. (2004). China's Post-WTO Technology Policy: Standards, Software, and Changing Nature of Techno-Nationalism. *the National Bureau of Asian Research Special Report.*

Swann G. M. P. (1999). Marshall's Consumer as an Innovator. In S. C. Dow & P. E. Earl (Eds.), *Economic Organisation and Economic Knowledge: Essays in Honour of Brian Loasby.* Cheltenham: Edward Elgar Publishers.

Swann, G. M. P. (1993). User Needs for Standards: How Can We Ensure that User Votes are Counted? In B. Meek et al (Eds.), *User Needs in Information Technology Standards.* Butterworth/Heinemann.

Swann, G. M. P., Temple, P., & Shurmer, M. (1996). Standards and Trade Performance: The British Experience. *Economic Journal, 106*, 1297-1313.

SWIFT e.message standards serve the banking industry – www.swift.com

Tanenbaum, A. S. (1989). *Computer Networks* (2 ed.): Prentice-Hall .

Tanenbaum, A. S. (1996). *Computer networks* (Third Edition ed.). Upper Saddle River, NJ: Prentice-Hall.

Tapia, A., Stone, M., & Maitland, C. F. (2005). *Public-private partnerships and the role of state and federal legislation in wireless municipal networks.* Paper presented at the Telecommunications Policy Research Conference.

Tapscott, D. (2001). Rethinking Strategy in a Networked World. Strategy and Business. *Third Quarter* (24), 1-8.

Tassey G. (1992). *Technology Infrastructure and Competitive Position.* Norwell MA: Kluwer

Tassey, G. (2000). Standardisation in technology-based markets. *Research Policy, 29*(4/5), 587-602.

Tassey, G. (2004). Policy Issues for R&D Investment in a Knowledge-Based Economy. *Journal of Technology Transfer, 29*(2), 153-184.

The Fundamental Value Chain Process – from Plan to Payment – Tom McGuffog – British Standards Institution ICT4 Paper. London, 2007 www.bsi-global.com

The TRADACOMS Electronic Data Interchange Message Standards – The Article Number Association (then e.centre.uk, now GS1 UK). London, 1982 - www.gs1uk.org. See also www.gs1.org

The Value Chain Forum of the Chartered Institute of Logistics and Transport – www.ciltuk.org.uk - to be published in Spring 2009

Thomas, J. W., Probets, S., Dawson, R., & King, T. (2008). A case study of the adoption and implementation of STEP. In T. M. Egyedi & K. Blind (Eds.), *The dynamics of standards* (pp. 117-134). Cheltenham, UK: Edward Elgar.

Thompson, G. V. (1954). Intercompany Technical Standardization in the Early American Automobile Industry. *Journal of Economic History, 14*(1), 1-20.

Timmermans, S., & Berg, M. (1997). Standardization in Action: Achieving Local Universality through Medical Protocols. *Social Studies of Science, 27*(2), 273-305.

Timmers, P. (1998). Business Models for Electronic Markets. *Electronic Markets, 8*(2), 3-8.

Tokuda, A. (2007). Standardization activity within Jas-Par: Initiatives of Renesas Technology Co., *Ritsumeikan International Affairs. 5*(1), 85-105.

Tompkins, J. A. (1998). Time to rise above supply chain management. *Transportation & Distribution, 39*(10), SCF16-SCF18.

Towill, D. R. (1997). The seamless supply chain - the predator's strategic advantage. *International Journal of Technology Management, 13*(1), 37-56.

Tuch, B. T. (2007). Personal communication.

Tuch, B. T., & Masleid, M. A. (1991). Wireless information transmission system. USA: US Patent and Trade Mark Office.

Tyndall, G., Gopal, C., Partsch, W., & Kamauff, J. (1998). Supercharging Supply Chains: New Ways to Increase Value through Global Operational Excellence. New York: Wiley.

UN (2005). *UN Global E-government Readiness Report 2005: From E-government to E-inclusion*, UN-PAN/2005/14, United Nations, New York

Updegrove, A. (1995). Consortia and the role of government in standard setting. In B. Kahin & J. Abbate, J. (Eds.), *Standards policy for information infrastructure.* Cambridge, MA: MIT Press.

Updegrove, A. (2003). *Major Standards Players Tell How They Evaluate Standard Setting Organizations.* http://www.consortiuminfo.org/bulletins/jun03.php.

Updegrove, A. (2005). *Evaluating Whether to Join a Consortium.* http://www.consortiuminfo.org/evaluating/.

Updegrove, A. (2005). Participating In Standard Setting Organizations: Value Propositions, Roles And Strategies. *Consortum Standards Bulletin, vol. 5*(no. 9).

Van de Ven, A. H., Polley, D. E., Garud, R., & Venkataraman, S. (1999). *The innovation journey.* Oxford, UK: Oxford University Press.

Van der Mandele, M. (2000). *E-Business and Strategy:* Arthur D. Little E-Business Center. http://www.netskill.de/ebusiness.nsf/7875A002F42DE041C125697E00562D54/

$File/e-business_and_strategy.pdf. Acess date: April, 2005.

Van Hooft, F. P. C., & Stegwee, R. A. (2001). E-business strategy: How to benefit from a hype. *Logistics Information Management, 14*(1/2), 44-53.

Van Nee, R. (2006). *Current status of Wi-Fi standardization.* Paper presented at the 9th Annual International Conference Economics of Infrastructures, Delft, the Netherlands.

Van Wegberg, M. (1999). *The Design of Standardisation Processes in ICT: An evolutionary transaction cost approach.* http://www-edocs.unimaas.nl/files/nib99001.pdf

Venkatraman, N. (1991). IT-Induced Business Reconfiguration. In M. S. Scott Morton, (Ed), *The Corporation of the 1990s: Information Technology and Organizational Transformation.* Oxford University Press.

Verhoosel, J. P. C., & Akkersdijk, V. (2004). eGovernment for Businesses: Lessons learned from a trajectory of Standardization of Business Information. In P. Cunningham & M. Cunningham, (Eds.), *eAdoption and the Knowledge Economy: Issues, Applications, Case Studies* (pp. 604-610). Amsterdam: IOS Press.

Verman, L. C. (1973). *Standardization: A New Discipline.* Hamden: Archon Books.

Vernon, R. (1966). International Investment and International Trade in the Product Cycle. *Quarterly Journal of Economics, 80*(2), 190-207.

Vijn, M., & Mourits, G. (2005). Wireless netwerk dekt Leiden. *Informatie, Okt.*

Von Burg, U. (2001). *The triumph of Ethernet.* Stanford, CA: Stanford University Press.

Von Hippel, E. (1988). *The Sources of Innovation.* Oxford and New York: Oxford University Press.

Von Hippel, E. (1988). *The sources of innovation.* Oxford, UK: Oxford University Press.

Von Hippel, E. (2005). *Democratizing innovation.* Cambridge, MA: MIT Press.

Vrancken, J., Kaart, M., & Soares, M. (2008). Internet addressing standards: A case study in standards dynamics driven by bottom-up adoption. In T. M. Egyedi & K. Blind (Eds.), *The dynamics of standards* (pp. 68-81). Cheltenham, UK: Edward Elgar.

Vries, H. J. (1999). *Standardization. A Business Approach to the Role of National Standardization Organizations.* Boston, Dordrecht, London: Kluwer Academic Publishers.

Vries, H. J. (2001). *Systematic services standardization from consumer's point of view.* Contribution to the ISO Workshop in Oslo May 2001, Oslo.

Walker, J. (2000). *Unsafe at Any Key Size: An Analysis of the WEP Encapsulation*: Intel.

Wallenstein, G. (1990). *Setting Global Telecommunications Standards: the Stakes, the Players and the Process.* Dedham: Artech House.

Web Science Emerges. Nigel Shadbolt & Tim Berners-Lee. Scientific American Vol 299 No 4, October 2008

Weiss, M. B. H., & Sirbu, M. (1990). Technological Choice in Voluntary Standards Committees: and Empirical Analysis. *Economics of Innovation and New Technology, 1*(1), 111-133.

Weiss, M. B. H., & Huang, K. C. (2007). *To be or not to be: A comparative study of city-wide municipal Wi-Fi in the US.* Paper presented at the Telecommunications Policy Research Conference.

Weizsacker, C.C. v. (1982). Staatliche Regulierung - positive und normative Theorie. *Schweizerische Zeitschrift für Volkswirtschaft und Statistik, 2,* 325-243.

Werle, R., & Iversen, E. J. (2006). Promoting Legitimacy in Technical Standardization. *Science, Technology & Innovation Studies, 2,* 19-39.

West, J. (2003). How open is open enough? Melding proprietary and open source platform strategies. *Research Policy, 32*(7), 1259-1285.

Whitfield, K. (2002). Looking both ways. *Automotive Design & Production, 11*(4), 36.

Whitworth, J. (1882). *Papers on Mechanical Subjects. Part I. True Planes, Screw Threads, and Standard Measures.* London: E. F. & N. Spon.

Wieringa, R., van Eck, P., & Blanken, H. (2004). *Architecture Alignment in a Large Government Organization: A Case Study.* CTIT Technical Report, http://wwwhome.cs.utwente.nl/~patveck/papers/wieringa_etal_caise-04forum.pdf

Wi-Fi Alliance. (2007). *Get to know the alliance.* Retrieved 2007-08-16, from http://www.wi-fi.org

Williams, R., Graham, I., & Spinardi, G. (1993). *The Social Shaping of EDI.* Paper presented at the Proceedings of the PICT/COST A4 International Research Workshop, Edinburgh.

Wireless Leiden. (2006a). *Techniek.* Retrieved 2006-06, from http://www.wirelessleiden.nl/techniek/

Wireless Leiden. (2006b). *Wi-Fi.* Retrieved 2006-06, from http://wiki.wirelessleiden.nl/wcl/cgi-bin/moin.cgi/WiFi

Woodward, C. D. (Ed.) (1965). *Standards for Industry.* London: Heinemann.

WTO (2005). *World Trade Report 2005: Exploring the Links between Trade, Standards and the WTO.* Geneva, Switzerland: World Trade Organization (WTO).

Zhu, K., Kraemer, K. L., Gurbaxani, V., & Xu, S. X. (2006). Migration to Open-Standard Interorganizational Systems: Network Effects, Switching Costs, and Path Dependency. *MIS Quarterly, 30* (Special Issue. Standard Making: A Critical Research Frontier for Information Systems Research), 515-540.

About the Contributors

Kai Jakobs joined RWTH Aachen University's Computer Science Department as a member of technical staff in 1985. Since 1987, he has been head of technical staff at the chair of Informatik 4 (Communication & Distributed Systems). He holds a PhD in computer science from the University of Edinburgh. Kai is (co)-author/editor of a text book on data communication and, more recently, eleven books on standardisation processes in IT. More than 190 of his papers have been published in conference proceedings, books, and journals. He has been on the programme committees of numerous international conferences, and has also served as an external expert on evaluation panels of various European R&D programmes, on both technical and socio-economic issues.

* * *

Knut Blind holds the chair for economics at the Technical University, Berlin and the endowed chair in standardisation at Rotterdam Erasmus University's School of Management. He also heads the department 'Innovationsystems and Policy' of the Fraunhofer Institute ISI, and the Competence Center 'Regulation and Innovation' in Berlin. He holds a diploma degree in economics and a PhD in political sciences, both from the University of Freiburg.

Raluca Bunduchi is a lecturer in management at the University of Aberdeen Business School. Her current research focuses on innovation management and the development and adoption of e-business technologies in organisations. Prior to that, she has been a research fellow at the University of Edinburgh looking at the development and adoption of e-business standards. She studied for her PhD in the Department of Management Science at Strathclyde Business School, examining the use of Internet technologies and their implications for the nature of business relationships within and across organizational boundaries.

Henk J. de Vries is associate professor standardization at Rotterdam School of Management, Erasmus University in Rotterdam, The Netherlands, Department of Management of Technology and Innovation. His education and research concern standardization from a business point of view. From 1994 until 2003, Henk worked with NEN, Netherlands Standardization Institute, in several jobs, being responsible for R&D during the last period. Since 1994, he has an appointment at the Erasmus University's School of Management and since 2004, he has been working full-time at this university. Henk is author of more than 200 publications, including several books on standardization.

Tineke M. Egyedi is senior researcher standardization. She has participated in several EU projects (the last one was on EU ICT standardization policy, finalised in 2007), industry projects (e.g. Dynamics of standards; Sun Microsystems), and Dutch government projects (e.g. Trends in Standardization).Her current research interests projects include standards and infrastructure flexibility (Next Generation Infrastructures project, TU Delft), and the interaction between international standardization and national innovation projects (Dutch National Science Foundation). She is president of the European Academy for Standardization (EURAS) and vice-chair of the International Committee for Standardization about Education (ICES). She has chaired standardization seminars, workshops and conferences. Currently she is associate editor of the *International Journal of IT Standards and Standardization Research* (IGI Global) and member of the editorial board of *Computer Standards and Interfaces* (Elsevier).

Vladislav V. Fomin is associate professor at the faculty of Informatics at the Vytautas Magnus University in Kaunas, Lithuania. His prior positions included visiting research fellow at Rotterdam School of Management, Erasmus University in the Netherlands (2008), associate professor at Montpellier Business School in France (2007), research scientist at the Faculty of Policy, Technology and Management, Delft University of Technology in the Netherlands (2006), assistant professor at the department of Informatics, Copenhagen Business School in Denmark (2004-6), and visiting assistant professor at the School of Information at the University of Michigan in the USA (2001-3). Current research interests include standard making processes in the field of information and communication technologies (ICT) and studies of ICT infrastructure development and design.

Stephan Gauch studied sociology at the University of Mannheim, majoring in statistics and methods of empirical social research. Since 2004 he has been a researcher and PhD candidate at the Competence Center Policy and Regions. His research interetses include science and technology indicators, empirical social and economic research, intellectual property rights, innovation sociology, and standardisation and technical change.

Martina Gerst holds a PhD degree from the University of Edinburgh and Diplom-Kauffrau from the University of Saarbruecken, Germany and from the Grand Ecole Institut Commerciale de Nancy, France. After starting her career at the central purchasing department of Siemens she joined the KPMG procurement practice in Paris. Afterwards, she worked as a Content Director for Commerce One and managed a large-scale e-marketplace launch for the Global Procurement & Supply department of DaimlerChrysler. Dr. Gerst has started her own business supporting international industrial clients in realising complex international supply chain projects (www.innovation-space.com).

Ian Graham, is a senior lecturer in operations management at the University of Edinburgh Business School.

Richard Hawkins is professor and Canada research chair (Tier 1) in Science, Technology and Innovation Policy in the Science, Technology and Society Program at the University of Calgary. He is also the senior fellow at The Centre for Innovation Studies (THECIS), and associate senior scientist in the Innovation Policy Group at the Netherlands Organization for Applied Scientific Research (TNO).

Ing. Vic Hayes is senior research fellow at the Department Technology, Policy & Management of the Technical University Delft (TUDelft), the Netherlands. In 1974 he joined NCR in the Netherlands and co-established and chaired the IEEE 802.11, Standards Working Group for Wireless LANs. He successfully mobilized the industry to support the WRC 2003 on the allocation of 455 MHz of spectrum on a co-primary basis. He is the recipient of 8 awards, including the "The Economist's" Innovation Award 2004, the Dutch Vosko Trophy, the IEEE Hans Karlsson Award, and the IEEE Steinmetz Award. In 1961 Vic received a BSEE degree from the HTS "Amsterdam".

Eric Iversen is a senior researcher at the Norwegian Institute for studies in Innovation, Research and Education (NIFU STEP) in Oslo, Norway, where he has worked in the field of innovation and economics of technological change since 1994. He is currently with the Australian Innovation Research Centre (AIRC) at the University of Tasmania finishing doctoral work. His work centers on the framework conditions of technological change with special focus on quantitative and qualitative analyses of standardization, IPRs, and their interrelationship. Recent work supported by the EU Commission has focused on the relationship between standardization and research and on standards for networked organizations. Iversen has also contributed to work of international organizations (e.g. OECD) and is a regular contributor to the Norwegian Research Council's Science and Technology Indicator report. He is a member of the editorial review board of the International Journal of IT Standards & Standardization Research.

Jan Kritzner is a researcher and a PhD candidate at RWTH Aachen University's Computer Science Department. His main research interests include telecommunication systems, intelligent networks, and distributed sytems.

Ir. Wolter Lemstra is Senior Research Fellow at the Department Technology, Policy & Management of the Technical University Delft (TUDelft), and Senior Lecturer at the Strategy Academy, both in the Netherlands. He is also a Faculty Member of the executive masters program in e-Governance at the Ecole Polytechnique Fédéral de Lausanne – Switzerland. He links his academic interests to 25 years of experience in the telecom sector, at Philips, AT&T and Lucent Technologies, most recently as VP Business Development and Marketing with responsibility for the European, Middle East and Africa Region. Wolter received his 'Ingenieurs'-degree cum laude at the Department of Electrical Engineering, TUDelft in 1978. In 2006 he received his Doctorate degree at the TUDelft, based on research exploring the impact of the Internet/telecom bubble on the development path of the telecommunication sector.

Mingzhi Li is an associate professor of economics at the School of Economics and Management (SEM), Tsinghua University, P. R. China. Professor Li got his PhD degree in economics from the University of Texas at Austin in 1999. He focuses his formal academic work on microeconomic theory, industrial organization, and electronic commerce. Professor Li has served as the primary researcher of several research projects aimed at exploring the economic aspects of electronic commerce and the evolution of China's information and communications industry: "Microeconomic Structure of the Electronic Commerce Markets", "China's Telecommunication Industry after WTO: Theory of Competition and Regulation." and "ICT Industry Development and Economic Growth". Professor Li's research has led to publications on international journals including *Computational Economics, Information Economics and Policy, Information Technology and International Development, International Journal of IT Standards and Standardization Research* and *Electronic Commerce Research.*

Tom McGuffog, MBE, was executive director for planning, logistics, purchasing, IT, and e-business at various times in Rowntree and Nestle. He was a non-executive director in the UK Ministry of Defence and the National Health Service, and also of SITPRO and e.centre.uk. He chaired the TRADACOMS EDI Standards Group and UK Partners for Electronic Business. He was head of the UK Delegation to UN/ECE/CEFACT in Geneva. He chairs the CILT Value Chain Forum. He is the author of many business and e.business publications. He has been visiting professor, fellow and lecturer at several universities such as Glasgow, Bath and Royal Holloway. He is a graduate in economics from the Universities of Glasgow and Massachusetts, and a fellow of the Chartered Institutes of Logistics and Transport and of Purchasing and Supply. He was awarded the MBE by The Queen for services to the development of e.business.

Mogens Kühn Pedersen is professor at the department of Informatics at the Copenhagen Business School (CBS). His current and past research topics include theory of distributed knowledge management systems and their use in services, including healthcare and construction, and in other industries. They also include studies in digital government (for business), governance of IT, and open source software and standards. Prior to joining CBS as professor and director of the PhD school in Informatics, he was at Roskilde University. He serves as chairman of the Danish Standards' committee S-142/u 34 on document description and processing language, a mirror committee to ISO/JTC1/SC34 (2007-) processing OOXML draft international standard (DIS 29500). He has been an adviser to the Danish Ministry on open standards (2005-6), open source projects (2003-4), advanced eGovernment applications (2003-4), and open source software in eGovernment (2002).

Kai Reimers is currently a professor of information systems at RWTH Aachen University, Faculty of Business and Economics. From 1998 to 2003, he worked as a visiting professor at the School of Economics and Management, Tsinghua University, sponsored by the German Academic Exchange Service (DAAD). He earned a doctorate in economics from Wuppertal University and a venia legendi at Bremen University. He has published in international journals including *European Journal of Information Systems, Electronic Markets, Electronic Commerce Research, Communications of the AIS, Journal of Information Technology, International Journal of Production Economics, International Journal of IT Standards & Standardization Research, International Journal of Public Policy.* He authored or co-authored five books in the field of information systems. His main fields of research are inter-organizational systems, IT management, and IT standards.

Akio Tokuda(PhD, Ritsumeikan University) is an associate professor at the Department of International Business, Faculty of Business Administration, Ritsumeikan University, Japan. He is also a visiting research fellow at RWTH Aachen University from 2007 to 2009. His research interests are centered around strategic management, strategic alliance, coordination theory, and standardization studies. Founded by New Energy and Industrial Technology Development Organization (NEDO) of Japan, he has been conducting international comparative research between German and Japanese standard consortia in automotive LAN-bus system since 2006. He is one of the academic members of the Japanese standard consortium called JasPar (Japan Automotive Software Platform and Architecture).

Robin Williams is director of The University of Edinburgh, Institute for the Study of Science Technology and Innovation (ISSTI). He has over 20 years experience in interdisciplinary research into 'the social shaping of technology' which has focused upon the interplay between social and 'technical' factors in the development and implementation of a range of commercial IT applications including inter-organisational network systems (e-commerce and EFTPoS systems) enterprise systems and multimedia.

Index

P

political divide 225
political markets 140, 142, 143, 144, 150
portals 254, 260, 261, 262, 266
proprietary systems 259

Q

qualitative methods 258
quality standards 178, 182, 201, 219, 220,
    221, 223, 224, 225, 226, 227, 228,
    229, 230, 231, 232

R

RACE project 3
radio frequency identification (RFID)
    53, 54, 133, 141
reasonable and non-discriminatory (RAND)
    194
regulation 204
reliable electronic signatures 206
RFID products 5
RFID supply chain 58
royalty free 96

S

sector-specific harmonization 253, 254
Semantic Web 6, 138, 139
service/product constructs 245
service standards 9, 12, 13, 20, 24, 25, 26,
    27, 28, 29, 30
signature-creation devices 208, 214
signature policies 208, 216
simple object access protocol (SOAP) 4
single point of entry 260, 265
software engineering (SwE) 236–252
spread spectrum 104, 105, 107, 116
stakeholders 31, 34, 35, 36, 37, 38, 40,
    41, 42, 43, 44, 45, 46, 65, 76, 82,
    84, 87, 88, 92, 93, 172, 188, 189,
    191, 193, 194, 210, 221, 254, 258,
    259, 261, 264, 267
standard for the exchange of product (STEP)
    136
standardized technology 257, 262, 265

standards 253, 254, 255, 256, 257, 258,
    259, 261, 262, 263, 264, 265, 266
standards-setting process 254
standards change 171, 172, 173, 174, 175, 1
    76, 177, 178, 179, 180, 181, 182,
    183, 186
standards developing organisations (SDOs) 2
standards dynamics 180, 182, 185
standards setting 254, 255, 258, 264, 266
standards setting bodies (SSBs) 2
suppliers 253, 254, 255, 257, 260, 261,
    262, 263, 264, 265, 266, 269
supply chain 254, 255, 260, 265, 266
supply chain management (SCM) 224
SupplyOn 261, 262, 263
suprasystem 247
SWIFT standards 135
systems engineering (SE) 236–252

T

taxonomy 12, 13, 20, 22, 24, 25, 26, 27,
    28, 29, 30
TD-SCDMA standard 140, 141, 147, 149
Third Estate 264
tier-1 suppliers 255, 261, 262
total quality management (TQM) 221
transaction cost 79, 141, 142, 143, 144, 150
transport and office protocol (TOP) 268
TTP/C 156, 169

U

UK Simpler Trade Procedures Board 129
United Nations Trade Data Interchange (UN-
    TDI) 129
universality 128, 162, 163, 165, 222

V

value chain 127, 133, 135, 138, 139, 148
value proposition 43, 44

W

W3C 255
Web content accessibility guidelines (WCAG)
    14